PRAISE FOR *RESCUE, RELIEF, AND RESIST...*

"Catherine Collomp's comprehensive   f the
Jewish Labor Committee's rescue act   r II
that have heretofore not been paid mu   ive
research in archives in the United State   .. pays tribute
to the incredible efforts of individuals to   ...s from Nazi-occupied territories which so far had remained unheralded."

— David Slucki, author of *The International Jewish Labor Bund after 1945:
Toward a Global History* and *Sing This at My Funeral: A Memoir of
Fathers and Sons* (Wayne State University Press, 2019)

"This is an important book. It calls attention to the role of the American
Labor movement in alerting the United States to the Nazi danger early on,
and in making significant efforts to save Jews and labor leaders trapped in
Europe by the Nazi military successes in 1940. As such it is both a valuable
addition to our understanding of the role of Labor in fighting fascism and
saving lives, and it is a significant corrective to interpretations which neglect
the role of labor, and political struggles over preserving democracy in the
battles against the threats of antisemitism and the attack on freedom. It
extends the argument as well to conflicts within the labor movement over
the Bolshevik repression of labor leaders. This book is worth the translation
from French and will interest a wide American audience."

— Peter Gourevitch, distinguished professor emeritus,
School of Global Policy and Strategy,
University of California, San Diego

"Collomp's work on the early decades of the Jewish Labor Committee, an
important and understudied topic, is both well researched and highly read-
able. Containing substantial amounts of new information on many fascinat-
ing subjects and filling a major gap in existing scholarly literature, this book
deserves to reach a wide audience."

— Jack Jacobs, professor of political science, John Jay College and the
Graduate Center, City University of New York

Rescue, Relief, and Resistance

RESCUE, RELIEF, AND RESISTANCE

THE JEWISH LABOR COMMITTEE'S ANTI-NAZI OPERATIONS, 1934–1945

CATHERINE COLLOMP

TRANSLATED BY SUSAN EMANUEL

WAYNE STATE UNIVERSITY PRESS

Detroit

English-language edition published by Wayne State University Press.
First published in French as *Resister au nazisme: Le Jewish Labor Committee,
New York, 1934–1945* by Catherine Collomp © CNRS Editions, 2016.

On cover: Baruch Charney Vladeck at the Jewish Labor Committee 1935 convention.
(JLC photo collection 048/B1.F1, Tamiment Library, New York University)

ISBN 978-0-8143-4620-4 (paperback)
ISBN 978-0-8143-4619-8 (printed case)
ISBN 978-0-8143-4621-1 (e-book)

Library of Congress Control Number: 2020944760

Wayne State University Press
Leonard N. Simons Building
4809 Woodward Avenue
Detroit, Michigan 48201–1309

Visit us online at wsupress.wayne.edu

This book is published with the support of La Fondation pour la Mémoire de la Shoah.

CONTENTS

Illustrations appear as a group on pages 129–149

ACKNOWLEDGMENTS

On both sides of the Atlantic many persons and institutions have contributed to the making of this book. My profound gratitude goes first to Gail Malmgreen. As the archivist who organized and catalogued the papers of the Jewish Labor Committee (JLC) when they were donated to the Robert F. Wagner Labor Archives at the Tamiment Library, New York, she knew this collection better than anyone else. Her advice, her knowledge of the relevant milieux, and her own publications guided me in exploring it. The anthology of documents that she published with Arieh Lebowitz offers a broad overview of the JLC contacts and achievements during the years of struggle against Nazism. Working with the staff of the Tamiment Library has always been a pleasure.

In Ithaca, New York, the Kheel Center for Labor-Management Documentation and Archives at Cornell University was another fundamental site for this research. In the study center holding the records of the garment trades unions that were pillars of the JLC, I benefited from the valuable and friendly help of archivists Richard Strassberg and Patrizia Sione, as well as from the technical support of their staff facilitating my demands. For me, coming from France, this documentation center was a researcher's paradise. In addition, these stays in Ithaca were the occasion to forge enduring friendships. In this respect I particularly thank Nick and Ann Salvatore, whose warm hospitality and unshakable enthusiasm made these visits memorable. Emoretta Yang, who introduced me to life on the Finger Lakes, has also become a very dear friend.

In France, I am grateful to Geneviève Dreyfus, former director of the Bibliothèque de Documentation Internationale Contemporaine (BDIC) in Nanterre, who was able to acquire the entire series of the JLC archives on microfilm. By doing so she made this library (now called La Contemporaine) one of the rare institutions holding the entire JLC collection, which concerns European history as much as that of the United States. Her successor Valérie Tesnière has continued to facilitate the consultation of these microfilms. This library, with its inexhaustible resources on twentieth-century social movements, was one of my favorite workplaces through the years.

In Paris, the Centre Medem-Arbeter Ring, still a lively forum for discussions of the Bundist heritage, Yiddish culture, and contemporary political events, has been essential for my understanding of JLC history. For more information, I could turn to Ida and Emile Papiernik, Léopold Braunstein, and Erez Lévy, as well as to other members always willing to share their knowledge of Bundist history and thought.

My colleagues at the Université Paris-Diderot encouraged me all along the way. Together we organized seminars, conferences, and publications on issues of international migration and collective identities. The Laboratoire de Recherche sur les Cultures Anglophones (LARCA) funded some of my trips to the United States. Its director, the late lamented François Brunet, always supported this project and facilitated the use of photographs and other visual documents for the French edition. I am happy that one of my students, Constance Pâris de Bollardière, has prolonged my work with her own research on the JLC and its wider integration into Holocaust history.

It was my pleasure to be published by CNRS Editions in 2016. My thanks go to Grégoire Kauffmann, who edited the volume, and to his colleague Martine Bertea, who helped get the book published in the United States.

The English edition of the book came into existence thanks to the support of several friends, colleagues, and institutions. I was greatly honored by the Organization of American Historians' 2017 award distinguishing the French version of my work as the "best book on American history written in a language other than English." I am grateful to the anonymous reviewers who reported on it. I also want to thank Professor Peter Gourevitch, who took a personal interest in the publication of the JLC history and strongly recommended an American edition. In Detroit, I would like to thank Thomas Klug, organizer of the North American Labor History Conference, and especially Professor Christopher Johnson, who recommended my work to Wayne State University Press. I am also grateful to David Slucki, whose pointed expertise and suggestions helped improve the final version of the text.

For the translation, it was my good fortune to find Susan Emanuel, who was then living in Paris and immediately devoted herself to the task; living in the old Jewish neighborhood of Paris, she immersed herself in the story. The Fondation pour la Mémoire de la Shoah greatly honored my work by contributing toward the cost of translating the book. As the foremost funding institution in France for research on the Holocaust and its commemoration, its contribution is a privilege.

I thank Kathryn Wildfong and Annie Martin for directing this project at Wayne State University Press. In the spring of 2020, the production process began as the whole world was suddenly paralyzed by the Coronavirus pandemic. Yet, under Kathryn's and Annie's guidance, the pace of production was not slowed down by the measures of confinement or social distancing. I am grateful to them and the whole team, if I am not forgetting anyone, Kristin Harpster, Carrie Teefey, Kristina Stonehill, and Emily Nowak, for their unfailing energy in these circumstances. My special thanks also go to Jenn Backer, a wonderful copyeditor, who efficiently read through and clarified my sometimes obscure sentences.

I am also indebted to Mark Greengrass, who kindly volunteered to read parts of the text. His exacting sense of the English language smoothed some of the difficulties.

In my family, Florentin, Emilie, and Virgile lived for a long time with this work in progress. I don't think it distracted them from their own paths of accomplishment. My husband, Alain, encouraged me all along the way. Life would not have been sustainable without them.

ABBREVIATIONS

ACWA	Amalgamated Clothing Workers of America
ADGB	Allgemeiner Deutscher Gewerkshaftsbund
AFL	American Federation of Labor
AJC	American Jewish Congress
AK	Armia Krajowa
BCRA	Bureau Central de Renseignement et d'Action
CAmS	Centre Américain de Secours
CAS	Comité d'Action Socialiste
CFTC	Confédération des Travailleurs Chrétiens
CGD	Comité Général de Défense des Juifs
CGL	Confederazione Generale del Lavoro
CGT	Confédération Générale du Travail
CIO	Congress of Industrial Organizations
CNR	Conseil National de la Résistance
CULM	Council for the Underground Labor Movement in Nazi-Dominated Countries
ERC	Emergency Rescue Committee
FO	Force Ouvrière
HIAS	Hebrew Immigrant Aid Society
HICEM	Hebrew Immigrant, Jewish Colonization Society
IFTU	International Federation of Trade Unions
ILGWU	International Ladies' Garment Workers' Union
ILO	International Labor Organization/International Labor Office

IRRC	International Rescue and Relief Committee
ISK	Internationaler Sozialistischer Kampfbund
ITF	International Transportworkers' Federation
JDC, or Joint	American Jewish Joint Distribution Committee
JLC	Jewish Labor Committee
LSI	Labor and Socialist International
NIRA	National Industrial Recovery Act
NSDAP	Nationalsozialistische Deutsche Arbeiterpartei
ORT	Organization for Rehabilitation and Training
OSS	Office of Strategic Services
PACPR	Presidential Advisory Committee on Political Refugees
POUM	Partido Obrero de Unificacion Marxista
PPS	Polska Partia Socjalistyczna
PSI	Partito Socialista Italiano
RSDLP	Russian Social Democratic Labor Party
SDAP	Sozialdemokratische Arbeiterpartei in Östereich
SFIO	Section Française de l'Internationale Ouvrière
SOPADE	German Social Democratic Party (SPD) in exile
SPA	Socialist Party of America
SPD	Sozialdemokratische Partei Deutschlands
Tsisho	Tsentrale Yidishe Shul Organizatsiye
TUC	Trades Union Congress
UGIF	Union Générale des Israelites de France
UGT	Union General de Trabajadores
UNRRA	United Nations Relief and Rehabilitation Administration
WRB	War Refugee Board
ZOB	Zydowska Organizacja Boyowa

ARCHIVAL COLLECTIONS

DDC	David Dubinsky Correspondence, 1932–1966, ILGWU Records, 5780/002, Kheel Center for Labor-Management Documentation and Archives, Catherwood Library, Cornell University, Ithaca, NY.

JLC R	Holocaust Era Records of the Jewish Labor Committee, Series I, 1934–1947, Robert F. Wagner Labor Archives, Tamiment Library, New York University (followed by Box [B] and Folder [F] number).
NARA	National Archives and Records Administration.
Papers of the JLC	Arieh Lebowitz and Gail Malmgreen, eds. *Robert F. Wagner Labor Archives, New York University, The Papers of the Jewish Labor Committee*, vol. 14 of *Archives of the Holocaust, An International Collection of Selected Documents*, edited by Henry Friedlander and Sybil Milton. New York: Garland, 1993.

INTRODUCTION

The Jewish Labor Committee (JLC) was founded in New York City in 1934 to fight anti-Semitism and Nazi ideology in Europe and their repercussions in the United States. The organization's discreet but effective contributions to wartime relief, rescue, and resistance efforts on both sides of the Atlantic have not received the attention they deserve. From the mid-1930s through the war years, the organization was involved in rescuing Jews and members of the European labor movement, welcoming refugees to the United States, and providing material support to several European resistance movements. This book offers a detailed portrait of these activities and their historical, political, and geographical contexts.

Created by prominent leaders of the Jewish labor movement in the United States, the JLC emanated from the vibrant Yiddish-speaking communities of pre–World War I immigrants from Central Europe who were mostly employed in the garment industry. Its initiator and first president, Baruch Charney Vladeck, was general manager of the *Jewish Daily Forward*, the widely read Yiddish newspaper in the United States. David Dubinsky and Sidney Hillman, the presidents of the two largest garment workers' unions, as well as representatives of political and fraternal organizations of the non-communist Jewish left and smaller trade unions, all participated in the foundation of the JLC. The organization was situated at the intersection between Jewish circles and the highly active labor movement of the period. Yet its ideological and practical independence reflected the founders' early involvement in revolutionary socialist internationalism before their emigration to the United States. The JLC thus stood in stark contrast to the studied political neutrality of much of the American labor movement, particularly the isolationist American Federation of Labor (AFL), which scrupulously avoided any association with European socialist trends. And compared to other Jewish American organizations, the JLC had a specific agenda.

Most of the JLC's leaders were former activists in the Jewish Labor Bund, a socialist workers' movement born in the Pale of Settlement in the Russian Empire. Forced into exile by the czarist repression after the 1905 revolution, they had migrated to the United States. After twenty years of actively contributing to the development of trade unionism in the clothing industry, they had reached its top leadership. Lasting memories of anti-Semitism in their native land and of the political repression of workers clearly inspired their immediate reaction when Hitler came to power. "Jews have been a true barometer for the Labor Movement," argued Baruch Charney Vladeck. "Whenever and wherever a government begins to persecute the Jews, it inevitably follows with persecuting the workers."[1] Given their early commitments, the JLC leaders grasped the implications of events in Europe more clearly than did other American labor groups, which were isolated from European politics both historically and geographically.[2] JLC leaders helped American labor become aware that the threat of Nazi anti-Semitism extended beyond the plight of European Jews and would lead to the destruction of all civil liberties. The struggle would require the combined forces of all labor movements throughout the free world.

The JLC's most impressive achievements involved dramatic rescues of some 1,500 people pursued by the Gestapo in Occupied France between 1940 and 1941. They also freed a large number of Polish Bundists who had sought refuge in Lithuania. From its offices in New York, the JLC oversaw two escape networks that both led to the United States, one based in Marseille that helped refugees flee via Spain and Portugal, and the other leading from Poland to Lithuania and then across the USSR and Japan. Both routes involved hazardous journeys through fascist and totalitarian territories. The intensity and danger of the rescue operations, which also required absolute discretion with respect to the American government, have left little trace in the public records.

Even before France was overrun by the Werhmacht in June 1940, the JLC was very much aware of the plight of German and Austrian opponents of the Nazi regime and of Italian anti-fascists who had already spent several years hiding in France. The organization maintained contacts with the leaders in exile of Socialist and Social Democratic parties as well as noncommunist trade unionists and liberal anti-fascist militants, assisting some of them through the networks of the Labor and Socialist International and the International Federation of Trade Unions. These personal and institutional contacts enabled the JLC to follow the vicissitudes of the lives of anti-fascist refugees. The organization also maintained close relationships with former members of the Menshevik Party who had initially fled the Soviet Union and sought refuge in Germany before migrating to France, where they were in danger again of being arrested by both the Soviets and the Gestapo under the terms of the German-Soviet Pact of 1939. In short, the JLC was engaged in rescuing an entire galaxy of European Socialist and Social Democratic leaders.

On June 22, 1940, with the fall of France, asylum in that country overnight became a death trap. The Armistice signed by representatives of the Pétain government contained the infamous Article 19, which committed the Vichy administration to surrender German citizens who opposed the Third Reich at the behest of German authorities. In the ensuing mass exodus of French people fleeing the occupying forces, the JLC used its networks to identify and offer assistance to individuals who had to be smuggled out of French territory.

By offering refuge in America to European labor activists, the JLC leaders in some way replicated their own survival in the democratic camp. Their rapid assimilation into American unions and politics made them no longer feel like exiles, but they retained from their past a sense of purpose and political awareness that only the precariousness of exile can foster.[3] It was precisely this Socialist and Jewish awareness that caused the JLC to become alarmed about the danger posed by National Socialism and every totalitarianism to the Jews, to workers, to civil liberties, and to democracies. Extracting European labor leaders from France allowed them to limit the number of victims while fueling hopes of a political renaissance in Europe.

A number of publications and studies in recent decades have focused on the narratives of European exiles who found asylum in the United States between the 1930s and the end of World War II. The biographies of these intellectuals, artists, and scholars who reinvented their lives in America abound with details of the problems they faced along the way. Ranging from the sociologists of the Frankfurt School who resettled in New York and academics invited to join the faculties of American universities, to writers, musicians, and filmmakers, European refugees have left an indelible mark on their adoptive country. This intellectual exodus has been thoroughly dissected, and its contributions to American culture have been evaluated and celebrated. The American institutions that welcomed new émigrés, including the New School for Social Research in New York, and the foundations and organizations that facilitated their immigration are also well documented, as are many of the groups and individuals who helped them escape from Europe.[4] Among them, Varian Fry, the agent for the Emergency Rescue Committee, who operated in Marseille from 1940 to 1941 and helped many of these refugees reach American shores, has posthumously been recognized as a towering hero and was the first American to be recognized as one of the "Righteous Among the Nations" by Yad Vashem.

The JLC's extensive participation in these operations, however, has received remarkably little scholarly attention. The JLC worked alongside Varian Fry to rescue anti-Nazi refugees who were being hunted by the Gestapo and the Vichy police in France. Early on in his book *Surrender on Demand*,[5] Fry remarked that another American, Frank Bohn, was also active in Marseille. Bohn had been sent by the AFL to help well-known German Social Democratic Party leaders, whose names were at the top of the Gestapo "wanted" lists, get out of France. These two American emissaries hastily divided their responsibilities, with Bohn suggesting to Fry, "Suppose you take the writers and artists and all the young members of the various left-wing groups you're interested in . . . and we'll go on handling the trade-union people and the older socialists."[6] The cooperation between the two men quickly unraveled, however, and Fry did not explain Bohn's connection to the AFL or their links with the JLC. In fact, the JLC is never mentioned in Fry's narrative, which also omits the fact that the JLC continued to engage in rescue activities after Bohn had left France. Although numerous publications and exhibitions have featured examples of Fry's successful rescues of writers and artists,[7] less is known about the fates of the

Socialists, union activists, and other political opponents who successfully fled the depredations of the Third Reich and Mussolini.

These figures included such eminent and diverse persons as Friedrich Adler, secretary-general of the Labor and Socialist International; Raphael Abramovitch, a leading member of the Russian Social Democratic Workers' Party (Menshevik); Julius Deutsch, leader of the 1934 workers' rebellion in Vienna; Friedrich Stampfer, editor-in-chief of the Berlin socialist daily newspaper *Vorwärts*; and prominent members—and leftist dissidents—of the German Social Democratic Party. Several activists and editors from the anti-fascist movement Giustizia e Libertà, including Alberto Cianca and Nicola Chiaromonte, were also among JLC protégés. Noah Portnoy, president of the Central Committee of the Jewish Labor Bund in Poland, and numerous Bund militants and intellectuals were among those saved via Vilna (Vilnius) in Lithuania. For every high-profile name on these lists, there were dozens of other companions in exile. Yet despite the combined efforts of the JLC in New York and Varian Fry in Marseille, a number of highly visible individuals failed to elude arrest. Rudolf Breitscheid and Rudolf Hilferding, for example, prominent political figures in the Weimar Republic, were arrested in Arles when the JLC was attempting to rescue them.[8] JLC financial aid, however, helped sustain some of these sought-after figures, including Italian Socialist Party leader Giuseppe Modigliani, who remained in hiding in France until the fall of Mussolini.

Even before June 1940, the JLC was aware that German and Italian authorities were pursuing labor organizers and other workers' representatives and attempted to provide assistance. Keeping track of their precarious situations in France—internment in camps for German citizens, escape through the Unoccupied Zone—allowed the JLC to establish lists of those in imminent danger of arrest and deportation and to dispatch an agent to Marseille. In reality, it was the JLC, under AFL cover, that contributed to Frank Bohn's mission.

The JLC did not limit its activities to rescuing activists, saving them from deportation and near-certain death. On the basis of such rescues, its wartime networks steadily expanded, eventually providing assistance to resistance groups especially in France, Norway, and Poland. In this way, by supporting clandestine networks that were part of the French Resistance, the JLC contributed to the reemergence of the French Socialist Party during the war. It equally supported members of the Bundist Circle in Paris (Cercle Amical-Arbeter Ring), who survived successive waves of Vichy and Gestapo roundups. At the same time it did its utmost to help Polish underground fighters in the Warsaw Ghetto until the very end.

During the 1930s and the war JLC activists operated from New York on behalf of the victims of Nazi violence to whom they felt connected by their former political involvement. Their motivations were part of a transatlantic context of affinities and connections that had not been erased through the immigration process, and whose transnational character, as well as political and sometimes underground nature, remained unperceived in the national narratives or in grand World War II chronicles. In this sense this book diverges from the perspective of American historians who criticized the Roosevelt administration—and public opinion—for failing to fully comprehend the sinister forces that were driving European refugees from their homes and the urgent need to intervene to prevent the massacre of Jews. "The Nazis were the murderers, but we were the all too passive accomplices," argued David Wyman in the introduction to his book *The Abandonment of the Jews: America and the Holocaust*.[9] His assertion is certainly justified in terms of strategic decisions made by the State Department and U.S. military authorities. "It is inaccurate to speak of low priority given to the rescue of Jews. It had no priority at all and was simply not considered," Henry Feingold also observed.[10] But the blame that Wyman heaps on the American government and the Allies does not apply to the many Jewish, Christian, and nondenominational organizations and other individuals and associations that tirelessly labored to save lives, sometimes in direct opposition to the government's wishes. Among these, as both a Jewish and a working-class organization, the JLC was doubly sensitive to the horrors of Nazism and contributed significantly to such efforts.

The JLC cooperated on many occasions with more established Jewish American organizations, despite their sociological and cultural differences. A social divide separated the elite of American Jewry, mostly descended from nineteenth-century German Jewish immigrants, and the recently founded JLC, which represented a working-class constituency of east European Yiddish-speaking immigrants. Immersed in socialism and worker solidarity, these immigrants formed the core of the garment industry's urban proletariat. On its own initiative, sometimes alone or in concert with other organizations, the JLC engaged in distinctly non-Zionist activities that were politically aligned with its leaders' labor and socialist backgrounds. Despite their internationalist commitment they did not seek to outgrow their Jewishness and therefore could not be labeled as what Isaac Deutscher has called "Non-Jewish Jews."[11] On the contrary, their Bundist beliefs were entirely committed to defending the Jewish people and preserving secular Yiddish culture in Poland and throughout the diaspora. Deutscher's model, however, partly explains the complex Jewish-socialist identity of the JLC's leaders, whose Jewishness, grounded in the eastern European history of anti-Semitism, was transcended, but not erased, by universal socialism. These two circles of collective identity combined to create a form of internationalist solidarity that remained largely unchanged after they emigrated to the United States. Indeed, this inextricably dual identity explains why the JLC received appeals from and extended help to both Jewish and Socialist political organizations and individuals.

Two different phases can nevertheless be detected in the JLC's anti-Nazi efforts. During the 1930s and through the early war years, the organization focused primarily on assisting prominent leaders of Socialist and Social Democratic parties and trade unions linked to the Labor and Socialist International, as well as politically committed opponents of Hitler's regime. Beyond this institutional orbit, however, a constellation of personalities and groups also depended on the organization for survival or assistance with emigration. This included lesser-known members and activists of Socialist movements: German, Austrian, Czech, and Polish anti-Nazi militants; Italian, French, and Belgian anti-fascists; former Russian Mensheviks; and Norwegian resistance fighters. Whether they were Jewish or not it was political belief that motivated the organization to assist or rescue these individuals and groups from arrest and persecution. It should be noted, however, that most Socialist leaders in the German-speaking world were Jewish, which reflects a preexisting symbiosis between Jewishness and socialism in

Weimar Germany. As Yuri Slezkine emphasized, "The left-wing intellectuals did not simply 'happen to be mostly Jews,' as some pious historiography would have us believe, but Jews created the left-wing intellectual movement in Germany."[12] The same could be said of eastern European Socialists, particularly the Bundists. A sublimated form of Jewish millenarianism provided the foundation for the Socialist idealism outwardly projected by the JLC.

After the invasion of Poland in 1939, however, and particularly after word of mass deportations in 1942 reached JLC leaders, the focus shifted to trying to save European Jews, especially those who were besieged in Poland. The JLC lived and breathed according to the rhythm of the unfolding Jewish tragedy, providing humanitarian assistance for Polish Jews forced to flee en masse to the Soviet Union and material support for clandestine organizations in the Warsaw Ghetto. It multiplied its activities despite dwindling hope for the survival of those imprisoned in the ghetto. Contributions to the struggle, however, and efforts to rebuild postwar Jewish life continued to be inspired by the original Bundist desire to preserve both Jewish secular culture and workers' rights.

All of this raises the question of whether the JLC's activities can be interpreted as forms of resistance—in both symbolic and practical senses of the word—as a form of intellectual, moral, and political engagement, and with respect to the European Resistance movements to which they contributed.[13] If one accepts the antithetical traits of lived experience posited by François Bédarida—submission/resistance, resignation/refusal, collaboration/revolt—the JLC's stance was decidedly aligned with resistance, both in opposition to the U.S. government's apparent disregard for the plight of European Jewry and in its solidarity with and support for European resistance movements. The organization's rescue and exfiltration networks were consistent with the political stance of refugees, who by entering exile were able to continue the struggle on behalf of their original countries.[14] At the same time, these activities were indicative of resistance toward the U.S. State Department's reluctance to admit refugees, especially those who were Jews and socialists. It is true that the JLC stood far from the occupying forces and the perils of the front lines and that their support was external to the day-to-day realities of the struggle. Nevertheless, their participation required a determination to cooperate with diverse networks that were engaged in combat with the oppressors and a moral and political endorsement of clandestine activities. For instance, with respect to German socialists, the JLC was fully aware that it needed to act on behalf of both the Social Democratic Party (SPD) in exile and dissident socialist groups actively engaged in an underground struggle. In France, the JLC provided funds to the Comité d'Action Socialiste (CAS; Socialist Action Committee) that acted through clandestine networks. In Poland, it supported armed insurrection in the ghetto and provided assistance to those partisans who were able to escape.

At the same time, the JLC also offered a specifically Jewish form of resistance. A number of historians have drawn a distinction between the participation of Jewish militants and combatants in organized resistance movements and the specifically Jewish daily struggle which the situation implied: survive, help others to survive, and escape deportation and extermination.[15] Through its rescue efforts and financial support of anti-Nazi activities, the JLC operated on both levels, nurturing hope that Jewish institutions in Europe would survive the war. Beginning in 1942, its dedication to socialism was combined with total commitment to humanitarian assistance aimed at saving the Jewish people, their culture, and their institutions. In supporting the Warsaw Ghetto fighters the JLC was symbolically part of the battle against the extermination of Poland's Jewish population. As has been emphasized, the frames of reference of the two types of Jewish resistance are not identical: one consisted in providing targeted assistance to political organizations engaged in the struggle against the occupying forces, while the other defended the very existence of Jewish people.[16]

Conveyors of ideas between two worlds—Europe and the United States—the JLC leaders also became smugglers of people, providers of money, and creators of hope. From one shore of the Atlantic to the other, the eventual success of their activism could not be taken for granted given the uncertainty of transatlantic communications and the hazardous conditions of reception and action. Each person whom they rescued increased the hope that others would follow, reinforcing a chain of resistance that reached across occupied territories in Europe. Every financial contribution from the JLC that reached its goal suggested that more would follow.

However, the overall situation deteriorated steadily through the twelve long years of the Third Reich. The memory of the past furnished no basis for predicting the Nazi State's extreme radicalization. Beginning in 1942, Nazi determination to exterminate European Jewry opened up a bottomless chasm—in terms of both its consequences for Jews and the vast emergency for defense and protection that the Allies never seriously attempted to provide. Given the sheer scale of the catastrophe, which only became apparent after the war's end, the contributions of the JLC and other organizations cannot be valued solely in quantitative terms. The will to help cannot be measured against the magnitude of absolute horror.

The Jewish Labor Committee's archives became available to the public only after 1985 when they were donated to the Tamiment Library/Robert F. Wagner Labor Archives at New York University.[17] Archivist Gail Malmgreen and her colleagues, including Karl Dunkel, a Yiddish-speaking former Polish Bundist, catalogued the material and attempted to publicize its rich contents. Her articles, as well as an anthology of documents coauthored with Arieh Lebowitz, helped raise awareness of the JLC's many accomplishments and paved the way for further studies.[18] A few researchers had been aware of these sources before they were catalogued, providing early fragments of the JLC history.[19] And in 1996, Jack Jacobs's focus on the rescue and support of endangered German and Austrian labor and Socialist leaders revealed the depth of the JLC's political connections in Europe.[20] Surprisingly, however, before or after 1985, no study of the American labor movement or of Jewish American history has taken into account the role of the JLC. For example, while Irving Howe's *World of Our Fathers* (1976) celebrated the role of Central European immigrants in the labor and Socialist movements in the United States, it never referred to the JLC.[21] To this day, the JLC appears in some studies inasmuch as it contributed to collective anti-Nazi actions, or in its relations with prominent labor leaders, especially David Dubinsky.[22] Other historians, exploring U.S. policies toward refugees, have made passing references to the JLC as one of a number of organizations pressing Washington to admit more refugees but have not described its successful rescue efforts and contributions to anti-Nazi and anti-fascist movements.[23] This in part may be a matter of scale: the role of the far larger American Jewish Joint Distribution Committee ("the Joint," or JDC) has been more thoroughly investigated.[24] Accounting for the Joint's diverse activities and the many countries in which it operated has certainly proven to be a challenging task. The more modest profile of the JLC, linked to its financial dependence on garment workers and to its pragmatic objectives, does not fully explain this relative neglect and lack of interest. This study has attempted to correct a lacuna in the historical record by bringing to light the JLC's most important activities during the 1930s and World War II. And new research is already expanding this perspective especially with regard to the organization's role in reconstructing postwar Jewish life.[25]

A full examination of the JLC archives would require proficiency in a number of languages. Readers of Yiddish can have access to a vast body of original printed and handwritten documents emanating from its members and correspondents in the United States as well as from countless persons writing for help from European countries. On the whole, at least one-third of the JLC archives are in the Yiddish language. In addition, given their many connections across the European socialist world, JLC leaders often received letters from German, Russian, Polish, Czech, French, and Italian correspondents in these original languages. Altogether these materials provide a broad perspective on the spectrum of JLC intellectual contacts and activities. But, without proficiency in so many languages, and after delving in these archives for some time, it appeared to me that a broad outline of the JLC history before and during the war emerged from the major part of its archives. Most of the JLC correspondence with European Social Democrats, and most of its exchanges with American interlocutors, was written in English. JLC formal administrative documents such as Executive Committee and Office Committee reports, conventions, and general correspondence were all written in English. At times, certainly, the use of Yiddish allowed JLC leaders a more intimate approach to the fate of their brethren in Poland. For instance, the minutes of the Executive Committee meetings in the summer and autumn of 1942, when JLC leaders discovered the horror of the Final Solution, are transcribed in Yiddish. For these key elements relating to Poland, I am grateful for the assistance of Erez Lévy, a linguist and historian at Medem Center-Arbeter Ring in Paris who translated for me what was said during these occasions. The very existence of such a rich collection of Yiddish-language documents, memoranda, and correspondence is a testament to their authors'—and readers'—political and cultural independence, to their inner apprehension of what was happening, and to their ability to sustain the Yiddish-speaking community across oceans and borders.[26]

Amid this multilateral and multicultural context and the broader Nazi-era environment in which the JLC arose, the book outlines its most significant activities. It analyzes the ethnic, social, and political origins of the organization's leaders and membership, their positions within the American and international labor movements, and their role in the 1930s antifascist struggle. Above all, the book highlights the JLC's wartime rescue and assistance operations, principally in France and in Poland. To trace the steps of this multifaceted activity, the narrative interweaves fields of historical inquiry that are usually treated separately and whose connection is perceptible only due to the transnational nature of both Jewish culture and the international labor movement. The story follows unpredicted paths, passing from the history of the Bund in Russia and Poland to that of U.S. labor in the 1930s; describing rescue episodes in both Marseille and Vilna (Lithuania); and finally tracing the JLC's involvement in the support of resistance movements in France and Poland. The JLC's ability to cross linguistic as well as administrative boundaries is reflected in the transhistoriographic character of its history, which may partly explain why its story has remained largely untold.

I

FOUNDATIONS

The Jewish Labor Committee was created in New York City in 1934 by prominent members of the Yiddish-speaking community of immigrants from Central Europe. The founders represented the main garment trade unions, as well as mutual aid societies and political organizations that were part of the "Jewish labor movement." The founders' objective was to create an umbrella organization that could coordinate their joint efforts to combat Nazism in Europe and anti-Semitism in the United States. Baruch Charney Vladeck, the manager of the Yiddish-language daily the *Jewish Daily Forward*, was the initiator of the new organization. His experience as a Bundist activist in czarist Russia and his long-standing European connections sharpened his appreciation of the true implications of the Nazi threat. Vladeck's political affiliations with left-wing labor movements and with Jewish organizations in the United States allowed him to play a key role in uniting these networks for the sake of the anti-Nazi struggle. In order to mobilize the working-class communities in the garment industry, traditionally composed of Jewish immigrants and other minorities, Vladeck stressed that anti-Semitism was only one facet of the Nazi menace, which also threatened all civil liberties and especially labor organizations. He believed that addressing a problem on this scale would require the combined resources of both organized labor and Jewish associations. The JLC embodied these two movements in a single organization that was based on the core values of European socialism and American Progressivism.

Understanding how the Jewish Labor Committee differed from other American Jewish organizations requires looking at its founders' shared political origins and recalling their reactions to early Nazi policies. Like other Jewish, Christian, and secular organizations, the JLC faced widespread resistance from legislators and citizens in general to admitting large numbers of European refugees. To circumvent this obstacle, the JLC engaged in political activity to a greater extent than did most humanitarian associations.

PRECEDENCE IN NAZI PERSECUTION

Early Nazi attacks on Jews coincided with the complete destruction of the German labor movement. Hitler encouraged the SA and SS, the armed wings of the National Socialist Party (NSDAP; Nationalsozialistische Deutsche Arbeiterpartei), to take action against groups and individuals considered to be subversive—primarily Jews and members of the labor movement. The exodus from Germany of Jewish and left-wing people began in the early months of 1933, almost immediately after Hitler took power on January 30. The primary obsessions of National Socialist ideology— anti-Semitism and anti-Marxism, combined in rabid anti-Bolshevism— had been clear well before the Nazi Party came to power. And when it did, the first political targets of the new regime and of its terror system were systematically Communists and left-wing organizations.[1] By the time the German labor movement had been quickly and thoroughly decimated, the persecution of European Jews had only just begun. Particularly after the Reichstag fire on February 27, anti-Communist fury led to the arrest of nearly ten thousand party members and supporters who were interned in newly created concentration camps. The fatal clash between the Hitler regime and the German Communist Party expanded to include the Social Democratic Party and the labor unions, which were outlawed. The Communist press was muzzled, and Socialist papers were suspended before they, too, were shut down. During the first week of May 1933, Nazi authorities arrested and jailed the leaders of the major labor organizations and confiscated their property. Within a few short weeks, the left had been crushed, constitutional law and civil liberties suspended. A month earlier, on April 1, the government-sponsored boycott of Jewish-owned businesses and trades had unleashed a wave of officially encouraged violence against Jews. Next, on April 7, an "Aryan Decree" authorized the firing of any government employee considered hostile to the regime, expelling Jews from public sector jobs and positions. A similar measure was extended to the liberal professions, the intention being to compel the German Jewish population to emigrate. In hindsight from the Holocaust, historians can detect the genesis of the Führer's anti-Semitic policies in his pre-1933 discourse, but when he first seized power it was impossible to predict the full extent of the Nazi-led horror and the devastation that would be perpetrated between 1942 and 1945.[2]

The chronological order of these events is important for understanding the motivations behind the anti-Nazi organizations that were created. For the JLC leaders, who were Jewish and socialist, well integrated into the labor movement, and prepared to combat anti-Semitism, it was the destruction of the German labor movement in 1933, followed by that of the Austrian movement in 1934, that drove them to act. More precisely, their mission—combining the defense of the Jewish proletariat and the values of international socialism—motivated their intervention on behalf of European labor. Seen retrospectively, Hitler's assault on organized labor is statistically less significant than the Final Solution and could be more easily explained in political terms. But to contemporary observers, the persecution of Jews and of the Left began simultaneously. The ultimate consequences of the two persecutions, however, only developed over different time periods.

While American Jewish organizations protested vigorously against the Third Reich's early anti-Semitic actions, reactions to the German assault on the labor movement were more muted. The American press, although skeptical at times, systematically reported German anti-Semitic activities after Hitler came to power in January 1933. In fact, German authorities, desiring to control their image abroad, pressured American journalists to censor their representation of the facts.[3] Well-informed and extremely concerned, the American Jewish community strongly denounced events in Europe. Several Jewish organizations organized protest marches on March 28, 1933, in New York and in more than eighty cities around the country. Heeding the call from hundreds of thousands of people for a national day of protest against the treatment of Jews in Germany, the Independent Order of the B'nai B'rith, the American Jewish Congress, and the American Jewish Committee coordinated this nationwide protest.[4] Representing a population of over four million people in the early 1930s, the American Jewish community wielded considerable influence—and felt a responsibility toward Jews throughout the world. In May 1933, Morris Waldman, the executive secretary of the American Jewish Congress, was prescient about the future:

> What has happened to the Jews in Germany, and indirectly to the Jews of the world, is worse even than the expulsion of Jews from Spain. It not only involves the possible extermination of 600,000 Jews, but also threatens to react dangerously upon the political, social, and economic status of the Jews in other countries. We have a tremendous job on our hands, not a passing episode, but one that threatens to be a problem for a long time. Many civilized countries of the world will have to be enlisted to offer shelter to the refugees.[5]

By contrast, public reaction to the crushing of German labor unions and the imprisonment of their leaders in May 1933 was more subdued, and the expressions of protest these actions elicited were not enough to mobilize the American labor movement. The AFL Executive Council filed a complaint with the State Department, requesting an investigation into "the destruction of the voluntary and independent organization of the German labor movement."[6] In the ensuing months, the AFL and Jewish organizations concentrated their efforts on a proposed boycott of German-made products. Only in early 1934 did American labor's more targeted assistance to besieged German labor and Social Democratic groups begin to gain momentum. As the manager of the *Jewish Daily Forward*, Baruch Charney Vladeck was naturally implicated in protests by Jewish organizations, but he thought that this mobilization needed to engage all the progressive forces in the nation and particularly labor organizations.

In February 1934, the urgency of his argument was dramatically confirmed by the crushing of the Austrian labor movement by Chancellor Engelbert Dollfuss's pro-fascist government. Caught between Nazi Germany and fascist Italy, Austria was overwhelmed by the Brown Shirts' onslaught. In a coup d'état, two days after the Reichstag elections had confirmed Hitler's victory on March 5, 1933, Dollfuss suspended the Austrian parliament and curtailed civil liberties, including the right to assemble and the freedom of the press. His goal was an authoritarian and corporatist government that could satisfy the religio-fascist movement, the Heimwehr (as well as the Vatican and the Mussolini administration), while preventing Austria from being completely swallowed by the Third Reich, which the National Socialist movement was pushing for. Month after month, the Social Democrats (SDAP; Sozialdemokratische Arbeiterpartei), led by Otto Bauer, could only look on as constitutional guarantees were abrogated and workers' rights were demolished. The SDAP had been Austria's largest and most powerful political party, with 600,000 members and electoral support of 40 percent in the 1932 elections. With more members than the Communist Party, it controlled major cities including Linz and Vienna. On February 12, 1934, however, the minister of public safety and leader of the Heimwehr, Emil Fey, seized the provincial government and dissolved the SDAP. Party offices were requisitioned, and party leaders and labor and even municipal representatives were placed under arrest. The Schutzbund, the SDAP's armed division in Linz and Vienna, led by Julius Deutsch, responded with a final, desperate uprising that was crushed after three days of savage fighting. Nine leaders were hanged, hundreds died in combat, and thousands were thrown into prison and concentration camps. After the devastation of the German labor movement, now the Austrian one ceased to exist.[7]

The American press provided better coverage of the brutal repression in Austria than they had of events in Germany the previous May, and the American response was immediate.[8] A protest against the Austrian massacre was held in Madison Square Garden on February 16, 1934, organized by New York labor unions and Socialists. But the meeting was violently interrupted by Communist agitators using similar tactics to those deployed in Vienna, where the Austrian Communists abandoned the Schutzbund and left the Social Democrats to take the blame for the debacle.[9] The largest garment workers' union in the United States, the International Ladies' Garment Workers' Union (ILGWU), stated that "the hundreds of thousands of workers affiliated with the unions that arranged the Garden meeting, will now more keenly than ever feel the sacred duty which the plight of their fellow workers in Austria has placed upon them and they will rally to their moral and material aid with every means at their command."[10]

CREATING THE JEWISH LABOR COMMITTEE

Foreshadowed over several weeks previously, the meeting that led to the founding of the Jewish Labor Committee finally took place on February 25, 1934, several days after the collapse of the Schutzbund. Over one thousand delegates from left-wing secular Jewish labor and fraternal groups met at the Central Plaza Hotel on Manhattan's Lower East Side, presided over by Baruch Charney Vladeck.[11] The meeting was billed as both a "People's Conference against Nazism and Fascism" and as a "Labor Conference for Jewish Affairs," a dual identity that was reflected in the name ultimately chosen for the new organization: the Jewish Labor Committee. The organization's charter as drafted at the meeting boldly asserted:

> [The purpose of the JLC is] to give aid to Jewish and non-Jewish labor institutions overseas; to assist the democratic labor movement in Europe; to provide succor to victims of oppression and persecution; and to combat anti-Semitism and racial and religious intolerance abroad and in the United States.[12]

Formulated in such general terms, the new organization's aim was vast. It sought to support social-democratic movements wherever they were threatened and to fight anti-Semitism wherever it existed. JLC records from the 1930s and 1940s confirm that its actions pursued these goals. However, JLC leaders were not utopians but pragmatists. Their objective was to create the necessary solidarity to provide assistance to beleaguered Jewish and labor groups in Europe. The JLC intended to raise its own funds in order to avoid competing with other Jewish organizations and to awaken American labor's solidarity with European labor movements.[13] This meant sensitizing American workers to the realities of anti-Semitism. At the same time, the movement established a left-leaning, secular, non-Zionist labor presence among the largest Jewish organizations. Vladeck's strategy focused on using political and social channels to generate American support for anti-Nazi movements, a struggle that was not limited to combating anti-Semitism in Germany. He underlined this in a declaration to the *New York Times*:

> In combatting fascism and Hitlerism in the United States, it is important to emphasize that these dictatorships aim at the destruction not only of the Jews but also of all organized labor and any and all liberal movements as well. We intend therefore to stress in our activities the trade union and liberal angles of the fight against Nazism as much as the Jewish angle. . . . In carrying on our fight as a labor body, we intend to impress upon the American people the fact that the great majority of the Jews in the United States, who reside in the large industrial cities, are wage-earners and are loyal members of the American Federation of Labor.[14]

A few months later, in October 1934, Vladeck officially announced the creation of the JLC at the AFL's convention in San Francisco. He reminded his audience about the international political crisis created by totalitarian regimes, especially Nazism: "Listen to the terrible, deadening silence that is falling upon a great part of the world like a sinister shroud of death. Italy, Germany, Austria, Russia . . . today, nearly half of the world has lost its voice."[15] Using a rhetoric that he had made his own, Vladeck highlighted the inherent connection between combating anti-Semitism and defending labor movements. He appealed to American workers to join the organization by opposing any racial discrimination and urged them to reverse the isolationist trend that prevented the United States from a unified response to events in Europe. His purpose was to encourage American workers to join the anti-Nazi struggle by emphasizing that fascist ideology was a threat not only to workers in Europe but also to themselves:

> In these torture chambers of Fascism and tyranny, the Jew occupies a conspicuous and painful place.... And as is always the case, the one who suffers most is the artisan and the worker. It is hard enough to be a Jew, but it is doubly hard to be a Jew *and* a worker.... Since the coming of the industrial age, the Jews have been a true barometer for the Labor Movement. Whenever and wherever a government begins to persecute the Jews, it inevitably follows with persecution of the workers.... This is why Organized Labor throughout the world, outside of sentimental reasons, is against anti-Semitism, because it knows that the first blast against the Jews is only the forerunner of a dark storm against Labor [and] that permitting a government to foster anti-Semitism is to strengthen a power that will crush Labor.[16]

He reminded the audience about the ominous events in Germany in March, April, and May 1933 when German labor leaders were arrested and union assets were confiscated. The largest labor federation, the Allgemeiner Deutscher Gewerkschaftsbund (ADGB), and its member organizations were destroyed, their property requisitioned, their bank accounts seized, and the labor press muzzled. The workers of the world, according to Vladeck, could not stand idly by in the face of an attack on the very principles of their existence. With his vision of the "double servitude" of labor and Jewish communities, Vladeck analyzed the situation through the lens of his own political experience. He also correctly understood that the Jewish labor movement had grown out of its marginality and was reaching a point when it could exert power in labor circles as well as with the Roosevelt administration.

ANCHORED IN THE JEWISH LABOR MOVEMENT

The JLC was founded at a time when the Jewish labor movement was at the peak of its influence. With approximately 500,000 members by the mid-

1930s, the "movement" included labor, political, and social groups that had been created by Jewish immigrants who had mainly arrived in the United States before World War I. Workers in the garment industry and other trades—bakers, butchers, typographers, bookbinders, painters, and leather workers—had joined trade-specific, ethnocultural labor organizations that reflected their constituencies' everyday concerns (including preserving languages like Yiddish and other cultural priorities). The original concentration of Jewish workers in the garment industry had given rise to powerful labor unions that grew rapidly and flourished under the aegis of the New Deal.

With the largest membership, the ILGWU, founded in 1901, represented men and women in the ready-to-wear women's clothing industry. After years of financial instability and near bankruptcy, the union was finally able to overcome employers' union-bashing tactics, its own internecine struggles with Communist factions, and the effects of the Depression. By May 1934, David Dubinsky, ILGWU president since 1932, could boast of a membership of 200,000, a figure that continued to expand for a decade. In recognition of the union's growing influence, Dubinsky was elected vice president of the AFL Executive Council that same year. The economic upturn that resulted from Roosevelt's first New Deal program helped the garment industry regain its prosperity, energizing union activities. In a number of manufacturing firms, labor agreements between employers and union representatives under the auspices of the National Industrial Recovery Act (NIRA) and the Wagner Act overcame management opposition.[17] As a result, union recognition became more common, despite the fact that these fragmented trades consisted of thousands of modest-sized textile and clothing workshops scattered throughout New York City as well as in cities as far-flung as Philadelphia, Cleveland, Boston, Kansas City, Chicago, and Los Angeles.[18]

Founded in 1914, the Amalgamated Clothing Workers of America (ACWA), the second-largest garment trade union, represented workers in the menswear industry. Under its president and founder, Sidney Hillman, the ACWA had remained independent of the AFL until 1934, when it briefly joined it. Like the ILGWU, it relied on the idea of industrial unionism to unite workers regardless of their workplace conditions, skill, gender, or ethnic origin, which were the causes of frequent antagonism and discrimination. The strategic promotion of industrial unity led to collective bargaining contracts and the arbitration of conflicts between labor and management in a number of cities. It also enabled unions gradually to modernize an industry that had been plagued by myriad divisions stemming from the sweatshop system and the lack of labor regulation.

Hillman's progressive approach to industrial management and his interest in workers' purchasing power and in the role of the state in labor relations were positive factors in this recovery. His 1933 appointment to the National Industrial Recovery Board to oversee the drafting of codes in the garment industry was a sign of the Roosevelt administration's recognition of his political and economic ability. He was able to promote better labor management, social progress, and union rights. The ACWA seized the opportunity to launch unionization campaigns in many cities, including New York, Rochester, Boston, Philadelphia, Chicago, Milwaukee, Cincinnati, and St. Louis. By late 1933, its membership reached 125,000.[19] Within a few months, both the ILGWU and the ACWA had overcome their economic difficulties, expanded their memberships, and helped modernize industrial relations by establishing norms in wage scales and workdays. The largest garment trade unions were now in the vanguard of the American labor movement and had a voice in Washington.

Moreover, their form of unionism had more in common with European social-democratic labor organizations than with the American trade unions that were affiliated with the AFL. Although Jewish labor unions' primary concern was improving the working conditions of their members, they provided other services including educational and cultural programs in English, Yiddish, and other languages spoken by garment workers. The ILGWU and ACWA offered courses and events such as lectures on American government, social insurance, political economy, and literature. Members could benefit from collective housing and banking services, as well as theater clubs, music, and outdoor activities. The unions and affiliated social organizations gave workers the sense that they belonged to a broad family that in addition to labor protection also provided education about American institutions, children's summer camps, and family cultural events.[20]

The close-knit networks fostered by the cultural and linguistic bonds among Yiddish-speaking immigrants were not weakened by the growing diversity of the labor force. Italian immigrants, who had arrived at about the same time as the wave of Jewish immigrants in the early twentieth century, provided nearly as large a workforce as recent Central Europeans. By 1930, only half of the ILGWU membership was of Jewish origin, a percentage that declined to one-third by 1940. For example, the ILGWU's largest local—New York Local 89, led by Luigi Antonini—consisted entirely of Italian dressmakers. In addition to Jews, Italians, and smaller numbers of Poles, Czechs, and Southern Slavs, African American women from the South—plus Puerto Ricans in New York City and Mexicans in Los Angeles—all diversified the labor force. However, the cultural and political orientations of the garment trades labor organizations remained predominantly "Jewish" inasmuch as their leadership still originated from early twentieth-century Jewish immigration.[21]

Smaller unions also joined the JLC, including the Hat, Cap, and Millinery Workers, whose president was Max Zaritsky, and a variety of trades that were represented by the United Hebrew Trades, an umbrella organization for Jewish-led unions affiliated with the AFL. Another important addition to the JLC was the Workmen's Circle (Arbeter Ring in Yiddish), a Jewish fraternal order with chapters in American cities with significant Jewish populations. The Arbeter Ring promoted a strong socialist program that included social services for workers, Jewish children's schools, and mutual aid associations for families. Although it was a national organization, the Workmen's Circle left it to local chapters to define their own programs and rules, which often emanated from earlier *landsmanschaftn* associations of European origins. The organization's secular Yiddish approach helped sustain communications between Jewish workers throughout the United States and eventually was vital in establishing and maintaining the JLC's foreign relief programs abroad.[22]

Several minor political organizations also helped establish the JLC. Among them was the Jewish Socialist Verband, which consisted of a group of former Bundist militants actively engaged in supporting democratic forms of labor organization to resist communism. Led by Nathan Chanin, the Verband, which split off from the Jewish Federation of the Socialist Party, had close contact with European socialist leaders in Poland or among Russian Mensheviks. Another small party was that of the Left Poale Zionists, an exception among the JLC's largely non-Zionist constituency. They combined a Zionist orientation with the ideals of international socialism.[23] Lastly, the *Jewish Daily Forward* was also represented in the JLC by its founding association and through Vladeck. With eleven regional editions and a readership of 250,000, the *Forward*, edited since its foundation in 1897 by Abraham Cahan, was not only the most widely read Yiddish daily newspaper in the world but also the most widely circulated socialist daily in the United States. Maintaining European correspondents, the paper was able to keep its readers informed about events that affected the Jewish communities in Europe. Significantly, the JLC installed its offices in the Forward Building, at 175 East Broadway, just as had the Jewish Socialist Verband. This meant that Vladeck had only to walk down a staircase for the *Forward* to publish JLC decisions in its pages.

Led by the charismatic figure of Baruch Charney Vladeck, the JLC's Executive Committee was composed of representatives of every major constituent organization. ILGWU president David Dubinsky held the strategic position of treasurer, while Joseph Baskin and Benjamin Gebiner from the Workmen's Circle served as secretaries. ACWA secretary treasurer Joseph Schlossberg represented his organization on the Executive Committee. Another influential member was Nathan Chanin of the Jewish Socialist Verband. Although Vladeck's sudden death from a heart attack in October 1938 temporarily left the organization in disarray, Adolph Held, former director of the ACWA union bank, took over the position of JLC president.

From the outset, the JLC enjoyed favorable economic and social conditions made possible by early New Deal policies. Invited to speak at the May 1934 ILGWU convention, Vladeck praised the remarkable "renaissance" that had caused the union's membership to soar in the previous year and made the creation of the JLC possible.[24] Financed by contributions from its local and national member organizations, the JLC could rely on a base of nearly half a million members throughout the 1930s and 1940s. Although it represented only a fraction of the labor movement and even of Jewish organizations in the United States, the combined power of the JLC's members ensured that their fundraising appeals and activities enjoyed full financial and political autonomy. Although it was linked to the AFL and later to the Congress of Industrial Organizations (CIO) through its affiliated unions, the JLC remained politically independent from both federations, while benefiting from their support for some of its activities.

POLITICAL ORIGINS IN THE BUND

The ideological and strategic commitments of the JLC leaders arose from shared political experiences in Europe. Most of them had a common political past as Bundist activists in the Russian Empire. It was this involvement that had prompted their emigration to the United States. In some ways the JLC functioned as a resurgence of their initial ideals. This Bundist background combining Marxist thought with the defense of Jewish people was clearly reflected in the JLC's goals, as well as in its attitude toward Communists. Moreover, the arrival of a number of Polish Bundists in the late 1930s reinforced these political leanings.

The Bund had been founded in 1897 in the Lithuanian city of Vilna (Vilnius), which was then part of the Russian Empire's Zone of Settlement. In the same year, Theodore Herzl founded the Zionist movement in Basel. Zionists believed that Jews could only save their people by returning to Palestine to establish a Jewish nation. Bundists, on the other hand, contended that Jews should defend their rights wherever they currently resided, whether as one of the recognized nationalities in the Russian Empire, or in Poland after 1918, or in the countries of emigration, as part of the diaspora. Another important difference between the Zionists and the Bundists lay in how they approached party politics.[25]

The General Jewish Labor Bund of Lithuania, Poland, and Russia—its official name—served primarily as a union that defended workers in the Pale of Settlement. Densely concentrated in Poland and Lithuania, the Jewish working class was mainly employed in artisanal trades and secondary labor sectors of Russian industry. The labor movement that emerged among these workers was economically and culturally specific. By adopting Yiddish—the vernacular language of the Jewish people—as its working language, the Bund actively sought to maintain the cultural identity of the Jewish proletariat. And preserving the spirit of the mutual aid societies organized by Jewish tradesmen in earlier times, within the space of a few years, it realized its goal of uniting Jewish workers throughout the Pale of Settlement. In addition to its purely economic functions, the movement actively participated in the rise of Russian revolutionary socialism.

The Bund also functioned as a Socialist workers' party. Founded one year before the Russian Social Democratic Labor Party (RSDLP), it remained one of its largest and best organized constituent groups, although relations between the two organizations were sometimes tense. The Bund sought recognition as the sole representative of the Jewish proletariat and defended Jewish national and cultural autonomy in the Russian Empire. Unlike the Zionists, Bundist leaders were not nationalists, a position that they considered to be utopian and backward. But recognition of Jewish nationality (as well as the cultural and political autonomy of other minorities in the czarist empire) remained a central feature of their program.[26] The RSDLP, on the other hand, believed that the Bundist project would fragment the working class and preclude the unity required by the revolutionary cause. The Bund's position on the national question troubled its relations with the Russian Socialist Party, whose leaders (principally Lenin but also including Jews such as Martov and Axelrod) were assimilationists.[27] In 1903, this discord drove the Bund to separate from the RSDLP, although it rejoined it in 1906. Nevertheless, its predominant involvement in the 1905 revolution and the organization of insurrectionary strikes in some sixty cities in the Pale of Settlement closely implicated the Bund in the revolutionary movement that shook Russia. By mid-1906, the claim could be made that the Jewish revolutionary socialist organizations had gathered under their flag almost the entire Jewish proletariat. And in Lodz and Warsaw, where the Jewish population constituted large minorities, the joint participation of Poles and Jews was doubly impressive because unusual.[28]

Vladimir Medem, a Bundist leader and promoter of the movement's cultural autonomy, recognized that the Yiddish language and culture were fundamental elements of Jewish identity. Unlike advocates of Hebrew scholarship and language who classified Yiddish as a kind of jargon, Medem elevated it to a national language, grounded in the daily lives and struggles of the Jewish masses. Consequently he supported a cultural definition of the Jewish population of the Russian Empire.[29] The regime's anti-Semitism—of which the Kichinev pogrom in 1903 and those that followed the 1905 uprising were brutal reminders—created a reaction that strengthened the Yiddish identity of the Jewish proletariat that only the local workers' movement defended. Historian Enzo Traverso argues that the Bund's power and originality resided in its quest for a dialectic process between proletarian internationalism and the defense of an oppressed culture. As members of the Russian revolutionary movement, Bundists articulated the need simultaneously to defend Jewish workers' positions as a class and a minority *and* their integration into the wider Russian and international proletariat, a dual position engendering tensions.[30]

The Russian Revolution and the restoration of the Polish state transformed the Bund's existence in eastern Europe. After the October Revolution of 1917, Bund partisans in Russia were torn between the Mensheviks' social-democratic tendencies, which they shared, but whose militants were forced into exile, and those who sided with the Communist revolution and were unable to resist the Bolshevik pressure to centralize. In 1921, the Comintern liquidated the Russian Bund, arresting most of its leaders and forcing it to disband. The Communist Party absorbed many of the Bund's members. Those who attempted to maintain a Social Democratic affiliation faced a choice between exile and persecution.[31]

At the same time, in liberated and independent Poland, the Bund rebranded itself as a legitimate political movement, transforming itself into a socialist party that represented the Jewish working class in the midst of the country's overwhelming Catholicism. The newly reinvented Polish Bund offered a plethora of social and cultural services—including schools, youth organizations, labor unions, and mutual aid societies, as well as a Yiddish-language press—that supported and propelled the Jewish minority into modernity. Its relations with the Polish Socialist and Communist parties, however, were as difficult as they had been in Russia. In 1930, following a period of internal dissent and of resisting separatist nationalist tendencies, the Polish Bund joined the Labor and Socialist International (LSI), which in 1923 had freed itself from the vestiges of the Second International.[32]

As the legitimate heir of the original organization, the Polish Bund functioned as a small Jewish Socialist International.[33] With a population of three and a half million in the 1930s, Polish Jews were the second-largest minority in the world (the United States had the largest Jewish population: over four million). New York and Warsaw were the twin capitals of international Jewish culture. Numerous exchanges between the two cities were established, and several well-known Bund leaders made fundraising trips to the United States, giving lectures, bringing fresh news, and generating support from the Workmen's Circle and the Jewish Socialist Verband. Vladimir Medem traveled from Poland to New York in 1921, where he died in 1923. It was Vladeck who delivered the eulogy at his funeral.[34] Anton Litvak, a writer and promoter of Yiddish culture, active in czarist Russia and later in Poland, also moved to the United States in 1925. Until his death in 1932, Litvak gave lectures to Jewish Socialist Verband and Workmen's Circle audiences. The Menshevik Raphael Abramovitch, a former Bundist and the leader of the Russian Social Democratic Party in exile in Berlin, went on a lecture tour of the United States in 1925. As a correspondent in Berlin for the *Jewish Daily Forward*, Abramovitch was an important figure who maintained contacts between the Jewish American and German workers' movements and with Menshevik political émigrés.[35]

BARUCH CHARNEY VLADECK AND THE BUNDIST GENERATION

Baruch Charney Vladeck (1886–1938) is an emblematic figure among the Bundist exiles who shaped the Jewish American labor movement. Born as Baruch Nachmen Charney near Minsk in Dukora, Vladeck was educated at a yeshiva and was initially influenced by Zionism. Abandoning traditional Talmudic studies, he sided with the leftist Zionists and was eventually arrested by czarist police in January 1904 and incarcerated with other political prisoners in Minsk. For Vladeck, as for many of his generation, prison offered an excellent "apprenticeship" in revolutionary theory and clandestine struggle. Renouncing the Zionist cause, he embraced the Jewish labor movement. The Bund posted his bond to secure his freedom, enabling him, at not quite twenty years of age, to become an official leader of the movement and one of the foremost activists in the general strike during the 1905 upheaval. After being arrested in Vilna, he escaped and went into hiding. Moving from city to city, his oratorical skills earned him the qualification of "Young Lassalle" (in reference to the founder of the German Socialist Party). A prominent Bund leader and a major intellectual and tactician of the revolutionary struggle throughout Polish territory in the empire, he managed clandestine meetings and published tracts and brochures. Along with such figures as Vladimir Medem, he was a Bund delegate to the RSDLP convention in London in May and June 1907, where the schism between Bolsheviks and Mensheviks that had begun in 1903 became permanent. Political repression in Russia after 1905 ultimately forced Vladeck to emigrate, and his reputation as an orator and agitator preceded his arrival in New York in November 1908. The *Forward* published a full-page article showing him descending from the ship and sponsored a lecture tour for him in the western United States and Canada upon his arrival.[36]

Vladeck rapidly immersed himself in American political and social life. His position as manager of the *Jewish Daily Forward* beginning in 1918 placed him at the heart of New York's Jewish and socialist politics. Elected alderman of the Brooklyn precinct of Williamsburg, he was one of the seven socialists in the New York City Council. During World War I he worked for the oldest refugee rescue organization, the Hebrew Immigrant Aid Society (HIAS), arranging contributions from the People's Relief Committee, a group formed among socialist circles. The JLC, which Vladeck founded in 1934, was in some ways a replica of the People's Relief Committee.[37] Resigning from the Socialist Party of America in 1936, despite having been elected on this party's ticket several times, he instead helped found the American Labor Party to mobilize the New York labor electorate in support of Roosevelt's presidential candidacy. After being elected to the New York City Council on this program in 1937, he was appointed director of the

Housing Authority by Mayor Fiorello La Guardia. Yet his sudden death on October 30, 1938, brought an end to a career that flowed from his early revolutionary activities in Russia through three different (if complementary) fields: managing the world's largest Yiddish daily newspaper, participating in municipal New York politics, and leading the JLC in its international struggle against fascism and Nazism. When Vladeck died, New York City liberals lost a leader who ardently believed that a solid alliance between progressive and labor forces could foster independent political action. According to the ILGWU journal, over 300,000 people attended his funeral service, and one month later, thousands more attended a memorial service at Carnegie Hall.[38]

Sidney Hillman (1887–1946) and David Dubinsky (1892–1982) shared similar pasts, but in the United States they applied their combative instincts and political skills to the labor movement. As former Bundist militants—Hillman in Zagare and Dubinsky in Lodz—who had actively participated in the 1905 insurrectionary strikes, their activism (like Vladeck's) caused them to be arrested and drove them into hiding. Dubinsky, barely sixteen years old, was deported to Siberia. The two militants eventually escaped further arrests by emigrating. Hillman arrived in Chicago in 1907 and Dubinsky in New York in 1911. Employed in the garment industry, like so many of their fellow Central European Jewish immigrants, they contributed to the decisive Bundist influence over the early development of the American labor movement. It was no coincidence that unionization in the garment trades grew so rapidly during the great wave of strikes that took place in the clothing industry from 1909 to 1914. Some fifty branches of the Central Union of Bundist organizations had been established in American cities by the first decade of the twentieth century. The presence of recent immigrants, who had been activists experienced in mass-strike tactics, underground activities, and disciplined party organization, helped energize a movement that might otherwise have collapsed, as had so many before them. An active member of this movement, Dubinsky steadily ascended the ranks of the ILGWU in New York, eventually becoming its president in 1932. Hillman founded the ACWA in Chicago in 1914 and remained its president until his death in 1946.[39]

The primary difference between the two men's American careers lies in Dubinsky's proximity to the AFL, despite the rift following the creation of the CIO, in which he would play a leading part. In his role as JLC treasurer, he was able to provide support for the organization and to facilitate its relationship with the AFL. Hillman, however, became a key figure in the CIO and was able to cooperate with the communists and the Soviet world.[40] His political skills during the war brought him into close contact with President Roosevelt, who appointed him in 1940 to the National Defense Advisory Commission. Supervising the Labor Division of the War Production Board and helping manage the economic transition to war production, he became known as a "labor statesman."[41] Hillman's involvement in federal policy put an end to his day-to-day participation in JLC activities, except during the war when he played a central role in some of the JLC's international operations. This did not prevent the ACWA from being one of the main pillars of the JLC, despite the fact that its delegate, Joseph Schlossberg, was a left-leaning Zionist and a supporter of Histadrut, the labor organization in Palestine.[42]

Adolph Held (1885–1969) would succeed Vladeck as chairman of the JLC in 1938. Only eight years old when he arrived in the United States in 1893, Held—unlike Vladeck, Dubinsky, and Hillman—was not a former Bundist and had not participated in the 1905 revolution. He was elected as a socialist representative to the New York City Council from 1917 to 1919. He had managed the *Jewish Daily Forward* before Vladeck and helped run the HIAS. After taking the helm of the JLC in 1938, Held piloted the organization through the war, as the tragedy of the Holocaust unfolded.

In the late 1930s and throughout the war, former leaders of the Polish Bund sustained the JLC's ability to maintain contacts with Polish leaders in exile and others living under German occupation. Among those in New York, Jacob Pat and Benjamin Tabachinsky, directors of the Association of Yiddish Schools overseen by the Bund Central Committee, headed the JLC's assistance programs in Poland. Others, such as former Bundist activist Lazar Epstein and ex-Menshevik Samuel Estrin, after periods in exile—Epstein to China and Estrin to Berlin and Paris—helped refugees by expanding JLC contacts in these areas.[43]

SOCIALISTS, NOT COMMUNISTS

Most JLC leaders shared a basic distrust of Communists and communism. Disillusioned by the Bolshevik failure to promote even a hint of democracy, they had grown suspicious of Comintern diktats. A profound rift between Bundists and Communists had developed in Poland in the 1930s. Henryk Erlich, one of the foremost Polish Bund leaders, argued that the entire Communist philosophy was merely a celebration of the Soviet Union that promoted an aversion to non-Communist movements.[44]

Contact with the American Communist Party confirmed the JLC's future leaders' instinct to keep Communists at arm's length. The tactics of American Communists reinforced a distrust based on earlier experiences with the Bolsheviks. The American Communist Party (or the Communist Workers' Party, as it was known in the early 1920s) followed Comintern instructions to infiltrate and take over labor organizations. Between 1924 and 1926, power struggles in garment unions provoked strikes and lockouts in locals that contained communist factions. This conflict is remembered in union records as a critical turning point and a veritable "civil war."[45] The ILGWU was particularly affected by rivalries between Socialists and Communists. A strike in July 1926, in which Communist militants took over several local unions in New York, Boston, Chicago, and Philadelphia, lasted for twenty-eight weeks. The strike, which involved as many as 30,000 workers, was a major setback for the ILGWU leadership and finances. The conflict became increasingly entrenched, although Dubinsky, leader of New York City Local 10 at the time, was eventually able to overcome the Communist faction. Nevertheless, the union was considerably weakened at the national level. The ACWA was more successful in maintaining its position in the face of opposition. Hillman's interest in the Soviet Union made him more tolerant toward Communists, but he suspended or expelled their branches when they threatened union leadership or attempted to undermine the union's authority.[46]

The strict fidelity of the Communist Party of the United States to Moscow, all the more abiding as its membership was small compared to other labor organizations, helped inflame these tensions.[47] The priority of most

Socialist-leaning garment unions was to preserve their organizations' democratic operations. They were also deeply offended by the Communists' characterization of German and Austrian social democracy as "social-fascism," a terminology that had helped Hitler crush the entire German labor movement. The Socialist-Communist clash was exacerbated when at Madison Square Garden on February 16, 1934, American Communist Party agitators violently interrupted the Socialist protest against Dollfuss's suppression of the Austrian labor movement. Although some American intellectuals found inspiration in communism during the 1930s, garment industry leaders remained suspicious even after the Communist Party attempted to create a united front in 1935. Nor were they part of the anti-Stalinist Trotskyist intelligentsia—the New York intellectuals who, according to Allan Wald, briefly wielded influence in university circles but were never strongly present in union ranks.[48] In fact, when the JLC was created, the Menorah Society—founded in 1906 at Harvard University by Jewish intellectuals, which by the early 1930s had become a pro-Communist group—was not invited to the JLC organizational meeting on February 25, 1934. This refusal reflected both the JLC's intention to control the sociological makeup of its membership and its fear that the new orientation of the *Menorah Journal* would lead the JLC in political directions they wanted to avoid.[49]

The narrow path taken by JLC leaders within the American Left partially explains why they were attempting to benefit from the AFL's larger membership base in order to legitimize their projects. As Vladeck stated, "In the anti-Nazi struggle, JLC members emphasize their opposition to any form of domination: on the one hand Communism and on the other exaggerated Nationalism. The great majority of Jewish workers in the United States is opposed to any form of dictatorship and determined to fight, not only within the limits of political democracy, but also for democracy itself."[50]

JEWS BUT NOT ZIONISTS

The JLC founders—and many of its members—were not Zionists. Like the Polish Bundists, they adopted the principle of *doykayt*, the objective of defending Jewish life wherever Jews resided, first in the Russian Empire and later in Poland, and then among Jewish immigrants in the Americas and Europe. According to the Bund, the Zionist choice of a "historical father-land" in Palestine directly contradicted proletarian internationalism. Ever since Karl Marx, *die Judenfrage*—the Jewish Question—had divided social-ists and generated endless debates about the fate of the Jewish working class in central and eastern Europe. Records from the Fourth Bund Convention in 1901 declared that Zionism represented "a bourgeois response to anti-Semitism" and an obstacle to class-consciousness. Zionists and Bundists in interwar Poland disagreed on every point, from language and social justice to prospects for a national entity in Palestine, which the Bundists consid-ered a misguided fantasy.[51]

In supporting the cause of minority rights, Austrian socialist theoreti-cians such as Karl Kautski and Otto Bauer also acknowledged the fact that Jewish identity included a national dimension, but they promoted assimila-tion as a solution to anti-Semitism.[52] Kautski acclaimed the Bund as a legit-imate proletarian movement, publishing its writings and celebrating Jewish socialist movements, including in Great Britain and the United States. The role of the Bund in the rise of Russian social democracy resembled that of minorities in the Austro-Hungarian Empire. A dialogue between Rus-sian and Austrian socialists had existed before World War I. Otto Bauer, a supporter of the rights of national minorities, nevertheless opposed Jewish cultural autonomy, preferring to resolve the Jewish problem by promoting assimilation through socialism.[53]

Following World War I, the Austrian Social Democratic Party (SDAP) distanced itself from the Jewish question, a persistent and fundamental problem that was revived by the ambient anti-Semitism. Friedrich Adler, vice president of the SDAP and secretary-general of the Labor and Social-ist International (LSI), was as hostile toward Zionism as were his father, Victor Adler (who had converted to Protestantism), and Kautski. Because of this stance, Friedrich Adler encouraged the Bund to join forces with the LSI in order to ensure that Jewish workers were represented. In 1929, he wrote to Henryk Erlich, the Bund's leader in Poland, stating, "It will be your particular task to represent the interests of the great masses of the Jewish proletariat outside of Palestine within the LSI."[54] This decision was made shortly after the Arab uprising in Palestine, which resulted in casualties on all sides that Bundists blamed on both British imperialists and Zionists, alleging that they had been wrong to encourage Jewish migration to Palestine. Adler also saw Bund membership in the LSI as a way to counterbalance Zionist influence.[55]

The Palestinian question continued to preoccupy socialist leaders, including Austrians such as Max Adler and Julius Braunthal, who sided with the Socialist Zionist movement. In 1936, Vladeck prolonged a trip to Europe in order to visit Palestine.[56] His interest in Palestine as a destination for immigrants on a par with the United States, Canada, Argentina, Paris, or London differed from the Zionist vision that saw the land as representing Jewish national destiny.

THE JLC, THE AFL, AND THE CIO

When Vladeck introduced the JLC program at the AFL convention in October 1934, it was not the first time that the AFL had reacted to Third Reich policies. Delegates to the previous convention in October 1933 had approved an Executive Council resolution to boycott German goods and services, claiming it should be maintained "until the German government recognizes the right of the working people of Germany to organize into bona fide [and] independent trade unions of their own choosing, and until Germany ceases its repressive policy of persecution of Jewish people."[57] AFL president William Green strongly supported the boycott and condemned Nazi persecution of the German labor movement and Jewish people. "The test of citizenship must not be whether you are a Gentile or a Jew, it ought to be what you are as a man," he argued, assuring the membership that "when those who are bound to us by the bonds of fraternity are persecuted or thrown in prison, when labor organizations are destroyed, I cannot conceive of an American labor movement remaining silent." The ovation that followed his appeal clearly indicated unanimous support for a boycott.[58]

By attending the 1934 convention, Vladeck hoped to create a positive relationship between the two organizations and was expecting the AFL to support the JLC-led anti-fascist struggle. On this subject, relations between the JLC and the AFL should be seen as complementary rather than conflictual, particularly in light of the tumultuous relations between the garment trade unions and the AFL. The ILGWU had always been affiliated to the AFL, and Dubinsky's nomination as first vice president in 1934 reflected the Executive Council's recognition of this "Jewish," or at least multiethnic, union. Also in that year, after historically maintaining its distance, the ACWA joined the AFL. The new partnership was, however, to be short-lived. Beginning in 1935, Dubinsky and Hillman sided with John Lewis, president of the United Mine Workers, to defend the principle of industrial unionism that they had always promoted. The official creation in 1938 of a new organization, the Congress of Industrial Organizations (CIO), resulted in the exclusion of the two principal garment unions from the AFL. The ACWA became a key member of the CIO, where Hillman's political skills and knowledge about the Soviet Union facilitated relationships with several of the new federation's communist-leaning leaders. The ILGWU chose not to join the CIO, remaining independent for a few years. Dubinsky maintained a close relationship with William Green, however, and rejoined the old federation in 1940. The JLC was therefore able to maintain connections to both the AFL and the CIO through the ILGWU and the ACWA that proved invaluable during the war despite its greater affinity with the AFL.

The historiography of the American labor movement has long suggested that the AFL was irremediably conservative. The advent of the CIO in creating the possibility of a more open industrial union environment reinforced the AFL's image as staunchly conservative and resistant to change. At the international level, however, the CIO was scarcely more progressive than the AFL. Following the break with the AFL in 1938, CIO president John Lewis certainly condemned the destruction of the German labor movement and the ensuing anti-Jewish "pogrom." But the isolationist stance concerning European affairs that he championed afterward paradoxically reinforced the "neutrality" of communist CIO leaders, all of whom fell silent concerning Nazi Germany during the German-Soviet Pact (September 1939 to late

June 1941).[59] It is well known that after World War II, AFL participation in the Cold War—before the CIO also joined in—created long-lasting obstacles to a progressive international vision. However, as we shall see in the following chapters, the AFL president fully supported solidarity with Socialist or Social Democratic leaders that the JLC promoted in the 1930s and early 1940s in the context of Nazi persecution. Independent from (but linked to) the two federations, the JLC stood at the avant-garde of the American labor movement with respect to fighting Nazism and anti-Semitism. In bringing the AFL leadership into the struggle, the JLC helped the organization break with its traditional isolationist stance.

In 1934, for example, Vladeck arranged for Walter Citrine to be invited to the AFL convention in San Francisco. Not only was Citrine the general secretary of the British Trades Union Congress (TUC), but he was also the president of the International Federation of Trade Unions (IFTU). Vladeck's and Citrine's combined presence and public appeals for anti-fascist action ended the AFL's long-standing isolationist stance. Like Vladeck, Citrine exhorted American delegates to join the opposition to fascism, emphasizing the similarities between the Italian, German, and Austrian regimes whose first initiatives were to crush labor in order to consolidate their power.[60] Although traditionally a British TUC delegate attended the AFL annual convention, the presence of the president of the IFTU was exceptional.[61] The rapprochement with the AFL that Citrine engineered at the 1934 convention was possible because of JLC contacts in the international labor movement. As the most internationalist of the AFL unions, the ILGWU was at the center of this new configuration, uniting labor groups in the name of the struggle against Nazi and fascist ideologies.

The JLC-AFL partnership, however, was restrained by the AFL's negative attitude toward immigration and therefore to the possibility of admitting large numbers of refugees to the United States. Indeed, since its foundation in the 1880s, the AFL had systematically opposed every new wave of immigrants, whether they came from Asia or from eastern or southern Europe.[62] The AFL clung to this position even after successfully lobbying for a federal quota system that dramatically limited both the overall volume and ethnic makeup of immigration to the United States. In addition, both major political parties shared this intransigence on immigration policy, exacerbating American anti-Semitism and impeding reform, while also distancing Jewish Americans from their communities of origin.

ANTI-SEMITISM AND U.S. IMMIGRATION RESTRICTIONS

The presence of a large Jewish community in the United States did nothing to dispel various forms of anti-Semitism. These were mild in comparison with the overwhelming brutality in Nazi Germany and its emulators, but they had a pernicious effect, contributing notably to shoring up the country's long-standing resistance to immigration reform—at a time when European Jews were desperately in need of a refuge.

In the 1920s, this prejudice often took the form of efforts by upper- and middle-class Americans to prevent the social integration of the descendants of immigrant groups. This included bans on Jews in luxury hotels and private clubs, real estate agents openly excluding Jewish renters and buyers, and the limiting of admissions of Jewish applicants to private universities to less than 10 percent—strategies with concrete effects on Jewish daily lives.[63] These kinds of ostracism and discrimination coincided with more vocal public displays, including Henry Ford's anti-Semitic rants about a global Jewish and Bolshevist conspiracy and, in the 1930s, Father Charles Coughlin's vehemently anti-Semitic sermons from his pulpit in Royal Oak near Detroit that sometimes were lifted directly from Hitler and Goebbels. Although Coughlin's audiences had begun to decline by late 1938, his discourse had support among the partly Catholic ranks of the needle trades.[64] And Coughlin was not the only prominent figure who distributed anti-Semitic or pro-Nazi propaganda. William Pelley's Silver Legion of America and the German American Bund emulated the German National Socialist Party in parades held in New York, Detroit, Chicago, and other major cities that had large German populations.[65]

American Jews became adept at circumventing these forms of rabble-rousing, but they were affected by them in a range of ways, including in educational and occupational settings. Indeed, one of the early JLC programs was to combat anti-Semitism in the workplace. Despite its impact on the relatively discreet daily lives of American Jews, the most significant influence of anti-Semitic discourse was perhaps on public opinion. Organizations that might otherwise have supported loosening European refugee quotas restrained their lobbying efforts or minimized the significant Jewish presence among refugees in order to avoid opposition.

OVERCOMING QUOTAS

One clear outcome of the spread of anti-Semitic ideas in the United States was the continued refusal by the U.S. Congress to reform immigration laws despite increasing demand for visas from Jewish people in Germany, Austria, and other countries under the yoke of the Third Reich. American historians have long noted the failure of the United States throughout the 1930s and during the war to welcome exiles as generously as had been historically the case. Arthur Morse in 1968 was the first to criticize "American apathy" toward the extermination of European Jews. He was followed by deeply critical historians, among whom David Wyman decried the administrative atmosphere that led to "the abandonment" of European Jews.[66] One explanation for this stance (beyond inertia) was the cultural insularity and isolationist attitudes of the Washington bureaucrats responsible for drafting and implementing immigration legislation. The resulting inflexible system was disconnected from the international situation and also reflected the administration's hostility to policies likely to increase the Jewish population.

National quotas that had been implemented since 1924 were not explicitly anti-Semitic. They did favor older sources of emigration such as the British Isles and Germany while sharply restricting the immigration from southern and eastern Europe, regardless of the religious or ethnic characteristics of these populations. Consequently, the quota for German immigrants was second only to that for British citizens. However, during the 1930s, a decade marked by economic crisis and low levels of labor migration, refugees, most of whom were Jewish, suffered directly from policies that were primarily intended to protect the labor market. This was largely due to the fact that political refugees lacked specific legal status. The prevailing American myth viewed all immigrants as Old World refugees who were seeking economic, religious, or political freedom. As the fate of more than 525,000 German Jews, as well as those living in neighboring countries annexed by the Hitler regime, was becoming increasingly bleak in the 1930s, American officials systematically clung to country-based quotas as a protective bulwark against what they perceived as uncontrolled immigration. But the Depression in the wake of the 1929 stock market crash exacerbated the implementation of the quota system.

In reality, during the 1930s and throughout the war, quotas were rarely applied at their original levels. An executive order from President Herbert Hoover in 1930 had dramatically reduced standing quotas by ordering consular officials to deliver no more than 10 percent of the number of visas initially permitted by the legislation of the 1920s. This caused the total number of European immigrants to plummet from 147,438 in 1930 to 12,383 in 1933, with only 1,919 from Germany.[67] This policy was a response to the economic crisis, which saw every immigrant as a potentially unemployed person, or "LPC" ("Likely to become a Public Charge") in administrative parlance. George Messersmith, assistant secretary of state in 1936, after heading the U.S. Consulate in Berlin and serving as ambassador to Vienna, successfully arranged for a modest increase in the number of visas granted to German citizens. But quota reductions were effectively maintained until the end of the war—with one exception. After the Anschluss in 1938, President Roosevelt decreed that the full quota of 25,957 for German citizens be fulfilled and that the Austrian quota of 1,413 be added to it, for a total of 27,370 visas. As a result, 1939 was the only year during which the German quota was fully honored; in 1940 it was only partially fulfilled, despite long lines of desperate applicants in front of American consulates. Maurice Davie, whose statistics have been accepted by later historians, calculated that only 16.8 percent of the quotas for countries under Nazi or fascist domination were used between 1933 and 1945.[68] The number of applicants for immigration to the United States during the years after the Anschluss at consulates in Germany, Austria, and Czechoslovakia came to ten times the existing quotas. This was also true of Poland, which, with a Jewish population of 3.5 million that the anti-Semitic Rydz-Smigly government would have rather seen expatriated, initially benefited from a full quota of a mere 6,524, that is, 652 under the 10 percent mandate. Even when the quota was fully met in 1939, it was discouragingly low. According to Maurice Davie's elevated estimate, a grand total of approximately 250,000 refugees—including some 157,000 Jews—entered the United States between 1933 and 1944.[69] This was a relatively large number compared to other Western democracies and even Palestine, which were not more open to immigration than the United States. Retrospectively, however, and given the human catastrophe occurring in Europe, the number of refugees admitted to the United States was small. Furthermore, such statistics fail to reflect the discrimination, delays, humiliation, and contradictory decisions faced by applicants at American consulates, embassies, and immigration offices.[70]

There were exceptions to the quota system. One provision of the 1924 law, for example, authorized the admission of self-employed persons, artists, students, and clergy "above the quotas." This clause benefited refugees in these categories who had professional, academic, or artistic backgrounds that made them employable, an indispensable criterion in gaining a visa. Persons in transit to other countries were also temporarily admitted as "non-immigrants," as well as those who could return to their home countries, a category that effectively excluded Jews, for whom return was unthinkable. Eventual permanent residency for individuals admitted beyond quota levels or as "non-immigrants" depended on openings under the official quotas, which led to extended periods of deep uncertainty for applicants.

Much has been written about the "illustrious immigrants" who were admitted above the quotas. Many were well known before arriving in America or had received invitations from American universities and cultural institutions. These figures—most of them Jewish—included such prominent scientists, artists, and academics as Albert Einstein, Enrico Fermi, Thomas Mann, Arnold Schoenberg, Igor Stravinsky, Max Ernst, Walter Gropius, Claude Lévi-Strauss, Max Horkheimer, Theodor Adorno, and the founders of the New School for Social Research, among many others.[71] Their stories and accomplishments have long inspired historians, paradoxically magnifying the perception of American hospitality to refugees both before and during the war. Indeed, approximately 25,000 intellectuals, researchers, writers, and artists were generously admitted during that period, greatly contributing to the cultural and scientific advancement of the United States. But ordinary individuals who did not receive invitations experienced far more difficulty negotiating the complex immigration process. In addition to being subjected to long delays before being notified whether their cases fell under existing quotas, they were required to submit proof of employment and affidavits from American citizens who would vouch for them. Those who were fortunate enough to be admitted outside of the quota system clearly benefited from a highly selective "exile system," one that the JLC was able to adapt to the specific demands of its protégés.[72]

According to historian Aristide Zolberg, in the State Department—the ultimate visa-granting authority—"the anti-Semitic habitus was not only respectable, but completely recommended."[73] In the early 1930s, the directors of the visa section did little to conceal their prejudices. Wilbur Carr and to an even greater extent William Phillips repeatedly blocked the relaxation of quotas, while Breckinridge Long, an early admirer of Hitler and Mussolini, who succeeded Carr and Phillips in 1940 as director of the visa section, waged an energetic administrative battle against increasing the number of refugees allowed to enter the country.[74]

Despite repeated requests to exempt refugees, the so-called "LPC clause" remained in effect. Supporters of increased refugee admissions, including Jewish organizations, avoided clashing openly with Congress. In the 1930s, Jewish representatives—Emanuel Celler and Samuel Dickstein—were repeatedly dissuaded from bringing the question of refugees before Congress for fear of awakening even broader opposition. In 1939, Congress failed to pass a bill sponsored by Senator Robert Wagner (D) and Representative Edith Rogers (R) that would have bypassed existing quotas to admit 20,000 German Jewish children. Opponents claimed that admitting the children would change the ethnic balance of the country, an unambiguous example of the anti-Semitic atmosphere in both Congress and public opinion. The refusal to admit the hundreds of passengers desperately waiting aboard the *Saint Louis* who had applied for entry visas to the United States was another shocking illustration of the prevalence of anti-Semitic attitudes.[75] Indeed, in four polls conducted in 1938—when the American public was obviously aware of the growing persecution of Jews in Europe—71 to 85 percent of respondents opposed refugee admissions above existing quotas, and 67 percent preferred that no refugees be admitted.[76]

The issue was considered too risky for Roosevelt to adopt a more welcoming policy. Party politics inside Congress created an unshakable consensus that left no room for more liberal voices. The president also feared that any move to increase refugee admissions would compromise his hopes of generating support for joining a war that he had promised to avoid.[77] He used his executive power to make a series of positive gestures, however, which included fulfilling the German and Austrian quotas between 1938 and 1940, organizing the Evian conference in 1938, at which the Intergovernmental Refugee Committee and the Presidential Advisory Committee on Political Refugees were created, and, somewhat belatedly, establishing the War Refugee Board in 1944.[78]

Attempting to pressure Congress, the ILGWU and the ACWA passed motions that defied popular opinion and the AFL at their conventions, demanding immediate reform of immigration regulations that prevented victims of racial or political persecution from entering the United States. The ILGWU promoted "free immigration," in the spirit of long-standing American hospitality.[79] In keeping with its customary restrictive position, however, the AFL staunchly rejected these motions. In 1935, it responded to a proposal by David Dubinsky and other ILGWU delegates to expand refugee admissions by stating that it "would run counter to the immigration laws now in existence as a result of the activities of the AFL." In the years that followed, the AFL not only maintained this anti-immigrant stance but lobbied actively against the reform of federal immigration policy.[80]

The AFL's intransigence regarding immigration put the JLC in a paradoxical situation. Keenly aware that most Americans, including organized labor, were opposed to reforming the immigration laws, the JLC therefore avoided pro-immigration initiatives, which in any case would have required an unlikely degree of international cooperation.[81] As a consequence, the JLC was forced to focus on the political aspects of the refugee crisis by using its contacts in the international labor movement to channel aid to persecuted European labor leaders—most of whom in fact were Jews—and support those who were able to satisfy State Department criteria.

Formed from a gathering of labor unions, Jewish political organizations, and secular associations, the JLC was known far beyond its circle of supporters. As former Jewish political refugees from czarist Russia or the USSR, before rising to the top of the American labor movement, its leaders were able to maintain contacts with their European counterparts, including members of the Polish Bund, the Labor and Socialist International, and the International Federation of Trade Unions. As a result, the JLC was the only organization in the international Social Democratic world that was able to alert the American working class to the reality of what was transpiring in Europe while successfully forging an anti-fascist community. Its particular focus on the twin targets of Nazi repression—Jews and organized labor—distinguished it from other American and Western anti-fascist organizations. While its political sympathies stopped short of the Communist Party, the JLC fashioned a movement that would defend both the Jewish world and the labor world.

2

CONSTRUCTING
INTERNATIONAL LINKS,
1933–1937

The JLC managed to forge international contacts that extended beyond its Polish roots through its involvement in the anti-Nazi and anti-fascist struggle. The weakness of international organizations and traditional American isolation did not make it easy. Little by little, however, JLC members were able to make contact with representatives of the International Federation of Trade Unions (IFTU) on the one hand and with the Labor and Socialist International (LSI) on the other, which in Europe were the labor and political (either Socialist or Social Democratic) branches of the movement. The links the JLC was able to create would become crucial for the survival of those who were struggling against Nazism or fascism. Although internationalism was a rather vague and idealistic concept at the level of the rank and file, for labor leaders who traveled to and participated in international conventions, these ideas became a human and concrete reality, even to the point of fostering friendships. The historian Victor Silverman speaks of a "community" of international labor organizations, stressing the mutual understanding among leaders that was rekindled at each meeting and subsequently maintained by official publications and correspondence. Apart

from these supranational institutions, labor leaders themselves were participating, by means of the circulation of persons, resources, and ideas, in the
emergence of a transnational space of struggle against Nazism and fascism.[1]

WEAKNESS OF INTERNATIONAL LABOR, AMERICAN ISOLATIONISM

The fall of the German labor movement in 1933 and of the Austrian one in
1934 considerably weakened international labor organizations. The German
Socialist Party (SPD), a pillar of the Socialist International, and the powerful German unions united in the ADGB had been the strongest and most
homogeneous of the national branches. After 1933 SPD leaders retreated to
Prague, and then in 1938 to Paris; from there they organized the representation of their party in exile, the SOPADE. The LSI, whose headquarters
had been in Berlin when the Hitler regime came to power, was also forced
to retreat to Paris. Moreover, since the 1920s the heads of both the Italian Socialist Party (PSI) and the General Confederation of Labor (CGL;
Confederazione Generale del Lavoro) had also found themselves in exile in
France. Much weakened, the IFTU and the LSI were henceforth composed
of several parties and national labor bodies in exile that were endeavoring
from the outside to combat the regimes of their respective countries. In the
years following the fall of the Italian, German, and Austrian labor movements, and then during the Spanish Civil War, the role of Great Britain
became particularly important thanks to the stability of the British Labour
Party and of the Trades Union Congress (TUC). In these circumstances,
Walter Citrine, who was both secretary-general of the TUC and president
of the IFTU, assumed the task of maintaining international contacts among
labor organizations.[2]

On the American side, the AFL had traditionally stood outside the international labor movement. It had not taken part in the formation of the Second International in 1889 because it distrusted the European socialists who
dominated it, not to mention those in the United States who wanted to
rally to it.[3] Yet it had briefly participated in the IFTU between 1913 and 1919,

requiring as a condition of its affiliation that the movement be restructured on a strictly trade union basis. But after World War I, finding it "too revolutionary for Americans," the president of the AFL, Samuel Gompers, did not renew its membership. Consequently the AFL also remained outside the Labor and Socialist International that had been formed in 1923 in the wake of the Second International. And, of course, the AFL was diametrically opposed to the Communist Third International created in 1920.

But the JLC was not situated in the same political orbit as the AFL. The membership of the Polish Bund in the Socialist International since 1930 had anchored the American Bundists to the European socialist movement thanks to ideological affinity. In 1931 the Polish Bundist delegates participated in the LSI convention in Vienna, which was the last one held before Hitler's regime crushed the German socialist movement. Meanwhile, the ILGWU had maintained its affiliation with the International Clothing Workers' Federation, which was a member of the IFTU, but without ever sending delegates to it.[4] These points of contact were important in the chain of events and decisions that would lead the JLC to mobilize on behalf of the European socialists and eventually lead the AFL to seek reaffiliation with the IFTU. This chapter traces the stages and motivations of this involvement from 1933 up until the Spanish Civil War.

The IFTU, in concert with the LSI, had launched a boycott of German products at its convention in Brussels on August 4, 1933. The Socialist International had made this decision in May 1933 and reiterated the motion at its Paris meeting of August 21. The LSI organization still thought that a rapprochement with the Communist International was possible, but nothing of the kind was agreed upon.[5] As a last hope, the LSI recommended a general strike and for workers to defend themselves, which (as we have seen) was tragically repressed in Austria in February 1934. The LSI and the IFTU acted in parallel, now seeking new and major support for uniting non-Communist anti-Nazi forces both in exile situations and among German workers. In 1933, as its secretary-general, Walter Schevenels, later recalled, the IFTU held clandestine meetings with German labor leaders and facilitated their organization abroad in Czechoslovakia, France, Holland, and Denmark. Thus, when in October 1933 the AFL launched its plan to boycott German products, it was responding to an international appeal. In fact, its president, William Green, recalled in his speech—without mentioning the IFTU—that "the unions of Britain, Czechoslovakia and other countries" had already taken this action.[6]

But there was a chasm between the support for European comrades solicited by international labor bodies and the geographic and ideological isolation of American workers. There was no political convergence between the European social-democratic movement with its national components, each with its own political tradition, and the bulk of the American union movement, which was primarily preoccupied with the economic fate of U.S. workers.[7] It became the JLC's task to fill this void, at least in part, as it endeavored to create links between European and U.S. labor institutions. Its activity was essentially situated at the level of the trade unions affiliated to it and among the Jewish and Italian communities they represented. Contacts were established at this level with European leaders, thus enabling a solidarity that was concrete, financial, and personal more than it was institutional. Ideas do not travel alone; human contacts are essential for their transmission, all the more so when human lives are at stake.

A FIRST GERMAN NETWORK OF INFORMATION AND SOLIDARITY

Martin Plettl was the first German labor leader to find refuge in the United States. President of the Garment Workers' Union (Deutscher Bekleidungsarbeiter Verband), he had been arrested on May 2, 1933, by the National-Socialists. Like most of the German labor leaders, he was sent to a detention camp, from which he managed to escape. Leaving behind both his union's and personal ruins, he clandestinely reached Amsterdam in June 1933, where he was sheltered by Tonnis Van der Heeg, the secretary of the International Clothing Federation of which Plettl was also a leader. But the contact between Plettl and the Americans who gave him asylum was the fruit of an encounter which, without being fortuitous, was surprising and strengthened transatlantic ties.

Abraham Plotkin, an American labor leader of Jewish origin, found himself in Berlin during the winter of 1932–1933. He was a witness to Hitler's seizure of power and the brutal repression of the whole working-class movement.[8] He made the personal acquaintance of Plettl and most of the German labor leaders, as well as many in the IFTU, whose headquarters had been in Berlin until these events. Plotkin himself was forced to leave Germany at the end of May. Passing through Amsterdam, he saw Plettl again and then went to Paris where the office of the IFTU had been moved. He returned to the United States in June 1933, where he was the intermediary between these German leaders (now in exile) and their American counterparts (Dubinsky, Schlossberg, and Vladeck).[9] A union organizer for the ILGWU, Plotkin had gone to Germany out of socialist sympathy for the German workers' movement, intent on studying how it functioned. But after Hitler seized power, he was the sole observer from the American union movement able to testify directly to the fate of the working-class leaders who were now subjected to terror or forced to flee or take clandestine action.

These circumstances made Plotkin the first link in the chain of solidarity established for German labor leaders between the United States and Europe. Upon his return, he published a long article about the destruction of the German workers' movement that appeared in the *American Federationist*, the AFL organ, in August 1933.[10] In the article he analyzed the reasons why it was impossible for workers to resist Nazi attacks. He described the persecution of people and labor organizations, the seizure and occupation of their offices, censorship of their mail, the interdiction of the labor press, the arrests, and the physical persecution by the SA. Plotkin explained the impossibility of a general strike (although this form of action was being considered until the end of March 1933): the unemployment of eight million people made any strike suicidal. Finally, Plotkin explained the conditions under which some fifty national leaders of the ADGB were arrested in Berlin on May 2, 1933, caught in a trap organized by Hitler for the May Day demonstration, turning it into a gigantic pro-Nazi event:

Every one of the heads of the thirty-one organizations in the ADGB had been arrested, and the important secretaries in the national office as well.

Plettl with whom I had been intimate, Otto Schweizer of the Engineers and Technicians, Brandeis of the Metal Workers, Husemann of the miners, Vomerhaus, organizer of the [Brandenburg] district, Otto Engel secretary of the Agricultural Workers Union, Franz Furtwängler, Walter Maschke, Frau Hanna, Kuno Broecker, Leipart and Grassmann, the two presidents of the ADGB—every one of the leaders arrested, not by the police but by the Nazi military troops. Fifty were arrested the first morning, the others were picked up in the succeeding days. This in Berlin alone—how many were arrested throughout Germany is not known and probably never will be known.[11]

Plotkin's report was instrumental in William Green's decision to call for a boycott of German products at the AFL convention. The AFL had protested on May 5, 1933, against the arrest of German union leaders to the U.S. State Department.[12] The terms that Green used to convince his audience at the October convention in fact echoed certain paragraphs of Plotkin's article. In a letter to Georg Stolz, assistant to Walter Schevenels at the IFTU, Plotkin noted that the AFL president had used the facts reported in his article to justify a boycott.[13] Written at the end of May or in June 1933, this text, which Plotkin had immediately transmitted to his colleagues at the ILGWU as well as to the *Jewish Daily Forward*, was the first to inform Americans of the actual attacks on German unions and their leaders. Samuel Lefkowitz, head of the ILGWU Joint Board of collective negotiations in New York, was astonished in the month of May by the arrest of Plettl: "As [far as] I know, he is not a Jew. Through the public press we are informed that only Communists and Jews are jailed and persecuted."[14]

Plotkin did more than just circulate information. On his recommendation the ILGWU and the ACWA invited Martin Plettl to the United States. And beyond this first rescue, Plotkin took part in the cooperation between these unions and the IFTU. In the month of July, he discussed with David Dubinsky and Joseph Schlossberg the possibility of bringing Plettl to the United States in order to help him and to have him testify to the reality of the situation in Germany. On October 31, 1933, Plettl disembarked in New York, where he was welcomed by a delegation from the two clothing workers' unions. Dubinsky and Schlossberg had agreed to organize a lecture tour for him across the United States for the purpose of informing American workers about events in Germany and collecting funds for other victims, as well as aiding the resistance movement that was getting underway.[15]

The committee responsible for this tour was a prefiguration of the JLC, which would be formed a few weeks later. Vladeck of the *Jewish Daily Forward* and Joseph Baskin of the Workmen's Circle were associated with it, along with Dubinsky and Schlossberg. Thus, they put into effect the call of Walter Schevenels, secretary-general of the IFTU, for international support for German labor leaders; from Paris, the IFTU had asked Plotkin to help it set up an emergency fund:

> We shall need to have the widest possible international basis, both moral and material. I have no doubt whatever that all the countries of Europe and America will give us such support as they can in these actions. In order to intensify feeling in America, I think it would be well to issue reports on the real events in Germany, showing up Nazi violence, not only towards Jews and Communists, but also towards Trade Unionists and their officials. I also think it will be very useful to arrange a series of conferences in America dealing with the state of affairs in Germany.[16]

Martin Plettl's tour of American working-class cities (the first of its kind) lasted more than three months, from November 1933 to the end of February 1934, and was a success according to the ILGWU's journal *Justice*. On February 21, 1934, a dinner in Plettl's honor was organized in the Central Plaza Hotel by those who, barely four days later, were going to found the JLC in that very location: Dubinsky, Schlossberg, Vladeck, and Morris Feinstone of the United Hebrew Trades, plus a few other New York union and Socialist figures. Matthew Woll, vice president of the AFL, and William Green, its president, sent a message of support from the AFL Executive Council. The sum of $4,325 was collected on the spot. It was meant to be sent to the Matteotti Fund jointly created by the IFTU and the Labor and Socialist International for the support of Italian and German labor and Socialist leaders.[17]

Martin Plettl did not return to Europe. He remained in the United States with Dorothea Heinrich, the secretary of the German Clothing Workers' Union, who became his companion. Plettl's activity mingled with that of the JLC and its member organizations to coordinate American support for their European comrades. The JLC had launched the creation of a mutual aid fund for the victims of fascism, for whom it hoped to collect the sum of $150,000. The appeal was relayed by the ILGWU and ACWA, whose conventions were held in May 1934 and at which Plettl spoke.[18] Somewhat later, Plettl thanked Vladeck for such support: "The substantial help voted by the American comrades is of utmost value to the Matteotti Fund, which is used for Italian, German and Austrian victims, as well as for the funds needed for the underground activities in Germany and Austria. I wish to express my sincere thanks on behalf of the IFTU and of my suffering German comrades."[19]

Simultaneously, Plettl created a committee representing German trade unionists in exile that was finally recognized by the IFTU in 1935. However, this Auslandsvertretung Deutscher Gewerkschaften, which assembled German union leaders in exile in Czechoslovakia, Belgium, Holland, and France, had no impact either on the Social Democratic milieu of German refugees in the United States or on the European situation in the events that later unfolded.[20]

WALTER CITRINE IN THE UNITED STATES

Plettl pursued efforts toward uniting international leaders. In a letter to Vladeck, he had suggested inviting the president of the IFTU, Walter Citrine, to the AFL convention that was to be held in San Francisco in October 1934:

> Citrine is an excellent orator, very tactful and sure of his ground. He knows the mentality of American labor as well as its traditions and peculiarities. If such a speech by Citrine were answered by an equally forceful speech of President Green, this would constitute, to my mind, one of the most remarkable

labor events. Not only the millions of oppressed German, Austrian and Italian workers, but international labor everywhere would draw inspiration and new courage. . . . It will also mean real workers' solidarity proclaimed on an international scale, instead of the usual Communist phraseology, which is contrary to the fight [and to] our movement for liberty and freedom.[21]

Things turned out as Plettl had hoped, although the second speech was given not by William Green, who had already alerted the AFL to the German situation the previous year, but by Vladeck, who, as we saw in the previous chapter, presented the fundamentals of the JLC mission. Citrine's speech vividly described the annihilation of workers' movements in Italy, Germany, and Austria, thus also trying to undermine the pro-Mussolini sympathies among some of the Italian American working-class electorate. And, along the same lines, aware of the American distrust of any Marxist doctrine, he carefully explained that socialism and communism were not synonymous. He evoked the possible means of responding to fascism, and he thanked the AFL for being associated with the boycott of German industries and services, whose efficacy was evident by the hostility it was arousing among the leaders of the Third Reich.[22]

The presence of Plettl in the United States and then Citrine's briefer visit had several concrete results for the anti-fascist cause. At the AFL convention of 1934, an international mutual aid fund, the Labor Chest for the Liberation of Workers of Europe, was created, which would add to the amount the JLC had already called for in February because it was drawing on a much wider community of workers. William Green was the Labor Chest's president and Matthew Woll its vice president. But in reality, it was the JLC that managed the use of these funds, notably because Dubinsky was the treasurer of both the JLC and the Labor Chest. The fund was initially used to finance Citrine's trip from England, and after his appearance in San Francisco, it supported his lecture tour of union branches in Seattle, Portland, Los Angeles, Chicago, Pittsburgh, Detroit, Baltimore, Washington, and Philadelphia. Long afterward, Citrine recounted a memory that would have pleased Vladeck, with whom he often shared the podium during this tour: "Although most of my meetings were crowded and much sympathy was shown, the only section of the community who were really against the Nazis were the Jews."[23]

Designed to inform labor milieux about fascism and Nazism, these tours were also fundraising efforts. Each meeting brought in $200 to $600, depending on the attendance. They became increasingly frequent, featuring various speakers. For example, Julius Deutsch, hero of the Austrian resistance, was invited by Vladeck to make an American tour. He spoke to working-class audiences in Chicago and in the Washington, D.C., area in December 1934. In February 1935, Gerhart Seger, a German journalist and former Socialist representative in the Reichstag, was invited by the Labor Chest to tour thirty cities on the East Coast and in the Midwest. Having escaped from the Oranienburg concentration camp in December 1933, he had witnessed Nazi violence firsthand. Tracts and brochures in English and in German for the numerous German-speaking workers were provided that also served to counter the pro-Nazi propaganda that was circulating in these regions. A Labor Chest correspondent in Detroit, head of the International Metal Engravers' Union, thanked Vladeck for sending three hundred brochures in German in advance of Seger's speech. "We would love to welcome others," he added, "since the Nazis in this city have become very active and our German anti-fascists do not have the means to print tracts themselves."[24]

But Seger's lectures did not benefit the German Social Democratic Party in exile in Prague (SOPADE) in the way that had been hoped for.[25] Returning a second time to the United States in 1935, Seger decided to remain there and became editor of the *Neue Volkszeitung*, one of the periodicals published by social-democratic German émigrés. Now this publication became the rallying point for such refugees in the United States. "I find on my desk, every time a boat from Europe has arrived, dozens of letters from people who are in a perfectly destitute situation," he wrote in 1938 to Isaiah Minkoff, a member of the JLC executive.[26] However, the SOPADE was slow to organize its representation in the United States and was split over the goals to be pursued. Meanwhile, during one of his trips to Europe in 1935, Vladeck established contacts with dissidents from the SPD who were more militant and politically more engaged in conducting clandestine work on German and Austrian territory. The support given by the JLC to Neu Beginnen, one of these groups, which will be described in the next chapter, came before what the SPD might have received with a better organized delegation.[27]

AN ITALIAN BRANCH

At the ILGWU convention in May 1934, resolutions to combat Nazism were adopted unanimously, reflecting actions taken by the JLC: to boycott goods of German origin, not to use industrial machinery coming from Germany, to voice protest against the Nazi brutalities in Germany, and, finally, to contribute $50,000 to the fund for victims of Nazism created by the JLC to assist exiled militants from Germany and Austria so they could continue to agitate against fascism.[28] Yet Luigi Antonini, ILGWU vice president and president of Local 89, the Italian Dressmakers of New York, whose labor force was exclusively of Italian origin, pointed out that Italy, the first country to fall under fascist domination, was not mentioned in these resolutions. Therefore a motion affirming solidarity with Italian anti-fascists was adopted unanimously. And Antonini took the initiative of inviting to the United States a major Italian social-democratic official, Giuseppe Modigliani, former Socialist representative from Bologna. Like most of the Italian labor and Socialist Party leaders, Modigliani had taken refuge in France in 1926 after the assassination of Giacomo Matteotti and the subsequent fascist offensive against left-wing parties, unions, and the liberal press. Modigliani, in the name of the Italian Socialist Party (Partito Socialista Unitario), had been the principal prosecution witness during the trial of the murderers of Matteotti.[29]

Luigi Antonini facilitated American workers' solidarity with Italian militants in exile. Born in 1883 in Avellino, Antonini had reached the United States in 1908. He participated in the unionization of the Italian workforce in New York dressmaking workshops and organized them on a linguistic and cultural basis. In 1934, Local 89, with a membership of 40,000, was the ILGWU's biggest local. These workers, 70 percent of whom were women, had a long tradition of struggle. The local had chosen the number 89 not by order of formation but in reference to the French Revolution. Likewise, Local 48, another Italian section that represented coat tailors, was led by Salvatore Ninfo and adopted this number in memory of the revolutions of 1848 that shook Italy and the rest of Europe. In the 1920s, when fascism took over the Italian peninsula and also made inroads into Italian American communities, the clothing workers' unions were at the forefront of the struggle against this ideology and against Mussolini's government. The ILGWU and the ACWA formed the core of the Anti-Fascist Alliance of North America and tried to dissuade the Order of the Sons of Italy, a mutual aid society, from supporting the Mussolini regime. The ILGWU and the ACWA each published an Italian version of their newspaper, respectively, *Giustizia* and *Il Lavoro*. Starting in 1934, Antonini even had a weekly radio program in English and in Italian; *The Voice of Local 89* was broadcast on stations WEVD and WHOM in New York City.[30]

Organized by Serafino Romualdi, editor of *Giustizia*, and by Augusto Bellanca of the ACWA, Modigliani's tour of the United States was a formidable enterprise. It had two main objectives: to counteract Il Duce's influence on the Italian American communities and to support the anti-fascist movement in France. The presence of Modigliani galvanized a demonstration organized by Local 89 at Madison Square Garden on November 8, 1934, to celebrate its fifteen years of existence. The whole audience rose when the Italian Socialist sang along with the chorus of the Metropolitan Opera the workers' anthem, "Inno dei lavoratori," whose lyrics had been written by the Italian Socialist representative Filipo Turati. From November 1934 to March 1935, Modigliani made a tour of some twenty cities with significant Italian communities. Without speaking English—Romualdi translated his speech when necessary—from the East Coast to the West Coast via Pittsburgh and Chicago, he made himself the spokesman of the anti-fascists in exile, affirming the necessity of strengthening underground activity and of supporting their delegates abroad. From New York, personalities from the Italian American Left were invited to bring out the local audiences. For example, fearing union "apathy" in Los Angeles, Romualdi wrote to Carlo Tresca, a well-known anarchist in the United States whose presence would generate high attendance. In Scranton, a mining area in Pennsylvania, on the other hand, he called on the president of the United Mine Workers, John Lewis, for support.[31]

In March 1935, Dubinsky gave a $10,000 check to Modigliani, fruit of the sums collected at his meetings. Modigliani sent it to Friedrich Adler, secretary-general of the Labor and Socialist International, who acknowledged receiving it. Dubinsky stated that this sum was to be applied "exclusively towards the carrying on of anti-fascist activity in Italy and outside of it and for the support of exiled victims of the Fascist regime, through the Italian Fund in care of the Labor and Socialist International of which you are the administrator." Despite its union origins, therefore, this money was earmarked for *political* activities. Modigliani in fact was careful to point out that other Italian organizations were receiving support from the Labor Chest: "The IFTU is evidently inclined to appreciate only 'trade union' activities; and since the activities of the Italian refugees are primarily of a political character, the IFTU underestimates their importance," he wrote to Antonini in 1936. After his tour in 1934–1935, Modigliani was decorated with the title of honorary president of Local 89 and received a gift of a radio set, the era's "magic" instrument, so that he could listen to the "news, voices and harmonies of the whole world" and especially "hear the announcement of the Liberation on the day when it comes." A column was also offered to him in the union organ *Justice*, by which he continued to transmit information on the general conditions in Europe and on the anti-fascist struggle.[32]

Transatlantic solidarity was strengthened by other encounters. For example, Antonini, as representative of the ILGWU, was invited by the Italian Socialist Party (PSI) in exile to attend an Italian conference in Brussels in October 1935 against the war in Ethiopia. There he met the whole apparatus of the labor and socialist internationals: Friedrich Adler, LSI secretary-general; Raphael Abramovitch, representative of the Russian Social Democratic Party exiled in Paris; and Edo Fimmen, secretary of the International Transportworkers' Federation and member of the IFTU Executive Board. He was welcomed by Modigliani of course but also by Pietro Nenni, secretary-general of the PSI, and Bruno Buozzi, president of the Confederazione Generale del Lavoro, and also met activists of the anti-fascist movement Giustizia e Libertà, which was widening the struggle beyond strictly socialist and labor circles. These encounters enabled him to understand the composition of the anti-fascist movement among Italian emigrants. He was taken to Toulouse and to Nice, where many refugees were located, and at the Brussels conference he was made aware that several Italian militants had come clandestinely from Italy.[33]

These new contacts reoriented the previously northern European views of the JLC founders. The anti-fascist movement had deep roots in the Italian locals of the garment workers. Like the defense of Sacco and Vanzetti, it had become part of the leftist activism among Italian workers' unions. Yet back in the 1920s, the Mussolini regime did not seem to threaten world peace nor American interests. After 1933, on the other hand, the impact of Nazism in Germany and Austria put the activities of Italian American anti-fascists in a much wider context. Less perceived as solely a somewhat marginal left-wing activism, it was now integrated into a struggle whose extent was just starting to be understood. All working-class communities in the needle trades, whether of recent immigration or not, were now invited to take part. Modigliani's visit in 1934–1935, for example, took place simultaneously with that of Gerhart Seger. These orators were of course addressing groups of different ethnic origins, but their presence nevertheless widened the overall understanding of European fascism in the United States.[34]

David Dubinsky also participated personally in strengthening international cooperation. In 1935, he was appointed AFL representative to the International Labor Organization (ILO), to which President Roosevelt had affiliated the United States a few months earlier. As such, Dubinsky went in April 1935 to Geneva where he spoke about American union progress under the auspices of the New Deal. The following year, he participated in the IFTU congress in London as a representative of the Clothing Workers' Federation. Walter Citrine encouraged him to develop Anglo-American cooperation, which had become all the more imperative since the beginning of the Spanish Civil War. As he moved around Europe, Dubinsky also went to Paris and to Poland, meeting Socialist and labor leaders in these countries.[35]

HELPING THE SPANISH REPUBLICANS

From the summer of 1936, the situation in Franco's Spain became a new stage in the expansion of fascist regimes in Europe and made the demand for solidarity among workers' organizations even more urgent. Support for the Spanish Republic can retrospectively be considered a crucial moment when international action could have developed more vigorously to prevent the outbreak of World War II. The abandonment of Spain by the democratic countries, due on the one hand to American neutrality laws and to the non-intervention of France, Great Britain, and Czechoslovakia on the other, left the Popular Front government of Spain to confront Franco's forces on its own. By contrast Franco's forces benefited openly from the military support of Germany and Italy. The USSR's strategy to intervene, although indirectly, in the war by sending weapons and by supporting the loyalist government (albeit taking increasing control of the government coalition via the Spanish Communist Party) testifies to the changing orientation of the Comintern (Communist International), which decided in 1935 to engage in Popular Fronts.

In this context, the IFTU found itself one of the only organizations through which non-military aid from democratic countries could be channeled. Because it did not oppose a pragmatic policy of unity with the Communist parties—which had been achieved in the Spanish workers' movement but also in France—the IFTU was the body best able to assemble international aid on the ground. In cooperation with the LSI, in July 1936 it addressed an appeal to all the workers' federations and Socialist parties. Denouncing the patent violation of international agreements that lay behind German and Italian aid to Franco's forces, this appeal demanded that moral and financial support be supplied to Spanish Republicans. In response, Dubinsky created a new solidarity fund called Labor's Red Cross for Spain—of which he was the treasurer—committed to collecting $100,000. All of these contributions would be sent to the IFTU.[36]

The JLC did not intervene directly in the war in Spain. However, the important role played by the unions that composed it (ILGWU and ACWA) meant for Dubinsky and other executives a first opportunity to be leaders in providing help and subsidies to a country at war. In this context, Dubinsky assumed the leadership of American labor's solidarity for Spanish Republicans. At first, even contributions from Communist sources were transmitted to the IFTU via Labor's Red Cross for Spain. Following the Moscow party line, the American Communist Party, which since 1935 had entered into a form of Popular Front, contributed to the support of the Republicans in proportion to its strength in the United States.[37] This situation earned Dubinsky insults and attacks that were both anti-Semitic and anti-Communist, and all the more venomous since he was committed to Franklin D. Roosevelt in the presidential election campaign that was unfolding in the summer of 1936. The Hearst press, supporting the (U.S.) Republican Party, labeled Dubinsky a Communist. Some Democratic congressmen took advantage of the situation to demand that Dubinsky's name be struck off the list of official FDR supporters. Dubinsky made it clear that the funds collected, far from being destined to political parties, were being shipped to the unions of Spanish workers in the form of clothing, food, and medicine. He also had to respond to attacks made by the American Catholic Church, which, at the instigation of Spanish bishops, tried to counter the pro-Republican movements in American public opinion by labeling them as anti-Christian and pro-Communist. Reflecting the conservative line, the Hearst press willingly maintained confusion over the legitimacy of the Spanish Republican government.[38]

Countering trends in popular opinion was one of the reasons for inviting leaders of the IFTU to the United States: Walter Citrine came over for the second time, as did Walter Schevenels, the IFTU's secretary-general.[39] The other reason for these visits arose from the IFTU's desire to tighten the links between American and European workers' movements. The IFTU had in effect all the more need for American help for Spain because with the disappearance of the Italian, German, and Austrian movements, its membership and its resources had collapsed catastrophically, whereas, inversely, needs had become urgent and costly. It became imperative for its leaders to seek new sources of financial support. With this prospect, Citrine actively solicited the AFL to become a member of the IFTU once again. His visit to the United States in October 1936 accelerated this process, as well as promoting the campaign to support the Spanish Republicans. Citrine turned to the representatives of the Labor Chest and of the AFL's Executive Council, encouraging them to contribute to Labor's Red Cross for Spain, affirming that $250,000 had already been collected, principally in England and France. The contributions from both unions and individuals had enabled food and medicine to be sent to Spanish workers, an ambulance to be equipped, and doctors and nurses to be recruited.[40]

The AFL's reaffiliation with the IFTU was sealed during the summer of 1937 and unanimously ratified at the AFL convention in October. The Committee for International Relations directed by vice president Matthew Woll recalled Citrine's earlier appeal for solidarity with German, Austrian, and Italian workers at its 1934 convention. Woll was delegated by William Green to negotiate the reaffiliation of the AFL with the IFTU's executive council when it met in Warsaw in August 1937. Upon Woll's return, the AFL committee recommended its reintegration into the IFTU, noting that the latter was "the militant spearhead of the free workers' movement in Europe," which had "splendidly contributed to the advance and the elevation of the economic and social standards of the people of all nations."[41] The conditions the AFL demanded in exchange for its return had been accepted: a guarantee of the independence of each national federation, an arrangement for dues from non-European members, and the freedom of delegates to not be associated with decisions they did not support. Ultimately Green was pleased about the American integration into international institutions like the International Labor Bureau and the IFTU, organizations of defense against fascism and dedicated to the support of victims of totalitarian regimes. The AFL's admission into the IFTU, however, did not occur without creating a stir in Europe, due both to the difference in political cultures and to increased tensions in the United States because of the burgeoning rivalry between the AFL and the CIO.[42]

In August 1938, the crisscrossing in New York of delegates from European labor organizations exposed these political and union divisions. A delegation of European workers' representatives, including Léon Jouhaux and Benoît Frachon of the French Confédération Générale du Travail (CGT), Edo Fimmen, president of the International Transportworkers' Federation

(ITF), and Ramon Gonzalez Pena, president of the Union General de Trabajadores (UGT) and minister of justice in the Spanish coalition government, all passed through New York on their way to Mexico to attend an international conference against the war and fascism sponsored by the Mexican labor federation. The AFL had declined the invitation to this conference in the knowledge that CIO representatives were going. Nevertheless, in a sign of international solidarity with the Spanish Republicans, Dubinsky, who had been contacted in advance by Léon Jouhaux and by IFTU assistant secretary Georg Stolz, organized a reception for the European delegates at a luncheon at the Astor Hotel on August 24. There Stolz would not only renew the demand for support of the Spanish fighters but also plead for lifting the American embargo on sending arms to Spain. Also invited were Allan Haywood, regional director of the CIO for New York State, Joseph Schlossberg of the ACWA (CIO), Norman Thomas, president of the American Socialist Party, Vladeck of the JLC, and Joseph Weinberg of the Workmen's Circle. After the European delegates returned from Mexico, two meetings were held several days apart, one on September 16, organized by John Lewis, president of the CIO, and the other on September 21, arranged by Dubinsky. Vladeck, who only witnessed the coming and going of the European delegation, ironically summarized these divisions: "I pray to the Lord that the Republic of Spain should have less advisors and more ammunition."[43]

These dissensions arose not only from divisions within American labor federations but also (and more deeply) from struggles in Spain among Communists, Socialists, and Anarchists. The fall of the Popular Front government of Francisco Largo Caballero in May 1937, provoked by Stalin's support of Spanish Communist leaders in the coalition, was the most visible sign of the Soviet grip on the Spanish Republican government. The arrest of the leaders of the Partido Obrero de Unificacion Marxista (POUM) (Trotskyist), the assassination of its head (Andrés Nin), and the liquidation of anarchists were the paradoxical and inexorable consequences. At the very time Dubinsky was receiving Ramon Gonzalez Pena, he had signed an appeal to the government of Juan Negrin, who had succeeded Largo Caballero. This appeal demanded that all prisoners—Socialists, POUM-ists,

UGT members, and anarcho-syndicalists—should receive the impartial assistance of foreign lawyers and that an international committee of workers' representatives be permitted to accompany these prisoners during their political trials.[44]

In July 1937, a new appeal for solidarity that aimed to collect $250,000 was launched in the United States for a hospital in Onteniente for Spanish combatants, as well as for the support of their families, and for subsidies. This appeal came from yet another committee, Trade Union Relief for Spain, led by Charles Zimmerman, head of ILGWU Local 22, which coordinated the actions of several ILGWU sections and of the United Hebrew Trades. Dubinsky, as always, was its treasurer. But this committee did not attain its financial objective. As fund coordinator A. S. Lipschitz noted in a letter to Zimmerman, there were too many organizations calling for solidarity with the Spanish Republicans—and their bases were overlapping.[45] Dubinsky also affirmed that in the American political context, it had become difficult to justify that the funds collected in fact had a civil—and especially non-Communist—destination. The State Department, which required the registration of these organizations, published a list of twenty-eight distinct committees engaged in collecting funds for Spain. The total collected reached $1,732,259 in April 1939. The Friends of the Abraham Lincoln Brigade had raised the most money ($215,456); the Trade Union Relief for Spain had collected only $32,903 since May 1937, according to State Department estimations. The Abraham Lincoln Brigade had in effect aroused much enthusiasm well beyond the Communist circles involved at the start; it had enrolled some three thousand American volunteers in 1937–1938 and had fought within the International Brigades organized by the Comintern, whose units included fighters from fifty-two countries.[46]

In 1938, support for the Spanish democratic cause assumed an internationally symbolic dimension in the context of Hitler's territorial annexations. "A victory in Spain would mean a victory in the worldwide conflict between fascism and democracy," noted Dubinsky at a meeting on September 21 organized with Trade Union Relief for Spain, which was receiving the European delegation for the second time. In the autumn of 1938, after the Anschluss, the Sudetenland was added to the list of territories annexed by the Third Reich. A representative of the German Social Democrats of the Sudetenland, Karl Deutsch, was present at this meeting. Edo Fimmen, of the International Transportworkers' Federation, who was deeply engaged in the underground struggle in Germany and in controlling freight to Spain, reminded the audience:

> Do not leave those fighters in Germany and in Austria; do not let them go to their doom; stand by them; do not forget them. All in the world can be saved from reaction, Nazism and fascism, and can be won for liberty, can be won for socialism, if Germany, which after all is one of the most important countries in the world, can be won back by our movement and won for socialism.[47]

After the fall of the Republican coalition in Spain, the ILGWU and Trade Union Relief for Spain were asked to help Italian combatants of the Garibaldi battalion of the International Brigades, whose members had taken refuge in France after the end of the civil war. In July 1939, these Italian fighters had been interned in concentration camps near the Spanish border, or, if they had no resources, they were awaiting the international aid that would prevent their being once again interned in France or, worse, extradited to Italy.[48]

During the years 1933–1937 the first personal and institutional links were formed between members of the JLC and European workers' movements and political victims of Nazism and fascism. These networks fostered a circulation of ideas, people, and means that broke the traditional isolationism of American workers, as well as the isolation caused on the other side by the destruction of German, Austrian, and Italian institutions in Europe and the defeat of their leaders. As incomplete as they were, these contacts created the conditions for the emergence of a transatlantic space among international labor organizations into which the JLC was integrated for the struggle against Nazism and fascism. Its leaders would play a decisive role in weaving together these contacts. At their core, members sustained and enlarged these networks by their financial and fraternal cooperation. As the failure of national and international working-class organizations to victoriously sustain the Spanish Republicans had demonstrated, the struggle was formidably unequal, given the obstacles erected by both the neutral nations and the belligerent powers.

3

POLITICS OF ANTI-NAZISM, 1935–1939

Anti-fascism in Europe, as Jacques Droz noted, was never a unitary move-ment, nor could it restrain the rise of fascism.[1] In the United States, too, frequent and diverse forms of action would lead to an impasse, running up against the traditional isolationism and the Neutrality Acts passed by Con-gress in 1935, 1936, and 1937. Nor could activism manage to soften American immigration policy. In this context, the Jewish Labor Committee could only try to influence public opinion, participating in demonstrations organized with other Jewish and labor organizations. It also initiated the Counter-Olympics in New York City, thus leading the way to the symbolic opposition to the 1936 Olympic Games in Berlin. At the same time, but more discreetly, the JLC moved along avenues that it would later develop: support for a resistance movement in Germany and for the Jewish workers' movement in Poland. Thus by the autumn of 1939, the JLC could envisage the possibility of exfiltrating political leaders caught in the trap of German occupation.

BOYCOTT OF GERMAN GOODS

In the United States as in Europe, the first reaction of many organizations to the anti-Semitic violence unleashed in Germany when Hitler came to power was to launch a boycott of German products. This kind of action would become a form of economic and ideological warfare on both sides of the Atlantic. In Germany the boycott of businesses owned by Jews that started on April 1, 1933, was cynically presented by Joseph Goebbels, minister of propaganda, as a "counter" boycott responding to the demonstrations organized in England and the United States, which since March had been denouncing violence against the Jews.[2] The Nazi measure, closely followed by the Aryanization of public services and the professions, stirred up the reaction of democratic countries, whose most common form of action was a spontaneous boycott of German goods and services.

The boycott never won unanimity in the United States, not even among Jewish American organizations, and did not come close to reaching its objective of economically isolating the Third Reich. Several organizations resorted to this form of protest. The most visible was the American Jewish Congress, which invited the Jewish Labor Committee to maximize the impact of the boycott it had launched at its founding in February 1934.[3] On the working-class side, at its October 1933 convention the American Federation of Labor had already called for a boycott of German products and services. In fact this stance did not differ from the positions taken by the Labor and Socialist International and the International Federation of Trade Unions during their respective meetings in Brussels in August 1933. After uncertain beginnings on an economic level, efforts became stronger in 1935. That year the JLC answered the invitation of the American Jewish Congress (AJC) to form a Joint Boycott Council that would centralize the dispersed activities and would be the principal interlocutor with the U.S. Congress and with other governmental and civic agencies. The agreement between the two organizations, sealed on November 27, 1935, was somewhat surprising, though: it downplayed their significant ideological differences. The JLC until then had refused any concerted action with the AJC because it did not share its Zionist position and reproached it for considering only the anti-Semitic aspect of Nazi violence and persecution. "The Jewish Labor Committee considers the Jewish plight in Germany as only one angle of Fascism and is of the opinion that only by conducting our campaign as a part of a general labor campaign against Fascism, can we succeed," Vladeck had earlier declared.[4] Rabbi Stephen Wise, honorary president of the AJC, for his part, considered Vladeck too little of a "nationalist" for the operation to be successful. But undoubtedly it was the possibility of extending the boycott in several directions that motivated the two organizations to combine their efforts. The JLC, for its part, could involve the AFL and the wider labor world more than it had before, and the AJC could develop the campaign in the direction of businesses, department stores, and consumers.

The anti-Semitic violence that took place in Munich in the spring of 1935 and the riots in Berlin on the Kurfürstendam in July of the same year propelled the AJC and the JLC to coordinate their efforts. In November, the publication of the Nuremberg Laws and decrees that defined the "Jewish race" and pursued the exclusion of Jews from public employment and from the professions, as well as removed their right to vote, all sharpened the indignation of American associations. Beyond diplomatic condemnations, presented by Secretary of State Cordell Hull to the German ambassador, however, the Roosevelt administration did not officially protest the exclusion of Jews from German citizenship. Could the economic impact anticipated by the Joint Boycott Council really compensate for the government's silence by imposing a form of sanction that emanated from individual producers and consumers?[5]

The agreement established by the Joint Boycott Council called for a number of actions: to launch the widest possible appeal against stores that sold German merchandise; to set up rotating picket lines, vigilance committees, and lectures; to mobilize women as consumers; to widen the boycott movement by a call for a national conference; to ask workers to refuse jobs in workshops and factories where the raw materials, semi-finished products, or the machines used were of German origin; and finally to persuade the longshoremen's unions to refuse to unload German products at the docks.[6]

According to Dr. Joseph Tenenbaum, president of the Joint Boycott Council, the boycott was the surest weapon against the Nazi regime—and could even precipitate its fall. He produced annual figures demonstrating the boycott's impact on the American importation of German products. "Time is working for us. Every month brings the economic collapse of Germany nearer," he asserted in 1936. "Germany will survive Hitler, but Hitler cannot survive a prolonged economic blockade." According to his estimates based on figures from the League of Nations, German exports to the United States fell by 40 percent between 1932 and 1935. And the United States was not the only nation exercising such pressure. Tenenbaum indicated that according to an official Reich source, German exports to twelve European countries, including the Soviet Union, had slumped from 71 percent to 55 percent of its foreign trade.[7]

Despite Tenenbaum's optimism, difficulties piled up for partisans of the boycott. Strong opposition certainly came from the business world but also from the State Department and the Department of Commerce in Washington. Moreover, in Germany the government and exporters found ways to circumvent the boycott such that only certain sectors of the market were affected. In fact, what moral sense did it make to refuse to buy German products, if on the other hand the United States was providing Hitler's regime with foodstuffs and industrial equipment?

Foreign trade was one of the domains where Roosevelt was trying to break American isolationism with measures to promote international exchanges. The appointment of Cordell Hull to the State Department was part of this plan. Hull was charged with drawing up bilateral agreements with various countries, invoking the need to liberalize international trade to dispose of American surpluses and to revitalize both the national and world economies. No particular agreement was signed with Germany, but then it did not seem possible to adopt measures of economic retaliation against this country alone if they contravened trade laws without applying them to others.[8] What the boycott campaign could in fact obtain from American diplomacy was the requirement that the Third Reich stop subsidizing German exporters. The Joint Boycott Council had noted that high German subsidies to exporting businesses contravened market laws, and it called for protectionist tariffs to be increased in proportion. It argued that these subsidies amounted to a depreciation of goods on the market, equivalent to a form of "dumping." By invoking the protectionist laws of 1921 and 1930, with the president's approval, the Department of Commerce and the Treasury imposed the right to levy customs duties in order to "compensate"

for German subsidies. As a consequence, Germany put an end to these export deals.[9] But other measures could still get around the possible impact
of the boycott, notably a barter system, by which an American exporter
could reimburse himself by importing German products that he could turn
around and resell on the American market. The supply of American cot-
ton, under pressure from the southern states, was especially subject to this
trade system.

Labeling imported goods with their country of origin, another conces-
sion by the Department of Commerce, sometimes facilitated the boycotting
of stores or businesses that were getting around the ban. Boycotting was
successfully applied against Macy's and Sears Roebuck and Company, for
example. But the distribution chains John Wanamaker and Butler Brothers,
and some manufacturers of photographic material—Eastman Kodak and
Agfa Ansco Corporation—were still on the list of businesses to be boy-
cotted in 1938. Most of the sanctioned products were consumer durable or
luxury goods, over which moral pressure on consumers did have a certain
impact: toys, leather gloves, textiles, needles, crayons, furs, precious stones,
pharmaceuticals, musical instruments, and sewing machines. But these
temporary victories were called into question by a certain weariness—or
by either side's circumventing import/export practices. In 1937, the Joint
Boycott Council acknowledged that imports from Germany had grown by
25 percent since 1932.[10] The incessant monitoring performed by the Joint
Boycott Council involved a sustained effort. On the macroeconomic level
they followed and interpreted the statistics of international trade; on the
political level they put pressure on legislators and the administration in
Washington; and on the consumer level they had to survey the products
on display in stores and monitor enterprises that contravened the boycott.
In addition they issued reports on these activities in order to strengthen
the boycott's impact. The JLC participated in the campaign in accordance
with its means; Vladeck and Isaiah Minkoff, in particular, actively pursued several cases. They campaigned among their members, who in turn
reported businesses that were resisting, which were then asked to cease
importing German products. But JLC leaders did not share Tenenbaum's
faith in this kind of action. After the death of Vladeck in November 1938,

the JLC records point to its decreased participation in the Joint Boycott Council. Yet Tenenbaum in his report of May 1939 described the boycott as a "grand social and international movement." He asserted that its check on the American and pan-American markets was such a handicap for the German economy that it was "on the verge of bankruptcy" and "Hitlerism was being defeated"![11] While copresident of the Joint Boycott Council, Vladeck never signed any of Tenenbaum's reports. The JLC's executive decided on September 7, 1939, that it would no longer participate in the Joint Boycott Council. More realistically, the JLC at this time was preoccupied with the fate of Jewish people in Poland especially after the German and Soviet invasions of September 1939.[12]

THE COUNTER-OLYMPICS OF 1936

Beginning in 1933, another form of boycott was being discussed in American and international circles: a boycott of the Olympic Games that were to be held in Berlin in 1936. By proposing the creation of a "counter-Olympics" in New York in August 1936, the JLC took a position whose ideological impact, at least until the Games were held, had more reverberations than the boycott of commercial goods from Germany. The World Labor Athletic Carnival, a workers' athletic and Olympic festival, took place on Randall's Island, in the East River, on August 15 and 16, 1936. In the end it was the only major counter-Olympics that would be held in protest over the powerful unfolding of the Berlin Games. The JLC thus took an active part in both movements that were opposed to the Berlin Games: the Popular Front of the international labor movement, on the one hand, and American public opinion on the other. Up until December 1935 it was not certain that the United States would actually send athletes to Berlin. News about the Berlin Olympics demonstrated that American public opinion did matter to the organizers of the Games.[13]

The decision to hold the Games in Berlin in 1936 had been made by the International Olympic Committee in April 1931, two years before the country sank into the Nazi regime. The desire to reintroduce Germany into the concert of nations (and into international sports competition) after the trauma of World War I had dictated this choice. Barcelona came in second. In that city, an International Workers' Counter-Olympiad was planned for July 1936, but this event was precluded by the start of the civil war.

In 1933 the American Olympic Committee (AOC), which prepared the American delegation, was already aware of the incompatibility between the spirit of the Games and Nazi racial ideology. It made it a point of honor to obtain from the German organizing committee a promise that there would be no exclusion of Jewish athletes of German or any other nationality. Two AOC representatives, Armitage Brundage and Charles Sherrill, visited Berlin in 1934 and 1935 to evaluate the situation. They were certainly fooled by the declarations of the German organizers, who denied there was any discrimination against Jews and affirmed the complete openness of the Games without any exclusion—racial, religious, or otherwise. Hitler himself made a show of participating in a meeting with Sherrill, who was still hesitant in 1935, in order to win him over.[14] The AOC therefore voted to send American athletes to the Winter Games in Garmisch-Partenkirchen in February 1936 and to commit to U.S. participation in the Berlin Games in August. Still, a national battle raged over this, which emanated not only from the Jewish milieux that were naturally sensitive to the issue but also from the general public. The Nuremberg Laws pronounced in September and November opened everyone's eyes to the reality of anti-Semitic persecution. On the sports side, German Jewish athletes, even if they wanted to compete, found themselves prevented from doing so because sports clubs and public training facilities were closed to them. A vast international opposition movement took shape in France, Britain, and the Soviet Union. In the United States, New York congressman Emmanuel Celler asked Congress not to vote the funds to send athletes—unsuccessfully. Nevertheless, an opposition of unprecedented scope included the Catholic Democrat Al Smith, former governor of New York State and former presidential candidate, and religious leaders like the theologian Reinhold Niebuhr and Reverend Harry Emerson Fosdick. A number of civil rights associations also participated, including the Anti-Defamation League, the American Jewish Congress, the American Jewish Committee, and the National Association for the Advancement of Colored People, as well as many magazine editors (*The Nation, Christian Century, The New Leader, Commonweal, Amsterdam News*) and topflight newspapers, with the *New York Times* leading the way. Seven governors, including Herbert Lehman of New York, six senators, forty-one university presidents, twenty Olympic champions, and the AFL all opposed both holding the Games in Berlin and sending an American delegation there.[15]

Any AOC decision was supposed to be supported by the Amateur Athletic Union (AAU), which in fact did not agree with the AOC's position.[16] Its president, Jeremiah T. Mahoney, an Irish Catholic close to the union movement and to New York City's mayoral office, tried in vain to maintain the AAU's position, which since 1933 had been rejecting American participation in the Berlin Games if it could be demonstrated that they were contaminated by Nazi anti-Semitic discrimination. In the end, Mahoney could not obtain a majority vote (55 to 58) and resigned from the AAU. He then approached the Jewish Labor Committee, which via other channels had been just as firmly opposed to the Games in Berlin.

The JLC committed all its energy to the venture of a counter-Olympics. If such an event was necessary, it would have to be resounding: "Big or nothing," it advised.[17] First the dates chosen, August 15 and 16, 1936, would correspond to the last two days of the Berlin Games, thus grabbing media attention before the return of the victors from Germany. Second, the event was doubled in size to ensure there were enough qualified participants. In fact, two separate competitions were to be held: an "open" one for national and international champions (but among the latter only a few Canadians were enlisted!), and a "closed" one designed for competition among amateur athletes who were members of labor unions or associations. The event attracted 20,000 spectators and 700 participants (of whom 450 were amateurs) on both days. It was placed under the high patronage of the New York State governor, Herbert Lehman, who was to hand a trophy to the winning team, and of the New York City mayor, Fiorello La Guardia, who offered the amateurs' cup. Four athletes of international standing participated in these games: much was expected of the black runner Eulace Peacock, who had three times beaten the records set by another African American athlete,

Jesse Owens, who had gone to Berlin. But this time an injured Peacock did not beat his record.

Chroniclers especially celebrated the world pole vault champion George Varoff, who by a vault of 14 feet, 4.5 inches achieved a better performance than those who had qualified for Berlin. The performances of the other competitors for these stadium events (swimming and track and field) did not outdo those of the American athletes in Berlin. Meanwhile, Jesse Owens, with four gold medals in Berlin, became the absolute champion, and the "stadium god" of the Olympic Games of 1936, and this despite Hitler's refusal to shake his hand when he had saluted other athletes.

But the stakes of the World Labor Athletic Carnival did not only lie in athletic performances. The participation of working-class amateurs, in particular, had another significance. It was the first time that the worlds of labor and sports were allied in a common purpose and, what is more, in political solidarity. As a sign of changes under the New Deal era, amateur sports among workers had only become possible since the legal reduction of the workday to eight hours by the National Industrial Recovery Act of 1933 and the union agreements reached under the Wagner Act that replaced it in 1935.[18] Thus the event was indeed both a tribute to union life and a New York festival. The New York Trades and Labor Council was associated with it, as well as the AFL, whose president, William Green, had traveled from Washington to attend. It was a Popular Front festival, too, since the Communist daily papers did not snub it, and even the president of the American Socialist Party, Norman Thomas, was present.[19] The political and sporting success of these popular Olympics enabled it to be held again the following year. Competitions were held in July 1937 at Randall's Island but with less resonance than the previous year (largely due to the vigorous protest movement that had led to it at the time). The JLC and the AAU had correctly interpreted the symbolic benefit that the Third Reich would draw from the Berlin Games. A symbiosis had been achieved between the Nazi nationalist power manifested in their organization of the event and the masses who celebrated it, as well as between the victories won by German athletes and the spirit of competition and virile strength that the champions incarnated. Moreover, Jesse Owens's glory paradoxically obscured the anti-Semitic discrimination involved in Germany's selection of its athletes. Above all, in the media the Games eclipsed the expansionism of the Third Reich, which had just begun.[20]

A NEW YORK LABOR PARTY

During the summer of 1936, Baruch Charney Vladeck had not attended the counter-Olympics in New York, nor had he participated in organizing them. Since 1935, his preoccupations had multiplied on both the national and international levels. In these years that would be the last of his life, Vladeck was highly involved in the politics of New York City. In addition, seeing the clouds accumulating in Europe, he crossed the Atlantic twice, in 1935 and 1936, strengthening his ties with German and Austrian socialist leaders. On the second trip he also went to Palestine to evaluate the situation between Jews and Arabs in the British Protectorate.

In 1936, without abandoning his socialist ideals, Vladeck did not renew his membership in the Socialist Party of America (SPA).[21] He had various motives: internal schisms had weakened the SPA's objectives; Vladeck was opposed to the rigid pacifism of its leader, Norman Thomas; the latter's Christian Socialism did not fit the Jewish Socialist "old guard"; and overall, Roosevelt's New Deal was doing more for social protection, union rights, and the American economy than the Socialist Party ever could. In the presidential campaign of 1936, Vladeck helped launch the formation of a New York–based labor party. The American Labor Party[22] was meant to rally the working-class electorate—of which a significant portion had previously voted Socialist—to Roosevelt's candidacy for the White House and to Herbert Lehman's for the New York governorship, and to promote Democratic representatives to Congress. Its 1936 electoral success continued into the city elections of 1937 when progressive Republican Fiorello La Guardia was reelected as mayor of New York. Vladeck himself was elected to the City Council on the new American Labor Party platform. His charismatic personality, which managed to bring together a heterogeneous coalition on the Council, earned him the post of majority leader. In this position at the center of municipal affairs, Vladeck was particularly active in the renovation of working-class housing. He is remembered for having created a complex of low-income apartments on the Lower East Side, which still bears his name.[23] The American Labor Party had taken root in an electorate and a district in which the New York City members of the JLC and its unions had a lively base. The leaders of the needle trades unions and people from the Jewish Daily Forward Association took the initiative: David Dubinsky, Sidney Hillman, Luigi Antonini, Alex Rose. Vladeck and Alexander Kahn of the *Forward* had also solicited the involvement of leftist intellectuals who were disenchanted with the Socialist Party, such as journalist Dorothy Thompson, philosopher John Dewey, and New Dealer and advisor to FDR Adolph Berle. Thus Vladeck found himself at the center of both city politics and a network of organizations (Jewish and non-Jewish, union and associative, political and cultural) that placed him in direct contact with New York's progressive circles. The electoral shift of the JLC leaders, and no doubt of their members, which took them from the Socialist Party of America to the Democratic Party as an integral part of the New Deal coalition, was not isolated. In the 1936 elections, which brought FDR to his second term, it was more or less the whole immigrant working class that left behind its marginality or its non-participation in elections in order to align with the Democratic Party. Among the Jewish electorate, support for Roosevelt was almost unanimous—despite class cleavages. The irreversible decline of the Socialist Party in the United States dates to this moment.[24]

In a communiqué to the British Labour Party a few years later, the JLC declared, "We are not a political party but an organization devoted to the principles of socialism and [that] supports energetically the New Deal program of President Roosevelt." The unions belonging to the JLC, the statement continued, "are the backbone of the American Labor Party, which has become an important political force in the State of New York."[25] Ambiguities abound in this declaration, such as denying that the JLC was a political party; it had helped found one on the local level, the American Labor Party, designed to support the Democratic Party. The JLC had several facets. Made up of union forces, but without any economic activity, it was guided by socialist principles; contrary to the general orientations of American unionism of which it was an integral part, it stood close to the Socialist International. No doubt its appeal to the British Labour Party, which led to this self-definition, explains the mixture of notions involved: without being able to reproduce the organic relationship that prevailed in Britain between the TUC and the Labour Party, the JLC was stressing the importance of its union base and of its political orientation.

ANTI-NAZI RESISTANCE: LINKS WITH NEU BEGINNEN

The JLC's contacts with anti-Nazi Germany had begun with the welcoming of the first Social Democratic refugees who reached the United States. Martin Plettl and Gerhart Seger were the first of a cohort that would grow, partially supported by the funds collected by the Labor Chest, to which the JLC and the AFL both contributed. But Vladeck established contacts with German and Austrian Socialists in exile independently of the AFL. He decisively committed the JLC to supporting resistance against the Third Reich, particularly by establishing links with a political group situated to the left of the German Socialist Party (SPD), which considered it dissident. The existence of the Neu Beginnen movement was a subject of dispute among official SPD members who had emigrated to the United States and led to controversies among American socialists. But Vladeck's support of Neu Beginnen reveals the central role he played among anti-Nazi émigrés and may explain why of all the German political organizations that found refuge in America, Neu Beginnen was the most effective in exile.[26]

In the summer of 1935, Vladeck had gone to Vienna and then Prague, where the German Social Democratic Party (SOPADE) had retreated. In July he attended the conference of the Labor and Socialist International (LSI) held in Brussels. There Friedrich Adler (LSI secretary-general) put him in touch with Karl Frank, one of the leaders of Neu Beginnen, whom Vladeck invited to come to the United States in order to spread the word about his movement and collect funds. Decimated inside the Third Reich by Nazi repression, the Neu Beginnen group barely counted forty young activists outside the country. While maintaining their membership in the SPD, they were critical of its position in exile, which they considered too bureaucratic, too focused on the past, lacking a vision for the reconstruction of German socialism, and incapable of fomenting domestic resistance—or even maintaining contacts with its working-class base. Like other groups that dissented from the SPD—the Internationaler Sozialistischer Kampfbund (ISK) and the Sozialistische Arbeiter Partei (SAP)—Neu Beginnen wanted the Communist Party and SPD to join together in the struggle against Hitler. The theoretical foundation of their position was circulated in a 1933 brochure titled *Neu Beginnen! Faschismus oder Sozialismus*, which was translated into English under the title *Socialism's New Start: A Secret German Manifesto*.[27] Knowing that the National-Socialist regime could not be overthrown only by resistance from the labor movement, its leaders sought support from abroad (but beyond the closed circles of the exile communities), which was all the more necessary because since 1935 the SOPADE no longer supported them financially. By inviting Karl Frank to the United States in the autumn of 1935, Vladeck was sponsoring this movement from across the Atlantic and contributing to the pursuit of its underground activity in Germany. It was Vladeck who suggested to Frank that he adopt the pseudonym "Paul Hagen" (which he kept his entire later life in the United States) and began to support his movement financially.[28]

Vladeck's interest in Neu Beginnen derived from his own historic affinity for dissident socialist or revolutionary movements marked by a certain idealism. The ability of this movement to conduct clandestine activities reminded him of the revolutionary operations he had conducted in the Russian Empire when he was a Bund militant. Moreover, the support Neu Beginnen found among the Austrian socialists—more than the German ones—also recalled the proximity of the Bund to Austrian socialist theoreticians. In 1937, Karl Frank wrote to Vladeck:

> Our development is satisfactory. You know too well how small the progress of an underground movement in months and years sometimes is, until the crisis of the dictator regime has come. But within these limits, we have

doubled our forces, have many new contacts and friends. We have a much greater reputation among the progressive wing of socialists in Europe, and especially much better relations with Brouckere, Adler, Bauer and Blum.[29]

Although Austrian by origin, Karl Frank had fought in Germany in the 1920s, first in the Communist Party until 1929 and then, because he was a critic of Stalinism, in the German SPD, which he had rallied in 1931, like many young militants, in order to defend the party and the workers' movement against the rise of Nazism. From this group Neu Beginnen was born. After Hitler took power, Frank worked to develop contacts between German workers at the grassroots level and the SPD leadership in exile. In 1934, after the defeat of the Schutzbund, Frank helped organize the clandestine Austrian Socialist Party and brought its methods of activism to Neu Beginnen. But rapidly the SOPADE took umbrage at these militants' initiative, seeing it as rivalry more than cooperation and, without formally expelling the group, forced it to seek support abroad.[30] The SOPADE leaders in exile no doubt were suffering from what historian Albrecht Ragg describes as a reversal of the importance of the main party (the SPD) in favor of radical splinter groups.[31] In any case, according to the JLC, Martin Plettl's rationale for supporting the SPD and German labor refugees paled in comparison with the militancy of Neu Beginnen.

In the United States during the autumn of 1935, Karl Frank/Paul Hagen founded another organization, the American Friends of German Freedom (AFGF), and managed to collect some $8,000 to promote underground work in Germany. The AFGF benefited from the aura surrounding Vladeck in New York: it received contributions from representatives of Jewish labor (Vladeck of the JLC, Julius Hochman of the ILGWU, and Max Zaritsky of the Hatters' Union) but also from Socialist Party president Norman Thomas, theologian Reinhold Niebuhr, Secretary of the League for Industrial Democracy Mary Fox, and pillars of the liberal press.[32] Again back in New York in 1937, Frank married Anna Caples, who had been active in the League for Industrial Democracy and who helped him publish regular reports sponsored by the AFGF on the evolution of the situation in Germany. During the war, these *Inside Germany Reports*, well informed on the

German situation, would be used by the Office of Strategic Services (OSS). Yet another fundraising appeal was made in 1937 that brought in $12,000, again arousing the hostility of the SOPADE, whose representatives abroad had not managed to collect sums equivalent to their official importance. Hagen's intention had not been to divide the German socialist emigration but on the contrary to assemble it, in Europe as in the United States, around its most dynamic members. Financing Neu Beginnen corresponded with this objective, and its anticipated "revolutionary" or insurrectional goals when Nazism eventually collapsed were brought to the attention of potential American sponsors. "The coming revolution can only be a people's revolution," Hagen asserted in 1938.[33]

The tense relationship with European communist parties detracted from any conception of a revolutionary goal. One significant example of this tension is the episode concerning the disappearance of Mark Rein, the son of Raphael Abramovitch, the president of the Russian Social Democratic Party who was at the time in exile in Paris. Rein, a young member of Neu Beginnen, had signed up as a journalist in Spain to cover the civil war. His articles for the *Jewish Daily Forward*—by no means favorable to the Communist manipulations of the International Brigades—made him an easy target for the NKVD, the Soviet political police. Rein disappeared in April 1937, barely a month after his arrival in Spain. His assassination, a form of revenge against his father, who was openly critical of the reign of terror in the USSR, was never explicitly acknowledged. On Vladeck's request Paul Hagen went to Barcelona to investigate, and he provided an account testifying to Rein's disappearance as a "sacrifice to Communist history," which, he argued, should cause Neu Beginnen to break off relations with the Communist Party. But the latter's predominant role alongside the Spanish Republicans, Hagen added, did not permit claiming that the USSR was responsible for this murder. Rein's forever-wounded father, Raphael Abramovitch, wanted to turn the affair into an international scandal.[34]

The death of Vladeck in November 1938 of a heart attack at the age of fifty-two opened the way to a period of intense slandering against Karl Frank/Paul Hagen by the SOPADE, a campaign relayed by those who for one reason or another had been opposed to Vladeck. "As long as Vladeck

was alive, he protected our interests," asserted Paul Hagen in his justifica-
tions to clarify his position.[35] In effect, the SOPADE considered itself the
sole representative of German socialism and believed that it should be the
sole recipient of American funds. Therefore its members tried to discredit
Hagen in the eyes of the JLC. Friedrich Stampfer, former editor-in-chief
of the *Vorwärts* in Berlin, the SPD's official organ, and representative of
the party's right wing, came to the United States in 1939 and again during
the winter of 1940. There he helped create a formal representation of the
SOPADE, the German Labor Delegation, whose goal was to attract the
support of the American labor movement. Accordingly, Stampfer pleaded
the cause of the exiled SPD to the AFL Executive Council in February
1940. He also intervened directly with leaders of the JLC in 1939 and 1940,
asserting that Neu Beginnen was using "Bolshevik" methods to destroy the
SPD. The party, he argued, had in the past assembled considerable forces,
but in the current situation a lack of money prevented it from conducting
vast campaigns of anti-Hitler propaganda.[36] In front of the JLC executives,
Stampfer's views were relayed by Abraham Cahan, the formidable editor-
in-chief of the *Jewish Daily Forward* in New York. Cahan's motives were
political but also personal: "If somebody works against Stampfer, then he is
a criminal. Neu Beginnen belongs to this category," he asserted to the JLC
leaders. "Adler [who had] introduced Hagen to Vladeck, was always close
to the Left, [so] his opinions are not taken seriously," he also maintained.[37]
Any argument against Hagen was fine: accusations of crypto-communism,
charges of misuse of funds, and disagreeable statements about Friedrich
Adler, who had supported him. Cahan was aligned with the moderate
wing of the SPD that Stampfer represented. Perhaps it was also out of
professional solidarity that he defended his colleague, Stampfer, who like
him headed a major social-democratic daily newspaper. But by doing so he
revealed an old jealousy of Vladeck. The latter had been his collaborator as
the administrator of the *Jewish Daily Forward*, but his political origin had
earned him close contacts with socialist leaders in Europe—which Cahan
envied or criticized.

Hearing these invectives, the JLC tried to reconcile the two factions,
delaying paying the promised sum ($10,000) to the SOPADE, as well as the

subsidy regularly granted to Neu Beginnen ($2,000); its leaders also asked Friedrich Adler and Walter Citrine for advice in the defense of Hagen's activities. Finally, Adolph Held, Vladeck's successor as head of the JLC, in March 1940 persuaded the Executive Committee to support the two groups equally, knowing that the ILGWU and ACWA would give their support to Neu Beginnen. The sum of $12,000 that was supposed to be shared was not paid as a lump sum, however. From June 1940, with the defeat of France, the JLC was using all of its funds to save refugees in France, including those from both the German SPD and Neu Beginnen.[38]

INFERNO BEGINS IN POLAND

The JLC leaders were also preoccupied with the fate of Jewish people in Poland. David Dubinsky and Julius Hochman of the ILGWU, as well as ACWA secretary-treasurer Joseph Schlossberg, made several trips to Poland in 1935, 1936, and 1937 to organize cooperation between their two unions to support their Polish colleagues financially. As confirmation of this agreement, the secretary-general of the Warsaw Clothing Federation, Herschel Himmelfarb, was invited to the ILGWU convention in May 1937.[39]

During the economic depression that severely hit Poland, poverty and the lack of jobs (9 million unemployed out of a population of 33 million, according to Himmelfarb) were not the only problems for the essentially proletarian Polish Jews. The virulent anti-Semitism perpetrated against them was what motivated the JLC leaders to intervene. Ever since the death of Marshal Josef Pilsudski (1935) and the military regime's rise to power, combined with the influence within the government of the National-Democratic Party, which emulated Germany's National Socialist Party, attacks against the Jews were openly inspired by Hitlerian methods. "Hitler is at work in Poland," affirmed a JLC brochure in March 1936, and the "Polish government is no stranger to the bloody massacres perpetrated there." The minister of foreign affairs, Jozef Beck, in effect proclaimed that 3 million out of the 3.5 million Jews in Poland should leave the country. Discrimination against them touched all aspects of daily life: interdiction on the ritual slaughter of animals, an official boycott of Jewish businesses and craftsmen, pillaging of their goods, restrictions on the access of Jewish students to the universities, and even bloody assaults against Jewish individuals and wholesale pogroms. In response to the pogrom in Przytyk on March 9, 1936, followed by several others, the Polish Bund successfully organized a general strike on March 17, with the support of the unions and other left-wing parties, including the Communists, but the government prevented the Bund from holding the Workers' Conference against anti-Semitism that it had planned for June 1936. The Bund's success in the municipal elections of 1936 and 1938 demonstrated that it could effectively restore political honor and dignity to Jewish workers.[40]

In New York support for the Bund, and more generally for the suffering Jews of Poland, was handled by the JLC, which on April 2, 1936, launched a fundraising appeal called "Hunger Day" with the intention of gathering a million dollars (the cost of meals during the collective fast). To the JLC leaders, support for the Jews of Poland was parallel to that of the Jews of Germany, which at the time was being orchestrated by means of the Boycott Council. The fruit of the collected funds was in fact meant to be divided between what was transmitted to Poland and support for the boycott of German goods. In Poland the JLC engaged pragmatically in a policy of assisting both educational institutions and Jewish workers. Its 1938 budget records almost $75,000 in subsidies to various organizations such as the Medem Sanatorium, the Central Committee of Jewish labor unions of Poland, the Jewish union of Chestochov, the central administration of Yiddish schools (Tsisho), and the Association of Socialist Workers. Most of these gifts, which came from the JLC's unions and fraternal organizations, were gathered and transmitted along with donations from the American Jewish Joint Distribution Committee. At the same time, $22,750 was sent to finance actions against anti-Semitism and Nazism, and $1,750 to support German refugees in Europe.[41]

Vladeck's initiative, along with AFL president William Green, to obtain an interview with Secretary of State Cordell Hull in April 1936, although very significant with respect to later events, had no concrete consequences at the time. Vladeck denounced the explosion of anti-Semitic violence that was unfolding with, as he said, "the explicit or tacit agreement of the Polish government." He attached to his memorandum a list of the pogroms perpetrated since March 9, 1936, in the course of barely three weeks. During this essentially informative interview, Vladeck asked the U.S. government to "take an interest" in the fate of the Jews of Poland, reminding Hull that the United States had sponsored the creation of the Polish Republic in 1918, which in his view justified an immediate diplomatic intervention. Vladeck affirmed—with extraordinary premonition—that "over three million human beings in Poland are on the verge of physical extermination only because of the fact that they are Jews." Noting that the JLC at the time represented 350,000 Jews who were citizens of the United States and members of the AFL, he hoped that the American government would be able to intervene to protect the Jewish minority of Poland, whose rights— recognized by President Woodrow Wilson when he inspired the League of Nations—were being systematically denied.[42]

At this stage in the United States, immigration legislation could not be changed, although the procedure for granting visas for natives of Germany would be somewhat relaxed by the State Department in 1938. The question of an exodus of Polish Jews was not even considered, and the meager quota for Poland (6,524) was only fully utilized in 1939. Debates in Congress and even within the major Jewish American organizations were at the time principally concerned with the possibility of providing refuge for German (and Austrian) Jews. The Zionist issue was a key element in these debates. For members of the American Jewish Congress, Palestine represented the natural refuge. Therefore, pressure should be exerted on Great Britain, whose mandate over Palestine restricted the possibility of emigrating there.[43] Moreover, in Poland the partisans of the Bund were fighting for the defense of Jewish rights at home. As non-Zionists who were speaking for a working population that was barely mobile, they did not see emigration to Palestine as a solution to the Jewish problem. For Wiktor Alter, leader of the Bund, a solution could only result from a struggle shared with the Polish Left for the construction of a socialist Poland. Vladeck himself had made the same case in an article in the *Forward*, of which he sent a translation to Dubinsky:

Everyone is agreed that the Polish Jews cannot solve their problem by emigration. Bundists have been saying this for a long time, and now even Zionists admit it. . . . If mass emigration were possible, we would support it whole-heartedly. But it is clear even to the blind that it is impossible. Of course, efforts should be made to take out of Poland every single Jew we can. One must always remember, however, that while this reduces the size of the problem somewhat, it does not render it less difficult.[44]

Despite some signs of improvement in the Roosevelt administration in 1938 when the German and Austrian quotas were combined, the regulation of immigration was only very slightly relaxed. Yet the Third Reich was inexorably expanding: annexation of Austria in March 1938 and of the Sudetenland in September, dismemberment of the rest of Czechoslovakia in the first months of 1939, and the invasion and division of Poland in September 1939. At the same time, the kind of violence unleashed by Kristallnacht in Germany in November 1938 was being multiplied in the annexed countries, forcing the Jewish populations to ask for asylum in Western democracies. Yet the U.S. Congress remained deaf to the demands to relax the quota regime—or even abandon it. The defeat of the proposed Wagner-Rogers bill to welcome twenty thousand children "above the German quota" and the debacle of the *Saint Louis* refugee ship, which was refused access to any American port, in May 1939, were additional stones in the "paper walls" that continued to surround Fortress America.[45]

The German-Soviet Pact, immediately followed in September 1939 by the invasion and division of Poland by the German and Soviet armies, placed the Jews of Poland "in a virtual hell, of which relief itself, as it is practiced by the Joint, will not rescue them," the JLC Executive Committee stated at their meeting on September 7.[46] Three Polish Bundist delegates who had recently come to the United States—Jacob Pat, Emanuel Nowogrodzki, and Benjamin Tabachinsky—who were in contact with colleagues and friends in Poland had received precise information about the situation. The German occupation was going to destroy every political, economic, educational, and social institution of the Jewish population, forcing thousands to flee. The Bund as a Jewish, socialist, and anti-Communist organization was targeted by both the Nazi and Soviet authorities. Its leaders and local militants were systematically imprisoned—including in eastern Poland. Notable among them were the Bund's national leaders, Henryk Erlich and Wiktor Alter, who were captured by the Soviets. Hundreds of others found a precarious refuge in Lithuania.[47]

The war forced the JLC to reset its priorities. Should it transform itself into a body for humanitarian aid, like the People's Relief Committee of World War I, of which Vladeck had been an administrator, and consequently combine its contributions with those of other institutions that made up the United Jewish Appeal? Or should it pursue its political anti-Nazi, anti-fascist policy? In such discussions, Isaiah Minkoff and Jacob Pat insisted on the independence of the JLC's mission which, before being involved in collective fundraising efforts, should pursue its specific task of helping the workers' movement, underground organizations, and the struggle against anti-Semitism, including in the United States.[48]

The JLC's other primary concern was assisting with the "political emigration" of Jewish labor activists from Poland. During the JLC Executive Committee meeting on December 28, 1939, Nathan Chanin raised the possibility, not envisaged until then, of obtaining temporary visas for a third country. Great Britain was offering twenty-four such visas, requiring a $2,000 deposit with the mayor of London for the operation. The committee ratified this plan, assigning $1,000 for this purpose to contacts in Europe, but it turned out that the actual amount needed was $10,000. However, the Bundist leaders they were trying to save with these visas would not leave. The Bund's central committee decided to remain in Vilna, transforming this city into the temporary headquarters of Polish Bundist activity.[49]

During the debates in New York on the possibility of saving Bundists, the Executive Committee specified that "the Jewish Labor Committee assumes the responsibility for the labor movement in Poland and for the emigration of labor people from Poland."[50] They were thus introducing the concept of "political emigration," which differed from the single "immigration" category, the only one recognized in American administrative language, and which would become the basis on which the JLC would succeed a few months later—after mid-June 1940, a date that signaled both the start of the

German occupation of France and the Soviet occupation of Lithuania—in extracting from these countries opponents of the Nazi, fascist, or Communist regimes who had taken refuge there.

Baruch Charney Vladeck had foreseen all the horrors of Nazism, but he did not live to see the most frightening realities. He died of a heart attack on October 30, 1938, a few days before Kristallnacht. He had understood that the Munich Agreement was the prelude to the complete dismemberment of Czechoslovakia, but he was spared the invasion of Poland and that of western Europe. He did not have to live through the Holocaust. The Jewish Labor Committee, now directed by Adolph Held, pursued its work, increasing its efforts to save political refugees and help Jewish working-class people in distress. It had to adapt its activity to its political, administrative, and financial means—and to the help being provided by other American rescue organizations.

4

TRAJECTORIES OF EXILE, RESCUE OPERATIONS

After the fall of France in June 1940, soon followed by the annexation of Lithuania by the Soviet Union, the Jewish Labor Committee achieved the administrative, humanitarian, and political feat of saving several hundred political refugees caught in countries that had fallen under either Nazi or Communist domination. This was an *administrative* feat because obtaining visas for admission to the United States even for persons in danger of immediate arrest was notoriously difficult; American immigration policy held fast to quotas that had long been inappropriate in the current international situation. It was a *humanitarian* feat because it was a matter of survival for opponents of Nazi Germany and fascist Italy who had taken refuge in France and were now sought by the Gestapo or by the Italian police and were in danger of imminent arrest and deportation by the Vichy police. The JLC leaders immediately perceived the magnitude of the infamous contents of clause 19 of the armistice signed on June 22, 1940, by which the Vichy government—abandoning its own sovereignty—accepted to "surrender on demand all German nationals designated by the government of the Reich." With this agreement, France suddenly had been transformed into a death trap for the thousands of exiles who had found refuge there. Finally, rescue was a *political* feat because it was the very core of the European workers' socialist or social-democratic movement that they were trying to save from the tempest. In itself, the JLC's commitment demonstrated its will to resist fascist dictatorial injunctions. Moreover, officially conducted in the name of the American Federation of Labor, this rescue activity committed American labor—traditionally an apolitical movement—to a path it had never taken: solidarity with the leaders of European working-class movements belonging to left-wing and socialist, but not Communist, organizations.

Most of the rescue operations took place over a year and a half, from July 1940 to the end of 1941. Not yet at war, the United States maintained diplomatic relations with the Vichy government, which made it difficult for the JLC to persuade the State Department to accept the notion of "political" refugees. At the same time, the rescue of Polish Bund representatives who had taken refuge in Lithuania took place in the context of the German-Soviet Pact: the two regimes were cooperating to seal the fate of their respective opponents and captives. Finally, Japan, for a while, served as a transit point for some of these refugees, although it was an ally of the Third Reich. But any hope of rescue across the Pacific was dashed by the Japanese bombing of Pearl Harbor in December 1941 and the U.S. entry into the war.

Some elements of this story also belong to the rescue operation conducted by Varian Fry, the well-known agent of the Emergency Rescue Committee, which was based in Marseille and had similar goals to those of the JLC. Although briefly mentioned in Fry's book *Surrender on Demand*,[1] the cooperation between these two organizations has never been described specifically nor properly explained. Yet the two networks were highly intertwined, in terms of both political inspiration and how the evacuation programs functioned.

AN OPENING IN WASHINGTON

It did not take long for the JLC to realize the extent of the disaster implied by the defeat of France in June 1940. The exodus of people to southern France, the French capitulation, and the German occupation were all catastrophes that dramatically affected the populations involved, and Western democracies more generally. For the representatives of the workers' movements who had taken refuge in France, whose survival and activities the JLC had long supported, the armistice was the death knell of the freedom they had sought in this nation. Political opponents of the Nazi regime, leaders of left-wing parties and of labor movements, and politically engaged writers and journalists all figured on lists of persons sought by the Gestapo. Forced like millions of French and Belgian people to move south toward the Unoccupied Zone, these refugees would have to hide their identities and whereabouts in order to escape arrest. Moreover, since September 1939, the beginning of the *drôle de guerre* ("phony war"), they had had to elude the French civil authorities, who indiscriminately categorized German, Austrian, or Czech refugees as "enemies of the nation"—although they were declared opponents of the Hitler regime—and interned them in detention camps ordered by the Daladier government and maintained under Vichy.[2] For Italian anti-fascists, the situation was quite similar. Italy's entry into the war on June 10, 1940, did not immediately result in the occupation of the southern region (apart from some border towns), but the hunt for militants by Mussolini's political police was strengthened by collaboration between Vichy and the occupying powers.[3]

On June 26, 1940, Isaiah Minkoff, executive director of the JLC, wrote to David Dubinsky: "For the leaders of the labor movement now living in Lithuania and France the situation has become more tragic from day to day. They are actually in a death-trap."[4] In fact Lithuania, which had temporarily served as a refuge for exiles from Poland, became occupied by the Red Army on June 15, 1940. From the Mediterranean to the Baltic, Europe was now being enclosed in a repressive and totalitarian vice.

Without waiting for more information on the situation of those persons he knew about, Minkoff implemented a procedure to obtain emergency visas that would prove efficient. Linking the situation of France after the German invasion to that of Lithuania under the Soviet occupation, he wrote a letter to Secretary of State Cordell Hull that was also signed by AFL president William Green, by ILGWU president David Dubinsky, and by Alexander Kahn, manager of the *Jewish Daily Forward*. Minkoff himself carried this letter to Washington to the State Department and obtained an interview with Breckinridge Long, assistant to Cordell Hull, on July 2. In this letter and in the course of the interview, Minkoff asked that eminent persons engaged in the democratic and social movement in Europe who were currently refugees in France and in Lithuania be allowed asylum in the United States, and provided lists of their names:

> Unless these men and women find immediate temporary haven in the United States, they are in danger of being imprisoned, placed in concentration camps or shot, whether it be by the Gestapo or the GPU.
>
> The men and women in whose behalf we are now appealing are world-famous writers, editors, labor leaders, former government officials, and ministers. Some of them are in intimate contact with the trade union movement, and are well-known to organized labor in the United States. Should they fall into the clutches of the German Gestapo or the Soviet GPU, they will face certain death, and their loss would be irreparable for the civilized world.
>
> Because of their opposition to Fascism, Nazism, and Communism, the majority of these men and women were forced to flee their countries—Germany, Austria, Czechoslovakia, Italy, Russia, Poland. . . .
>
> In view of the above, we earnestly appeal to the State Department and sincerely urge you, Mr. Secretary, to do all within your power, in line with American tradition, to make it possible for these people to enter the United States as visitors.[5]

Minkoff's letter was skillfully composed to break the State Department's intransigence on the visa matter. Thanks to its political history, the JLC was well placed to compare the fate of Socialists and Social Democrats repressed by either Nazi or Communist regimes, and so it could validate the similarity between the two kinds of totalitarianism. Obviously, the current Molotov-Ribbentrop Pact favored this comparison. And the signatures of William Green and David Dubinsky, known for their opposition to communism, warranted that stance: in this context the socialist leanings of people the JLC was recommending for admission would appear less of a political danger to the United States. Nevertheless, the JLC was indeed trying to save top officials of the international labor movement, especially leading members of the Labor and Socialist International (with whom the AFL had always refused to form an alliance). And by avoiding any mention that most of these left-wing activists were not only Socialists but Jews—as was obviously the case with Polish Bundists in Lithuania had they been named but also the case for many others—Minkoff was evading the often anti-Semitic reactions of the State Department. By insisting in general terms on what these leaders had contributed to the "civilized world," he was contrasting the democracies that the United States claimed to lead with totalitarian barbarism. Finally, the conclusion of this collective portrait was almost abrupt: he was requesting *visitors' visas* for these eminent persons, thus skirting the issue of quotas. The State Department's response was immediate and favorable. The next day, July 3, Breckinridge Long, who was piloting the visa policy, wrote to William Green: "As I informed Mr. Minkoff, the Department has been glad to telegraph to the appropriate consular officers regarding the persons included in the list and has requested the consuls to give every consideration to their applications for visas."[6]

Minkoff had outpaced the State Department on the whole matter. He was not the only one to do so, but his speed managed to short-cut the cumbersome official procedure. Several rescue organizations had mobilized after June 1940 to try to get refugees out of occupied countries. For example, the American Jewish Congress prepared a list of rabbis and directors of rabbinic schools to be delivered out of Poland and Lithuania; the Rockefeller and Carnegie foundations were concerned about the fate of eminent scientists and academics in France; and the Emergency Rescue Committee, to which we will return later in the chapter, focused on writers and artists.[7] In Washington, the committee appointed by President Roosevelt in 1938 to handle refugee matters, the Presidential Advisory Committee on Political Refugees (PACPR),[8] which had remained rather inactive until then, was suddenly charged with coordinating all the requests for asylum emanating from these various associations. On July 26, the PACPR president, James G. McDonald, and his executive director, George L. Warren, decided that all these demands for exceptional visas should henceforth be addressed to them and would then be sent for validation to the Department of Justice, which now had authority over the Immigration and Naturalization Service, and then to the State Department. If a request was considered valid by these two departments, local consulates would be required to deliver the visa to the applicant in question—as long as his papers were in order.[9]

Having preempted this reorganization, the lists submitted by the JLC on July 2 had been accepted in advance of the approval of the PACPR. The AFL—more officially recognized at the State Department than the JLC and vouching for it—made itself the guarantor of the names mentioned in the lists.[10] This meant that the simple mention of persons on the "AFL list" would qualify as an affidavit (political, moral, and financial) in lieu of any other document required by the State Department. The advantage of this expeditious intervention meant that Washington granted visas to the named persons immediately while allowing the JLC time to refine the lists in July and August, pending information it received from Europe. The JLC could thus benefit from a good number of the visas granted by the PACPR before the program was rescinded in the autumn of 1940. All of a sudden, summarizing the situation in his diary on September 18, 1940, Breckinridge Long stated that what he considered a parenthesis should now be closed:

> We have been very generous in offering hospitality in the United States to persons who have been in imminent danger there [Europe]: who have been leaders of public thought there in the form of Rabbis in Germany, Poland and near-by territories and who were leaders of Rabbinical schools and colleges; and also to a category of leaders in the labor union movement in Europe who were recommended by William Green and a committee of the American Federation of Labor; and also to certain intellectuals who were guaranteed by the President's Advisory Committee. The list of Rabbis has been closed and the list of labor leaders has been closed. And now it remains for the President's Committee to be curbed in its activities so that the laws again can operate in their normal course.[11]

ESTABLISHING LISTS

The JLC hastily compiled lists of approximately 350 names of refugees in France, and a hundred more in Lithuania, which were attached to the letter addressed to Cordell Hull. At this stage, as far as France was concerned, three lists of prominent figures from the labor and Social Democratic worlds were organized by nationality: Russians (mostly Mensheviks), Germans and Austrians, then Italians. Another list included the names of refugees from Poland in Lithuania. These first lists were the subject of urgent negotiations by telegram or postal mail back and forth across the Atlantic and were revised three times until the end of August 1940, at which point they were declared "closed" by the State Department. On the American side, as soon as news spread that the JLC might obtain visas, requests flooded in from everywhere. For example, Thomas Mann, leader of the German literary exiles, hoped that the JLC might obtain for him fifteen visas for "highly important liberal writers." Dubinsky replied that the JLC was limiting its lists to "labor refugees."[12] The Italian art historian Lionello Venturi, an opponent of the Mussolini regime who had taken refuge in the United States and held a post at Johns Hopkins University, sent Minkoff a list of seventeen prominent anti-fascists whom he hoped to rescue.[13] The JLC and these figures collaborated for their rescue; the Emergency Rescue Committee got involved as well, overseeing the rescue of writers and artists. It was important to avoid duplication among the several rescue committees, not to mention the fact that when people were initially mentioned, it was before having ascertained their location or whether in fact they wanted to go to the United States. There was great urgency in the chaos of the French debacle; an American visa was the only conceivable exit for thousands who were sought by the Gestapo with the collaboration of the Vichy government. Seeing one's name on the list signified potential access to the United States—as long as the obstacles in Europe could be overcome. Hundreds of telegrams reached the JLC during these months of anguish and dislocation. The few words correspondents managed to send signaled the survival (under the direst conditions) of persons with whom the JLC had long been in contact. They also indicated the presence of other comrades whose names needed to be added to the lists in order to obtain visas for them. The telegram (or cable) was the modern means of communication and an effective vector for organizing the visa program in the limited time it was able to function. Initially, the address of one of the refugees—for example, Modigliani in care of A. Garsin and Company, 59 Rue Grignan in Marseille, or of Abramovitch at the Hôtel Regina in Toulouse—could serve as a central "mailbox" for the whole network that was gathering around these figures.

Mensheviks

The Abramovitch list, named after the leader of the Russian Social Democratic Labor Party in exile, Raphael Abramovitch-Rein, who was also a member of the executive committee of the Labor and Socialist International—in other words, the Menshevik list—was perhaps the most readily established; the departure of the people on this list to the United States was relatively quickly organized. Stripped of their nationality of origin and actively sought by the Gestapo, these people had to leave France as quickly as possible.[14] Despite internal dissensions in exile, the Mensheviks remained a solid political and intellectual group and their internationalism did not eliminate their Jewishness, even if this identity was rarely foregrounded.[15] During their successive exiles—from Russia to Germany, then to France—they had relied on the American Jewish labor movement as an important source for their material and intellectual survival, and would continue to do so in the United States. For example, Abramovitch was a European correspondent for the *Jewish Daily Forward* and was also the director of the editorial team of the *Jewish Encyclopedia* financed by the JLC. In New York, it was another Menshevik, Samuel Estrin, who had come to the United States in 1939 and was part of the JLC executive office, who drew up the first list.[16]

Estrin identified approximately sixty persons (and their families), many of whom since the exodus had found refuge in the region of Toulouse. Among them were important Russian Social Democrats in exile—starting with the party's two leaders, Raphael Abramovitch and Feodor Dan—and many of their political friends who had been active in revolutionary Russia before October 1917, such as former deputy minister of labor Anatoli Dubois, economists David Dallin and Solomon Schwartz, who was also an ex-leader of the Russian trade union movement, and historian Boris Nicolaevski, as well as journalists, professors, and other intellectuals who had all held important political offices since 1905. As editor of *Sotsialistitchevski Vestnik*, the organ of Russian non-Bolshevik revolutionaries in exile, Abramovitch was at the center of a constellation of socialist-oriented movements including Russian Bundists and members of the Party of Socialist Revolutionaries. Prominent members of that party figured on the list of Russians stranded in southern France: former minister of the Provisional government Nicolai Avkentiev, former mayor of the City of Moscow, V. Rudnev, and political scientist and writer Mark Vichniak, among many others, were included on the list hastily drawn up in 1940.[17]

On July 19, Abramovitch wrote that the consul in Marseille had indeed received the list of persons mentioned—but he could not furnish visas. For these temporary visas, each candidate had to have a passport authorizing him to come back to France, or hold a visa for a third country where he could go when the temporary visa expired, and an affidavit guaranteeing that an American citizen would be responsible for him if necessary—documents that these fugitives were far from possessing. Maybe the JLC could make itself their collective guarantor and supply them with visas for Canada or the Dominican Republic? The JLC confirmed with the consulate that the AFL's endorsement was equivalent to an affidavit and supplied other guarantees. It also had $5,000 transmitted to Abramovitch by the Hebrew Immigrant Colonization Society (HIAS/HICEM) in Marseille.[18] By August 28, Abramovitch and his family as well as "six comrades" had already left Lisbon aboard the *Excalibur*. On September 6, 1940, they reached New York.[19] A few days later, on September 12, nine other families reached New York on the *Nea Hellas*. Szmul "Artur" Zygielbojm, member of the Bund Central Committee, as well as other figures in the Jewish Polish movement were among them.[20] Others would follow. In December 1940, however, Abramovitch wrote to George Warren of the PACPR asking that visas be granted to other "Russian Social-Democratic refugees who are living in unoccupied France and who are believed to be in imminent danger of persecution by the German and Soviet secret police agencies acting in France."[21]

This cohort of the first refugees benefited from particular circumstances in France and from a favorable moment at the State Department. Adolph Berle, assistant to the secretary of state, told consular personnel "to extend every facility and assistance permitted under the law to the alien refugees living under difficult conditions who desire to come to the United states either as immigrants or non-immigrants, temporary visitors or transients, when applicants are qualified under the law." He also affirmed that instead of individual affidavits and visas for third countries, the collective guarantee procured by the AFL should be recognized on these two points "as established."[22] These provisions and these "affidavits in lieu of passports" were meant to apply to all those on the JLC/AFL lists. But the Russian refugees benefited from the additional fact that the men among them were not required for military service for their national army and so they had no difficulty getting the "exit visa" from French territory that was required prior to receiving the American visa. This was not the case, however, for the Italians and the Germans, especially if they were of an age to be drafted.

Italian Anti-Fascists

Establishing the list of Italians in France was likewise the product of transatlantic collaboration.[23] On the American side Serafino Romualdi, editor of *Giustizia*, the Italian version of the ILGWU's publication *Justice*, as well as anti-fascist refugee Professor Lionello Venturi, helped compile the list. But this list could not be finalized without the authority of Giuseppe Modigliani in Marseille, who was a central figure among Italian refugees and well known to his ILGWU friends since his 1935 American trip. Initially the list contained 28 names (without counting wives or companions) of opponents of the fascist regime, such as Modigliani himself, leader of the moderate Socialists, Bruno Buozzi, president of the Confederazione Generale del Lavoro (CGL), Pietro Nenni, president of the Italian Socialist Party, and even Randolfo Pacciardi, president of the Italian Republican Party. But the list also included many names from the Giustizia e Libertà (GL) movement, which was neither a party nor a labor organization but a network of activists engaged in the fight against fascism through their writings and other forms of action. Thus, one of the GL leaders, the former socialist representative from Sardinia Emilio Lussu, and economist Silvio Trentin—whose bookshop in Toulouse was a gathering place for Italian activists—were among them, as well as Franco Venturi, Lionello's son, and political scientist Aldo Garosci, both editors of *Giustizia e Libertà*, the GL's organ. Journalists and editors of the liberal press were also mentioned: Alberto Tarchiani of the *Corriere della Serra* and Alberto Cianca of *Il Mondo*. Modigliani wrote directly to the American consul in Marseille on July 31, 1940, adding to this list the names of Nicola Chiaromonte, editor and contributor to French radio programs and to American magazines, who had been active in the Spanish Civil War until his disagreement with the Communists; Carlo Emmanuele Prato, former editor of the *Journal des Nations* in Geneva and *New York Times* correspondent; and Odette Bigard, former executive director at the League of Nations and Prato's collaborator. Knowing that some people mentioned on the list would not leave France because they preferred to pursue the fight where they were, and that others were too unwell or too elderly to be able to leave, or were burdened with family responsibilities, Modigliani proposed new names to be added to the lists.[24] From New York, Romualdi, stating that with a contribution of $5,000 the ILGWU could take responsibility for the transatlantic crossing of fifteen persons on this list, asked Modigliani to appeal to the ACWA for a similar arrangement, and suggested that the GL members solicit anti-fascists in the United States like "Ascoli, Salvemini, Venturi, etc.," for the same sum. A telegram on August 16 from Pacciardi to Romualdi about adding five other anti-fascists, two of whom had fought in Spain, arrived later.[25]

But the main problem was not establishing lists, however well documented they might be. It lay primarily in France, where, actively sought by the police, these persons were living clandestinely, fearing arrest at any moment, and could not move without a safe-conduct pass even to collect the requested visa, which, moreover, would not be granted anyway if they did not possess all the necessary documents. These former Italian nationals no longer had passports, or any official document of any sort, and moreover, the Vichy government would not give an exit visa to people sought by the Italian police. According to the armistice convention, the Italian authorities were claiming able-bodied men for military service and demanded from the French intelligence services a list of people known for their propaganda against Mussolini. On October 5, 1940, the Italian political police transmitted to the German police a list of 123 "dangerous subversives" they wanted arrested and handed over to the Italian authorities at the border. This list, except for the Communists, was scarcely different from the one that the JLC/AFL had submitted to the State Department in Washington and to the consulate in Marseille.[26]

For candidates for departure, this situation meant at the very least producing false passports, a clandestine exit from French territory, and then crossing Spain and Portugal illegally. Modigliani never wanted to submit to any of this. "Any thought of illegal escape must be brushed aside. I don't believe in them and they are repellent to my conscience. I would prefer to trust . . . Destiny," he wrote on August 5 to the JLC. In fact, despite the fact that his wife, Vera Funaro, asked David Dubinsky to convince him, Modigliani did not go to the United States. After the German occupation of the southern zone in November 1942, although under house arrest in Nimes, he was exfiltrated to Switzerland.[27]

In short, representatives of all the components of the Italian non-Communist Left were named here. Only some of them reached New York, where they continued the struggle alongside the anti-fascists who were already there, but for some of them it was only after a long period of wandering that they were able to cross the Atlantic.

German and Austrian Anti-Nazis

The difficulty of establishing a single list that represented the German and Austrian Left (apart from the Communists) reflected the political tensions between various groups that composed it in exile.[28] In New York, Rudolf Katz, secretary of the German Labor Delegation, who considered himself the sole representative of German emigration, prepared a list that was revised many times during July and August 1940. Heading it were eminent members of the SPD executive office during the Weimar Republic, including Hans Vogel, its president; Rudolf Breitscheid, head of the SPD parliamentary group in the Reichstag; economist and theoretician Rudolf Hilferding, who had been finance minister in 1923 and 1928–1929; and Friedrich Stampfer, former editor of *Vorwärts*. To this list were quickly added the names of other SPD members and intellectuals and writers close to the party and active in the exile press who had been designated by

Rudolf Katz—and in the case of writers, on Thomas Mann's advice.[29] The Austrian Friedrich Adler, LSI secretary-general, also appeared on this list, as well as Josef (Georg) Stolz, IFTU secretary.[30] With the exodus, these figures and many other German refugees headed toward Agen in south-west France, while others tried to be closer to the American consulate in Marseille. Friedrich Heine, former member of the SPD executive, became one of the collaborators of Frank Bohn and then of Varian Fry in Marseille (which we will discuss below) and suggested other names.[31] The intern-ment camps in southern France were holding in isolation a large number of German and Austrian opponents whose freedom was requested by men-tioning them on the list.

In Marseille, Rudolf Breitscheid and Rudolf Hilferding were the most prominent of all these German exiles. Like Modigliani, and just as ostensi-bly as he, they would not hear of false papers for themselves or of clamber-ing over the border to Spain. "Nonsense! Hitler wouldn't dare ask for our extradition," cried Breitscheid. In the café of the Marseille harbor where they openly conversed every morning with Modigliani, these three leaders were certainly conspicuous.[32] Aware, though, of the particular difficulties for their compatriots and for themselves—no visas to leave France, hence no visas to transit across Spain or Portugal—they thought their renown protected them—or that there was no point in masking their identity.

In order to facilitate contacts between the refugees scattered across the south and the consulate in Marseille, an envoy was sent from New York: Frank Bohn, who was close to Rudolf Katz and to many prominent Ger-man émigrés. His designation was made by the German Labor Delegation, in conjunction with Lionello Venturi and his friends for the defense of Italian anti-fascists and with the support of the JLC. Several organizations worked together for the defense of their own protégés.[33]

At the same time, in New York, Paul Hagen (Karl Frank) was wor-ried about the fate of his friends from Neu Beginnen, most of whom were interned in French camps, especially at Le Vernet in the Ariège region. These militants—situated to the left of the SPD—did not figure on the lists established by Rudolf Katz, who continued to monopolize the atten-tion of the JLC. Hagen was able to convince Minkoff and the JLC to add the names of eight Neu Beginnen militants designated as "among those who were most in danger" to the lists to be presented to the State Department. And to assuage all doubts, Minkoff got confirmation from the famous Italian American anarchist Carlo Tresca that these militants were not Communists: "I would put my hand in the fire: I know damn well that they are all anti-Stalinists," the latter replied authoritatively.[34] We can surmise that six militants of the SAP group (Sozialistische Arbeiter Partei) and two of the ISK (Internationaler Sozialistischer Kampfbund), including Ewa Lewinski,[35] also owed their rescue to Hagen's intervention with the JLC. Belonging to leftist groups close to Neu Beginnen, these militants were eventually included in the lists. Some were protected by the JLC, others by the Emergency Rescue Committee (ERC), which Paul Hagen and his New York friends (American Friends of German Freedom) had founded after the fall of France. It was this organization (the ERC) that sent Varian Fry to Marseille.[36]

FRANK BOHN AND VARIAN FRY IN MARSEILLE

Frank Bohn was already in Marseille when Varian Fry arrived there in mid-August 1940. The two Americans divided up their responsibilities. According to Varian Fry, Bohn was responsible for "old socialists and union leaders" such as Breitscheid, Hilferding, and Modigliani, while he (Fry) looked after "writers, artists, and young activists from left-wing groups."[37] This division of labor in fact corresponded to the organizations that had sent them but also to their personalities and own political preferences. Yet the two networks they represented were closely linked.

Bohn, who oversaw the JLC/AFL list, represented the interests of the German Labor Delegation to which he was close. His approach was officially supervised by the State Department, which had alerted the American consul in Marseille to his arrival and had prepared his trip across Spain by arranging a meeting with the U.S. ambassador in Madrid in order to obtain his support for the passage of refugees who would be crossing Spain in their flight to Lisbon. Bohn had been chosen by Rudolf Katz because of his social skills and Washington contacts: his father-in-law, Daniel C. Roper, was a senior official and ex-ambassador to Canada, and had been secretary of commerce under Roosevelt (1933–1938).[38] Accordingly Bohn proceeded with his mission in France in an official manner. His first step was to go to Vichy to the office of the U.S. ambassador, then to the Ministry of the Interior, where he learned from Minister Adrien Marquet the details of the Vichy government's collaboration with German authorities, which Bohn quickly conveyed to the State Department:

> The German government has now demanded a list of all German nationals in non-occupied France . . . France is subject to severe penalties for failure to comply. . . . Marquet said France is in no position to authorize the departure of any German or Italian national. The terms of the Italian Armistice Convention are of course similar in this respect. He promised, however, that he would release persons of any other nationality in whom the American Federation of Labor has stated an interest.[39]

This description explains the relative ease with which the group of Mensheviks were able to obtain their American visas and the accompanying exit permits and affidavits in order to reach Lisbon. This also underlines the necessity of making false passports that would provide covert identities— Czech, Lithuanian, Chinese, or Polish—for German and Italian nationals. This is what Varian Fry managed to do in order to get them out of France.

Meanwhile, not well-informed about the modifications to the "AFL list," Bohn had difficulty identifying and contacting the persons whose names were on it. The consulate had warned, however, that the "action" would be closed on October 1 and that those who had not obtained their visa by this date would lose it.[40] By September Bohn had exhausted all of his means of action. He found himself with no alternative course after the plan to evacuate people by sea (designed to avoid false documents, subterfuges, and the exhausting walks over the Pyrenees) failed, which he had conceived for Modigliani, Breitscheid, Hilferding, their wives, and other eminent German refugees—especially the writers Lion Feuchtwanger, Heinrich Mann, his wife and his nephew Golo (son of Thomas Mann), and Franz Werfel and his wife, Alma Mahler, whose departure along with them was planned. But his contacts in Marseille had collapsed. "I am at the end of the rope as regards saving them (nearly all of them leaders of German, Austrian, Italian labor movements and democracy). My belief is that the President and Secretary Hull can save them by making a strong effort with Vichy," he cabled to William Green.[41] Moreover, the difficulties suddenly created by Spain for transits, almost systematically closing the border, were a response to German and Italian demands for extradition. The Spanish authorities were not granting laissez-passer to refugees of these nationalities.[42] Sometime later, Breitscheid and Hilferding were assigned to forced residence in their homes in Arles. Their tragic fate is well known: on the eve of a plan conceived by Varian Fry for them to embark on a ship for Martinique in February, they were arrested by the Gestapo and brutally transferred to (and tortured in) the Prison de la Santé in Paris. On February 11, 1941, Hilferding was found dead in his cell. Assassination or suicide? We will never know. Breitscheid was sent to Buchenwald, where he died in August 1944 during an Allied bombing attack.[43]

Perceiving in September that Bohn's mission was compromising—and likely to hinder—its relations with the Vichy government, the State Department asked its ambassador to put a stop to it. It also warned Varian Fry that his schemes would no longer be tolerated: "This government cannot countenance the activities as reported of Dr. Bohn and Mr. Fry and other persons, however well-meaning their motives may be in carrying on activities that evade the laws of countries with which the United States maintains friendly relations."[44] The State Department told the consul in Marseille to notify the two Americans that they were ordered to return to the United States. Frank Bohn complied with this injunction at the end of September. Yet he had only begun to understand the meaning of his mission: "I should stay on indefinitely. ... No one in New York or in Washington can know what conditions are here or how hard my job is to do. I shall stay until it is done."[45] In a letter to William Green on September 12 Bohn stressed the importance of sending these leaders of democratic parties to the United States: "These 50 to 60 men (Germans, Austrians, Italians) will be worth several times their weight in gold to us in the USA if and when we enter the war. They are the known leaders of democratic parties. . . . All these groups must be carefully organized to appeal (doubtless under your direct leadership) to the masses who oppose the dictators." Also criticizing the lack of means and determination of American diplomacy, whereas the Mexican government was announcing its intention to receive 130,000 Spanish refugees,[46] Bohn informed Green of the situation in the internment camps.

> My immediate problem—an agonizing one—is that of the thousands of Germans, Austrians and Italians—working men—left starving and ragged, and often sick in concentration camps here. I am anxious only to remain on the job here. As soon as the direct and immediate problem of rescuing the leaders is accomplished, I urge you to assist me in caring for the rank-and-file. They have been (90% of them) active labor union workers or they would never have gone into exile. Typhoid fever has broken out in some camps. Cold rains have fallen for four days past. They have no winter clothing. Thousands have only the one dirty shirt on their backs. The New York Clothing Workers have done most of what has been done here. Can't some other organizations be persuaded to advance funds? Five or six thousand dollars would let me begin (through a selected group of volunteer agents). The greater need is for $50,000—that would allow me about $10 per man—spread over six months. I visited the camp Vernet (near Toulouse) last Friday. One must *see* in order to *know*.[47]

The decision to recall Bohn was a manifestation of the vigorous opposition that had developed within the State Department to the emergency visa system. Breckinridge Long pointed out in a letter to President Roosevelt that the temporary visas were being granted too easily and might favor the arrival of undesirable persons in the United States. According to him, the PACPR had deprived the consuls of their power. Therefore, on September 19, the president signed new directives concerning requests to the PACPR for emergency visas, which recommended that consular personnel not grant visas until after the strictest examination of a person's political past and of his future intentions. "We have been generous, but there are limits!" Long noted in his diary. These new guidelines went into effect in October 1940.

In Marseille and even in Lisbon, persons who had been previously approved found themselves being refused visas by the consular authorities. This meant that having one's name on such lists did not lead to the automatic granting of a visa—far from it. According to David Wyman, Long could not have been unaware that by the end of September only 40 out of the 561 people presented by the PACPR and approved by the State Department had obtained their visas in the consulates concerned. In other words, consuls had already been exercising "some latitude of judgment."[48]

When Frank Bohn departed, Varian Fry continued to work, with the help of Friedrich Heine and Breitscheid's secretary, Erika Bierman, on behalf of refugees who were members of, or close to, the SPD. Certainly Fry was more suitable for the situation than was Bohn, who had been too respectful of official procedures. Overcoming the new administrative conditions issued by Washington, Madrid, Lisbon, or Vichy required a political sense that was akin to resistance. Fry was engaged in a mission that was much more perilous than he had imagined. As he explained in his book: "Most of all it was a feeling of sympathy for the German and Austrian Socialist Parties which led me to go to France in the summer of 1940—a sympathy born of long familiarity with their principles and their work."[49] And it was because his heart was set on saving the "friends of Paul Hagen" that he stayed in Marseille despite the American embassy's injunction. In fact, he was personally closer to these dissidents from the SPD than to the official party members. After a trip in Nazi Germany in 1935, where he had witnessed the violence done to the Jews in Berlin on the Kurfürstendam, he made the acquaintance of Paul Hagen in New York. Eventually it was to him that Fry primarily dedicated his book *Surrender on Demand*, written after returning from his mission: "For Anna Caples and Paul Hagen who began it."[50] Hagen had married Anna Caples in 1937. Alongside her, in the intellectual and liberal milieu of the New York Left, he had created first the American Friends of German Freedom and then in 1940 founded the Emergency Rescue Committee (ERC). This new committee extended the work of the International Relief Association, founded in New York by Albert Einstein, Carl von Ossietzky, and a group of the New York intelligentsia, including Freda Kirchwey, editor of the weekly *The Nation* and

Frank Kingdon. The latter, a former Methodist minister and president of Newark University, became the ERC president. Support from the liberal press gave the organization an image of cultural anti-fascism.[51]

In Marseille, Fry found himself in charge of two lists of persons to be saved from likely arrest and the horror of the camps. The list drawn up by the ERC included the names of writers and artists; Fry is most often celebrated for having saved many of them: Marc Chagall, Jacques Lipchitz, André Breton, Max Ernst, André Masson, Victor Serge, Hannah Arendt, Walter Mehring, Lion Feuchtwanger, Wanda Landowska, and Franz Werfel, to mention only the most well-known names.[52] But in fact he was also now in charge of the "AFL list," which had not been directly communicated to him, but persons on that list appealed to him in the hope of obtaining the visas that the JLC had secured for them. Both lists included very prominent people as well as less well-known ones, which would mean resorting to increasingly illegal methods as the German occupation and the Vichy regime hardened. "Our very existence is hanging from slender threads, which may break at any moment," affirmed Victor Serge, one of Varian Fry's protégés who finally obtained a visa for Mexico. "Several times the total occupation of France is rumored to be in the offing. And the long-awaited visas are not here—still not here! This much must be said: because of their reactionary or bureaucratic leanings, most of the American republics have displayed neither humanity nor sense in their immigration policies. Visas were granted in the merest trickle, in a manner so criminally stingy that thousands and thousands of real victims, all fine human beings, were left to the mercy of the Nazis."[53]

The imbroglio over the lists was increased by the fact that Paul Hagen, through his contacts, had been able to enlist the help of both the ERC and the JLC so that the largest number of those he hoped to save could obtain a visa. To contact them, though, since several were held in Le Vernet or Les Milles or other camps, Fry was able to draw on militants who were experienced in clandestine activities. Thus, one of his acolytes, code-named "Beamish," alias Albert Hermant, was in reality Albert Hirschman, future economist of international renown, himself a refugee from Germany, who was close to several activist networks of the Socialist International. In

Berlin, he had known Raphael Abramovitch and his son Mark Rein and the circle of the Russian social-democratic exiles. As a young militant in Neu Beginnen, Hirschman had to leave Berlin for Paris after Hitler took power. Signing up in Barcelona in 1936 with the Republicans, he soon criticized the Communist ascendency over the International Brigades. Also close to Eugenio Colorni, one of the leaders of Italian anti-fascism, Hirschman was at the heart of a cluster of activists involved in several resistance networks. His presence was precious to Fry in locating and extracting "friends of Paul Hagen," to the point of being sought by the police himself; he was forced to leave Marseille in December 1940. Fortunately he was able to obtain the visa that the American consul Hiram Bingham had received for him from the Rockefeller Foundation.[54]

Hans and Lisa Fittko also played an important role. German nationals and anti-Nazi activists since 1933, they had been forced out of Germany to Czechoslovakia, then out of Switzerland to France for having distributed the underground press. They had experienced internment in French camps (Lisa in Gurs, Hans close to Nevers) despite their opposition to Nazism. During the winter of 1940–1941, under an agreement with Fry, they smuggled a hundred people across the Pyrenees between Banyuls and Port-Bou to avoid the border controls on the French side.[55] In Marseille after Fry left at the end of the summer of 1941, Daniel Bénédite, who had been particularly active in liberating numerous refugees from the camps, took over with Jean Gemähling the leadership of the operations of the Centre Américain de Secours (CAmS) that Fry had created to house some of the refugees. After the German occupation of the southern zone beginning in November 1942, Bénédite and Gemähling were actively involved in the Resistance.[56]

After Frank Bohn's return to the United States, the JLC continued to orchestrate from New York the departure of the persons for whom it had obtained visas. But those who were able to leave did so thanks to the ERC and the CAmS team around Varian Fry, who prepared false passports and clandestine passage to Lisbon. Refusing to comply with the order to return to the United States, Fry stayed a year longer, intensely devoted to the evacuation of as many people as possible from the southern zone. From September 1940, the JLC's protégés who had quickly received visas reached New York. On October 2 Isaiah Minkoff sent William Green a list of the first persons who had reached the United States, which included the names of nine Germans, twelve Austrians, and fourteen "Russians, Poles, and Jews" (meaning the Mensheviks and Bundists); these were families who had crossed the Atlantic on the ships *Excalibur* and *Nea Hellas* in September.[57] In the same letter, a second list itemized those who were still in Lisbon awaiting a visa for the United States, a ticket for the crossing, or a place on a ship—or all of these at the same time. Among the twenty-one Germans on this list were the editor Friedrich Stampfer, political writer Konrad Heiden, journalist and SPD's education director Alexander Stein, writer Alfred Polgar, and Maria Zweig (Stefan Zweig's first wife). Friedrich Adler (LSI secretary-general) was also waiting in Lisbon, as well as sixteen "Russians, Poles, and Jews."

President of the SOPADE Hans Vogel and Eric Ollenhauer, as well as Friedrich Heine, also found themselves blocked in Lisbon, but they reached England in December 1940. According to historian Albrecht Ragg, it appears that the German Labor Delegation (GLD) in New York, under the leadership of Albert Grezinski and Rudolf Katz, did not favor the reunion of the SOPADE leaders in the United States.[58] Motivated by their personal ambition to be the sole representatives of German social-democratic emigration, they created a schism in its executive bureau between New York and London that weakened its means of action in exile. Ragg attributes the failure of German representation in the United States to the GLD's maneuvers, especially during the rescue operation, and wonders which was stronger, Katz's cynicism or Bohn's naivete. Meanwhile, Katz was also hindering the possibilities for departure of the members of Neu Beginnen, while also leaving a significant number of SPD comrades languishing in French internment camps.[59]

Upon the arrival of each ship in New York, the JLC sent a representative to the dock to welcome the arrivals and help them with disembarkation formalities. The ERC did the same when it had been the source of the visa. On October 2, 1940, Paul Hagen announced the arrival of several members of Neu Beginnen: Erich Schmidt, Otto Schoenfeld, Gerhard Danies, and Sigmund Jeremias, accompanied by their wives and some by their children, but

Hélène Boegler, whose husband, Franz, would remain long interned in Le Vernet, arrived alone. Hagen asked Minkoff to share the financial burden of the transatlantic evacuation of this group, of whom several others were still in France. On October 8, the ERC announced the arrival of eighteen refugees aboard the *Nea Hellas* and asked the JLC to assume responsibility for its own protégés.[60] This meant helping them look for lodging, for work, and sometimes for transportation to more distant destinations. On October 26, Adolph Held, president of the JLC, sent a telegram of welcome to Friedrich Adler and his wife, who had arrived the previous day aboard the *Exochorda*: "The Jewish Labor Committee heartily welcomes you to America and wishes to express its great joy at your presence here."[61]

Julius Deutsch had a more hazardous journey. This leader of the Austrian workers' rebellion in 1934 and combatant in the Spanish Republican Army managed to reach Havana with his wife and daughter. But without a visa for Cuba, he was interned there for several weeks and threatened with being sent back to Europe. On October 12, Deutsch wrote to Adolph Held asking for his intercession to obtain a visa for the United States. Demonstrating the services he could offer, Deutsch affirmed that if the United States ever entered the war, he would certainly prefer to fight "in the U.S. Army rather than that of the Dominican Republic." Held must have convinced the State Department, since Deutsch and his family reached Miami in January 1941.[62]

The Italian refugees destined to the United States followed tortuous and often incomplete itineraries. Count Carlo Sforza, former ambassador to France, and Alberto Tarchiani, ex-editor of *Corriere della Serra*, had the good fortune to catch one of the last boats for England from Bordeaux at the end of June 1940. They reached Montreal and finally New York, where they collaborated with the Mazzini Society to help rescue Italians still in France. Among these were Alberto Cianca, Aldo Garosci, Leo Valiani, Nicola Chiaromonte, the Pierleoni brothers, and a dozen militants from Giustizia e Libertà who had escaped from internment camps. All of these men were sought by the police and were trying to avoid Spain, where they risked being arrested, like many others before them, and extradited to Italy. From Marseille, Emilio Lussu directed their evacuation, an episode he later recounted.[63] Procuring their passage to Algiers in January 1941, Lussu then sent them to Casablanca (not without pitfalls) where, lacking visas, money, and means of transport, these Italians remained stuck for months. In June, Lussu made a secret trip to Lisbon, opening up a new channel along the way that would avoid border controls. In the Portuguese capital he used his contacts with the British War Office to obtain transport for the refugees stuck in Casablanca. When they reached Lisbon they could finally get their American visas. And most of them arrived in New York in August 1941. For his part, Pacciardi followed on his own initiative the North African route along with some of his friends from the Republican Party, but he was the only one of this group who avoided arrest in Oran and reached Lisbon. The funds for this whole operation, as Lussu recognized, came from the "American friends" of the ILGWU, the ACWA, and the Mazzini Society thanks to contact with Max Ascoli.[64]

ACROSS SIBERIA AND JAPAN: "ONE MIRACLE AFTER ANOTHER"

At the same time as the JLC was trying to extricate from France as many opponents to Nazism and fascism as it could, it was also rescuing Bundist leaders from Lithuania, which had fallen under Soviet authority. While the former feat seemed an unattainable challenge, there were even greater odds against obtaining passage for Bundists (long-standing enemies of the Bolsheviks) across the Soviet Union as far as Vladivostok, then access to Japan (an ally of Nazi Germany), and eventually a ship to the West Coast of the United States. Yet the JLC managed to lead both operations at the same time. In the autumn of 1940, it simultaneously welcomed to New York and to San Francisco refugees coming from the two totalitarian poles.

The occupation of Lithuania by the Red Army in June 1940 once again plunged the Polish Jews, who had been refugees of the German and Russian invasions since the autumn of 1939, into danger and despair. Among some 16,000 Jewish refugees in Vilna and Kovno who belonged to multiple political parties or groups, generations, and professions, were about 400 representatives and militants of the Bund. The establishment of a Soviet government in Lithuania on July 14, 1940, signified the total destruction of political parties and of the educational, religious, and commercial structures that these refugees had been trying to reconstruct there. Because of their political history, Bundists and Socialists were among the most threatened opponents of communism. The Soviet secret police, which viewed the Bund as a reactionary and anti-Bolshevik party, inspired terror among militants. The wave of arrests and deportations of Bundists in Polish cities under Soviet domination had been ferocious. And many were aware that the two national leaders of the Bund, Henryk Erlich and Wiktor Alter, had been arrested by the Soviets in the autumn of 1939, accused of being part of the Socialist International and for their proximity to Western Socialist parties. According to Daniel Blatman, "no other Jewish party or movement was persecuted so relentlessly."[65] Yet for a brief period of time the USSR did not oppose the departure of some 2,500 Lithuanian or Polish Jews— including at least a hundred Bundists protected by the JLC. These persons benefited from the audacity of those who could take bold measures in their favor.

On July 2 during his visit to the State Department, Isaiah Minkoff argued for the need to procure visas for refugees from Lithuania as well as from France. Like the other lists, those of Polish Bundists under threat by the Soviets were revised during the months of July and August. Emanuel Nowogrodzki, secretary of the Bund's Central Committee who had arrived in New York the year before, participated along with Jacob Pat and Nathan Chanin of the JLC executive in creating lists of persons whose survival depended on their immediate emigration. The Bund's records show that discussions were bitter between the Bund's representative and the JLC leaders. The Bund was trying to bring over the maximum number of leaders or activists classified by their rank in the party (and the corresponding danger they were in) but said their family members could wait. The JLC, on the other hand, counted 108 families and was requesting visas for all of them. In any case, the JLC committed itself to raising the funds to cover these evacuations. Ultimately a hundred names of Bundist figures, but also members of the Polish Socialist Party and others belonging to Poale Zion and their families, were submitted to the State Department.[66] A temporary visa for the United States, however, was useless without a visa of transit through the other countries before reaching the United States. An attempt coordinated by Nowogrodzki to organize evacuation through Sweden was only possible for a few; passing via Berlin was obviously out of the question.[67]

An unexpected solution was offered by the consul of Japan, who had an office in Kovno, Lithuania. Sempo Sugihara had been sent to this city in September 1939 by the Japanese ambassador to Berlin, who was trying to observe from a neutral country the movements of the German army vis-à-vis the USSR. But after June, the Soviet grip over Lithuania no longer warranted the façade of Japanese interests needing this location, and the consul was required to close his office by August 31, 1940, at the latest. Through the month of August, despite the opposition of his superiors in Tokyo, Sugihara responded generously to the requests for transit across Japan from Jewish migrants who were trying to leave Lithuania. Clearly understanding their fate, the Japanese consul provided transit visas to all refugees who asked for them. But they also needed to be armed with a visa for a final destination. Students from the rabbinic school of Vilna had thought of going to Curaçao, a Dutch colony that did not require visas and accepted Jews; others thought of heading for Palestine.[68] The Bundists, protected by the JLC, received an American visa guaranteed by their being on the "AFL list." Knowing that this gesture could save lives, the heroic Sugihara delivered some 3,500 visas of transit through Japan.[69]

Yet reaching Japan was impossible without a Soviet permit to leave the country. Moreover, this document would only be delivered upon proof of a Japanese visa, which itself depended on possessing a third visa for a host country. What negotiations were undertaken to obtain these precious permits from Moscow to leave the Soviet Union remain unknown. Neither the JLC archives nor those of the State Department leave explicit traces. The names on the AFL list were cabled by the State Department to the American embassy in Moscow. But Ambassador Laurence A. Steinhardt had some reservations about furnishing visas in a collective and indiscriminate way to applicants whom he suspected of political activism.[70] And once an American visa was obtained, Intourist, the USSR official travel agency, controlled the procedure for leaving Soviet territory, but not without extorting foreign currency from these emigrants and requiring that they had paid for the trans-Siberian train journey (the fare was over \$200).[71] The American Jewish Joint Distribution Committee and the Hebrew Immigrant Aid Society branches in Poland and Lithuania were both asked to advance this money, as well as to defray the costs for migrants waiting in Vladivostok and Japan. To make matters worse, Isaiah Minkoff was informed that the visa to exit the Soviet Union was only valid for ten days: "It is indispensable to do all that it is in our power to save these persons, or else the years of imprisonment or exile they will have to suffer will remain on our conscience."[72] At this stage, the fate of the hundred Bundists became intermingled with that of some 2,400 other Jewish refugees who transited from Lithuania and were trying to reach Kobe. In this Japanese port, the tiny Jewish community of fifty families hosted refugees while they awaited ships to take them to their final destinations. Those who could not leave the island before Pearl Harbor (December 7, 1941)—more than half of them—were later evacuated to Shanghai, where the Japanese occupation authorities, by now sharing the anti-Semitism of their Nazi ally, confined Jewish residents, without resources or work, to the miserable ghetto of Hongkew.[73]

Nevertheless, the majority of those benefiting from the JLC's protection managed to emigrate to the United States. The first of them reached Seattle on October 31, 1940, aboard a Japanese ship, the *Heina Maru*. Among them were Naomi Pat, director of the Young Workers' organization of Warsaw, and Dr. Emanuel Pat; they were Jacob Pat's daughter and son. On the same ship were Froim Zelmanowicz, a member of the Bund Central Committee, with his wife and two sons, as well as Zalman Lichtenstein, a member of the executive board of Jewish labor unions of Poland who was also a Warsaw municipal councillor, plus his wife and daughter. Among those who arrived on November 17 on the *Hikawa Maru* was the president of the Bund's Central Committee, Jan Portnoy (Noah). Emanuel Scherer, another Bund officer and Warsaw councillor, arrived at the same time as Szlama (Shlomo) Mendelsohn, director of the Jewish school network Tsisho, aboard the *Kamakura Maru* in San Francisco on April 10, 1941.[74]

The arrivals occurred at the rate of about one ship a month. The wait could be long, depending on the availability of Japanese maritime transport, and no doubt on the transfer of funds, and even on obtaining a visa, since some emigrants reached Kobe without having yet obtained an American visa. Minkoff went to Seattle, San Francisco, and Los Angeles to resolve issues with the authorities of the Immigration and Naturalization Service and the Department of Justice on the West Coast, who had not always been informed by Washington of the refugees' special circumstances. The crowning blow, he wrote to a member of the JLC (no doubt Jacob Pat) when the first boat arrived, would be for them to be turned back just when they reached the United States. This epic journey carried so many uncertainties:

> It is only now that I begin to feel that our work was indeed successful. Since it was very difficult to get rid of the terrible feeling that we succeeded in saving people from the Nazis but were completely helpless in the case of the Commies. From the first stories that I get from them, it is just one miracle after another. I am afraid that we will probably lose some more people before they arrive in Japan. They will tell you all about it.[75]

With the arrival of each ship, Minkoff furnished the port authorities with the names of those ready to disembark, names that had been fixed by the "AFL list" and ratified before the presidential decision to turn things over to the PACPR. In reality the JLC also took responsibility for other refugees whose names did not appear on the initial lists. Some of them had no valid papers. For those, Minkoff had to use elaborate administrative persuasion and furnish individual affidavits guaranteeing their political past and their material means of survival in the United States.[76] On the list of "Persons Rescued by the Jewish Labor Committee" dated July 1941 and conserved in the Isaiah Minkoff Papers are the names of 86 families that arrived on the West Coast, having followed this trans-Siberian and trans-Pacific itinerary.[77] But many others were still en route or had been arrested somewhere along the way, according to the meager records available. In March 1941, Jacob Pat affirmed that 340 persons had been rescued out of Lithuania thanks to the JLC: among them, 84 had reached the United States, 9 were still at sea, 12 families had chosen to head for Palestine, and 102 individuals were in Japan waiting for visas, of whom 8 were in transit, 7 in Sweden, and

20 "in prison"—in the Soviet Union?—since he also noted that 11 individuals were stuck in Vladivostok without the possibility of reaching Japan.[78]

THE SOCIALIST INTERNATIONAL IN NEW YORK?

In November 1940, the JLC decided to celebrate the arrival of the first refugees in the United States by organizing an extraordinary conference. The plenary session was planned for Carnegie Hall on Friday, January 17, 1941, to take place in the presence of the leaders of the American labor movement. "The meeting will also be attended by the many friends who succeeded in escaping from the vengeance of the dictatorial powers in Europe with the help of the JLC. This meeting will serve as a demonstrative affirmation of the principles and ideals which underline the work of the JLC," affirmed Adolph Held and Isaiah Minkoff in their invitations.[79] Some three thousand persons were expected at the meeting, which was meant to be followed on Saturday and Sunday by the regular JLC convention with an examination of reports of activities and projects for 1941. Leaders of American labor organizations and Jewish associations were invited to the Friday evening event (which some considered inappropriate for a Jewish meeting). Representatives of émigré associations such as Max Ascoli of the Mazzini Society and Rudolf Katz of the German Labor Delegation were invited, as well as refugees (who had been helped by these associations), who would speak at the conference. On the whole 349 delegates from various organizations participated, including of course the entire Executive Committee of the JLC and its affiliated organizations. The well-prepared event received the honor of a telegram from President Roosevelt, who addressed his "hearty greetings to all who attend the conference of the Jewish Labor Committee to be held in Carnegie Hall next Friday evening. I trust that the deliberations will be fruitful of wise counsels and constructive action in the solution of the great problems under consideration."[80]

For the first time in the history of the American labor movement, on the podium, alongside JLC president Adolph Held, appeared its own leaders (William Green of the AFL and David Dubinsky of the ILGWU), as well as leaders of the Labor and Socialist International (LSI): Friedrich Adler, secretary-general, as guest of honor; Noah Portnoy, president of the Central Committee of the Bund of Poland; and Raphael Abramovitch, president of the Russian Social Democratic Labor Party. Walter Citrine, secretary-general of the International Federation of Trade Unions (IFTU) and president of Britain's Trades Union Congress, had planned to attend but he was giving a lecture tour on the West Coast.

In his speech Friedrich Adler paid homage to the JLC by emphasizing the internationalist character of its enterprise, which as he said was not guided only by Jewish solidarity.

> The Jewish Labor Committee has undertaken a world-embracing activity. This is true both figuratively and literally. For example, those of the Jewish Bund of Poland who were separated after Hitler's invasion of their country have met again in the city of New York. Comrade Zygielbojm came across the Atlantic while our old and honored comrade Noach [Portnoy] came through Siberia, Japan, across the Pacific Ocean and the United States. The same is true of us Austrian Social Democrats. Several days ago, almost at the same hour, there arrived in New York City after many days of wandering two comrades whom we had last seen in Paris: Julius Deutsch came across the Atlantic Ocean while comrade Ansboek, a man who was recently active in the Austrian underground movement, crossed the Pacific.
>
> When it came to rescuing the victims of European totalitarianism, the JLC did not guide itself by the religion of the person nor by his race and nationality. Help was extended to all who had rendered service to the International Labor Movement. . . . True peace will not come with military victory alone but with the establishment [in] all countries of a socialist society—a society that the workers of all countries must attain if the world is not to be brought once more to the brink of ruin by fascist barbarians and treacherous politicians.[81]

Not every speaker viewed socialism as the pinnacle of their hopes, as Adler did. Instead, William Green and David Dubinsky, for example, celebrated the solidarity unlimited by race, nationality, or religion that was manifested by the JLC in its support for "European democratic movements." In a speech that was inspired more by multicultural idealism than by the political history of the JLC, Dubinsky emphasized the aid it furnished to "Polish, Italian, Jewish, Czecho-Slovakian, Spanish, French, German, Austrian labor refugees. . . . This help was provided by the collective efforts of American workers originating themselves from all parts of the world and representing all creeds, races and colors."[82]

In his opening speech, Adolph Held had set the tone, stressing the human and universal motivations for solidarity: "There is no citizen in the world who one day or another could not find himself without a roof, without food, without protection, and become a refugee! Nobody knows what tomorrow will bring. Salvation comes from understanding the misfortune of others. This is what distinguishes humans from a pack of wolves." Held's words were designed to place the celebration on a humane rather than a political level. In a note to William Green prior to the conference to suggest topics for his speech, Held underlined that the JLC had been founded on the principle that the goal of resolving the Jewish problem was only one part of the movement for the liberation of all of humanity, that is to say, for political engagement: "Unfortunately, for reasons of security, much of our work, such as for instance direct assistance to the underground movement in the totalitarian countries, cannot be made public at present."[83]

Certainly, this great gathering was not the place to assert political positions, nor to rekindle the Labor and Socialist International on this side of the Atlantic, nor even to build a united anti-fascist front. Despite affirmations of solidarity, it was actually a dilapidated vision of the International that was being manifested. Most of the national delegations were missing, starting with the German Social Democratic leaders Hans Vogel and Eric Ollenhauer, who had chosen to represent the SOPADE in England rather than in New York. It was in London in fact that a union of German socialists took place, including militants situated to the left of the SPD, a display of unity that was impossible in New York, where disagreements between the SPD and dissidents had not been resolved, thereby weakening the whole German Social Democratic representation.[84] In fact Paul Hagen had not even been invited to the Carnegie Hall event. "I do not consider myself important but I do consider our group and our work important," he said regretfully. "And I would ask you to invite also one representative of our group to address this meeting. The Jewish Labor Committee has always recognized the fact of the existence of two groups in the German movement and I hope you will certainly invite one of us." He proposed asking either of two members of Neu Beginnen who had recently arrived from France: Eric Schmidt, representing the young workers, or Heinrich Ehrmann, a lawyer and historian. Neither was invited to speak at the assembly. Paul Hagen's letter to Minkoff was struck with a penciled "NO" to indicate a categorical refusal of this suggestion. Was Minkoff—or some other member of the JLC executive—trying to preserve the hierarchy between the official and dissident Socialist movements, despite the support Adler had once given to Hagen in his quest for help? The fact that William Green of the AFL, who was supporting Stampfer and the SOPADE, and Abraham Cahan, so ferociously opposed to the JLC's support of Neu Beginnen, were among the guests of honor contributed to Hagen's marginalization from the American public event, while letting him continue to bear the brunt of the tension between his group and the German Labor Delegation.[85]

It would be difficult to make a political assessment of the rescue operation at this stage: not only because it was still underway—more JLC protégés arrived in the United States or North America during 1941 than in the year before—but also because it gave rise to a constellation of individuals and groups, with different backgrounds and horizons, who would now act in disparate ways to continue their fight. Stéphane Dufoix has spoken of "exo-politics" to describe the activity of exiles vis-à-vis their countries of origin, a concept that does describe the refugees' political involvement during the war.[86] Activism was effervescent at this time and in this space of extraterritorial action by exiles who found themselves on American soil. Despite the feelings of alienation and uprooting provoked by exile and so well analyzed by Hannah Arendt (who was among these cohorts),[87] once they arrived in the United States, the political refugees usually became involved in already existing organizations or created new ones. Ranging from the Mazzini Society around Gaetano Salvemini, where many Italians were trying to bring the Italian American community into the anti-fascist fight, to the Representation of the Bund of Poland already implanted in New York, many associations were carrying on the fight by means of propaganda or parallel diplomacy aimed at the real theaters of operation. Structuring membership according to nationalities and political affinities, these organizations acted in diverse ways. Their operations closely depended on how the United States' position on their government of origin evolved, and then on American involvement in the war effort. The presence on American soil of these European leaders would certainly have a strategic value that would enable support to be given to underground movements in occupied Europe[88] and would even contribute to the evolution of American politics after the war.[89]

ASSESSING THE NUMBERS

When the JLC celebrated the arrival of the first refugees in January, the flow had only just begun. In fact, the first six months of 1941 saw the highest number of refugees leave and travel to the United States. The ever-changing and contradictory demands of the State Department and the governments of Vichy, of Madrid, and of the German occupiers now gave way to a period that was relatively favorable, during which Varian Fry seized the opportunity to evacuate as many refugees as possible. For example, for a certain period of time the State Department no longer required a French exit permit before granting a visa. And suddenly Vichy put up fewer obstacles to granting authorizations to leave France, which enabled some refugees to leave Marseille for Martinique as legally as could be! It is even probable that at this stage Vichy was encouraging refugees to leave. After the Kundt Commission (working for the Gestapo) toured all the internment camps in search of those it wanted to transfer to Germany, managing the camps became a heavy economic burden to the Vichy government. The problem was made worse, in fact, by the thousands of Jewish refugees who traveled south during the exodus and were apprehensive of returning home because of German anti-Semitic laws but who now found themselves trapped in the Unoccupied Zone by the Vichy legislation enacted on October 3 and

4, 1940. In particular, the law ruling the status of "foreigners of the Jewish race" authorized prefects to intern immediately those whom they judged to be undesirable—which quickly multiplied the population of the camps. In addition, thousands of Jews expelled by the Reich from Baden and the Palatinate poured into the "free" zone. Thus Vichy tried to foster the emigration of certain categories of refugees; we can see this in the French ambassador to Washington Gaston Henry-Haye's request to the State Department that they admit more refugees from France, as a way to relieve the congestion of the camps. Starting in the month of December 1940, the Les Milles camp near Marseille was specifically designated for the transit of internees who had obtained a visa; a certain number of departures were recorded from this camp in the first trimester of 1941. But on the American side, Vichy's demand was turned down flat. State Department official Robert Pell stated that the United States would firmly resist Germany's continual efforts to push refugees to the West. Therefore, the administration of visa requests would not deviate from the previously ratified lists.[90]

This relative openness would not last. In June 1941, the State Department put an end to the PACPR program by refusing to grant new visas, while leaving open the possibility of admission to the United States for those who were already on lists, including that of the AFL.[91] But time was running out. The attack of the Wehrmacht on the Soviet Union in June 1941, and then that of Japan in December on Pearl Harbor against the United States, would turn Polish Jewish refugees into hostages of the Axis powers. The U.S. entry into the war resulted in stricter standards for admission, since any refugee was suspected of being an infiltrated enemy agent. Thus, in July 1941, fearing the uncertainties created by serial family immigration, Breckinridge Long ordered that visas not be delivered to persons who still had relatives in Germany, Austria, Italy, or the USSR. One year later, in November 1942, the German occupation of southern France forced persons chased by the Gestapo into even deeper hiding; consequently, some joined the *maquis* of the Resistance or fled to Switzerland. By this time the Kundt Commission had extradited to Germany approximately eight hundred political opponents, a figure well below its goal. Even if among them were people as eminent as Rudolf Breitscheid, many others were reported missing: they were hiding or had already emigrated. All those whom the JLC had succeeded in evacuating were effectively saved from these deportations.[92]

In July 1941, Isaiah Minkoff assessed the rescue activity up to this date. The accounting was not simple, since the process of delivering many persons was still underway, with all the attendant uncertainties. The most explicit document in this assessment—in the records that remain—is the list Minkoff established of "Persons Rescued by the Jewish Labor Committee,"[93] which contains exactly three hundred names and provides the most complete and precise estimation on the subject. Organized alphabetically (on the basis of file cards kept up-to-date by the JLC staff), it indicates the family name, first name, and nationality of the visa holder (almost all of them men), as well as his function in the socialist and labor movement, or his role as an intellectual, and his situation in exile when that information could be obtained, for example, the name of the internment camp. The list also notes the names of family members admitted under the same visa. Thus, it appears that a total of 540 persons were rescued by the JLC at this time. Also on this list were indications of the presence of these refugees on American soil: the date of their arrival in the United States, the port of entry for those who arrived via the West Coast—New York being the port of arrival for all who embarked in Lisbon—and the name of the ship of the transatlantic or transpacific crossing. Because these final details were lacking in some cases, we may perceive that in July, out of the three hundred names listed, fifteen represented families or persons who had received and obtained a visa, who were known to be about to leave or to have left Europe (no doubt since the cost of the transport had already been advanced) but had not yet reached the United States. Among the latter figured the Italians Chiaromonte, Cianca, and Garosci, who only reached New York in August 1941 after having been rescued from Casablanca by Emilio Lussu. Seven names among the fifteen are those of Polish Bundists still waiting in Japan, who may have reached the United States before the end of 1941.

In addition, a list prepared by the JLC on July 8, 1941, bore the names of thirty-two persons who had already come to the United States but were awaiting the arrival of family members who were either blocked in Europe or on the perilous journey across Siberia and Japan.[94] Another list from

June 30, 1941, enumerated "individuals on AFL List not yet arrived in the United States."[95] Bearing 216 names, this list partly incorporated the fifteen persons missing from the first list and those of family members still expected in July. But taking these possible overlaps into account, this list indicates that the JLC was able to intervene much more widely than it had initially intended. Beyond the number originally agreed to with the State Department in July–August 1940, it appears that the JLC was able, with the approval of the PACPR, to obtain visas for more names (although the lists were declared closed as of October). Among the 216 persons figure Jewish refugees from Poland who had been stuck in Lithuania or in Japan, and others in France for whom the difficulties had piled up, making it impossible for them to benefit from the visa that the JLC had requested.[96] Camp internees and persons in hiding could not take the necessary steps to get their visas, and others did not want to leave behind their families or their companions of struggle and misfortune. Moreover, some wanted to conduct their resistance from France. This was the case for many Italian political figures: Giuseppe Modigliani, Pietro Nenni, Giuseppe Saragat, Silvio Trentin, and Emilio Lussu.[97] Others, notably Hans Vogel, Friedrich Heine, Kurt Geyer, and Georg Stolz (whose wife had reached the United States), would emigrate to Great Britain. Finally, other names figured as memorials of the JLC's failures: it had been informed, for example, that Bruno Buozzi, secretary of the Italian Labor Confederation, had been arrested in Paris in February 1941 and then deported to Germany and to Italy. Likewise they were perfectly aware of the fate of Rudolf Hilferding and Rudolf Breitscheid. Hilferding's widow, on the other hand, reached New York in June 1941.[98]

In a memorandum sent to the British Labour Party and to the TUC, also dated July 1941, Minkoff affirmed the JLC's initiatives: "At this writing, there are some 800 leaders who have either reached the shores of the United States or found safety in other countries. All financial obligations attendant upon this act of rescue were assumed by the Jewish Labor Committee, which, to date, on this undertaking alone spent a sum amounting to approximately $300,000."[99] Similarly, a JLC brochure recapitulating its activities in 1941 affirmed that "the work of rescuing labor leaders and intellectuals threatened with extermination at the hands of the Nazis, first undertaken in July 1940, was carried on in 1941. During that year some out-standing labor leaders and men of letters were brought over to the United States or to Canada, Mexico and Cuba. In all about 1,000 leaders, Jews and non-Jews."[100]

A mixture of approximations and certitudes, these varying figures call for some explanation. It is certain that in July 1941, given the difficulties in France and on the international level—new regulations from the State Department, administrative complications at the American consulate, dan-gerous journeys across the Pyrenees and Spain—it was impossible to state precisely the result of the JLC operations. To the 540 persons of July 1941 (a figure that includes the 300 leaders and their close kin), all certified by the date of their arrival, Minkoff was adding an imprecise number of those who had "not yet arrived" but for whom visas had been requested. Minkoff also knew that he had asked for—and obtained—from Washington many more visas than those initially noted in July–August 1940. Several other lists in his papers record this activity. The arrival of the first refugees in New York created a snowball effect, since these refugees could indicate the presence of their companions who had been left behind in France.

In August 1942, Minkoff summarized the names of persons for whom the JLC had made new visa requests: a list of 38 persons who had obtained visas for Mexico, another list of 83 people, almost all of whom were born in Poland but resided in France and were active in what was called the "Jew-ish workers movement in Paris," and two lists of Austrian trade unionists in France. By the end of 1942, the JLC now claimed to have organized the rescue of 1,500 "labor leaders and men of letters."[101] These 1942 lists gave for every person the address of the Centre Américain de Secours of the Emergency Rescue Committee, 18 Boulevard Garibaldi in Marseille. Again, this confirms the cooperation between the JLC and the ERC, with the latter helping refugees obtain their visas at the consulate and to leave France, by land or by sea. Daniel Bénédite, who after Varian Fry's departure in Sep-tember 1941[102] took charge of the Centre Américain de Secours, noted that as of the autumn of that year, after a period of difficulties, visas that had been previously obstructed or had expired were being reconfirmed: "We often receive agreement for Mexican and Cuban visas that compensate for the restrictions observed elsewhere." In two months, he went on, "a good hundred of our clients were able to leave France."[103]

SHARED HONORS

The collaboration between the JLC and the ERC in France—which in 1942 became the International Rescue and Relief Committee (IRRC)—makes it difficult to determine which organization should be credited with these rescues. Rather than suggesting rivalries between the two, the evidence shows that lives were saved because of their cooperation. The number of successes on each side is not very different. Varian Fry is generally credited with having obtained the rescue of 1,200 to 1,800 persons.[104] The origin of an operation is one way of viewing who was responsible, depending on which organization took the initiative in requesting and obtaining visas. The JLC began with the "AFL list" and pursued this enterprise with the PACPR. For its part, the ERC did the same for its own protégés with the help of the Museum of Modern Art and the Rockefeller and Carnegie foundations. Meanwhile, those who in Marseille knocked on the door of the Centre Américain de Secours (CAmS) could have been sponsored by either organization. The CAmS, in any case, deserves credit for having helped them on the ground, including financial assistance: Fry mentions having financially supported some 4,000 persons and studied 15,000 cases!

Certainly, the actual receipt of a visa at the consulate and provision of the means to leave France—legally or illegally—were due to the persistence and ingenuity of Fry and his office. But the cost of the voyage and the related expenses—including reimbursing the State Department for the telegrams it sent—and supporting refugees for months was borne by each organization depending on which one had initially signaled the existence of a candidate and obtained the visa from Washington after biographical evidence and affidavits were presented. The JLC and ERC were accountable for all these operations, each reimbursing the other for the cost of the ocean crossing of its protégés (the cost of the transatlantic crossings had often been advanced by the HIAS).

In the JLC records, the rescue operations appear under the rubric "rescue work." For 1940, expenditures totaled $138,449; for 1941, $102,189; and for 1942, $87,590.[105] The cost of the transatlantic voyage from Europe to New York was about $300 per person, and that of the peregrination from Lithuania to San Francisco more than $450—not counting living expenses during the months of waiting. Several rescue organizations in Marseille and Lisbon—the IRRC itself, the Unitarian Service Committee, the American Committee for Christian Refugees, and the American Jewish Joint Distribution Committee—helped cover the daily expenses of refugees. The JLC relied entirely on the contributions from its members in order to provide the necessary financial assistance. The local unions of the clothing industry and the Workmen's Circle raised money for these budgets, principally in New York but also in every city where a Jewish working-class community had developed. Without the support of any foundation, the work of the JLC was therefore the fruit of the social and political solidarity of a segment of the American labor movement. In April 1941, Minkoff reviewed the debts incurred in these operations: "We owe the Workmen's Circle $10,000; $10,000 to the International (ILGWU); $6,000 to Agro-Joint; We owe $5,000 to the ORT, and about $10,000 to the Cook's Agency with whom we have made agreements for those who arrive from Japan. We owe $20,000 to the Joint Distribution Committee for the last group which came from Japan." A month later he added that the JLC also owed $15,000 to the HIAS and that "if all our people in Europe had the possibility to leave now, we would need about $90,000."[106] It was certainly difficult—if not impossible—for the JLC to raise funds beyond its network of members and sympathizers in order to rescue European labor leaders whose renown had been limited to their countries of origin. The ERC, on the other hand, had scarcely any members but was trying to mobilize public opinion in support of the arrival of artistic and scientific figures of some renown. "If Albert Einstein could be brought to the United States today," wrote Harold Oram to Fry, "we might collect a million dollars in a short amount of time by having him make a tour throughout the country. [Pablo] Casals is probably worth $100,000 and Picasso $50,000."[107] Undoubtedly equivalent sums could never be expected in the case of figures from the labor world. Yet, on both sides, financing these operations was a challenge. ERC president Frank Kingdon even asked the JLC to conduct joint fundraising campaigns.

LIMITS OF POLITICAL EMIGRATION

"We thought that when we presented all our lists in Washington, we would be finished with our work," Minkoff stated at an executive meeting. "We were the first organization to receive practical results from the work. Many people appealed to us that we should help them in emigration work." Other aid organizations existed, he said, such as the International Relief Association and the National Refugee Service or the HIAS, to help people with "more general matters that would require a lot of [extra] work from us."[108] This remark underlines the JLC's limited focus. In the context of a U.S. immigration regime that was practically closed at the time, the decision to plead for the admission of people confronted with likely persecution, imminent arrest, or death justified this selectivity among cases. The political opponents of Nazi and fascist regimes were particularly exposed. The JLC had given itself the task of saving those with whom it had political and intellectual affinity. The number and prominence of persons who reached the United States attested to the success of its enterprise. In July 1941, faced with new visa restrictions from the State Department, the JLC reaffirmed its project of political emigration in order to submit new visa requests and to obtain renewals of those about to expire: "Our action is specifically a political one, which general organizations could not carry out. We have confined our efforts to men and women with an active political background, who are subject to special persecution from totalitarian regimes."[109] With this objective, the JLC became a pioneer in the history of American immigration legislation, ahead of its time in using the category of "political refugee," a concept later adopted to distinguish political refugees from immigrants who wanted to leave their country of origin for economic reasons.[110] But for JLC leaders in the 1940s, obtaining visas for European political refugees was a constant struggle against the dominant culture of the State Department and public opinion. In this they were guided not only by their own history of political emigration and their confidence in the United States as a nation that guaranteed democratic values but also by their ideological commitment to the national and international labor movement. Their defense of European refugees did not serve a cause internal to the American labor movement; it was primarily a matter of humanitarian and political protection, of providing a refuge in time of war, enabling the transmission and survival of European democratic movements.

Nevertheless, as the war unfolded, large segments of the civilian population found themselves directly threatened, making it increasingly difficult to determine who was a political refugee. The issue had been first posed in 1939 about Spanish Civil War refugees in France who had been dumped in abominable internment camps. Jacob Pat wrote to David Dubinsky: "Until now we have not undertaken to aid Spanish refugees in Southern France, because this is a very big and complicated issue. However, as you know, we are taking care of the cases of Largo Caballero, and his secretary Rodolfo Llopis. We have come to the conclusion not to involve ourselves in the problem of the Spanish refugees. We would appreciate your opinion on the matter."[111] Indeed, the JLC (like the ERC) had requested visas for the former Spanish prime minister and leader of the Spanish workers union and for his secretary, and tried to intercede in their favor with the Vichy government, which was yielding to German and Spanish pressure to refuse to grant them exit visas. But they were not successful. After house arrest in the Drôme region, Largo Caballero was arrested in February 1943 and deported to Sachsenhausen—from which he returned in 1945. But in the United States, the question was never raised of opening the doors of immigration to Spanish refugees, who were, in fact, welcome in Mexico. One might think that the absence of a large Spanish ethnic group in the United States, in contrast to the presence of millions of Jewish Americans and Italian Americans, partly explains the lack of support for Spanish refugees. Relations between Vichy and the Franco regime explain the rest. But it was also a matter of the distinction between the immigration of vast cohorts of refugees and the more limited political emigration of a small group of prominent figures.

The problem was even more acute for the Jewish population of France, native or foreign, who rushed into the southern zone. The JLC's silence on this subject at the time may seem paradoxical. The establishment of lists, as we recall, was limited to labor and political leaders and intellectuals who were being targeted for their activities or publications that were hostile to the Nazi and fascist regimes. A majority of these persons were Jewish, but this was not the sole reason for their rescue and was not either an obstacle to their obtaining a visa on the American side or the primary cause of their being designated on the lists of the Gestapo or of the Mussolini police. The term "political refugee" was not a euphemism to refer to all the refugees that the Third Reich was hunting down for political or "racial" reasons. However, with the "Jewish status" decreed by Vichy on October 3, 1940, combined with the law of October 4 authorizing the internment of "foreigners of the Jewish race," the anti-Semitic policy of the Pétain government then filled the camps not only with political refugees but with men, women, and children rounded up because they were Jews.[112] Far from being insensitive to that— as we shall see in the following chapters—the JLC maintained its narrow focus on rescuing people from France for whom it was able to obtain visas, a fortiori if they were Jewish, but not only. The pragmatism of this attitude reveals the limits of what its leaders knew they could actually achieve. No consensus in the State Department, in Congress, in public opinion, or even within the AFL would have been able to introduce modifications to the current legislation governing immigration. The line of "exceptional rescue" that the JLC had adopted was not a solution to the massive and urgent demand for Jewish emigration resulting from the expulsion policy conducted by the Third Reich before it came to the Final Solution. It is not surprising that the JLC leaders were overwhelmed by requests for emigration help that they could not provide. Their sole means of obtaining a visa had relied on a brief opening at the State Department and it had been made explicit for policy reasons that they were of limited scope and duration. The approximately 1,500 persons the JLC succeeded in bringing across the Atlantic were all saved from being hunted down in France—and from the soon to be implemented deportation program under Prime Minister Laval's collaboration with the enemy. The occupation of the south from November 1942 closed the trap, putting an end to any possibility of emigration.

Baruch Charney Vladeck at the Jewish Labor Committee 1935 convention. The board at
the background bears the name of the organization in Yiddish: Yidisher Arbeter Komitet,
and the date of its foundation, February 1934. (JLC photo collection 048/B1.F1, Tamiment
Library, New York University)

Baruch Charney Vladeck, founder and first president of the JLC. This undated photograph was taken in the 1930s. (JLC photo collection 048/B1.F5, F11, Tamiment Library, New York University)

"Fight Nazism and Fascism," poster used by unions and other JLC member organizations in their public actions and publications. (ILGWU Records, 5780/2, B8, F2, B, Kheel Center, Cornell University)

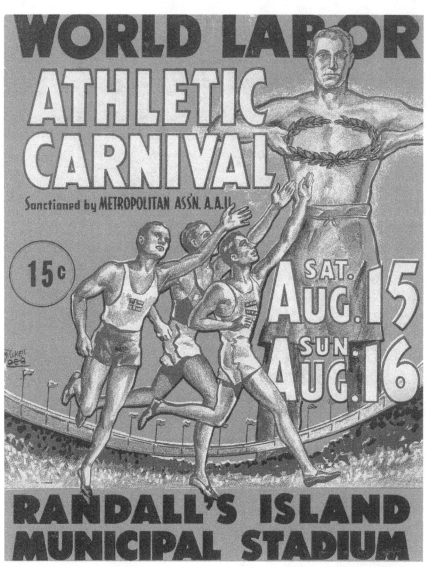

Poster, the 1936 Counter-Olympics, August 1936. (JLC Records, Series I, B13, F6, Robert F. Wagner Labor Archives, Tamiment Library, New York University)

Giuseppe Modigliani receiving a $10,000 check from David Dubinsky at the end of his lecture tour on Italian fascism, March 1935. (ILGWU Records, 5780 PB024F18C, Kheel Center, Cornell University)

Sidney Hillman (*left*) and David Dubinsky. The ACWA and the ILGWU presidents did not agree on all issues, especially on relations with Communists and the USSR. But they collaborated on the rescue of political refugees, the support of resistance movements, and postwar assistance to Displaced Persons. (ILGWU Records, 5780 PB012F25A, Kheel Center, Cornell University)

A modern workshop of women workers in the New York clothing industry, early 1940s. The cutting and pressing departments were staffed by a male labor force. (ILGWU Records, 5780 PB031F06, Kheel Center, Cornell University)

JLC executive director Isaiah Minkoff was the mastermind of the rescue operations. (Isaiah M. Minkoff Papers, Robert F. Wagner Labor
Archives, Tamiment Library, New York University)

NICHT LETTER   August 30, 1940

N. Chanin
c/o Apelbaum
Victor Hotel
Miami Beach, Fla.

Abramovich and 6 friends left Lisbon August 28th on ship Excalibur. Entire

Abramovich Ziegelbaum group leaving September 3rd on ship Nehilis. Mendelson

wired everything satisfactorily accomplished for 10 who have Finland visas.

Victor Shulman, Sholem Hertz, Baumgarten, Secretary of Central Rath Warsaw,

wired xxx yesterday from Vilna about ship tickets Yokahama New York. They

received permit to leave Lithuania. We must raise necessary funds.

Pat

Jacob Pat to Nathan Chanin, August 30, 1940, telegram announcing the arrival of R. Abramovitch and six friends, together with the Zygielbojm group, as well as ten others who had visas from Finland. The telegram also confirms the Lithuania to Japan itinerary for refugees in Vilna. (JLC Records, Series I, B39, F2, Robert F. Wagner Labor Archives, Tamiment Library, New York University)

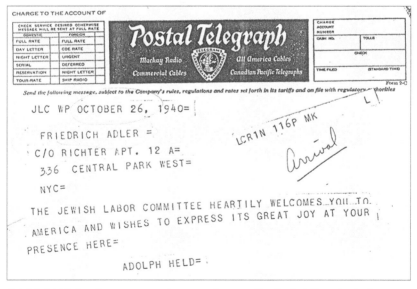

First telegram:

I.J.Wixon
Immigration and Naturalization Service
Hutchins Building, 10-th and D street
Washington, D.C.

EATTLE, WASH.
OCT 28 1940

The following persons are expected to arrive next
Thursday october 31 in Seattle on S.S. Heian Maru:
Pat Dr.Emanuel and wife, Pat Noema alias Naomi,
Zelmanowioz Froim Lezer, wife and two children,
Lichtenstein Zalmon Josef, wife and child, Federman
Rafael and wife, Rozenboim Jakob M. Piekarz Leiba H.
Nowogrodski Markus C. Hero Jacob Shulim, wife and
two children stop All these names were submitted by
President William Green to State Department on July
third stop State department cabled these names to
Kaunas on july Sixth stop Name p Pat Naomi alias Noema
was submitted July 23 stop State department cabled this
name first to Kaunas and recently to Tokio stop
Many thankbbbr thanks for your kind confirmation of these
names by wire to Director Bonham in Seattle in order to
facilitate their landing

I. Minkoff
Hotel Stratford, Seattle

Isaiah Minkoff to Immigration and Naturalization Service, October 28, 1940, telegram announcing the arrival at Seattle of some twenty refugees from Poland, reaching the United States from Japan. (JLC Records, Series I, B39, F2, Robert F. Wagner Labor Archives, Tamiment Library, New York University)

Second telegram:

JLC WP OCTOBER 26, 1940=

FRIEDRICH ADLER =
C/O RICHTER APT. 12 A=
336 CENTRAL PARK WEST=
NYC=

LCR1N 116P MK
arrival

THE JEWISH LABOR COMMITTEE HEARTILY WELCOMES YOU TO
AMERICA AND WISHES TO EXPRESS ITS GREAT JOY AT YOUR
PRESENCE HERE=

ADOLPH HELD=

Adolph Held, October 26, 1940, telegram welcoming Friedrich Adler, who had arrived in the United States. (JLC Records, Series I, B39, F6, Robert F. Wagner Labor Archives, Tamiment Library, New York University)

Daniel Bénédite and Varian Fry in Marseille, 1940. (Private collection of Pierre Ungemach)

Sixth shipment of food and clothing to Poles and Jews in Russia, 1942. Benjamin Taba-chinsky and Jacob Pat are first and second on the left (JLC president Adolph Held is the fourth). (JLC photo collection 048, B1, F3/13, Tamiment Library, New York University)

Left: Paul Vignaux, 1940. (Private collection, Vignaux family)

Below: Paul Vignaux standing in front of the Rockefeller Center, where the New York OSS office was situated. (Private collection, Vignaux family)

NEWSLETTER PUBLISHED MONTHLY BY
THE JEWISH LABOR COMMITTEE
175 EAST BROADWAY   NEW YORK, N. Y.

Vol. 1, No. 3   All matter in "Voice of the Unconquered" may be reprinted without acknowledgment   MAY, 1943

Last Appeal From Polish Jews

Early in March the Jewish Labor Committee received a message from two members of the underground organization of the General Jewish Workers Union of Poland which left Warsaw, through underground channels, on February 7th.

This message revealed for the first time the news that armed resistance had broken out in the Warsaw Ghetto and that scores of Nazis and several hundred 's were slain in resisting deportation.

'e printed this underground report the last issue of THE VOICE OF THE .NCONQUERED. Now the news has been officially confirmed by the Polish Government in London.

On April 21st the secret Polish radio made a dramatic appeal to the Allies to rescue the Jews of Poland. It said that men, women and children in the Warsaw Ghetto were battling the Nazis with bare hands. Another story to this effect was published in the *New York Times* of April 23rd:

"Armored cars and tanks have moved into Warsaw, where the Ghetto populace is resisting deportation of the city's remaining 35,000 Jews. The battle was still raging when the Polish exile government in London received its latest news.

"Those resisting are the most active elements left after the mass murders and deportations of last fall. The Polish Underground Movement has supplied arms and sent trained commanders for a last stand, which is said to be costing the Germans many lives . . ."

The Jewish Labor Committee now makes public the last appeal from the Jews of Poland. It re- dly reached through under- und channels Mr. S. Mikolaj-

(Continued on Page 4)

"Le Populaire" formerly edited by Leon Blum Published Again by the Underground

In the last issue of *The Voice of The Unconquered*, we published a report which had reached us through underground channels, that the trade union movement in France is alive and fights on.

Leon Blum, former Premier of France, great leader of the French Socialist Party and intimate friend of the Jewish Labor Committee, has been recently transferred to one of the most cruel of the Nazi concentration camps in Germany.

The Jewish Labor Committee is now in possession of additional information on the activities of the pro-democrat and anti-Nazi movement in France.

As we were going to press we received a letter, dated March 25th, 1943, from a prominent member of the "Directing Committee of the *Comite d'Action Socialiste* (reorganized French Socialist Party) which reads:

"Jewish Labor Committee,
175 East Broadway,
New York, N. Y.

"Dear Friends:

I am only too well aware of your generous interest in, and concern for the development of the democratic forces in Europe, I therefore take this opportunity of sending you a detailed note on the position of the Socialist Party in France, and our need for support in the difficult circumstances that we find ourselves. I am certain that I am expressing the hopes of large masses of French workers whose eyes have been turned towards America during these terrible years . . ."

For reasons of security the Jewish Labor Committee is able to publish only part of the following report on the French Socialist Party:

"During the few months that followed this vote (Petain's capitulation—editor) the Socialist Party, disorganized by repressive measures of the Petain 'government,' was not able to show any signs of life.

"However, since the beginning of 1941, due to the initiative of socialists both in the occupied and unoccupied zones the 'Party' has been coming into its own.

"Propaganda is being carried on despite the many dangers it entails. Indeed, the past two years have made us realize that the solid and true masses of socialists remained intact and powerful. Without going into much detail we can say that, due to the untiring efforts of party militants, the Socialist Party is once again organized, and constitutes a nucleus of primary importance for French democracy.

"Today it is the Socialist Party that has set up a number of organizations in various cities among them . . . and so on. We are once again printing *Le Populaire*, which, despite its being clandestine, and despite the scarcity of paper,

(Continued on Page 4)

Front page of JLC organ, *Voice of the Unconquered*, no. 3, May 1943. At the same time as the article heralded the underground reappearance of the Socialist newspaper *Le Populaire*, to which it had contributed, the JLC circulated the news of Léon Blum's deportation to Buchenwald on March 31, 1943. (JLC Records, Series I, microfilm roll 159, Robert F. Wagner Labor Archives, Tamiment Library, New York University)

London, March 11, 1943

RECEIVED TODAY CABLE DATED FEBRUARY SEVENTH FIND (JANCZYN AND BEREZOWSKI)
AS FOLLOWS "JANUARY GERMANS STARTED LIQUIDATION OF REMNANTS WARSAW GHETTO
STOP JEWS RESISTED TENS OF GERMANS AND A FEW HUNDRED JEWS KILLED AMONG THEM
MERMELSTEIN CHOLODENKO GITERMAN STOP AFTER THREE DAYS GERMANS STOPPED AC-
TION TAKING AWAY SIX THOUSAND JEWS STOP ALL OVER POLAND LIQUIDATION PRO-
CEEDING STOP LIQUIDATION OF WARSAW REMNANTS PLANNED MIDDLE OF FEBRUARY STOP
ALARM THE WORLD STOP APPLY POPE FOR OFFICIAL INTERVENTION AND THE ALLIES FOR
EXTRAORDINARY STEPS AGAINST GERMANS IN THE ALLIED COUNTRIES STOP WE SUFFER
TERRIBLY THE REMAINING FEW HUNDRED THOUSAND JEWS THREATENED WITH IMMEDIATE
ANNIHILATION ONLY YOU CAN RESCUE US STOP RESPONSIBILITY TOWARDS HISTORY
THROWS UPON YOU "

XXXXX ZYGIELBOJM

Szmul Zygielbojm's last telegram to the JLC, March 11, 1943, informing of the telegram
he received from Berezowski (Leon Feiner) in Warsaw about the German attack on the
ghetto of January 1943 and announcing the imminent "liquidation of the remnants of
the ghetto." (JLC Records, Series I, B11, F24, Robert F. Wagner Labor Archives, Tamiment
Library, New York University, also reproduced in Papers of the JLC, 247)

Underground Polish press received by the JLC, *Voice of the Unconquered*, November 1943. (JLC Records, Series I, microfilm roll 159, Robert F. Wagner Labor Archives, Tamiment Library, New York University)

Inauguration of the Arbeter Ring's first children's home, supported by the JLC, at Les Buissons, near Le Mans, June 1945. JLC delegate Nathan Chanin is standing at the center. (Centre Medem-Arbeter Ring collection, Paris)

JLC delegation in Paris, winter 1946. Jacob Pat (second row, on the left); Fajwel Schrager is standing by him at the center. (JLC photo collection, 048, B1, F1, Tamiment Library, New York University)

Vladka Meed, the very young underground agent who helped Jews hidden outside of the ghetto, is here being shown pictures of David Dubinsky and President Roosevelt when she came to New York for the JLC 1947 convention. (JLC photo collection, 048, B5, F1, Tamiment Library, New York University)

Jacob Pat (first row center) among surviving Jewish workers in Poland, 1946. (JLC photo collection, 048, B2, F3, Tamiment Library, New York University)

Jacob Pat (first row, third from the left) among Jewish men and women, Poland, 1946. (JLC photo collection, 048, B2, F3, Tamiment Library, New York University)

Daniel Mayer at the JLC 1947 convention. (JLC photo collection, 048, B3, F26, Tamiment Library, New York University)

Léon Blum among children at the Vladeck Home, Brunoy, December 31, 1949. Fajwel Schrager is seated to his left. Thomas Tursz, the director of the home, is standing behind Blum with former resistant Bertha Mering. Blum died in April 1950. (Centre Medem-Arbeter Ring collection, Paris

5

WITH THE FRENCH
RESISTANCE

Although it unfolded principally in Marseille, the rescue operation conducted by the JLC in 1940–1941 hardly involved the French labor movement. Yet during the war a rapprochement occurred that placed the
Socialists, trade unionists, and Jews of France at the heart of the JLC's
efforts. In effect it would come to support Socialists who were gathering
clandestinely as well as sections of the labor movement that were rebuild-
ing themselves, thus contributing to a non-Communist current within the
Resistance. Similarly, the JLC focused on assisting the Jewish organizations in France to which it was close because of the political leanings of
their activists. In other words, the JLC developed ties with segments of the
French labor and socialist movement, as it did with Jewish organizations, to
support their resistance to the Nazi occupiers. These links were forged in
the underground struggle.[1]

PAUL VIGNAUX: A MESSENGER FROM
FRENCH LABOR

Beginning in June 1940, French labor was brought down by the defeat
of France, the armistice, the elimination of democratic and republican

institutions, and the crumbling of the Socialist Party (SFIO).[2] The Communist Party had been banned in September 1939 and labor organizations were dissolved in the autumn of 1940.[3] Meanwhile, from New York the JLC was organizing the rescue of European leaders who had taken refuge in southern France. This operation, however, did not mean that the fate of French labor or socialist leaders became a priority. No list of French people to be helped out of the country was compiled as there had been lists of Russians, Poles, Germans, Austrians, and Italians.[4] Two time schemes were at work: the JLC had followed the trajectories of the persons it sought to help since their first exile from Germany, Austria, or Italy and had acted quickly as soon as France fell when it understood the danger they were in, whereas the French suddenly found themselves plunged into chaos and a "new order" that they were just starting to comprehend.

From New York it was difficult to perceive what was happening to the French labor and socialist movement under the Occupation. The SFIO no longer existed. The rallying of a majority of parliamentary Socialists to the Vichy government on July 10, 1940 (90 out of 168 voted full powers to Pétain, 36 voted against, 6 abstained, and the rest had disappeared), had finished off a party, which in any case since the Munich Agreement had already exhausted itself in internal struggles. Those who wanted to resist were divided. Some went to London, although not all of them had faith in General de Gaulle, and others soon began to work underground in northern or southern France. And a few Socialists found refuge in New York. But the latter were isolated in a French emigrant community that was divided by a strong anti-Gaullist current. Let us recall that Vichy had an ambassador in Washington, Gaston Henry-Haye, who fully supported Pétain. On the other hand, the representation of France Libre (Free France) in Washington and in New York would not succeed in promoting the Gaullist political alternative in a convincing way. The JLC, moreover, had barely any contact with Adrien Tixier, who was the France Libre delegate to Washington starting in 1941, although he was close to the labor community through his former position as assistant director of the International Labor Office in Geneva. On the whole, the JLC had little contact with the community of French wartime émigrés. The eight to nine thousand who made up this group of exiles emanated from a generally upper-class milieu that was less politically than intellectually involved. Many of them were "privileged by birth, by wealth, and by intellect," as was later recalled by Jean-Louis Crémieux-Brilhac, who had been part of Free France in London.[5]

Standing at the intersection of these two worlds—as a labor activist and an intellectual—Paul Vignaux was able to prime the JLC's interest in France. A specialist in medieval philosophy and holding a chair at the Ecole Pratique des Hautes Études, Vignaux was also a union organizer who had been active in the Christian-affiliated Confédération Française des Travailleurs Chrétiens (CFTC). Among French emigrants, he was one of the rare intellectuals to devote the years of his American exile to militant action.[6] He worked tenaciously to establish contacts between French and American labor and left-wing organizations, in order to provide information on the one hand and obtain subsidies on the other. The JLC would be the purveyor of some of these funds. At the CFTC, Vignaux had advocated non-faith-based rules of membership; in 1937 he had founded the Syndicat Général de l'Enseignement National (a teachers' union) to be non-partisan and open to the American model of industrial unionism. He himself was vice president of the CFTC federation of civil servants. A refugee in southwest France and professor at the University of Toulouse during the first year of the Occupation, in August 1940 he contributed at the local level to the revival of labor organizations initiated by Léon Jouhaux, the secretary-general of the left-wing Confédération Générale du Travail (CGT).[7] Jouhaux was trying to re-create underground a French labor movement from the ruins of its own institutions by bringing together members from the CGT—the historically stronger organization—and from the Christian CFTC. The resulting *Manifeste des Douze* (Manifesto of the Twelve), signed on November 15, 1940, sealed an agreement among nine executives of the CGT and three of the CFTC in a plan for common resistance to Vichy's anti-union Charte du Travail announced by the labor minister René Belin (who as a former deputy to Jouhaux in the CGT had become a turncoat). Jouhaux hoped that this alliance between the two federations would consolidate the existence of underground union forces in an independent movement that would be capable of moral and strategic resistance, while excluding those of Communist allegiance from the old CGTU because of their adherence to the German-Soviet Pact. On his side, Vignaux contributed thereby to preventing the CFTC's rallying to the Vichy regime—as was desired by some clerical authorities. In addition, Jouhaux undertook to enter into relations with the British Trades Union Congress and with American labor organizations, from which he was hoping for material support to guarantee union autonomy, free of any interference by the government and even independent of the political power of the Allies. From April 1940 onward, he had announced that the time had come to establish transatlantic relations: "Across the ocean, consciousness is starting to awaken. Isolationism is coming to an end," he asserted.[8] Vignaux's departure for the United States enabled the creation of hoped-for links with American labor.

This ideological and pragmatic convergence was complemented by other events that were not fortuitous either. During the year they spent in a retreat in southwest France, Vignaux and his wife lived in Toulouse not far from Silvio Trentin, the anti-fascist resister and inspirer of Giustizia e Libertà, whose bookshop in the Rue du Languedoc was a meeting place for Italian anti-fascists, Spaniards, Germans, Austrians, and Russians pushed back to southern France, and a kernel of an early French resistance network. As Vignaux recalled it in a later account, at Silvio Trentin's he could perceive "the existence of milieux that were apparently tiny, multiple, dispersed, ignorant of each other, and ungraspable overall, which in an apparently generalized concern, constituted so many points of resistance, and virtual nuclei of activism."[9] Even before his arrival in New York, he had been in contact with this "convergence between such diverse minds that was intellectually constitutive of the Resistance," a cosmopolitan constellation of activists hunted down by the Occupation, several of whom the JLC was trying to get out of the French trap. In this milieu, Vignaux also met Walter Schevenels, the secretary of the International Federation of Trade Unions (IFTU), who had not been spared by the tribulations of exile and exodus. In Lisbon, in the month of August 1941, before embarking for the United States, he also encountered "the great Sardinian militant" Emilio Lussu and several of the JLC's Italian protégés whom Lussu had managed to evacuate from Morocco, including Cianca and Garosci, who were also leaving for the United States.[10]

Thus Paul Vignaux was fully aware of the JLC's European connections when he contacted its leaders in New York. He did not owe them his own emigration with his family but rather was indebted to Jacques Maritain, a Christian philosopher who was already present in the United States and had obtained for him a position at the University of Notre Dame in Indiana that was financed by the Rockefeller Foundation. Vignaux entered the United States during the summer of 1941 with a professional invitation and an "above the quotas" visa as an intellectual, without having had to brave the Spanish and Portuguese border posts. But in addition to his teaching, he was charged with another mission. In the words of Jean Lecuir, "Going to the United States was for Vignaux a militant act." He had a dual agenda: "to exert influence in favor of the U.S. entry into the war by informing politicians and public opinion about the realities of the French situation" and "to develop an external resistance which would sustain and support the French workers' underground struggle by propaganda and financial means."[11] Armed with a letter of introduction from Léon Jouhaux to AFL president William Green that authorized him to undertake "information and documentation work," from his arrival Vignaux was on a par with the leaders of the JLC, in front of whom on August 26 his wife, Georgette (who was more fluent in English), read a report on the labor situation in France.[12]

In New York, Vignaux was joined by a former member of the CFTC executive office, Joseph Botton.[13] The two men started working on unifying the presence of Socialists, trade unionists, and other democratically oriented French exiles by organizing them into a French Labor Movement Committee.[14] From across the ocean this movement aimed at "unifying the struggle for national independence, and the fight for free trade unions, by opposing both German domination, the Vichy régime, and the capitalist powers that support it and collaborate with Germany." Vignaux projected a militant vision intending "to maintain and to rekindle the tradition of the French Revolution by rejecting any vitiation of the principle of the equality of citizens, regardless of race and creed.... To uphold the tradition of the French labor movement, which is based upon the freedom of association and opinion and independence from employer or State control."[15] To do so, the committee launched a weekly publication called *France Speaks*. Jean

Rollin and Albert Grand, former journalists with the Havas news agency, edited this mimeographed bulletin, published in English and documented by "confidential sources in Occupied and Non-Occupied France," sources that were verified and circulated in France itself. For two years the JLC contributed financially to the regular appearance of this bulletin as revealed by Paul Vignaux's demand in 1943 that the subsidy be raised.[16] From its inception in the autumn of 1941 *France Speaks* presented an optimistic affirmation of the people's resistance, opposed to the treachery of the Armistice. The bulletin reprinted the *Manifeste des Douze* in its first issue and tracts circulating in the Toulouse region. In November, it reported news of the "Fifty for One Massacres," that is, the execution by the Germans of a hundred hostages in Nantes and Bordeaux in retaliation for the attack against two German officers.[17] The weekly mentioned the existence of several resistance networks (Liberté, Libération Nationale, and Libération). It stressed the unanimity of the working class against Vichy's corporatist social and economic policy and celebrated the Socialist Revolution that was underway.[18] Through this publication Vignaux and his team wished to draw the attention of French people in the United States and of the American public to the surging opposition to the Vichy government. They called for the formation of an "Atlantic Confederation" to overthrow the pan-Germanic order imposed by Hitler on Europe—and more precisely (before it finally did so in December 1941) to involve the United States in the war.[19] From the beginning of 1942 came alarming news concerning the Jews of France—decrees, arrests, roundups and raids, detention in Drancy, deportation to internment camps.[20] The bulletin also relayed information about the slow progress made by France Libre and the reemergence of the Socialists. However, on these two points the JLC's own information network, initially issuing from that of *France Speaks*, somewhat differed.

THE COMMITTEE FOR SOCIALIST ACTION AND FRANCE LIBRE

Information on the French Resistance also came directly from Free French, which was organizing the resistance networks in France from London. During a visit to New York by one of their delegates, Henry Hauck, who represented the CGT in London, the JLC was directly introduced to the demands of the French labor movement. Hauck had come to New York to participate in the International Labor Organization (ILO) Conference in November 1941.[21] During this occasion he solicited the JLC for its assistance, meeting its president, Adolph Held, and members of the Executive Committee who immediately granted a $200 subsidy per month—or about 20,000 francs—for a period of six months to the clandestine labor and socialist movement. At Hauck's request, this sum was to be divided among the CGT (45%), the CFTC (15%), and the Socialist Party (40%).[22] This split reflected the agreement in the *Manifeste des Douze* adding the Socialist Party to the non-Communist labor unity. "The subsidy is to be used for underground propaganda work. It might also be useful to add a monthly sum for relief in order to help our arrested or persecuted comrades," he added. The names of the recipients in France were to be supplied by Robert Jean Longuet, secretary of the French Labor Movement Committee, or by Albert Grand, his substitute.[23] Hauck also explained that it was easier for the Americans to send money to France than it was for the French in London whose finances were controlled by the Foreign Office. Preferring no doubt that these transactions remain unknown to the British backers of France Libre, Hauck requested this financing for the sake of the socialist and labor resistance in Occupied France. At this stage, the whole issue of financing the Socialists and the labor federations remained uncertain and the subject of difficult negotiations among the various branches of the Resistance.[24]

Moreover, beginning in 1942, transatlantic contacts began to be established between the French Labor Movement Committee and former members of the Socialist Party in France, who—discounting those who had granted full power to Pétain—were gradually assembling in the south into the Comité d'Action Socialiste (CAS; Committee of Socialist Action) led by Daniel Mayer. Mayer, whom De Gaulle later described as "the methodical artisan of Socialist action," had been a member of the SFIO since 1927. He had been in charge of the social questions in the party's organ, *Le Populaire*. Indignant about the Munich Agreement, he stood against the pacifist resolutions that divided the party, a position that brought him close to that of the party's leader, and former head of the Popular Front government, Léon Blum.[25] During the Occupation, as Jewish refugees in Marseille, Daniel Mayer and his wife, Cletta, both worked for local committees of assistance to other refugees. After contacting resisting members of the party (Gaston Defferre, André Blumel, Henri Ribière), Mayer decided to consult Léon Blum for his advice on how to start a socialist revival.[26] At the time, Blum, having been indicted by the Vichy government in November 1940, was interned in the austere fortress of Bourassol near Riom in the Massif Central. Until March 1943, when Blum was deported to Germany, Mayer visited him fifteen times, thus making himself a courier between the socialist leader and the underground militants. Since Blum was denied the right to receive visitors or correspondence, Mayer's consultations with him were done in writing by an intermediary, Blum's daughter-in-law Renée, who transmitted questions and answers. From his place of detention, Blum was thus able to influence the crucial choices of a socialist party that covertly was taking shape. It was in large part thanks to his magisterial defense at his trial in Riom in February–March 1942 that the party revived. The CAS now benefited from the prestige Blum acquired with his defense against Vichy. The influence of this key moment on the Socialists, and more generally on the swinging of public opinion against the Vichy regime, was decisive in the history of the French Resistance. From that time forward, Blum conferred on it an aura of rigor, legitimacy, and justice by overturning the accusations leveled against him and using them against his accusers. The legal victory in this prosecution (the trial was abandoned on orders from Berlin) contributed to a resurgence of the party, which had declined since 1938. Despite his detention, Léon Blum once again ensured his authority over the party thanks to Daniel Mayer's mediation, erasing the image of an impotent, discredited, and divided SFIO.[27]

Mayer smuggled out Blum's defense in a brochure recalling republican principles and calling for resistance against Vichy and the German Occupation. This brochure was transmitted to the United States by militants of the Internationaler Sozialistischer Kampfbund (ISK), a minority party to the left of the SPD, a few of whose activists had taken refuge in France and were active in the Resistance. Others such as Ewa Lewinski-Pfister[28] had reached the United States thanks to the JLC rescue efforts of 1940–1941 and now relayed information via her contacts with Paul Vignaux and Paul Hagen. Extracts from Blum's self-defense in the courtroom appeared in *France Speaks*.[29] And Lewinski-Pfister transmitted to the JLC parts of the prosecution and the defense of Léon Blum and Edouard Daladier at the Riom trial.[30] The JLC left to others the task of translating and publishing them.[31] No doubt the JLC found it more urgent to support the resistants— the CAS and Blum himself—in their present difficulties.

The initial subsidy that the JLC granted the CAS (followed by others) enabled it to resume publication in the Non-Occupied Zone of the main socialist organ, *Le Populaire*, of which Blum had been editor for years. "Our friends inform us that publication of this paper has been made possible only with your help, the generous contribution of the Jewish Labor Committee towards the French Labor Movement," wrote Ewa Lewinski to Jacob Pat, sending him the first issues of the underground socialist paper, to which he immediately replied, "Please do not hesitate to call on us whenever we can be of further assistance in this great work."[32] In contact with several resistance movements, Lewinski also sent copies of *Combat, Libération, Franc-Tireur,* and the June 1942 issue of *Cahiers de Témoignage Chrétien*, as well as tracts, instructions, and local reports.[33] In October she sent other titles (including *Socialisme et Liberté*, which came from the Occupied Zone) and copies of these publications, as well as several documents protesting the deportation of the Jews, among which were the appeals by the cardinals and archbishops of the Occupied Zone to Pétain, as well as Cardinal Gerlier's communiqué, and the letters by the bishops of Toulouse and Montauban, all condemning Vichy's treatment of the Jews.[34] Lewinski thanked the JLC several times "for the generous assistance given to our comrades in France, $3,000 provided for R. and the $3,000 handed over to Ryba Nathan." These sums correspond to those mentioned by Jacob Pat to the JLC's executive office on May 14, 1942, specifying that $3,000 was sent on March 20, then again $3,000 on May 13, followed by $3,810 for individual aid—or a total of $9,810 at this stage.[35] A few months later Ewa Lewinski stated:

> [Our friends] want us to know that the French labor movement continues; they say that the Occupation has not had any devastating effect on the trade union movement, the monthly bulletins are being issued to the officials of the t. u. movement, that information bulletins and clandestine papers continue to appear. The conscription of labor has however increased the difficulties of French labor and we are told that many try to hide with French peasants in order to escape conscription. Nevertheless, in January a congress of the CGT at about the same time as the Christian trade unions was held which were attended by delegates of many unions and where resolutions were passed and distributed. Jouhaux has been arrested, and some other friends.
>
> As far as the refugee situation in France is concerned, we are told that wholesale deportations have been resumed which affect also those who are not interned. However, it is still possible to escape to Switzerland.[36]

It is clear, as with the resurgence of the Socialist Party, that the aura of Léon Blum, his personality, and his vindicating eloquence gave new impetus to the JLC's intervention in France in favor of the socialist networks. In effect it was around Blum rather than General de Gaulle that the JLC began organizing the fundraising and activism on behalf of the French Resistance. Keeping clear of quarrels with the London "Jean Jaurès" socialist group that wanted to limit the general's role to military operations, and especially not letting itself be misled by the State Department in Washington, which maintained diplomatic relations with Vichy until the end of 1942 but did not support De Gaulle thereafter, the JLC followed a line that corresponded to that adopted by the French socialists of the CAS. Blum himself directed them to rally to France Libre and coordinate their action with that of the already established Resistance movements (such as Combat and Libération) and recommended that they not create autonomous organizations, even if the prevailing movements and the Communist Party were clearly marginalizing the Socialists.[37] By May 1942, Blum affirmed that the interim government after the liberation of France should "be constituted around only one person, around only one name, that of Général de Gaulle."[38] At the same time, De Gaulle's evolution toward a democratic and republican conception of Free France strengthened the Socialist's adherence to its project and to the resistance networks that constituted it. The nomination of Adrien Tixier in Washington, like that of Georges Boris (former advisor to Léon Blum) and André Philip (former SFIO representative and professor of political economy) to the Interior Ministry at Carlton Gardens, gave the government in exile a "socialist aspect" that was able to reassure the CAS militants.[39]

In this context, when Blum was promoting the unity of resistance movements by integrating the activity of the Socialist Party in those already constituted, the JLC was emancipating itself from the position taken by Paul Vignaux, while continuing to collaborate with him through his contacts with the French Labor Movement. Vignaux was wary of General de Gaulle's political control over the Resistance movements and the likelihood of an authoritarian power after the Liberation. He feared that the Gaullists' pronounced nationalism in wartime might veer in peacetime toward a narrow conservatism. "We do not think," Vignaux wrote, "that the interest of the French and of the people of the colonies under French tutelage can be defended during the war and after the war in the name of such narrow nationalism. We hold that the international tradition of the workers' movement must be guarded against any nationalistic contamination."[40] In June 1943, a letter from Robert Jean Longuet of the French Labor Movement Committee accused Vignaux and his collaborators of giving an anti-Gaullist tone to the columns of France Speaks, "although almost the whole French Labor Movement is now behind de Gaulle."[41] The JLC's line of action was less motivated by these ideological viewpoints than by the information it directly received from the Socialists and the French Labor Movement; its leaders were also becoming increasingly concerned about the fate of the Jews in France. In Washington during this time, after the Allied landing in North Africa, President Roosevelt played on the rivalry between the two generals—De Gaulle and Giraud—in the government in Algiers.

He only recognized the authority of De Gaulle's power in the autumn of 1943, yet Roosevelt still did not include Free France in devising the Allied strategy.[42] The publication of *France Speaks* was interrupted in June 1943. It is not clear whether this decision was a result of the JLC's interruption of its subsidy and subscription. But beginning in the spring of 1943 the sources of information that had contributed to Vignaux's bulletin were now going to be poured into articles about the resistance in France that would henceforth appear in a new organ launched by the JLC.

VOICE OF THE UNCONQUERED

Since March 1943 the JLC had been in a position to publish its own monthly paper: *Voice of the Unconquered*. This publication was announced as "bringing the voices of the men and the women who have succeeded by a miracle in escaping from the ghettos, dungeons and concentration camps." Having supported resistants to Nazism and fascism since its foundation, the JLC now published the information they provided in order to keep up their fight. Their voices "come to us through short wave broadcasts of the underground radios, through illegal newspapers and publications which go from hand to hand until they reach a free border."[43] Edited by Léon Dennen and then by Joseph Godson, the paper was immediately acclaimed by Jewish American organizations (the World Jewish Congress, the *Jewish Daily Forward*, the American-Jewish Committee, the Council of Jewish Welfare Funds, the United Jewish Appeal), as well as by labor organizations, especially the CIO, and social research institutes like the American Labor Archive and Research Institute of the Rand School of Social Science.[44]

Without duplicating the coverage of the war in major press outlets, *Voice of the Unconquered* instead drew attention to working-class movements in the conflict and to the fate of Jews in the occupied countries, Poland in particular. News about France was frequent, at least that which could be published without compromising the clandestine work of those who supplied it. On the official level of diplomacy among the Allies, for instance, the JLC was happy to announce the restoration of French citizenship to the 120,000

Jews of Algeria that, established since 1870 by the Crémieux Decree, had been abrogated by the Vichy administration. In October 1943 the Comité Français de Libération Nationale (Committee for National Liberation) restored the decree. The JLC had intervened on this subject during General Giraud's visit to the United States in July 1943 in a letter to Secretary of State Cordell Hull, in which Adolph Held stressed that discrimination against the Jews of Algeria would continue as long as the restoration of the Crémieux Decree was not fully implemented.[45]

Throughout 1943, *Voice of the Unconquered* published news about France under the Occupation, furnishing proof of the propaganda and sabotage activities by groups of resistants, and of the continued existence of the underground French Labor Movement and Socialist Party. The latter (the CAS) drew American attention to the imbalance between the meager funds it possessed and the fulsome funds received by the Communist Party from the Communist Internationale. Hoping to counterbalance this weakness, increased by the preponderant place of the French Communist Party within the Resistance, the CAS called upon American labor to help.[46] In May 1943, a picture of Léon Blum appeared on the front page of the monthly with the information about his internment in "one of the concentration camps [Buchenwald] in Germany." Yet the article also played the hopeful card of reproducing along with Blum's picture the information that *Le Populaire* was being published again by the Underground and reproduced a letter by the CAS to the JLC reporting on its activity.[47]

Two years later, when the news of the liberation and return of Léon Blum to France arrived in May 1945, the leaders of the JLC—Adolph Held, Joseph Baskin, and Jacob Pat—expressed their joy in a telegram in French to Daniel Mayer, who had become secretary-general of the Socialist Party:

LÉON BLUM HELD HIGH THE BANNER OF HUMAN DIGNITY EVEN IN THE NAZI PRISONS STOP WE WILL NEVER FORGET HIS COURAGEOUS ATTITUDE DURING THE HISTORIC TRIAL IN RIOM STOP WE ARE SURE THAT LÉON BLUM WILL SOON AGAIN BE LEADER OF THE FRENCH SOCIALIST MOVEMENT AND WILL RESUME HIS PLACE AT THE FOREFRONT OF THE LEADERS OF THE NEW FRANCE.[48]

Blum himself and Daniel Mayer echoed this telegram on the occasion of the first Labor Day since the war ended in September 1945: "Happy to salute the American workers without distinction of race. . . . Hoping that the union of all people in the world will permit the establishment of a just and lasting peace by collective security resulting in the United Socialist States of the world."[49]

SUPPORTING UNDERGROUND LABOR MOVEMENTS

Beyond the revered figure of Léon Blum, the JLC did not fail to support Socialists and the French labor movement during the war. Whether requests came via Paul Vignaux and Ewa Lewinski or via London, they were honored, as we know from the acknowledgments that followed them. To do so, but also to extend its aid to the underground movements in Germany, Austria, Poland, Belgium, Luxembourg, Czechoslovakia, Norway, and Italy, Isaiah Minkoff in the spring of 1943 proposed enlarging the fundraising base to the entire American labor movement, including the AFL, the CIO, and the railroad workers' unions, whose cooperation he sought. In January 1943, the Bund's representation in New York had suggested a similar project based on the presence of European Socialists who had taken refuge in the United States.[50] This meeting affirmed a desire to punish the Nazi criminals "when the Judgement came." But the JLC's initiative gave a positive orientation to this project, rather than a punitive one, by furnishing it with a financial and labor base that could call on the major labor federations with the constructive goal of sustaining the underground labor movements in Europe. The project was ambitious. It was trying to finance more widely and regularly the various underground labor movements in the occupied countries, that is, non-communist resistance movements, in their more or less structural ties with parties and labor organizations. To manage this, it created a new committee, the Council for the Underground Labor Movement in Nazi-Dominated Countries (CULM).[51]

CULM was formed by a number of refugees whom the JLC had managed to bring out of Europe and who had remained in contact with the movements or parties in their countries of origin. Their presence on this council—an a posteriori strategic justification of the rescue effort that had allowed them to come to the United States—also guaranteed that this new institution was made up of people who had firsthand knowledge of the countries they were speaking for. Their representation on CULM was based less on nationality than on the resistance movements and political parties to which they had belonged. Composed of these representatives, the Council was to pass along requests coming from the underground groups struggling against the Occupation. Thus, it included Friedrich Adler for the Austrian labor and socialist movements (who refused, however, to become the Council's president), Paul Hertz and Paul Hagen for Neu Beginnen, and Ewa Lewinski for the ISK. The SPD was represented by Max Brauer—and Rudolf Katz in his absence. Katz was opposed to a seat being granted to J. Walcher, a delegate from the German Socialist Workers' Party (SAP). But that delegate gave proof of his contacts with comrades exiled in Sweden who were part of underground networks and might "act more effectively if they were better financed."[52] Sigfried Taub sat for the Socialist Party of Czechoslovakia (German in language), along with Ignatz Schutz, former labor representative in the Czech parliament. Vanni Montana represented the Italian labor and socialist movement, Paul Vignaux the French Labor Movement, and Hans Nilsen and then Haakon Lie the Norwegian one. Omer Bécu represented Belgian labor, as well as the International Transportworkers' Federation whose seat was in Great Britain but also had an office in New York. Three delegates sat for Poland: Emanuel Nowogrodzki for the Bund, S. Arski and then Wladislaw Malinowski for the Polish Socialist Party, and J. M. Gottlieb for the left-wing Zionists (Left Poale Zion). Professor Rustem Vambery sat for the Hungarian Social Democratic Party, as well as Bela Halasi, a Hungarian labor leader and member of the IFTU. Isaiah Minkoff inaugurated the first meeting of this council:

It so happens that we in the Jewish Labor Committee and I particularly were fortunate to know most of the members of the Council personally. In fact, we take great pride in having been of assistance to them in taking some of their people out of the Nazi hell, and thus making them useful in their common struggle for a democratic world. The council is not a political body that has aspirations of creating an international association of labor. It does not deal with programs for a future Europe. . . . One of the primary purposes of the council is to be of service to you in your own endeavor to strengthen the underground democratic labor movement in these countries.[53]

Then the delegates were invited to establish a budget of requests to support the movements they represented.

THE AFL AND THE CIO COME INTO PLAY

The appeal to the AFL, the CIO, and the railway unions offered the possibility of using reserves from the Labor War Chest and the War Relief Committee that these federations had collected since the U.S. entry into the war and whose budget considerably outstripped that of the JLC. A budget of one million dollars for 1943 was proposed.[54] Abraham Bluestein represented the AFL in this Council; Monroe Sweetland and Irving Abramson the CIO. This collaboration between the two rival federations was unprecedented and enabled the creation of a "Joint Relief Commission" to manage the collection of funds. The International Federation of Trade Unions (IFTU) had telegraphed from London its agreement in principle on the creation of CULM: "Presume your [the JLC] and their [the AFL's Labor War Chest] action coordinated, thus avoiding overlapping."[55] Although the JLC was the initiator of CULM, it only offered itself as a consultative voice in its debates. It left the representatives of the countries concerned responsible for decision making.

> The main function of the Council is to act in an organized manner and upon a democratic basis in the interests of the European underground labor movement and to represent these interests before the Labor War Chests of the American Federation of Labor, of the Congress of Industrial Organization and other trade union organizations in the United States. . . . The transactions and decisions of the Council are not to be made public unless there is a special decision of the Council as a whole.[56]

And so the enterprise was set up. Yet initial disagreements about how it would function and its ultimate goal slowed down its beginnings. The AFL delegate (Bluestein) and the CIO's (Abramson) not only wished to use official channels—that is to say, the representations in exile of the occupied countries—for the transfer of funds to European labor movements but also considered these sums as humanitarian relief money that would be officially recognized as such, rather than as political help for underground movements.[57] Abramson asserted:

> As a condition for this relief it was decided that it must be only a relief project, and the project for each country must have the approval of the respective governments in exile. The help must be given not only to the members of the labor movement. The money will be given through the government relief agency of the respective countries and an accounting of the spending of the money is to be received from the recipients of it.[58]

These stipulations outraged the European socialist refugees. They claimed that it was impossible to conceive in an identical way of such cases as the aid to England during the German aerial bombing but whose labor movement was not clandestine; the aid to the Polish resistance movements (including those in the ghettos) that were crushed by the German occupation but whose country possessed a government in exile in London; and, behind the Axis lines, the aid to German and Austrian labor movements that were engaged in a mortal struggle against the Third Reich, with which the United States was at war. With respect to France, Paul Vignaux stressed that the independence of the trade union movement depended on the independence of channels through which help was to be given: "It is a very dangerous thing to give help for the labor movement through government agencies because this gives the government the control of the labor movement as such." Regarding the Free France government in London, Vignaux renewed his insistence on the necessary independence of the labor movement from political power. Wladislaw Malinowski used the same language, fearing governmental control over the Polish labor movement if it became the recipient of the funds. And Friedrich Adler coldly pointed out that the effort over the previous few months had been a fiasco.

[Austria has] no government in exile. The representatives of the CIO and AFL announced here that the resolution to assist the labor movement in Axis countries had not yet been considered at all. . . . Therefore we must say that the entire matter in which we were originally engaged has been a complete failure. We are aware of the difficulties of the American labor movement, but we must also know what consequences will follow from this failure.[59]

The problem was linked to a fundamental difference in the relationship between politics and labor, moreover, in time of war, on either side of the Atlantic. For the resistants of occupied countries, action could only be clandestine. In contrast, the leaders of the American labor movement at the time were conceiving of international action in an official manner. In fact, from the beginning, the AFL and CIO payments had been contributions to a larger national fund, also backed by the American Red Cross. The total of these contributions was to be submitted for the approval of the War Department and by the president's War Control Board. But since the U.S. entry into the war, it was officially impossible to send money to countries at war with the United States because the Trading with the Enemy Act forbade any commerce and any financial transaction with enemy countries, including countries occupied by the enemy—which meant almost all of Europe except neutral countries (Switzerland, Sweden, Spain, and Portugal) and the Allied countries (Great Britain, France Libre, the USSR, and China).[60] The JLC, by contrast, was accustomed to underground activity: the rescue of European socialist and labor leaders, plus the relation with the CAS in France and with the Free French in London, had hardened it to underground, secret, or semiofficial activity. Its aid to the insurgents of the Warsaw Ghetto, as we shall see in the following chapter, also had to go through underground channels.

In addition, the American labor compromise negotiated for the war effort also came into play. Abandoning the right to strike and make wage demands during the wartime, American trade unions had obtained the recognition of their local branches and the maintenance of membership in compensation. This was ensured by direct deduction of workers' union dues from their wages by their employers.[61] Managed by the War Labor Board, this compromise therefore put the unions in direct relationship with the federal government. And the sums levied for the war funds assumed an official and humanitarian character outside of the political mission that the JLC and the European representatives of underground movements would have preferred.[62] Trade union independence certainly did not have the same meaning in the United States as in Europe, which illustrates the limits of the cooperation on this point between the JLC, the AFL, and the CIO. All the European movements, however, from the most radical to the more reformist ones (with the exception of Communists), pragmatically solicited the assistance of the American labor movement.

A type of political division of labor was established. Through the official channels with the Allies, the Labor War Chest of the AFL and the War Relief Committee of the CIO provided subsidies for "labor projects" among the Allies, meaning first of all aid to the labor movement in Great Britain and in the British Empire but also for the benefit of governments in exile that were headquartered there: Poland, Czechoslovakia, Free France. In November 1944, the AFL renewed its appeal to levy a million dollars to help labor movements that were "liberating themselves from Nazi tyranny."[63] Assuming the presidency of the New York section of the Labor War Chest and Relief Committee, Sidney Hillman played a central role in the administration of this AFL/CIO agreement for the distribution of American aid. His position as head of the labor division in the War Production Board of the Roosevelt administration since 1942 gave him a better view of the possibilities of international labor action—and of the regulations of the American administration.[64]

For its part, the JLC continued to take responsibility for and to support "democratic socialist" movements in Europe, meaning the non-Communist underground parties that it was already financing through its own channels. In its annual reports, the JLC noted an increase in the overall sums that it was contributing to underground movements. In 1942, the column "Aid to Underground Labor Movements in Nazi-Occupied Europe" gave the sum of $61,905, to be distinguished from what was devoted to the rescue effort that was still operating that year ("Political refugees," $87,590). The following year, the expenses for "Underground Labor Institutions" rose to $148,308. In 1944, the various expenses for "Underground Labor Institutions," "Rescue," and "Activities against Antisemitism" were combined for a total of $332,295. In January 1945, the JLC's financial statement showed that it had supported underground movements in Europe in their struggle against the Occupier to the tune of $321,210. The JLC was solely responsible for these sums.[65] In 1944, after the liberation of France, Adolph Held summarized the situation and announced: "While the Chest will concentrate its aid chiefly in behalf of the Trade Union movement in Europe, we have directed, and will direct, our aid principally to the Socialist Labor organizations in the liberated lands, which will have to be the motivating force, the soul of the Labor Movement."[66]

THE FREE FRENCH

Although the records do not specify how these sums were divided among the various countries, we may conclude that the French labor and Socialist movement got its share. Responding to an appeal from the Council for the Underground Labor Movement on behalf of the CGT, the CFTC, and the Committee for Socialist Action (CAS), "whose situation requires urgent examination," Paul Vignaux and Ewa Lewinski proposed a budget in conjunction with the ISK that had been confirmed by Félix Gouin, Léon Blum's representative in London.[67] For all of these groups, Vignaux asked CULM for a subsidy of $7,500 per month. In addition, in Gouin's estimation, a special fund of 150,000 francs for the families of arrested and imprisoned militants would be necessary. Vignaux also stressed that a 10 percent increase would be welcome to assist French labor's representation in the United States.[68]

The requests made and thanks expressed to the JLC by the recipients lead us to believe that sums of this order were actually paid. In the spring of 1943 the French Labor Movement had formed a delegation in London to the Free France government. Albert Guigui and Georges Buisson of the CGT were joined there by Marcel Poimboeuf of the CFTC.[69] Pressed by the need for subsidies for their movements in France, they wrote to Sidney

Hillman in the hope of obtaining the means to sustain the resistance of young workers who escaped the forced labor in Germany program (STO). In short, as Hillman understood it: "In such conditions it looks desirable that the help to the French labor movement follows another channel than De Gaulle's services; and that it be clearly made known this is a direct help from the American labor movement to the French labor movement."[70] In other words, the action consisted less of sustaining France Libre as such than of supplying U.S. labor's aid to the French Labor Movement. Albert Guigui was expecting to immediately receive a sum of $3,000 from the JLC.[71] In a letter to Paul Vignaux (June 25, 1943), Guigui confirmed from London the reception of American labor's assistance while seeking to be sure of its provenance:

> Robert speaks of the U.S. Trade Union Fund. Is this the Committee we know under the name of the CIO-AFL Joint Relief Committee and which is led by Sidney Hillman [CIO] and Matthew Woll [AFL]? Let me tell you that this Committee already contributes a share in a subsidy to the French Labor Movement by virtue of a tripartite Franco-Anglo-American agreement concluded here [London] in March upon my arrival. This grant serves on the one hand to strengthen actions against [STO] deportation, and on the other to permit the CGT and the CFTC to develop their organizations. Said Committee has recently asked us to have the CGT warrant this contribution. Buisson and I immediately provided it. But I wonder if in Robert's mind it is a matter of the CIO-AFL Committee. Of course, if this Committee wanted to give a more direct labor aid above and beyond the tripartite grant, our friends in France would welcome it heartily. But we will not ask you to take the initiative of an approach in this direction.[72]

In response to this letter, Vignaux confirmed the following:

> With respect to financial aid, I am always in contact with Sidney Hillman, co-director with Woll of the New York Labor War Chest. As a member of a Council for the Underground Labor Movement, and member of its executive board, I have contact with the AFL and the CIO at the national level.

In accord with your letter, I continue to keep contact without formulating new demands.[73]

This exchange of communications reveals the reality of the transmission of funds of labor origin—from the AFL and the CIO—from the United States to London, where they were divided among the organizations concerned in France. But it also indicates the lack of transparency of the origins of these funds with regard to the interested parties. Behind the Labor War Chest (of New York State and the national one), otherwise referred to as the "AFL and CIO Joint Relief Committee," CULM operated. In this interlocking of facades and organizations, the JLC continued to provide money to feed the French labor and Socialist movement as it had done since the agreement with Henry Hauck in 1941. Thus Georg Stolz, IFTU assistant to Schevenels, informed CULM that upon his arrival in London (in 1943), Félix Gouin had confirmed that the money sent by the JLC to the French Socialists had contributed to revitalizing the party at its most crucial moment. After the Liberation, Albert Guigui, who in 1944 had become a member of CULM, reiterated from London his thanks to the JLC for the solidarity manifested to the underground movement and for its support in the darkest hours, "more important support than he realized at the time." And Daniel Mayer thanked the JLC on behalf of the SFIO, of which he had become secretary-general, and was happy—"now that communication was open"—to be able to establish official relations. Some years later, when Mayer was invited to the first convention held by the JLC after the war (February 1947), in his speech he once again thanked the JLC for "its magnificent contribution to the Resistance movement to liberate France. [Its leaders] fought splendidly in our underground, thus contributing their acquired skill in the fight against tyranny and terror in czarist Russia, Poland, and other countries of Europe."[74]

But what Guigui did not clarify in his exchange with Paul Vignaux was the nature of the "tripartite" agreement he had obtained in London. Which three parties were involved? Did he mean the AFL/CIO Joint Committee on the American side, and the CGT/CFTC delegation and the Socialist Party on the French side? But which was the British party? Or was it a relationship among the secret services of the three Allies to implement a "Franco-Anglo-American" agreement: the Office of Strategic Services in Washington, the British Special Operations Executive in London, and Free France's Bureau Central de Renseignement et d'Action (BCRA) also in London? In any case, the seal of secrecy was indispensable, as Guigui and Buisson requested:

> AFL and CIO must not under any circumstances publicize this gift, for this would endanger the security of the trade unionists in France. It would be very easy for the Nazis to arrest several thousand unionists merely on suspicion. If the CIO or the AFL want to claim any public credit, they should not say that they have helped trade unions, which would be easy to identify, but merely say they have given assistance to resistance movements. Please let us know by cable when the funds may be obtained.[75]

THE OSS BEHIND THE SCENES

Compared to the enormous sums required by the French Resistance and the thorny question of financing its diverse currents, these contributions may appear vastly insufficient. Their particular origin, though, distinguishes them from the general financing of the Resistance by France Libre. These sums came from American working-class communities gathered under the aegis of the JLC on the one hand, and the AFL and CIO on the other, according to the project elaborated by CULM, thereby responding to requests formulated by representatives of labor movements in resistance. But still, the manner of their transmission, and hence their independence from American political power, according to the fundamental principle enunciated by Paul Vignaux, should be clarified. The U.S. secret services were not strangers to this kind of transaction.

Since 1942, once committed to the war, the United States developed information agencies, which had remained embryonic until then. The Office of Strategic Services (OSS), founded in June 1942, assembled these services under the direction of William Donovan. The agencies based in

Washington, New York, London, Berne, and Algiers cooperated in collecting information on France.[76] Roosevelt had set three objectives for the OSS: intelligence for military operations underway, psychological warfare against the enemy, and help for the Resistance in occupied countries. To do this, a dozen special services were set up. Among them, the Labor Desk, directed by Arthur Goldberg, was tasked with surveillance of labor organizations in occupied countries and eventually sustaining their underground operations.[77] In addition, Donovan created a vast service for the observation and mobilization of foreigners and refugees who were located in the United States. This "Foreign Nationalities Branch" collected the most recent and pertinent information on civil society and on the resistance movements that were developing in these émigrés' countries of origin. Thousands of pages and documents were gathered in this way, with reports and analyses coming from communities of foreigners—and especially figures of some notoriety.[78] Thus most of the members of CULM were solicited for their linguistic, political, and social knowledge and for their proximity to the resistance movements. This was the case with Paul Vignaux, as we shall see, but also of Paul Hagen and the group he had created, American Friends of German Freedom. Omer Bécu, representative of the International Transportworkers' Federation (ITF), was particularly active with the OSS, as was Vanni Montana in relations with the Italian-American Labor Council organized by Luigi Antonini, and no doubt Haakon Lie for Norway.[79] The Jewish Labor Committee itself supplied the OSS with reports on the situation in France, Luxembourg, and Poland that newly exfiltrated militants had provided to it in May 1942.[80] Numerous French émigrés supplied information to the Foreign Nationalities Branch, offering diverse perspectives on both Free and Occupied France. Paul Vignaux and Joseph Botton were the most active: they furnished reports on the labor movement and its relationship with the Resistance both inside France and with France Libre. In fact this relationship is particularly well documented in their reports based on publications coming from the southern zone. Thus, the information that Vignaux and Botton possessed, including underground publications like *Combat*, *Franc-Tireur*, and *Libération*, that had been obtained by Ewa Lewinski-Pfister, and which she simultaneously transmitted to the JLC, were analyzed and placed at the disposal of OSS authorities.[81]

Moreover, the OSS obtained information from its own agents on the ground, especially in London, where it had established a branch that maintained good relations with the secret services of France Libre directed by Colonel Passy.[82] It was this rapprochement between London and New York that enabled CULM to overcome the legalism of the AFL and the CIO on the issue of using the Labor War Chest for purposes other than humanitarian aid. The tripartite Franco-Anglo-American agreement mentioned by Albert Guigui in the spring of 1943 resulted from the intervention of secret services on all sides. In fact, a telegram from Omer Bécu to Jacobus Oldenbroek, secretary-general of the International Transportworkers' Federation now based in London and sent by the OSS from New York, affirmed that Matthew Woll (after some hesitation) and Sidney Hillman had agreed that the "Joint Relief Committee" of the AFL and CIO would furnish financial assistance to the ITF in the amount of $25,000. Later aid would follow, he said, as a function of the information received.[83] In the London branch of the Labor Desk, George Pratt established close contacts with representatives of the international labor movement who were located there, including Georg Stolz, IFTU secretary-general, and Omer Bécu (who crossed the Atlantic several times) and Jacobus Oldenbroek, both of the ITF. Willi Eichler of the ISK, plus Albert Guigui and George Buisson of the CGT, also collaborated on collecting information and supporting resistance operations.[84] Correspondence between Arthur Goldberg in New York, Gerhard Van Arkel of the U.S. consulate in Algiers, and George Pratt in London revealed in effect that Albert Guigui and Georges Buisson had offered information to the U.S. secret services in exchange for their subsidy:

> You will note from the enclosure that Guigui and Buisson, on behalf of the C.G.T., propose to place at our disposal for intelligence purposes and other operations the network of the C.G.T. throughout France. You will recall that for some time we have been partially financing the program of the C.G.T. to resist the conscription of French labor by and for the Germans. At the

present time our subsidy for this purpose is $25,000 monthly. The proposal of the C.G.T. represents the quid pro quo for this subvention.[85]

In a previous letter, Goldberg had noted that the "Joint Committee CIO-AFL" might take over from the OSS in this financing, since this committee also contributed financially to the Swiss office of the OSS for the French Labor Movement.[86] In fact it was the AFL/CIO funds solicited by Guigui that were already subsidizing the ITF. But Guigui's plan ran up against a number of difficulties. The first one, noted by Goldberg, was about communicating to the Americans information coming from France when the British services were reserving their primacy in this. The second obstacle resided in De Gaulle's conception of the financing of the French resistance. American subsidies risked breaking the independence and unity that he was trying to construct with the help of Jean Moulin[87] among the several movements engaged in the Resistance, which would lead to the creation of the Conseil National de la Résistance (CNR) in May 1943. Nevertheless, the CGT indeed obtained "from American unions," as was sometimes acknowledged, significant financial support from March 1943 to July 1944.[88] Thus for BCRA executives in London and for General de Gaulle, the financing of the CGT was dissociated from that of the organized movements that composed the Resistance. The principal objective of the tripartite agreement for France Libre was for French workers to avoid the STO, while strengthening the opposition to the Charte du Travail imposed by Vichy on businesses and administrations. The financing of the paramilitary operations that were going to compose the CNR apparently derived from another rationale. At least this is what is revealed in the "Swiss affair" over the financing of the Combat network.

The Swiss Affair and Agent 328

Since it was close to the internal French resistance, the OSS branch in Berne, Switzerland, was particularly effective. Directed by Allen Dulles, this agency was situated at the heart of enemy nations and served as a site of convergence for the intelligence directed to Washington, while also circulating it to London, Algiers, and Caserte (its base in Italy) as needed. In Berne, Dulles was surrounded by professional agents and spies but also by people recruited among the refugees and the local civilian population. Having quickly managed to establish a link between Geneva and Lyon, he worked toward the financial support of resistance networks in this region.[89]

The episode of his contact with Henri Frenay, head of the Combat movement, is well known to historians of the Resistance.[90] Offering to generously finance his movement—in exchange for military intelligence on German positions—Dulles began sending Frenay substantial amounts of money starting in January 1943. This gesture provoked the anger of both General de Gaulle and Jean Moulin, his representative in France, who interpreted it as a "stab in the back" when they became aware of it in the spring of 1943.[91] Beyond the acute material need, increased by the influx of young men who were defying the STO by joining *maquis*, the issue of gathering fighting France around De Gaulle required fidelity to a single commander and a single source of finance. Fearing that networks would become autonomous from the authority in London, Jean Moulin was radically opposed to this American interference in domestic affairs, all the more so because De Gaulle, in difficulty in Algiers, where the Americans were playing the Giraud card, had good reasons to distrust American aims. The exchange between Dulles and Frenay was perceived, moreover, as a violation of the prior agreement of the OSS with the British secret services guaranteeing them priority in the intelligence coming from France. Reacting to the crisis provoked by this "Swiss affair," the BCRA in London called a halt to the financing from Switzerland. This interdiction put an end to the payments from Dulles to Frenay.[92] But it wasn't an obstacle for more modest funds that were independent of the American government, those coming from the JLC and "AFL/CIO Joint Relief," which flowed directly to the CAS and the French Labor Movement.

Among Dulles's informants in Berne was "Agent 328." This person was none other than René Bertholet, the famous "R" mentioned in Ewa Lewinski's and Albert Guigui's letters. Sometimes called "Pierre" or "René" or "Robert," he was a Swiss citizen who had been active before the war in labor and socialist circles in France and Germany, close notably to ITF leaders.

A militant of the ISK like Ewa Lewinski, he was, along with her, the key contact between the New York labor world and the networks of the French Labor Movement. According to the official historian of the British Secret Services, Michael Foot, Bertholet, also recruited for British intelligence, was "one of the best and most precocious agents of the clandestine communications section."[93] Judging from the thousands of messages cabled from Berne that have been decoded by Neal Petersen, Agent 328 managed to maintain through the entire war a fundamental connection with "Eva" in the United States. By this channel, a considerable number of messages were exchanged, and significant sums of money of labor origin were paid in several deliveries destined for the *maquis* and for underground labor elements in France, as well as for aid to refugees in Switzerland.[94] In November 1942, Dulles informed Washington of his relations with Agent 328.

> Today I had a long conversation with 328. This confirmed his usefulness for contact with French syndicalist and other labor organizations, provided that his contact can be maintained despite the present border patrol. He stresses the fact that the French labor organizations are reluctant to receive funds except from other labor organizations. Suggest that you consider the possibility that contributions be made by American labor organizations. Provided that complete discretion as regards method of transmission can be observed, we could pass on these funds through 328. I believe that this would have a helpful psychological effect. Meanwhile we will help to modest extent which they are willing to receive from us.[95]

In other words, Dulles recognized the soundness of the payments made by the American labor movement to the underground labor movement in France. He proposed that the OSS in Berne serve as a conduit for the transmission of these funds and the money be remitted to recipients by "328," who could cross the border. The Berne agency took charge of converting the currency from dollars to francs. Accordingly, several exchanges of mail and dispatches of funds were recorded. For example, on August 16, 1943, Agent 328 thanked "Eva" for the 50,000 (francs) sent for the Socialists, the CGT, and the Christian trade unionists. He reported the progress of the Socialist

Party, the wide distribution of *Le Populaire* in France, the gratitude of comrades for these dispatches, and the growing support for General de Gaulle. He also warned his interlocutors about the American attitude (at least in Washington) of hostility to the Comité de Libération Nationale, which was incomprehensible to the resistants who might become receptive to Soviet overtures.[96] In a telegram of August 19, 1943, "328" informed Eva of the fate of several persons with names of Germanic (Jewish?) origin.[97] Over the ensuing months, as the dispatched funds became both more frequent and more generous—despite the problems of security for the OSS—Dulles maintained that it was important to continue to support Agent 328 in his transactions, especially since the latter did not want to be remunerated by the OSS. At the most he accepted an advance on these funds to pay for his frequent travel expenses.[98] At a certain point, Dulles reported the activity of Agent 328 in Germany in light of a democratic renaissance of the labor movement there: "328" had asked "Eva" if part of the sums in the American dispatches could be used for this purpose. His wife of German origin, "as capable as our Eva in New York," Dulles commented, was part of the network. In June 1944, it was the "Joint Relief Fund" of the AFL/CIO that transmitted the money through the OSS in Berne: $200,000 was sent to support the underground movements and the victims of Nazi persecution in Holland, Belgium, and Luxembourg.[99]

As a partial conclusion we may say that a real network of international labor solidarity functioned effectively during the war. The example of the French case presented here testifies to the contribution of this network to the survival of the French Labor Movement and the Socialist Party when they were underground. The core of this success was composed of persons and organizations of different origins. Put into operation in New York by Paul Vignaux of the Committee for the French Labor Movement and by the Jewish Labor Committee, it was the fruit of the—initially improbable—cooperation between Christian and Jewish trade unionists, French exiles, and Americans, using both the resources of exo-politics of some and the fervor for political solidarity of others. This alliance knew how to utilize channels for transmitting communication and for dispatching funds. It used the links with France Libre in London in the framework of cooperation among the Allied forces, on the one hand, and the underground channels of contact with resistants, on the other. Ewa Lewinski in New York and René Bertholet across the Franco-Swiss border—both members of the ISK, a tiny party on the left of the German SPD—were the key dispatchers of information received from underground sources. From Lewinski and Vignaux, the JLC obtained information on the state of the union movement and on resistance activity in the southern zone; reciprocally via Vignaux, the JLC offered the French Labor Movement and the CAS access to American labor organizations and to resources provided by the AFL and the CIO. In spite of their historic, cultural, social, and political differences, the network they maintained worked toward the rapprochement of the CFTC, the CGT, and the French Socialist Party and for their recognition by the government of France Libre. Moreover, the logistical support procured for them by the American labor movement, through the OSS channel for the underground transmission of messages and funds, did not change the objectives of this international cooperation, nor did it change its labor-oriented methods, which remained independent of the State Department. This complex but determined coalition worked to attain the victory of civilian forces over the Nazi occupier in Europe. "It was merely a dream, two years ago, that the American labor movement should become vitally interested in the labor movement in Europe and come to its aid in the struggle. Now, however, the dream has become a genuine reality," Adolph Held stated proudly at the end of 1944.[100]

At the same time that the JLC was supporting the French Labor Movement in resistance, it was also supporting the Jewish resistance—or actually the survival of Jews (particularly Bundists) in France as well as in Poland. These simultaneous activities, especially from 1943 onward, demonstrate that the JLC's political orientation did not exclude either humanitarian gestures or support for armed resistance. All the more so as from New York the JLC leaders, working to support their comrades in France and in the Warsaw Ghetto, had understood what arrests, roundups, and deportations really meant.

SAVING THE CERCLE AMICAL-ARBETER RING

The JLC had not established a "French list" of official figures in the labor movement in 1940, as it had done for the Germans, Italians, Russians, and Bundists of Poland. But it was particularly worried about the Jewish milieu of Bundist orientation in Paris who were ideologically close to it. In August 1942, Isaiah Minkoff recapitulated several lists of names for whom visas had been requested between November 1941 and April 1942. In a last hope against rigorous American regulations, and especially against the quasi-impossibility for these persons to leave France, Minkoff tried again to obtain American asylum for some of them. In general, it was too late because Jewish families had already gone underground and could not escape.[101]

In contact with members of the Cercle Amical situated at the Rue Vieille du Temple in the traditionally Jewish neighborhood of Paris, the JLC received direct information about the acts of violence by the Nazi occupiers and the Vichy regime against the Jews of France. Founded before the war by immigrants from Poland, the Cercle Amical-Arbeter Ring was a center for mutual aid, comparable to the U.S. Workmen's Circle, a pillar of the JLC.[102] During the Occupation, its members (workers, artisans, and shopkeepers of eastern Paris) were struggling for their own survival and that of the Jewish community. They were part of the Rue Amelot network of Jewish resistance, formed in July 1940 by the gathering of several political and cultural associations representing Jewish immigrant milieux, Zionist or not, but all non-Communist: the Bund, the left wing of the Poale Zion, the Fédération des Sociétés Juives de France, the Yiddisch Vinkl (debate circle), and the Colonie Scolaire (working with children). Throughout the war, the Amelot Committee functioned illegally, procuring false documents and providing hiding places, financial help, and support of all kinds to the hunted Jewish population. Notably it organized the placement of children outside their families and outside Paris. During the darkest years, the incessant checks, humiliations, arrests, and especially the increasingly massive roundups, culminating in the Rafle du Vel d'Hiv in July 1942,[103] forced many members of the Arbeter Ring to disperse across the southern zone. In June 1943, David Rapoport, head of the Amelot network, was arrested and deported; from that point on the work of the committee fell to L'Union Générale des Juifs de France (UGIF), which, although created at the request of the occupying forces, managed to maintain some of its clandestine activities.[104]

An account published after the war by one of the Paris Bundist leaders, Fajwel Schrager—who later became the JLC's correspondent in France[105]— describes the activism of these refugees who were fighting for their survival. In addition, Jacob Pat's letters from New York to his correspondents in Switzerland—Boris Tschlenoff, head of the OSE (Oeuvre de Secours aux Enfants) and delegate to the International Red Cross, and professor Liebman Hersch of the University of Geneva, both close to or members of the Bund—testify to the help given by the JLC in this struggle. Therefore from New York via Switzerland, allowances and relief reached these Jews in hiding, contributing to their rescue—and survival.

Fajwel Schrager

Schrager—whose real name was Fajwel Ostrynski—was a veteran of struggle. Born in Krynki in the province of Grdno on the edge of eastern Poland, he had come to France as a student at Grenoble at the end of the 1920s.[106] After having been active in a branch of the Communist Party's MOI (Main-d'oeuvre immigrée), he moved closer to socialist circles and became secretary of the Bund Committee in Paris in 1938. Enlisting voluntarily in the French army in the "phony war," he was taken as a prisoner to Germany, then escaped and came back to France, to Agen and Toulouse in the southwest. He did not manage to reach Marseille in time to obtain the visa for the United States that the JLC had secured for him.[107] Then he went to Lyon, where he barely escaped the Gestapo roundups that included several members of the local committee of the Bund, which was recomposed as part of the coordinating committee of several Jewish organizations.[108] In 1943, Schrager was involved with his companions in a unitary movement in alliance with Communists to form the General Committee for the Defense of the Jews (CGD). During these years, he led the dangerous life of a Jewish resistant, doubly exposed to torture and to deportation. Moving with his wife and child to Grenoble in the Italian zone of occupation, he found several Bundist comrades, including Jules Jacoubovitch, initiator of the Amelot Committee, Alexandre and Rachel Minc, Dinah Baruch, and others with whom he participated in creating a resistance network that succeeded in smuggling children to Switzerland and in publishing (when they could) the Bundist organ *Unzer Stimme* (Our Voice).[109]

The telegrams exchanged between New York and Switzerland reveal that the JLC furnished material aid to several "families" or "groups" of refugees. Escaping the clutches of the Gestapo that was hunting them, the Frenkel (Nathan Frenkel) and Ryba (Rafal and Dinah Ryba) families arrived in Switzerland in January 1943 and there took charge of their friends in France who needed immediate help. Thus "R" (René Bertholet, Agent 328), whom they mentioned, was simultaneously a bearer of messages and money for certain refugees who found themselves in Switzerland, bridgeheads for those who were still hidden in France, and for the Labor Movement and the CAS, as we saw previously. The JLC sent $3,000 in February, then $12,900 in April. Meanwhile it dispatched $10,000 to the International Red Cross in Geneva to help refugees, requesting that this sum also cover medical expenses and job retraining in various professions. The news was rarely positive: "Peskin, Stark, Dobin, Honikman [Honigman] Madame Jelin and Dr. Bonsheskyan and son have been deported. Their families in France now in great danger." On April 9, "the equivalent of 5,000 dollars from Uncle Pat [Jacob Pat]" was transmitted to Ryba and Nathan Frenkel—also destined for Ojzer Szwarc in Geneva and the family of Joseph Friedman.[110] In September 1943, a dozen "families" were present in Switzerland, including the protégés of the left-wing Zionist Marc Jarblum, to whom funds were sent.[111] Among them was the Leo Puder group, assisted by both the JLC and the International Rescue and Relief Committee, of which René Bertholet was the correspondent in Switzerland. After the collapse of the Italian occupation in the summer of 1943, and therefore, the German takeover of the region, refugees from the Nice borderland started reaching the Swiss border. In January 1944, a telegram from one of the Bundist representatives in the Polish government in exile in London, Emanuel Scherer, also asked for regular monthly aid and an immediate large sum for some 120 refugees who were in Switzerland, while the whole political "family" was in great danger back in

France.[112] Initially hesitant, the Swiss government ended up accepting the presence of more Jewish refugees on its soil—provided they were financed from abroad.[113] The rescue of children also assumed greater scope. It was largely directed by the OSE, but according to Liebman Hersch, much more could be done if funds were available. Rachel Minc, Bertha Mering, and Cirl Steingart of the Arbeter Ring and the Colonie Scolaire took part in this effort to smuggle children into Switzerland. Rachel Minc noted that "American Judaism" was providing the funds needed to pay for the travel and housing of these refugees. In the forefront of these Jewish American organizations was the American Jewish Joint Distribution Committee (the Joint), which supported the OSE but also (in proportion to its means) the JLC. In June 1945, Liebman Hersch summarized in a telegram to the JLC that it had supplied aid to 131 refugees of the "Medem group" (Bundists of France), of whom 80 women and children were still in Switzerland, and contributed to aiding 123 refugees of the Puder group. "Thank cordially assistance which permitted rescue several hundred friends," Hersch wrote.[114]

Boris Tschlenoff and Liebman Hersch

From Switzerland, Boris Tschlenoff and Liebman Hersch organized the circulation of money that was becoming more substantial and more regular. If René Bertholet sometimes served as liaison for Jewish refugees, the majority of the transactions for this purpose were dissociated from the payment he transmitted (via the OSS) for the labor movement in France. The need to find another correspondent in Switzerland became imperative after the American landing in North Africa (November 1942), which, as a reprisal, had unleashed the occupation of the southern zone by the Germans and hence the abandonment of U.S. diplomatic relations with Vichy. As a result, France fell under the Trading with the Enemy Act by which the State Department banned any financial transaction with enemy nations. Consequently, American rescue or relief organizations had to resort to various strategies. Thus, the Joint, installed since the start of the war in Lisbon, found itself unable to send funds to France and had to function with the help of an intermediary in Switzerland, Saly Mayer, beginning in 1943. The legality of the activity depended not only on the place of the operation but also on the nationality of the operator. The same action could be legal if it was done by a Swiss national and illegal if it involved an American.[115] Swiss citizen Boris Tschlenoff and Liebman Hersch, who was a Polish citizen but lived in Switzerland, became the financial correspondents for the JLC who carried out bank transactions. Moreover, thanks to the cooperation of certain Socialist customs officials, Hersch succeeded in bringing to Fajwel Schrager and to Alexandre Minc near the border post in France the funds provided by the JLC, which could thereby be used to help refugee comrades on both sides of the border.[116]

Hersch and Tschlenoff were more than financial correspondents for the JLC. As the representative of the OSE for the Swiss Red Cross, Dr. Tschlenoff was situated at the center of the network of international relief organizations, closely cooperating with the Joint. Originally a Russian, born in Ukraine in 1864, he had been strongly influenced by the Bund in his youth, which became the reason behind his lifetime commitments. He believed that only the Jewish socialist intelligentsia could bring "enlightenment, self-management, awareness and a sense of organization" to the Jewish population of the Russian Empire. Already active in the effort to protect refugees after the 1917 October Revolution, during the Nazi era, his life became entirely devoted to the relief and rescue of victims of the regime.[117]

Liebman Hersch was also a Bundist and an eminent specialist in the history of the Jewish people. His involvement in the rescue of Jewish comrades from labor and Bundist milieux had deep political and philosophical, as well as humanitarian, origins. From his youth in Russia Hersch had been close to the original Bundist leaders, Vladimir Medem, Raphael Abramovitch, and Henrik Erlich, and was part of the Foreign Committee of the Bund. Born in Lithuania in 1882, he had studied mathematics in Warsaw, then statistics at the University of Geneva where in 1913 he defended a thesis titled "The Wandering Jew of Today." During the 1920s and 1930s, continuing to observe Jewish migratory movements, Hersch was an anti-Zionist, opposed to the idea of a Jewish state in Palestine, affirming on the contrary the vitality of the Jewish national identity in the Diaspora.[118] But the cruelty of the Nazis, which launched the Jewish people on a new and tragic wandering, incited Hersch to defend the persons and groups he could help save. A member of a network of Bundist activists, he transmitted to the JLC the information he received on the Jewish population in Poland: the forced displacements, the formation of ghettos, and the liquidations by mass shooting or in the death camps. It became a duty incumbent on Bundists who could act to rescue their brothers, to protect them with forged identities, to establish contacts of solidarity, to train them in armed resistance when that was possible—all things that Liebman Hersch was engaged in for the sake of the Jews of France, Poland, and Hungary.[119] In January 1946, in the columns of *Voice of the Unconquered*, the JLC expressed its gratitude to Professor Hersch by publicly revealing his role during the years of the Nazi occupation as the person who transmitted the JLC's financial aid to persecuted Jews—and to the clandestine labor movement engaged in mortal combat with the enemy.[120]

RECONSTRUCTING JEWISH LIFE

At the end of August 1944, Fajwel Schrager participated in the liberation of the region of Lyon with other members of the General Defense Committee for the Jews. This was victory! But it was a "bitter victory" when, month after month, all illusions about seeing the return of those deported vanished: "Each one of us was absorbed by the catastrophe that had overcome us. We did not yet know the whole horror of the extermination camps." But Jewish life had to be reconstructed. Returning to the French capital, Schrager discovered "the deserted streets of the Pletzl of Paris. One would have believed a natural cataclysm had taken place. Everything appeared annihilated."[121] The comrades who gathered—Hill Najman, Doctor Oguse, Rafal and Dinah Ryba, and others—took an inventory of needs, establishing lists of those who had come back and those who were still missing. They started the services of the Arbeter Ring again, especially its canteen at 110 Rue Vieille du Temple. They informed the JLC in New York of the physical and moral exhaustion of the survivors, the lack of food, and the difficulty of restoring the right of foreign Jews to return to their former lodgings.[122]

In the first months of the Liberation, the JLC sent hundreds of packages of food and clothing to political friends whose names it had been given. This meant not only members of the Arbeter Ring but also Socialists and labor unionists whose movements were known. Georg Stolz of the IFTU provided the names of comrades in the labor movement who had been active in the Resistance; Paul Vignaux did the same before leaving the United States in October 1945.[123]

More fundamentally, in a move that oriented its objectives in a more humanitarian way, in a plenary session in December 1944 the JLC launched a solemn appeal to raise a million dollars to help the survivors of the tragedy that had befallen the Jewish people. It intended to make the cultural and secular reconstruction of Jewish life the goal of its future program: "We call upon the Jewish workers of the United States to fulfill their historic obligation, placed upon them by the tragic fate of European Jewry." Engaged simultaneously in work to rescue the Jewish survivors in Poland, but also in Hungary and Romania and in the refugee camps in Sweden, the JLC developed programs for the reconstruction of Jewish life in France, the first country to be liberated.[124]

The surviving Jewish population of France, some 220,000 to 240,000 persons, broken by the annihilation of more than 75,500 deportees and weakened by suffering and spoliation, was nevertheless the largest in Europe, thus offering the hope of re-creating significant communities. Moreover, after the liberation of the camps, from which so few came back, and then after the end of the fighting with the evacuation of the refugee camps, France would become a country of immigration or transit to Palestine or the New World.[125] Several American organizations, with the Joint at the forefront, contributed to the recovery of the Jewish institutions of France and of their communities.[126]

In the spring of 1945, the JLC sent one of its leaders, Nathan Chanin, director of the Workmen's Circle and the JLC's administrative chairman, to France to assess the overall needs and to determine what the JLC could offer. He stayed there from May to September 1945 and also went to Belgium and Switzerland where he settled accounts with Liebman Hersch. His missions were various: the first was to obtain information on the fate of families or persons being sought. The news he obtained was transmitted each day to the *Jewish Daily Forward* to respond to requests from Jewish Americans searching for their relatives. For example, this telegram from July 5, 1945, with the uncertain spelling of names:

TELL DAVID DUBINSKY THAT COUSIN S WEISSBERG SON OF IDA SCHEIN-WALD LODZ 29 SIENKIEVICZ STREET ARRIVED IN PARIS. EVERYBODY EXCEPT HIM IS LOST STOP TELL WEINRICH KARMANOVITCH NAFTOLY WEINIK DIED IN CONCENTRATION CAMP ESTONIE STOP DOCTOR PER-ELSTEIN FROM KOVNO AND DAVID KAPLAN DIED IN CONCENTRATION CAMP STOP MRS SHABAD WAS IN VILNO GHETTO UNTIL THE LAST MOMENT BUT NOBODY KNOWS WHERE SHE WAS SENT.[127]

After contacting various Jewish organizations and associations linked to the labor movement in France and Belgium, Chanin recommended that they receive subsidies totaling $125,000 for 1945, a sum the JLC ratified and began to transfer. Thus several institutions were immediately supported: the Representative Council of the Jews of France (Conseil Representatif des Juifs de France), the Jewish Interunion Committee (Comité Intersyndical Juif of the CGT), the Federation of Artisans of the Rue Vieille du Temple, the Jewish Cultural Verband, the Organization of Jewish Artists, and that of Jewish actors, the Union of Socialist Foreigners (particularly German and Austrian refugees), the Union of Jewish Students of Grenoble, the Socialist Party (SFIO), the Belgian Socialist Party, the Federation of Polish Jews, the Arbeter Ring, and the leftist Zionists. The Colonie Scolaire, to which the JLC allocated 500,000 francs, received the most support.[128]

Helping children was the most urgent task. At the Liberation, the directors of the Oeuvre de Secours aux Enfants (OSE) informed the JLC: "Children in France hit most catastrophically. Need instant relief and rehabilitation. Besides the adults, there are about 10,000 children who must receive assistance." It was estimated that "about 2,050 of them fell into the category of so-called abandoned children who had either lost their parents or who probably will never see them again"—a figure much lower than the actual one. Others had been placed in institutions or in foster families that had to be remunerated. Even the families that were still intact could not provide enough food for their children. A certain number of French Jews received government aid, like the families living in regions that had been bombed. But foreigners—who constituted 60 percent of France's Jewish population—did not have the right to this welfare.[129] Receiving 70 percent of its funds from the Joint, the OSE was able to create twenty-five children's homes, thus becoming one of the most significant children's organizations in the country, but not the only one. In conjunction with the OSE through a division of tasks, the JLC took responsibility for part of this reconstruction work, thereby reflecting Bundist values among the various associations that financed these institutions.[130]

A major part of the JLC's effort in France after the war was designed to finance children's homes for orphans managed by the Arbeter Ring. This funding began in 1945 and continued until the last one closed in the 1950s. The first of these homes, Les Buissons in Le Mans, was inaugurated in May 1945 in the presence of Nathan Chanin. It was later transferred to Maisons Laffitte, where the JLC bought two houses and created the Morris Sigman and S. Mendelsohn homes. With the purchase and management of the Vladeck children's sanatorium in Brunoy, the Arbeter Ring was responsible for three homes that were supported in full by the JLC. And it contributed to financing four other centers: Ika in Corvol l'Orgueilleux in the Nièvre, Ringelblum in the Oise, Aronson in the Eure, and the Colonie Scolaire in Paris. It also partly financed the purchase of several properties for the latter organization near Paris. Moreover, we know that the JLC also helped finance homes in Belgium, Italy, and Poland.[131]

The Arbeter Ring decided to reconstruct among the children their link to secular Yiddish culture. The Vladeck children's sanatorium in particular symbolized this heritage. Named after Baruch Charney Vladeck, the JLC's founder, it recalled the model of the Medem Sanatorium near Warsaw that was destroyed by the Nazis, who exterminated all the children and staff. Supervised by a doctor, nurses, and a teacher assigned by the Education Ministry, it was designed for children who needed medical care, those suffering from malnutrition, tuberculosis, or the trauma of deportation. Survivors of family tragedies were first in line to receive a spot in this home, followed by

Polish children arriving in France or those coming from Displaced Persons camps. They were taught traditional Yiddish songs and songs of the ghetto. In all homes sponsored by the Arbeter Ring, most of the children were Jewish and came from socialist families, but not exclusively, since there were also orphans who were the children of political war victims and a few Spanish Catholics. The homes managed by Left Poale Zion members, Aronson in Les Andelys and Ringelblum (named after Emanuel Ringelblum) in La Verberie, to which the JLC also contributed, stressed Jewish and Zionist identity and added Hebrew to the teaching of Yiddish and French. Some of these children were promised emigration to Palestine. In these centers, education was deliberately secular and progressive. The children attending the local schools were thus anchored in French civic culture. Their adaptation was facilitated by the creative methods that relied on the modern pedagogy developed in Central Europe. Ernst Papanek was a proponent of this approach; he had directed homes for Socialist refugees before the war with methods developed in the young Austrian republic. Serge and Rachel Pludermacher, who came from the Bundist ranks of Vilna, based the education of children at Les Buissons on music, theater, and the visual arts. Many of the staff had been active in the Resistance during the war. Among them was Bertha Mering, who had saved the lives of some children by smuggling them into Switzerland.[132]

The autonomous financing of these homes relied on a system of sponsorship by individuals or institutions belonging to the JLC. To support the large budgets required by these operations, the JLC called upon its membership of American workers, suggesting that they symbolically adopt a child to cover the cost of his or her education. These sponsorships might be taken on individually or collectively by union branches or sections of the Workmen's Circle. In 1949, a thousand children had already been "adopted by American workers."[133] These sponsorships (about $300 per year per child) covered most of the children's expenses while they lived at the homes. For example, in 1951 the JLC financed the "adoption" of 570 children, of which 312 were adopted by ILGWU locals, 10 by various unions, 94 by sections of the Workmen's Circle, 78 by mutual aid societies of common origin (*landsmanschaftn*), 36 by workshops, and 40 by individuals. It is interesting to note that in the 1940s, the unions' memberships were no longer mostly Jewish but as often were made up of people of Italian or Puerto Rican descent, or were African American. The network of solidarity on which the work of the Arbeter Ring relied emanated from the transatlantic Jewish Diaspora, of course, but it was also multicultural and multireligious.[134]

In order to solidify the relationship between the Arbeter Ring in Paris and the JLC in New York, Nathan Chanin appointed Fajwel Schrager as the JLC representative in France. His role was to strengthen the links between the communities on both sides of the ocean. Seeking to raise funds for the children's homes, Schrager made several trips to the United States in 1946 and 1948, where he toured working-class communities to raise funds and promote the sponsorship system. He closely collaborated with ILGWU president David Dubinsky, whose Local 25 helped finance the Morris Sigman House in Maisons Laffitte. He also met several Bundist leaders, including Shlomo Mendelsohn. In February 1947, Schrager participated in the first postwar JLC convention, accompanying the guest of honor, Daniel Mayer, whose speech he translated into Yiddish.[135]

The JLC's assistance to the French Resistance during the war corresponds to its double identity, both Socialist and Jewish. It supported the labor and socialist movement in the struggle against the German Occupation and the Vichy regime, and helped the Jewish population in its fight for survival and against the German occupying forces. The juxtaposition of these two goals in this chapter reveals that compared to their gradual encounter with the French labor and socialist movement, the JLC leaders' knowledge about the Jews of France developed relatively slowly, and only when their networks of information had acquired enough independence to grasp the situation in France of those tracked by the Gestapo for political and/or "racial" reasons. More precisely, there appears to have been a turning point in the JLC's agenda. Up to 1942, its actions were essentially political (rescues, the start of its aid to the Resistance). But from that year on, the Jewish tragedy turned the JLC's mission in a more humanitarian direction. Belated and insufficient aid, certainly—limited by the administrative closure of immigration to the United States and Palestine, and then by the wartime situation—but oriented toward the future in the goal of reconstructing Jewish life. Now the JLC defined the range of help it could provide according to the political choices it had previously made. It targeted the institutions or associations that were close to it on an ideological level with which it came into contact: the Socialist Party, the CGT-CFTC labor movement, and in Paris the Jewish socialists (Bundists or left-wing Zionists) whom it helped when they had gone underground and then openly after the Liberation.

CODA: LÉON BLUM: "HERE I FEEL AT HOME"

On December 31, 1949, Léon Blum was invited to visit the Vladeck home, the sanatorium for children of the Arbeter Ring at Brunoy. The photos of the event show the grandfatherly figure of Blum surrounded by Jewish children who had survived abandonment and their parents' death, educated in France within a Jewish and socialist culture—in a home financed from New York by the Jewish Labor Committee. As a high point, shortly before his death, the meeting between Blum and these children in this place symbolized the "privileged ties" extending from one side of the Atlantic to the other that had been woven between the JLC and French socialism, here in the person of its eminent leader.

These ties had been strengthened since the war years. In the spring of 1946, Léon Blum, the éminence grise of the new French Republic, had undertaken a mission to the United States as ambassador-extraordinary of the provisional government of Félix Gouin. He was charged with a delicate financial mission that was formalized in the Blum-Byrnes Agreements, favorable to postwar France.[136] Blum's trip to the United States was an occasion for the JLC leaders to hold a dinner in his honor, among other celebrations. During the dinner on April 13 at the Waldorf Astoria in New York that assembled figures of the Jewish and labor world, Adolph Held saluted the leader of the French Socialist Party, affirming his almost "legendary" character, as the first French Jewish statesman and an ideal-type of international socialism. He also recalled Blum's own defense during the trial in Riom as a crucial moment that heralded the spirit of resistance against Nazism and fascism, and his almost miraculous return from detention in Buchenwald. In his own speech to the JLC, Blum affirmed: "I have been marvelously welcomed in this country. But with you, here, it is different. Here I feel at home."[137]

This warm and personal relationship testifies to a shared culture strengthening the political ties already expressed across the Atlantic. This explains in part why Léon Blum at the end of his life agreed to supply articles to the *Jewish Daily Forward*, which Fajwel Schrager translated into Yiddish.[138] In his contributions to the *Forward*, Blum addressed general subjects in French domestic and foreign policy. Regarding the French position in the postwar tensions, he asserted his opposition to the notion of the collective responsibility of the German people: "The dogma of the responsibility of a people, he maintained, leads fatally to the notions of racial types and indelible racial characters"—notions that a Jew could never accept.[139]

6

FIRE AND ASHES IN POLAND

I have been walking through a nightmare. That first day I saw Warsaw heaped in ruins; and I did not recognize a single street in this city whose every block, whose almost every house I used to know. I started out toward the former Jewish Ghetto. And when I reached the ghastly desert which once was Leshno Street, Nalevki, Novolipia, Karmelitzka, I stopped dead and turned back.

Thus wrote Jacob Pat in the foreword to his book *Ashes and Fire*, devoted to his trip to Poland in the winter of 1946. "I seem to see those Jews, rising one by one from their own ashes to do sentry duty on that bit of wall. I see their cold eyes stare across this barren desert of destruction, this monument of shame—the one-time Warsaw Jewish ghetto."[1]

During the war years, Jacob Pat, who had now become the JLC's executive secretary, was in charge of the JLC's relations with Poland—his home country and where his family lived. Having come temporarily to the United States in 1938 as director of the organization of Jewish schools in Poland (Tsisho), which he had helped create, he had never gone back. A writer and a man of letters, he was also deeply involved in the Bund, a member of its Central Committee, and coeditor of its organ, *Neue Folkszeitung*.[2] Since the beginning of the war in September 1939, Pat and his comrades in the JLC in New York experienced the Polish nightmare from a distance. The JLC members had similar substantial links with the Jewish minority of Poland: almost all of them shared that background, whether their emigration to the United States had taken place during the tsarist era or between the two world wars. For example, Benjamin Tabachinsky, who became the JLC's campaign director in charge of fundraising, had the same political and cultural experience as Pat. A Bund militant and representative of the Jewish school network who had also come to New York in 1938, he was likewise forced to remain in the United States when the war broke out.[3] Directly in contact with the organizations from which they emanated and those who now worked there, Pat and Tabachinsky closely followed their tragic destiny and tried to help them. What positions should the JLC adopt, what means could it use to attenuate the suffering of the people who seemed doomed to extermination? And how did its leaders become aware of the Final Solution?

THE GERMAN-SOVIET PACT

The JLC was stunned by the signing of the German-Soviet Pact: it buried any hope of an alliance between the Western democracies and the Soviet Union in the fight against Hitlerism and fascism. Worse, it subjected the entire Polish nation to combined Hitlerian and Communist dictatorships and abandoned millions of Jews to the hell of the Nazi terror. "At a time when hundreds of thousands of Jewish lives are reduced to dust in the gears of the death machine, the USSR has stabbed in the back all liberty-loving humanity," the JLC declared.[4]

While the German armies were concentrating the Jewish Polish population in ghettos and pushing hundreds of thousands of others to flee to the Soviet zone, amid the immense human chaos into which Central Europe was thrown, no contact was possible with the individuals or institutions previously known by the JLC. The Nazis, having massively expelled the Jews from the western provinces, thus rendering them *Judenrein* and directly incorporated into the Reich, now concentrated and isolated the Jewish population in the central region known as that of the "General Government."[5]

Some 1.8 million Jews were pushed into ghettos and cut off from any contact with the outside world. Ghetto inhabitants had no right to receive mail
(which was so vital for the refugees in France). Only the neutral countries
could theoretically still send packages there. Therefore only packages from
the Soviet Union (considered neutral until its invasion by the Wermacht in
June 1941) or the United States (before its entry into the war in December
of the same year) could actually be sent there. Yet the Allies, respecting the
British blockade of the Reich, forbade the sending of money and even food
packages on the pretext that it would absolve the Nazis of their responsibility to feed these people—though this was an unrealistic assessment of Nazi
treatment of the Jews and their manipulation of the Polish population in
order to stir up that hatred. Under the terror of the Occupation, Poles and
Jews were forced into competition with each other for their survival.[6] Let us
also recall that while the Polish government in exile led by General Sikorski did not maintain the prewar state's anti-Semitism, it still maintained
plans for massive emigration designed to resolve the "Jewish problem" once
the war was over.[7] Taking refuge first in France (in Angers) until the German Occupation, then in London after June 1940, this government was
composed of representatives of all Polish parties (Communists excepted)
and would manage at a distance relations with the well-organized Polish
resistance. Recognized by the Allied powers, it had ambassadors in their
various capitals.

The American Jewish Joint Distribution Committee was the essential
source of help in the ghettos and provided considerable, although always
insufficient, assistance. In Warsaw the Joint could rely on several Jewish figures who were acting clandestinely, notably Isaac Giterman, Leib Neustadt,
David Guzik, and historian Emanuel Ringelblum,[8] to coordinate relief,
along with self-help societies for aiding children and the sick, by providing everything from food to education. This did not prevent malnutrition,
epidemics, and typhus; absolute physical and moral destitution was killing
the inhabitants of the ghettos at the rate of several thousand per month. In
fact, death by organized famine was the Nazis' first form of programmed
annihilation. Some 100,000 persons in the Warsaw Ghetto would die of
hunger between 1940 and 1942. In the region under General Government

administration, the Joint supplied half of the budget of the officially recognized welfare organization, the Jewish Self Help Society (JSS; *Aleynhilf* in Yiddish). In the spring of 1941, the Joint acknowledged that its food program was able to help only a fraction of that population. And on the Soviet side, eastern Poland was hardly any better: 200,000 to 300,000 Jewish refugees fleeing the German army were now added to the local Jewish population of 1.3 million, and all of them remained isolated from Western aid as long as the German-Soviet Pact lasted.[9]

The Bund was the first Jewish political organization to reconstruct itself for the sake of underground work in the Occupation, even before the formation of the Warsaw Ghetto in October 1940. With the exception of the left-wing Zionists, most parties and organizations found themselves without leadership. Many Bundist leaders, however, had fled in advance of the Soviet invasion, trying to reach Lithuania; among them, Wiktor Alter and Henryk Erlich, the two foremost leaders, were captured by the Red Army and imprisoned in the Soviet Union. Szmul (Artur) Zygielbojm, the only member of the Central Committee to reach Warsaw during the invasion, refused German orders to collaborate with the *Judenrat* in forming the city's ghetto; he sought refuge first in France and then temporarily in the United States before being named Bund representative in the government in exile in London in 1942.[10] After his departure, the Bund was enlivened by the presence of members of the youth organizations Tsukunft and Skiff, and relied on the tenacious activism of a few Warsaw militants: Sonya Nowogrodski, Abrasha Blum, Loeser Clog, Berek Snaidmil, and Bernard Goldstein. According to the latter's account, the Bund helped create tenement committees to organize collective life over crucial issues like how lodging, food, and childcare should be shared. These committees were useful relays for the distribution of aid from the JDC and the *Judenrat*. The Bund continued to organize the resistance through illegal publications, underground schools, and weapons searches.[11] Meanwhile, the formal direction of the Bund was split between Vilna, where the majority of the Central Committee had taken refuge, and New York, where several executives (Emanuel Nowogrodzki, Jacob Pat, and Benjamin Tabachinsky) formed the American Representation of the Bund, which started raising funds. This connection with the

United States was vital for the survival of many Bund leaders, including dozens who, thanks to the channel created by the JLC, would reach New York in 1940–1941 (see chapter 4). With the arrival of Emanuel Scherer, Shlomo Mendelsohn, and Noah Portnoy of the Central Committee, the Bund was now effectively headquartered in New York City.

In September 1939, Jacob Pat and Benjamin Tabachinsky informed the JLC about the catastrophic situation that was developing in Poland. Faced with the urgency and gravity of the situation, it was decided that the help offered by the Bund Representation and the JLC would be combined under a single organization under JLC direction, which now permanently integrated Pat and Tabachinsky into the Executive Committee: "the JLC assumes responsibility for the labor movement of Poland and for the emigration of labor people."[12] In other words, if "relief and rescue" designated two modes of action, in this initial period the JLC favored the latter. Not that it refused to send relief to the populations of the ghettos, but it did so by the intermediary of the Joint or the United Jewish Appeal, to which it contributed. The JLC intended to maintain control over its activity by targeting groups and individuals from the labor movement that it wanted to support. "The funds we raise are not only for relief, but are also for aid to labor groups, for underground work. We set certain sums for the United Jewish Appeal or for the Joint. We do not have to submit our books to the above-mentioned organizations, because we are not their agency, but they are *our* agency for relief," affirmed Isaiah Minkoff. Refusing to be merely an agency of the Joint, the JLC was adamant about maintaining its political identity. During 1940, it supplied the Joint with 35 percent of the funds it collected. And beginning in 1941 it launched a major campaign across the United States and Canada. Tabachinsky, assisted by Charles B. Sherman, traveled across the United States, meeting with Jewish and labor communities in an attempt to raise half a million dollars. After deducting the gifts to the Joint, the rest would go to rescuing the refugees in Lithuania and financing their exodus across Russia, Siberia, and Japan, similar to those whom the JLC was exfiltrating from France at the same time.[13] One of the ways in which the JLC collaborated with the Bund Representation was sending money to reconstruct and revive the Medem Sanatorium of Warsaw, which sheltered a hundred children and had been destroyed by a German attack. Gifts from the ILGWU for this purpose were precious.[14]

Apart from these accomplishments in providing relief, the JLC's activity until June 1941 remained focused on its rescue operations. Starting in 1941, the role of refugees from Poland who had reached the United States became essential, both for receiving information from the underground Bund activists and for raising funds to send to them in Poland. Szmul Zygielbojm, who had been in the United States since the autumn of 1940, toured twenty-five American cities to solicit financial aid from the local branches of the garment trades unions and from the Workmen's Circle.[15] Eventually appointed (after equivocations) in March 1942 to the National Council of the Polish government in exile in London, Zygielbojm was a relay between the Bundists of Poland, the Polish government in London, and the Bund Representation in New York. The Zionist Ignacy Schwarzbart also sat on the National Council; despite the political differences between him and Zygielbojm, he shared the duty of representing the Jewish masses of Poland. The Polish leaders in the Sikorski government in London had appointed Zygielbojm precisely for his connections with the ghetto resistance and for his contacts with the American Jewish world, whose support they needed as a counterweight to the difficult alliance with the USSR.[16]

HUMANITARIAN AID FOR THE JEWS IN RUSSIA

The entry of the Soviet Union into the Allied camp, a consequence of the German attack that began in June 1941, altered the possibilities for humanitarian intervention. This turn of events, followed by the U.S. entry into the war in December 1941, enabled communications with the USSR via diplomatic channels. The Polish government in exile now had an embassy in Kuybishev that could help transmit aid to the Poles (Jews or not) who were refugees in the Soviet Union. Similarly, the Soviet embassy in Washington disseminated information and transported aid. Meanwhile, the most brutal savagery was being perpetrated by the Nazis on the Jews. Mass murder by shooting was committed by the Einsatzgruppen, and gassing in trucks preceded the concentration and then annihilation of Jews in extermination camps. Without yet knowing about these horrors, in the summer of 1941, the JLC alongside the Joint began a major operation to provide relief to the Jewish people caught between the two fronts.

This humanitarian orientation was more customary for the Joint than the JLC. The members of the Executive Committee that met on July 28, 1941, discussed the JLC's position in relation to humanitarian work. The JLC adopted a pragmatic approach instead of an ideological one, which would have precluded any involvement with the Soviet government, which the JLC essentially distrusted. "Every relief work is political work," affirmed Tabachinsky. Moreover, Isaiah Minkoff insisted that "the JLC is really a political organization, and as such we must be part of the relief organizations which will be organized. Only the Communists [so far] and the Joint are now able to work in Russia." At this meeting, Raphael Abramovitch called for a clarification of this decision concerning the Soviets, also remarking that it was a matter of operating somewhat "like a Popular Front" in order to create a united delegation of several American aid organizations.[17] In part, the JLC was responding directly to the appeal of Bundist refugees who found themselves in the Soviet Union. Jacob Pat had in fact received from the Polish embassy in Kuybishev the translation of a telegram addressed to the Polish embassy in Washington: "Confidential. The situation of the Polish refugees in Russia is a hard one. Immediate help is needed. The undersigned members of the General Jewish Workers' Union of Poland in Kuybishev ask the Jewish Labor Committee to come in contact with the Polish government about the organization of relief."[18]

Starting in the summer of 1941, the JLC launched a campaign to collect clothing, shoes, medicine, and foodstuffs, in view of the likely needs for the winter. Tabachinsky obtained from his negotiations with Soviet ambassador Constantin Oumansky in Washington an agreement that the USSR would transport these shipments from Los Angeles.[19] Moreover, an agreement was made between the Polish government in London and the JLC as to the contents and destination of these shipments. At the end of 1942, the JLC stated that it had sent more than 500 tons of clothing in nineteen maritime containers that also included tons of condensed milk and other nonperishable food. For the year 1942 it committed $104,347 for this purpose (without including the cost of clothing, probably negotiated with the makers since used clothing was not accepted). At the end of 1942, Polish ambassador Stanislaw Kot in Kuybishev telegraphed the JLC a message confirming the arrival of the first transports and their distribution in several regions.[20] In the course of these campaigns, Jacob Pat strongly solicited sections of the Workmen's Circle, which Charles B. Sherman visited one by one in 1941–1942, as well as the ILGWU locals. The latter supplied $25,000 worth of tents and emergency hospital equipment in 1942.[21] In 1944, the JLC began collaborating with the United Nations Relief and Rehabilitation Administration (UNRRA). At the end of the war, Adolph Held summarized that the JLC had managed to send clothing and other urgently needed goods to Poland valued at $1,550,000. To these collective shipments were added individual parcels sent to hundreds of persons whose names had been supplied by the Bund Representation in New York and by the JLC.[22]

It is not absolutely certain that aid was distributed in the USSR without discriminating against the Jews, for two interrelated reasons. An accord had been established between the Polish government in exile and the Jewish Labor Committee for the aid to be "distributed as equitably as possible among the refugees, so that the needs of the Jews among them, as Polish citizens, be equally covered." This agreement in itself implied that recurrent favoritism prevailed among Polish agents on the ground. But discriminatory practices may have been reinforced by Soviet manipulations. For reasons of territorial ambition, the Soviet Union had decided to Sovietize Polish citizens on its territory by assigning them Soviet nationality. The Russian authorities rescinded this decision on December 1, 1941, however, concerning the minorities of Poland--Ukrainians, Byelorussians, and Jews—whose nationality remained questionable. Such a policy might well have reinforced Polish ambivalence to minorities or fostered their exclusion from aid organized by the Soviets.[23] Yet the Polish government at the time was trying to obtain the support of Jews in the free world. Ambassador Stanislaw Kot in Kuybishev had asked Wiktor Alter, liberated (like Henryk Erlich) from Soviet jails in September 1941, to take charge of inspecting aid centers in order to prevent discrimination. The liberation of the two Bundist leaders,

Erlich and Alter, followed by that of other militants, took place in the brief period before their new imprisonment, providing a source of political inspiration for the government in exile as to the role Jews might play in the war as an international anti-fascist force. But Soviet leaders decided otherwise.

THE ERLICH AND ALTER AFFAIR

This affair eventually became the root of the distrust of the Soviet Union. For Bundists in the United States, it was the sign of their powerlessness to get the United States to intervene in favor of Jewish labor leaders of international renown. It also meant that Jewish American public opinion had little influence over the geopolitics of the war. This failure signaled in advance the Allied powers' disinterest in the defense of Jewish populations that were caught in a vise between the two dictatorships.[24]

Wiktor Alter and Henryk Erlich had been arrested by the NKVD in September and October 1939, respectively, during their flight to the east like hundreds of other militants. Their status as Bundist leaders, hence anti-Stalinists who were linked to the Social Democratic Socialist International, doubly incriminated them in the eyes of the Soviet leaders. After months of prison and interrogations, they were accused of reactionary activity, of conspiring with Polish intelligence and plotting against the Soviet regime, and were condemned to death. In September 1941, however, after the German attack on the USSR, their sentences were commuted and the two leaders liberated. It had become apparent to the Soviet government that the notoriety of the two Polish leaders in the Labor and Socialist International, as well as in the international Jewish world, might favor the mobilization of Jewish public opinion and of American labor in favor of the Soviet Union, now weakened by the German attack. In fact, Erlich and Alter (now residing in Kuybishev) agreed to participate at the request of NKVD chief Lavrenti Beria in the creation of the Jewish Anti-Fascist Committee, whose role was to promote anti-Nazi propaganda in Jewish international circles. Moreover, in the short lapse of time before they were again incarcerated in December 1941, Erlich had been appointed by the government in exile in

London to sit on its National Council (in preference to Zygielbojm), and the Polish embassy asked Alter to monitor the distribution of social aid in Russia. But, suspicious of the manifest independence of the two leaders and of the international support they enjoyed, Stalin had them arrested again on December 4, 1941, barely two months after having freed them—and soon had them assassinated.

Their deaths only became known in February 1943. Meanwhile, an intense campaign for their liberation had developed, appealing to the Soviet authorities and ambassador Maxime Litvinov in Washington. In various stages this campaign involved the secretary-general of the British TUC and IFTU president Walter Citrine, AFL president William Green, the American Socialist leader Norman Thomas, the Polish ambassador Stanislaw Kot in Kuybishev, and various Bund representatives—Szmul Zygielbojm in London, Emanuel Nowogrodzki and Emanuel Scherer in New York—plus leaders of the Workmen's Circle and the JLC, as well as ILGWU president David Dubinsky and many influential figures in the United States.[25] But news of their death was communicated, without comment, by Litvinov to William Green on February 23, 1943. Accused of wanting to foment a separate peace with Germany, they had been executed in accord with the verdict of 1941. Was the sentence implemented in December 1942 (as indicated) or previously? According to historian Daniel Blatman, in the light of Soviet documents, Erlich had actually committed suicide in his prison cell in May 1942. The publication of this news at the end of February 1943 corresponded to a moment when the Soviet Union, since its success in Stalingrad, no longer feared the backlash of public opinion. The two leaders had been the Soviet Union's pawns in its stormy relations with the Polish government and objects in a demonstration of force with respect to the West.[26]

In New York, the event produced tensions within the Jewish labor world represented by the JLC. Sidney Hillman, for his part, refused to participate in the meeting of commemoration and protest organized by the JLC on March 30 at Mecca Temple in New York. As a member of Roosevelt's cabinet and director of labor relations in the War Production Board, he judged that it was inopportune to manifest criticism of the USSR in the context of the Allied war strategy. Hillman's defection on this occasion was reinforced by that of the great confederation of industry, the CIO, fully engaged in the war effort with the support of its several Communist leaders. The State Department had even recommended that William Green not divulge the information he had received about the deaths of the two men. But Green quickly got a copy of the letter to Jacob Pat, who informed the union world about it.[27]

Faithful to its political and moral line, the JLC did not want to submit to the imperatives of realpolitik promulgated by the State Department, but it did not withdraw from solidarity with the Allied nations. The declaration the JLC agreed upon for the meeting at Mecca Temple included an expression of indignation about the execution of Henryk Erlich and Witkor Alter and a complete rejection of the accusations against them of collaborating with the Nazi enemy or defaulting on the Allied nations' strategy to defeat the Axis powers: "Despite the grievous injustice perpetrated by the Soviet court on the two servants and leaders of labor, we are, as ever, loyal and devoted to the declared and clear aims of our country's alliance with the Soviet Union, and all the United Nations."[28]

To make matters worse, the discovery in April 1943 in the Katyn Forest of the massacre of thousands of officers and members of the Polish elite perpetrated by the Soviets in 1940 worsened relations between Poland and the Soviet Union, which accused the Nazis of these mass murders. The event, manipulated by both Soviet and Hitlerian propaganda, led to a rupture of relations between the USSR and the government in exile, making any communication between the Allies and Polish exiles in the Soviet Union almost impossible. The deaths of Erlich and Alter, the Katyn affair, and soon (in May 1943) Zygielbojm's suicide in London all had the effect of leaving the Jews of the ghettos in Poland and in the USSR in increasingly profound isolation.[29]

EARLY KNOWLEDGE OF THE UNTHINKABLE

Walter Laqueur and other historians have identified and analyzed the several sources of various origins that transmitted information on the Final

Solution over the course of 1942. They have pointed to the initial incredu-
lity and the slowness of the Allies to grasp the reality of the facts revealed to
them, as well as their political or psychological resistance to absorbing this
evidence.[30] Without reviewing this established knowledge, here my purpose is to perceive how information about the Holocaust gradually reached
the JLC and how they reacted to it. Among the most decisive elements in
the information that reached the West were messages emanating directly
from the Bund in the Warsaw Ghetto during the months when the Germans were proceeding to eliminate its inhabitants. As a Bundist delegate
in the Polish government in London, Szmul Zygielbojm was at the center
of the reception and dissemination of this information to the Allies, to the
English-speaking Jewish world, and of course to the New York Bundists
and the JLC. Horrifying news came directly from their political friends,
gradually revealing the sealed fate of all the inhabitants of the ghettos as
well as of all European Jews.[31]

The first report from the Warsaw Ghetto was received in London by
Zygielbojm in May 1942; it had been transmitted by Leon Feiner. The
report affirmed that more than 700,000 Jews had already been murdered in
Poland. The report was precise, mentioning the killings in the gas trucks in
Chelmno and the massacres in Vilna and in the Lvov region, noting that the
deportations from Lublin had begun in March. The report also mentioned
the executions perpetrated in the Warsaw Ghetto by the Gestapo that
occurred during the night of April 17, 1942, when several Bund members
and union leaders were shot on the spot. Leon Feiner—alias "Berezowski"
or "Mikolaj"—was a member of the Bund's Central Committee. Having
recently returned to Warsaw after escaping Soviet territory where he had
been incarcerated and "interrogated," he became a liaison between the ghetto
and the government in exile. A well-established lawyer before the war, Feiner
resided on the Aryan side but managed to slip into the ghetto for meetings
with Bundist leaders. It was he who transmitted this report from the underground Central Committee, as well as the subsequent ones that reached
"Artur" Zygielbojm in London, passing either via a courier (a person travel-
ing to neutral or allied countries) or by a radio message from the domestic
and resisting Polish Army (Armia Krajowa; AK) to London.[32] From the

perspective of the ghetto militants—Bernard Goldstein, Mauricy Orzech, and Abrasha Blum—Feiner's ability to contact the Polish resistance and especially the underground Socialist Party (Polska Partia Socjalistyczna; PPS) was essential. The militants wanted to alert the Polish government in exile (and more generally the Allies), and they knew that there was no chance of armed struggle without the help of the Polish resistance.[33]

But in London, the Polish government minimized this report because it had limited faith in it. It only alluded to it in successive declarations that mentioned "tens of thousands" of victims—instead of 700,000. In fact, Sikorski was controlling all communications to the British press and radio to make sure that coverage of the Jewish tragedy did not exceed that of the Polish nation on the whole.[34]

In New York, meanwhile, the Feiner report was indeed mentioned in the press, although discreetly. The news was buried among other dispatches on page 5 of the New York Times on June 27.[35] Other reports were coming from the continent alerting Jewish American organizations. Jacob Pat was indignant about the silence with which these pieces of news were being received. Speaking of the emotion raised by the massacre of the inhabitants of the village of Lidice in Czechoslovakia (perpetrated by the Nazis on June 10, 1942, in reprisal for the assassination of Reichsprotektor Reinhard Heydrich),[36] Pat could not understand why recurrent news of Nazi massacres in occupied countries was being neglected. "The world is angry, but most of the Nazi massacres of the Jews pass almost in silence," he affirmed, mentioning the execution of 258 Jews in Berlin, 60,000 Jews in Vilna, and 60 Jewish children who were trying to escape the Warsaw Ghetto. Pat proposed that the JLC take the initiative of giving all Nazi crimes resounding echoes in democratic countries, particularly in America.[37]

In concert with several Jewish organizations, principally the American Jewish Congress, the JLC circulated a petition addressed to the president of the United States. This letter reported "the deliberate massacre of some one million European Jews by the Nazi government" and demanded that the president, in accord with the Allies, "demand a reckoning of the leaders and people of Germany for any further excesses committed against the Jewish civilized population of Europe."[38] Not minimizing the number of victims and even calling for reprisals, this letter was based on details contained in the Feiner report. These Jewish organizations also held a protest meeting on July 21, 1942, at Madison Square Garden. Roosevelt's response to Rabbi Stephen Wise, president of the American Jewish Congress, stated that "the American people not only sympathize with all victims of Nazi crimes, but will hold the perpetrators of these crimes to strict accountability in a day of reckoning which will surely come."[39] The Bund Representation did not participate with the JLC in this initiative, reproaching it for allying itself with militant Zionists. Daniel Blatman emphasizes the isolationist stubbornness of the New York Bundists during this ordeal, putting up obstacles to Zygielbojm's initiatives in London to make the situation more widely known, including among European socialists, and to his attempts to more deeply inform Jewish American opinion.[40] What was the cause of this quarrel? Political illusions—or narrow-mindedness—about a tragedy that concerned not only the Bund or the Jewish working class of Poland but the entire European Jewish population?

In August 1942, the JLC leaders received another message from Warsaw via the Bund Representation. The minutes (in Yiddish) of the executive meeting held on August 26 reveal that they were by this date aware of the wholesale deportation that had begun in July, planned by the SS, to empty the Warsaw Ghetto of its inhabitants.[41] It was also in August that Gerhart Riegner, representative of the World Jewish Congress in Geneva, sent information to both London and the United States on the massive extermination of Jews in the gas chambers. Yet the State Department did not transmit this information to its destined recipient in the United States, Stephen Wise, who also presided over the World Jewish Congress. Rabbi Wise only found out the gist of it thanks to Sidney Silverman, who sent him a message on August 28. The British representative of the World Jewish Congress and a Member of Parliament, Silverman was another destined recipient of Riegner's telegram. But after consultation with Undersecretary of State Sumner Welles, Wise was constrained not to divulge this information before it was verified by the State Department.[42]

Therefore the information possessed by the JLC had reached it earlier than, and independently from, the Riegner telegram and it contained more details about the deportation from the Warsaw Ghetto. The JLC was also informed of the suicide of Adam Czerniakow on July 23 in Warsaw. This man, president of the *Judenrat* and thus forced to execute the orders of the occupying forces, had tried in vain to plead for exemptions from deportation, especially for children. But the SS commanders, requiring 10,000 Jews per day for "selection" for the supposed work camps, were not interested in such details. By a systematic manhunt, repeated day after day in the ghetto alleys and apartment buildings, they assembled by force on the *Umschlag-platz* convoys of thousands of persons of all ages, trades, and professions, in all physical conditions. Bound for an "unknown destination," these convoys were inexorably headed for Treblinka, the new center of extermination close to the Warsaw-Bialystok train line. Powerless to stop the death machine or to intercede in any other way, Czerniakow put an end to his life at the beginning of the operation. Between July 22 and September 21, 265,000 persons were gassed, 10,380 perished during the "action," executed or terrorized, and 11,580 were sent to forced labor camps. Out of a population of more than 400,000 inhabitants, only 55,000 remained in the ghetto, and several thousand were hiding outside the walls on the Aryan side.[43]

Almost religious in tone, the meeting of the JLC executive on August 26, 1942, which included some members of the Bund Representation, was a commemoration for Czerniakow, a funeral wake for those dying in the ghetto, and a night of mourning on the extent of the massacres. Were its organizers aware that these "martyrs" were only the first in a programmed genocide? The Warsaw Ghetto operation was not yet over, since there was talk of a demand to the *Judenrat* to deliver 100,000 more Jews. But the JLC leaders were also aware of the mass murder caused by the lack of food (17,542 dead in Lodz even before the deportations took place there in September), of the absolute destitution in the ghettos, where the dead and dying were thrown into the streets: "It is death that fills the ghettos . . . but death itself has lost its sacred character." The only feeling of dignity and redemption in these events came from the survivors' will to resist. Adam Czerniakow's suicide was presented to the meeting as a warning to the world. "May our tranquility be troubled. We shall not rest in peace!" By these words, Shlomo Mendelsohn engaged his comrades to celebrate and support the heroism of ghetto resistants preparing for the struggle.[44]

On September 24, the JLC had received a report from underground movements in Poland giving more information on the Bund and its determination to resist.[45] The liaison established with the Polish Socialist Party—which had no doubt passed along the information—was perceived with hope. "It is with great satisfaction that we have heard that the walls of the ghetto until now have proved incapable of separating the Jewish and Polish clandestine movements. Fraternally, they conduct the combat jointly for a new Poland built on the foundations of democracy and socialism," remarked the JLC officers. Not only did "the burning lines of this report in which each word is impregnated with blood and illuminated by faith in the spirit of resistance" blunt the horror of the description of massacres and deportations, but the message also brought a seed of hope, linking the struggle in the ghettos to Jewish and international socialist history. "At this very moment we feel that the clandestine combat of Poland is linked to that conducted in Czechoslovakia, in France, in Holland, in Norway, and in other occupied countries." The cause of the Jewish martyrs was thus linked to that of the underground movements under Nazi occupation that the JLC had been supporting since the beginning of the war.

As soon as this information was received, Jacob Pat affirmed that every effort should be made to bring the details arriving from the clandestine movement to the attention of the American public, particularly to the working class. All information relative to both the massacres committed by the Nazis in Poland and the heroic resistance demonstrated by the Jewish socialist movement was to be made public. The outcome of this meeting was that the JLC Executive Committee decided to present the news to the AFL convention to be held from October 5 to 14; the report "would contain *verbatim* documents on the situation of Jews in the ghettos, on the uninterrupted Nazi terror, and on the resistance of the socialist movement in Poland against the Nazis in which the working class plays a remarkable role."[46]

During the AFL convention, ILGWU delegate Julius Hochman read the report that the JLC had prepared.[47] Precise and documented, the report detailed the atrocities country by country: massacres perpetrated, summary executions, deportations, and punishments of all kinds, emphasizing the overall horror committed and its methodical cruelty. Because it included relatively recent information, the report related the roundup at the

Vélodrome d'Hiver in Paris in July, the Lidice massacre in Czechoslovakia, and that of Skela in Yugoslavia. For Poland, it gave the number of Jewish victims city by city. It mentioned the murder of 700,000 Jews as reported by Leon Feiner's message in the month of May, and the 300,000 victims (of the *Einsatzgruppen*) in Ukraine and in Byelorussia, according to Soviet sources. But it did not present precise information on the massive roundups in the summer of 1942 in Warsaw, although they were at least partly known by the JLC. Mixing descriptions of Nazi murders and acts of political resistance in the Occupied countries, from the north to the south and from the west to the east of Europe, the report was factual. At this stage, it fell short of announcing the specificity of the Final Solution concerning the Jews; but it did describe the extermination as "a world-wide pogrom" in which men and women, children, and elderly Jews were being massacred.[48]

By providing this precise information, the JLC ignored the State Department's decision not to divulge facts whose veracity it had not checked. Perhaps because the report was read in Toronto (Canada) in the framework of a workers' convention that dealt with other subjects, it does not seem to have startled public opinion or the world of North American labor.[49] The JLC leaders remained paralyzed by the weight of the knowledge they had received from firsthand informants and by the immobility of public opinion and the government. The direct access they had to the Bundist sources of information had not succeeded in helping them mobilize public attention.

It was at the end of November 1942 that Jan Karski, the secret courier of Poland's underground government and army (Armia Krajowa; AK), arrived in London to speak to the members of the government in exile. He was also to contact Allied authorities, particularly the British and the Americans, to give them information on the activities and experiences of the resistance.[50] Before leaving Poland, Karski had received instructions to meet two eminent figures in the Jewish community, one Zionist and the other Bundist. The latter was Leon Feiner; the Zionist might have been Dr. Adolf Berman. Guided by Feiner, Karski had twice entered the Warsaw Ghetto "so that he could literally see the spectacle of a people expiring, breathing its last before his eyes." He was also introduced, wearing the uniform of a Ukrainian guard, into the Belzec death camp, where the victims, dumped into wagons, were burned with quicklime. These visits made him a firsthand witness to the horror—even beyond what this Polish resistant, toughened by torture, had been able to imagine—that had to be conveyed to the Western democracies. The two ghetto militants were sharp:

> Our entire people will be destroyed. A few may be saved perhaps, but three million Polish Jews are doomed. As well as others brought in from all over Europe. The Polish Underground is in no position to prevent this, and the Jewish Underground even less so. The Allied Powers must bear the responsibility. Only from outside the country can effective help for the Jews be brought. . . . Tell the Jewish leaders that this is no case for politics or tactics. Tell them that the earth must be shaken to its foundations, the world must be aroused. Perhaps then it will wake up, understand, perceive. Tell them that they must find the strength and courage to make sacrifices no other statesmen have ever had to make, sacrifices as painful as the fate of my dying people, and as unique. This is what they do not understand. German aims and methods are without precedent in history. The democracies must react in a way that is also without precedent, choose unheard-of methods as an answer. If not, their victory will be only partial, only a military victory. Their methods will not preserve what the enemy includes in his program of destruction. Their methods will not preserve us.[51]

In London, Karski reported to Zygielbojm and to Ignacy Schwartzbart, with whom he had a personal conversation on December 2, that the ghetto representatives had revealed to him their preparations for armed struggle: "The ghetto will go up in flames. We are not going to die in slow torment but fighting. We will declare war on Germany—the most hopeless declaration of war that has ever been made."[52]

By the time its executive meeting took place on December 2, the JLC had already heard reports of the intelligence Karski had communicated to London: "In recent days we have received the newest information on the subject of massacres. Zygielbojm has telegraphed that he has received a report from the Jewish underground signed by a person who is well known by the Bund Representation [Feiner]. In this report he says a total annihilation of the Jewish population is currently being perpetrated in the ghastliest manner."[53] It was indeed only now that Leon Feiner's second report (dated August 31) was reaching London. It affirmed that out of 3.5 million Polish Jews, only one million (or maybe 1.25 million) were surviving. It described the great deportation (*Unsiedlung*) from Warsaw that resulted in 250,000 deaths. At Lvov 55,000 to 60,000 Jews had been massacred. It mentioned the destination of trains of deportees: Treblinka, Belzec, Sobibor.[54]

In fact, such proof was accumulating from all quarters. On November 24, 1942, with the prior agreement of the State Department, Stephen Wise finally divulged in two press conferences (in Washington and New York) the annihilation of the Jewish population revealed in the Riegner report. According to his information, two million had already been exterminated. The Nazis were transporting Jews from all over Europe to Poland to execute them en masse.[55] In the face of news from the Bund and elsewhere, the JLC leaders were distraught but powerless. "The worst has already been done. The world should be turned upside down. But how can we demand that the non-Jewish world be involved if the Jewish streets are not burning with rage?" asked Shlomo Mendelsohn. Any proposed symbolic demonstration—fasting by observant Jews, closing of stores, a ten-minute strike in factories, offices, and workshops (only ten minutes so as not to interrupt the war effort for long)—could at most salve consciences.[56]

Instead, the Jewish organizations banded together to demand intervention by President Roosevelt. On December 8, Adolph Held on behalf of the JLC participated with leaders of four other Jewish organizations in a meeting that Stephen Wise had arranged.[57] They had prepared an appeal asking for immediate intervention to stop the extermination of the Jews, to which they added a twelve-page memorandum gathering the facts known at that date. In his somewhat bitter report on this meeting "that lasted exactly 29 minutes," Held noted that Roosevelt and his administration said they were already perfectly aware of the facts that the delegation was reporting and that it would accede to their demand to make a new declaration.[58] The result of this request took the form of the joint declaration formulated on December 17, 1942, by the United States, Great Britain, the Soviet Union, and other Allied governments. They "condemn[ed] Germany's bestial pol-

icy of cold-blooded extermination of Jews. . . . They [resolved] that those
responsible for the shedding of innocent blood shall not escape retribution."
These words, similar to the ones Roosevelt had already pronounced in July
1942 without full knowledge of the facts, did not commit the parties that
signed it to anything beyond their current strategy. As Karski's interlocutors in the Warsaw Ghetto foresaw: "We demand that people know . . . how
little we stand to gain from an Allied victory as things are now, because if
it comes in a year, in two or three years . . . we will have ceased to exist."[59]

OF MONEY AND WEAPONS

For the Ghetto Combatants

"The combat will be conducted jointly with the underground Polish labor
movement": this is how the JLC leaders and the Bund Representation in
New York understood the information sent them by Zygielbojm at the
end of August 1942 and confirmed by Jan Karski in December. In New
York, they placed their hopes in the fact that "the walls of the ghetto have
until now proved incapable of separating Jewish combatants from Polish
socialist resistants."[60]

The goal of the Bundist combatants in the ghetto was indeed to conduct the fight alongside the Polish Socialist Party, on whose support they
were depending to obtain weapons. The carnage of April 1942 and the massive deportations over the summer had taken away the great majority of
Bundist militants who had already prepared for combat. Among the small
number of survivors (25 out of 500), four new groups were reconstituted.
They were mainly youngsters of the Tsukunft, determined to fight rather
than disappear without resistance along with the rest. They joined the Jewish Combat Organization (ZOB; Zydowska Organizacja Boyowa), which
assembled most Jewish political organizations in the ghetto.[61] Young Marek
Edelman was named Bundist representative to the ZOB leadership under
the command of Mordechai Anielewicz. In Warsaw and in other ghettos of
the General Government region, from the moment young people decided
to participate in an insurrection of Jews against the Nazis, they were able

to eliminate the political differences that had previously divided the groups they belonged to.[62]

Obtaining weapons was the most urgent matter, as was procuring money for surviving inside the ghetto and outside it. Survivors' stories relate this dangerous, constant, and desperate quest. Bit by bit, one by one, they managed to buy weapons (or cobble them together): grenades, Molotov cocktails, handguns, submachine guns. On the Aryan side, as Bernard Goldstein reports, all possible sources were explored: the black market, professional dealers, the Armia Krajowa, Polish Socialists, and underground military organizations.[63] When, on January 18, 1943, to the surprise of the SS detachment, four armed groups of Jewish Ghetto resistants succeeded in interrupting a new roundup in Warsaw—and killing some twenty Germans—the Polish underground was unanimous in their admiration. From this moment, Goldstein notes, the ghetto was transformed into a terrain of combat. Its combatants knew that reprisals and the final attack "against the rest of the ghetto" would not be long in coming.[64] The AK now delivered to the ghetto some 90 pistols, 500 defensive hand grenades, 100 offensive grenades, 15 kilos of plastic explosive, with charges and detonators, a light machine gun, and a submachine gun and explosives.[65]

Despite the hopes of the fighting Jews, their preparations for an armed uprising did not lead the Polish resistance to join the insurrection. "They make promises to us," affirmed Leon Feiner to Vladka Meed, a young Bundist militant in charge of the search for weapons and hiding places on the Aryan side. But the Polish leaders judged that the conditions were not favorable for them to join an insurrection. Despite the pressure exerted by Bundist delegates through Zygielbojm on PPS leaders in London, the Warsaw Jews remained alone in their final combat.[66] A despairing Zygielbojm launched a new appeal on March 11, 1943; having received that day a cable from "Janczyk" and "Berezowski" (Feiner) dated February 7, he relayed their cry to the West:

ALARM THE WORLD STOP APPLY POPE FOR OFFICIAL INTERVENTION AND THE ALLIES FOR EXTRAORDINARY STEPS AGAINST GERMANS IN THE ALLIED COUNTRIES STOP WE SUFFER TERRIBLY THE REMAINING

FEW HUNDRED THOUSAND JEWS THREATENED WITH IMMEDIATE ANNIHILATION ONLY YOU CAN RESCUE US STOP RESPONSIBILITY TOWARDS HISTORY THROWN UPON YOU.[67]

The German command sent tanks into the Warsaw Ghetto on April 19, 1943, intending to "liquidate" it in three days. But it took them almost four weeks to put down the armed resistance that had been in preparation since the previous autumn. Against the haphazard armaments of the combatants, the German divisions used massive means: more than two thousand men with armored trucks, tanks, artillery, machine guns, flame-throwers, grenade-launchers, bombs, and air cover. This did not prevent the ghetto insurgents from fighting house by house, bunker after bunker. Moved by a will not to die without fighting back, the Jewish combatants launched an appeal by radio to the Polish population, calling for help, "For our freedom and yours," in the hope of countering the imbalance of forces. But, caught in a trap behind the walls, the Jews remained alone, without any external intervention to save them from gunfire, flames, or deportation.

Zygielbojm's suicide on May 12, 1943, symbolized the desperate end of his people, who had been abandoned by the world and those in power. In its June 1943 issue, *Voice of the Unconquered* announced that the Warsaw Ghetto was now no more than a cemetery, and it published Zygielbojm's testament.

> I cannot be silent—I cannot live—while remnants of the Jewish people of Poland, of whom I am a representative, are perishing. My comrades in the Warsaw ghetto took weapons in their hands in that last heroic impulse. It was not my destiny to die there together with them, but I belong to them, and in their mass graves. By my death I wish to express my strongest protest against the inactivity with which the world is looking on and permitting the extermination of my people.[68]

In New York during these months of desperate fighting, the JLC's actions, while incapable of preventing the tragedy, were nevertheless central in relaying help. "We are bone of their bone and spirit of their spirit. Their struggle is our struggle; their sufferings and hopes are our sufferings and hopes," stated its leaders.[69] Committing itself to complete solidarity, the JLC played a central role in sending money destined for the Jews of Poland. The JLC not only raised money but also transmitted sums from other organizations. Since the U.S. entry into the war, the Joint (JDC) had not been able to act through official channels as it previously had. Closed by the Nazis, its agency in Warsaw had lost control of the social work it had managed to do in the General Government region. Its representative in Warsaw, Isaac Giterman, remained in contact with underground self-help associations of the ghetto organized around Emanuel Ringelblum, but their resources for the redistribution of wealth among ghetto inhabitants were excruciatingly insufficient. Giterman himself was associated with the struggle of the Jewish Combat Organization and succumbed during the attack of January 18, 1943. According to Yehuda Bauer, the JDC help came too late, like that of the whole Jewish American world and Western democracies. From 1943, the Joint resumed its activity in Poland by aligning itself with the networks of the Jewish Labor Committee and by cooperating with it.[70]

The JLC had managed to get around the State Department's proscription against sending money (and even help in kind) to an enemy country, which had paralyzed the Joint's usual forms of intervention. The JLC's link with Zygielbojm permitted direct contact with the Bund militants in Warsaw, as well as with other Jewish organizations in the ghetto. Thus the JLC was able to send money in increasing amounts from 1941 to 1945, contributing what it could to the survival of the inhabitants of the ghetto and those who had gone over to the Aryan side but also to their resistance efforts by helping them purchase weapons. An inventory of these dispatches shows that the JLC sent $18,455 to Poland between March and September 1941 in unequal monthly installments. In 1942, the total rose to $28,393. In 1943, it sent $113,000, and $182,000 in 1944.[71] The money was sent to Zygielbojm in London, who transmitted it to Leon Feiner in Warsaw.[72]

These sums were parachuted into Poland, recalled Marek Edelman, commander of the Bundist group in the Warsaw Ghetto insurrection and one of its few survivors. They were used to finance the purchase of weapons on the black market and elsewhere. In his memoir, Edelman reports he witnessed the parachuting of $120,000. He also recalls that years later, in the 1960s, during a trip to the United States, he was welcomed by trade union leaders. He remembers meeting these "twenty-some emotional men with reverential faces, presidents of unions who had sent money for buying weapons in the ghetto."[73] Vladka Meed likewise reports that starting in 1943, "funds began to reach us through underground channels, first mainly from the Jewish Labor Committee in the United States, subsequently from other Jewish organizations and to some extent from the Polish government in exile as well. The money reached the Coordinating Committee in American dollars, which were exchanged for zlotys on the black market."[74] After the uprising, these sums served to help the Jews who had gone over to the Aryan side, hiding in conditions of extreme material and moral insecurity. Meed circulated among them, using American dollars to rent lodging, purchase food and weapons, and pay off blackmailers and denouncers (*szmalcownicy*), predators always on the lookout to profit from the vulnerability of hunted Jews. "In Warsaw and nearby areas we ministered to some twelve thousand persons," she noted.[75] Invited to the first national convention the JLC held after the war (1947), Vladka Meed was more specific about how valuable the JLC's help had been:

Only when the supplies sent by the JLC from America began to reach us through the underground were we able, in small measure, to satisfy these demands. It is unnecessary to describe the tremendous importance of those gifts of money. It will be enough if I tell you that this was the only way in which it was possible to hide a great number of Jews and enable them to survive the war. The money you sent was the basis for all our later illegal activities. Your help reached the various cities of Poland, the hideouts, dugouts, forests and camps where Jews still lived.[76]

The American Jewish Joint Distribution Committee from 1943 onward adopted the JLC's networks and methods. Being assured that funds sent by these means would actually reach the people for whom they were intended, the Joint used the Polish government in exile to send significant sums. A first payment of $100,000 destined for clandestine Jewish groups was sent to London on September 14, 1943, for transmission to Poland. Comparable amounts followed in December of the same year, and then in March 1944. In July, the $125,000 total contained a share coming directly from the JLC ($25,000). By the end of 1944, with a payment of $200,000 in September, the Joint had managed to send a total of $650,000 to Jewish organizations in Poland.[77]

At the same time, the JLC was expanding American labor's aid to underground movements in countries under Nazi domination, including Poland. In the spring of 1943 it created the Council for the Underground Labor Movement in Nazi Dominated Countries (CULM), whose aim, we recall, was to represent the interests of resistance movements organized in Occupied Europe to the AFL and the CIO.[78] The estimate of the demand made by each representative of a political group engaged in the resistance was based on the amounts already sent in the preceding year and on forecasts for the coming months. Emanuel Nowogrodzki, Bund representative in New York, wrote that "in 1942 we transmitted a sum of $60,000 to the Jewish Underground Movement in Poland. It is difficult for us to show how that money was spent by the Movement in Poland. We deem it important to add here that this amount was sent with the aid of the Jewish Labor Committee, which is, therefore, in a position to verify the remittance of that amount. We would also like to note, that we have already in our possession acknowledgements for the greater part of this sum."[79] Similarly, I. Gottlieb, who represented the Left Poale Zion, also acknowledged the JLC's considerable aid to his movement in Poland.[80]

Recapitulating the aid offered to Poland in 1944 ($250,000), Jacob Pat recalled the humanitarian and political choices the JLC had made to support Jewish organizations and people living in hiding.

> Out of an income of half a million dollars, the JLC appropriated $360,241 for this purpose. One quarter of a million dollars of this money went to the Jews in the ghettos. The general Jewish budget in Poland in 1943 and 1944, was covered by the Jewish Labor Committee to the extent of 50%. I emphasize "general Jewish budget." That means for all Jewish needs, such as hiding, as well as rescuing Jews, and providing them with food, etc. In the city

of Warsaw alone, the JLC was instrumental in giving sustenance to 10,000 Jews. One half of the resources for this purpose was provided by the JLC, and the remainder by other Jewish funds.

It is a lie to say that the Jewish Labor Committee gave support to only ONE group in Poland. As pointed out above, the JLC covered 50% of the general Jewish budget, for general relief purposes. In addition, it gave assistance to the underground groups of the Bund, Right and Left Poale Zion and Hashomer Hatzoir. The Youth of the Hashomer Hatzoir played an important role in the fight of the ghettos.[81]

After the liquidation of the Warsaw Ghetto, its gifts were destined for the survival of those who had been able to escape the massacres and round-ups. Their existence on the Aryan side closely depended on the help that they could get from resistance networks.

Aid for the Polish Resistance

The JLC had also been supporting the struggle of non-Jewish Polish socialists. Their representative to CULM, Stefan Arski, transmitted the request of the Polish Underground Labor Movement, which estimated its needs at $200,000 per year and hoped that American labor could supply most of this sum. The anticipated expenses included "the cost of maintaining clandestine printing shops; the maintenance of hidden radio stations; assistance to members of the Underground who are hiding to escape arrest and to the families of executed and arrested members; support for professional organizers and couriers; various items, the nature of which must remain entirely confidential."[82]

In the hope that a link might be established between Jews and Poles in their struggle, but also out of political fraternity with the Socialist Party, the JLC helped finance both sides of the resistance. However, it was primarily due to the faith of the Bundist resistants on the ground, transmitted to their delegation in London and to the Bund Representation in New York, that the JLC supported the Polish resistance: "The Jewish Labor Committee's assignments of aid to Poland were made on the basis of the appeal from the Jewish underground movement in Poland through the Representation of the Bund in America. We had reasons to believe that the Jewish underground movement in Poland gives certain sums to the Polish underground movement when necessary for their purposes," wrote Jacob Pat to Wladyslaw Malinowski. The latter was the accredited representative in New York of the Polish Socialist Party and labor movement in the exiled government.[83] Since February 1942, the JLC financially supported ($300 a month) the publication of *Poland Fights*, a bulletin launched by the Polish Labor Group in New York.[84] The links between the JLC and the Polish Socialists were not superficial. Adolph Held, for example, sat on the board of *Poland Fights*. He was also invited to preside over the "confidential" conference given by Jan Karski, the underground courier from the Polish resistance, when he went to New York and Washington in the summer of 1943. After arriving in London, Karski was sent by General Sikorski to the United States to complete his mission by meeting with several members of the U.S. administration and other public leaders. Invited to an interview with President Roosevelt, he informed him of the methods of the Polish resistance and on the losses the Polish nation had suffered. He also confirmed news about the fate of Jews in Poland.[85] On the strength of these proofs of the Polish struggle as relayed by Malinowski and Karski, the JLC fulfilled the PPS's requests for funds several times. In August 1943, the JLC transferred $5,000 to the Polish labor movement for its underground press. Other contributions of the same size were made in December 1943 and February 1944.[86] In September, responding to an appeal transmitted by Tomasz Kurzniaz, financial advisor to the Polish embassy in the United States, Adolph Held and Jacob Pat had sent $33,000 to help the Jews of Poland and for the underground Jewish movement against the Nazis.

> In our letter to the Finance Minister, we asked that our friend Comrade Berezowski [Feiner] in Warsaw take care of our relief sums and that we expect to receive receipts and reports from him. . . . It would help us tremendously to hear from you from time to time about conditions in Poland and about the possibility of relief for the Jewish and non-Jewish population and for the underground movements in Poland. We assigned $5,000 for the PPS

recently and $2,000 for the Polish Peasant Party. . . . We believe that in the future the underground labor movements in Europe will be able to receive even greater aid than before from the Council [for the Underground Labor Movement] created by our efforts.[87]

And in fact on August 10, 1944, Jacob Pat informed Malinowski that the Labor War Chest (the AFL's fund) was going to allocate $100,000 to the Polish government in London, with two-thirds being destined for the PPS.[88]

PUBLISH, INFORM, ACT

Since the winter and spring of 1943, the JLC, certain that the fate of all Jews in countries under German domination had been sealed by Hitler, multiplied its efforts to mobilize American public opinion and government power, while feeling powerless to influence events. "Living and breathing at the pace of the Polish tragedy," it organized hundreds of meetings and conferences, for this purpose relying on the sections of the Workmen's Circle across the country. Overwhelmed by the immobility of the government, it had the feeling of "running up against a wall."[89]

The JLC tried to fill the void in the major U.S. daily newspapers on what was happening in Poland.[90] For example, Jan Karski's report to Zygielbojm was transmitted by the JLC to the *New York Times*, which requested exclusivity for its publication, but it only appeared on page 12 of the paper's morning edition on February 10. Indignant about such contempt, Leon Dennen, who was in charge of JLC public relations and had just launched its monthly *Voice of the Unconquered*, published the document in the first issue of the new organ. Titled "Eye-Witness Report of a Courier Fresh from Poland," here was Karski's text reporting the words of Leon Feiner, confirming the horror of the massacres and the exterminating drive of the Nazis in Poland.[91] In subsequent issues, *Voice of the Unconquered* ceaselessly covered the unfolding of the Holocaust. In May 1943, its headlines included "Last Appeal from Polish Jews" and "Heroic Warsaw Ghetto Fight Ends"; in July–August it announced the end of the deportation of the Jews of Holland to the death camps of Poland, the liquidation of the ghettos of Latvia (in which almost every inhabitant had been executed by the Nazis), and the situation of the Jews of Prague who could no longer find food or clothing and were dispossessed of their apartments. In February 1944, the JLC received from Switzerland a report from the OSE indicating that Jewish children in France were subject to systematic roundups. In June an undercover source reported information on the liquidation of the Lodz ghetto and on the extermination of the Jews of Krakow. And during the summer of 1944, the monthly addressed the mass deportations of the Jews of Hungary and Rumania to the death camps. The October issue headlined "Nazis Speed Up Extermination of Remaining Jews in Poland." It also reproduced a list received from an underground courier bearing the names of 320 Judeo-Polish victims of the massacres: artists, educators, scientists, political leaders, social workers, rabbis, writers, and journalists. Among them were Mauricy Orzech, head of the Bund's Central Committee in Warsaw, who had been responsible for relations with the PPS, and Emanuel Ringelblum, historian and organizer of rescue and resistance.[92]

The exceptions to the terrifying succession of such announcements were rare. Among them *Voice of the Unconquered* noted the protection offered by Sweden in 1943 to the Jews of Denmark who thus escaped the tragic fate awaiting them under the German Occupation.[93] The monthly also celebrated the restoration of the Crémieux Decree in Algeria, which reestablished the French citizenship of the Jews there. The progress of the Resistance in France was also front-page news in some issues. But elsewhere, in eastern Europe, extermination proceeded at an infernal pace.

In these months when an eventual victory became foreseeable, but while the extinction of Jewish life in Europe loomed, the JLC put unrelenting pressure on those who had the power to make strategic decisions. These interventions ran up against the American government's "wall of incomprehension" as it refused to address the fate of the Jewish people. The Bermuda Conference in April 1943, for which the JLC had prepared documents with other Jewish organizations, was totally fruitless. And the meeting with Secretary of State Cordell Hull in November 1943 obtained by Adolph Held with a delegation of the entire American labor movement (AFL and CIO) did not result in any action either. All of these pleas were asking that the murderers responsible for mass crimes be precisely identified so that justice could be done; that the Jews of occupied countries be considered by the Allies as prisoners of war, which would have facilitated the intervention of aid to feed and protect them; and that the Allies welcome in the territory under their control any Jewish refugees who managed to escape the Nazi inferno. Cordell Hull terminated this meeting with the assurance that he intended to bring "all necessary consideration" to these requests.[94]

Hull's bland words actually concealed the debate raging inside his own department as well as between State and the Treasury. At the end of 1943 Secretary of the Treasury Henry Morgenthau challenged the division of European affairs at the State Department, responsible, under the authority of Breckinridge Long, among others, for the visa division whose Malthusian interpretation of the immigration laws had blocked the visa requests of many Jews asking for asylum. In addition, in January 1943 Long and his acolytes had delayed, and even blocked at the highest level, the information on the Final Solution that Gerhart Riegner continued to provide in his telegrams to the State Department.

It was "death by bureaucracy," affirmed Stephen Wise when he later learned how this conduct had postponed knowledge of the Final Solution—and hence sending help—for several months.[95] Morgenthau informed President Roosevelt of this scandal, before it burst onto the public stage, and he proposed creating a new agency, the War Refugee Board (WRB), specifically charged with dealing with refugee matters. Created by a decree of January 22, 1944, the WRB, under the direction of John Pehle, was meant "to take all measures in its power in order to save the victims of enemy oppression in imminent danger of death" and to "supply help and assistance consistent with the successful prosecution of the war." The WRB had a budget of a million dollars and also made great use of private funds. In fact, the majority of its operations in Europe were financed by Jewish American organizations.[96]

The JLC welcomed the creation of the WRB as a sign that the government was finally committed to taking action. It congratulated itself for having contributed to the State Department's intelligence on the fate of the

Jews in Poland, Romania, Hungary, and other countries. As a counterpart, the recognition that it obtained from the WRB for the precise information it procured on the fate of the resistance in Poland amounted to official authorization to send subsidies to underground movements, which is to say, to ignore the interdiction on sending money to countries at war with the United States.[97] To support the WRB's action, the JLC launched a campaign presided over by Abraham Cahan to collect a million dollars. At this point Adolph Held set aside his diplomatic reserve and openly criticized Breckinridge Long, challenging the fallacious figures that the latter had advanced in his own defense on the number of refugees that the United States had admitted. In effect, as David Wyman notes, during the war years, 91 percent of the quotas for the nationals of occupied countries were not even utilized![98]

The JLC supported the WRB's project to create "free ports." However, although 70 percent of American public opinion had been won over to the idea that free zones in ports, within the United States and elsewhere, could be opened temporarily to receive refugees, Roosevelt remained hesitant about this project without congressional approval. The only camp opened in the United States was to be Fort Ontario at Oswego in northern New York State, which welcomed a total of 982 refugees in August 1944. Evacuated from southern Italy, these persons of seventeen different nationalities had survived deportations, including to concentration camps. Jacob Pat and Nathan Chanin from the JLC hoped that the opening of this camp would be followed by others. They visited Oswego, learning from refugees' accounts about what they had experienced, and made suggestions for necessary improvements. But this American gesture was not followed by the creation of other free ports. "The smallness of the offer destroyed its value," remarked a member of the Unitarian Aid Committee. "If the United States cannot receive more than a thousand persons, how can it ask other countries to do so?"[99]

On the other hand, the WRB was active in Europe. There was daily urgency on the fronts of both eastern and western Europe. Now breaking with the interdiction imposed by the Trading with the Enemy Act, the WRB permitted aid to be extended. And the positioning of its envoys in neutral countries like Sweden, Switzerland, Spain, Portugal, and Turkey facilitated the reception of refugees in these places. The WRB in part functioned thanks to funding from the Joint and other Jewish organizations. It may have saved the lives of 200,000 refugees. According to Yehuda Bauer, "the WRB was the expression of moral and political support by the Administration to save Jews—with Jewish means." Rebecca Erbelding, for her part, explains that the number of persons saved by the WRB cannot be determined with accuracy but that the United States dedicated many more resources toward humanitarian efforts during 1944–1945 than at any other point during the war.[100] The JLC suggested solutions for saving survivors, asking for the opening of Palestine to refugees, the abrogation of the British *White Paper*, and the establishment of UN citizenship for Jews. In concert with other Jewish organizations, the JLC also worked on rescuing Jews from Hungary, Romania, and the Balkans.

The fate of the Jews in Hungary had become horrendous since the occupation of the country by the Wehrmacht in March 1944. On July 6, a telegram from Emanuel Scherer, successor to Zygielbojm at the Polish government in London, alerted the JLC to the deportation of 400,000 Hungarian Jews to Poland; 350,000 others "faced immediate annihilation." The cable asked the JLC to make suggestions for rescue: "Switzerland, Sweden, Turkey [could] give them honorary citizenship and this way full protection. Do all possible immediately. Don't neglect financial help."[101] Apart from the envisaged diplomatic solutions that would emanate from the WRB in collaboration with the State Department, the JLC took part in sending an envoy in Turkey, Leon Denenberg, to handle difficult situations.

In Istanbul, Denenberg (alias Leon Dennen, who had given up his job as editor of *Voice of the Unconquered*) did work similar to what Frank Bohn and Varian Fry had done in Marseille in 1940–1941. He was mandated by both the JLC and the International Rescue and Relief Committee with which the JLC had made an agreement[102] to assist refugees in their quest for evacuation. In the spring of 1944 Turkey was a neutral country and was experiencing the arrival of refugees from Hungary, Romania, and Bulgaria, as well as anti-Nazi Germans, Austrians, Czechs, and Poles for whom the Hungarian refuge had been only temporary. Istanbul, which had become a site of transit for thousands of persons whose fate was more than precarious, was trying to limit the influx of refugees.

Denenberg's activity from June to October 1944 relied on the presence of the WRB in Turkey. It intervened with the Turkish prime minister to protect German political refugees who were being hunted by the Gestapo, which operated even as far away as Istanbul thanks to the covert cooperation of the local police. Denenberg submitted to the WRB lists of Bulgarian, Romanian, Hungarian, and Polish intellectuals who were interned in camps or prisons now that the arrival of German troops in Romania was putting them in danger of deportation. Some sixty Poles were evacuated from Constanza by the Black Sea. In September, the JLC said it had been able to obtain a certificate of departure for Palestine for 750 Hungarian families. Denenberg pursued this work with the Jewish Agency for Palestine for two hundred additional Hungarians. He encouraged refugees to set up a committee of eminent personalities among them to help anyone who might benefit from the assistance of the International Rescue and Relief Committee. While trying to inform the American press about these circumstances, Denenberg also became involved in individual cases; for example, he helped Hungarian Nobel Prize Laureate Szent Gyoryi obtain an invitation to the Chemistry Department of the University of Istanbul. Denenberg, faithful to the JLC policy, was essentially preoccupied with locating and supporting Jewish refugees in their exodus, as well as helping persons in danger for political or intellectual reasons.[103]

"WHEN THE LONG NIGHT IS OVER"

Meeting in plenary session in December 1944, the JLC leaders called upon the Jews of the United States to accomplish the "historic mission" imposed on them by the tragic fate of European Jews.[104] The JLC proclaimed its desire to reconstruct Jewish life in Europe—in its economic, political, labor, and cultural aspects—and to help democratic and socialist labor movements recover and develop. "We are convinced that the best guarantee for a lasting peace as well as for equal rights for Jews is a strong, free, democratic, socialist labor movement in the countries which have been freed and will be freed from Nazi bondage."[105] Linking the survival of the Jewish people in Europe to the political conditions of its existence was an immense task, for which concrete objectives were fixed that would outlast the immediate postwar period.

Struggling against Anti-Semitism in the United States

With the advance of the Allied forces, revelations multiplied about the extermination of the Jewish people of Europe and the total destitution of the survivors. At every stage, the JLC tirelessly put pressure on government institutions to improve the fate of those who had survived. For example, along with the U.S. State Department and the Polish government in London, it requested help via the International Red Cross for internees from the camps.[106] It capitalized on the occasion of the founding of the United Nations (at a San Francisco conference, from April to June 1945) to issue a thirteen-point demand for the restoration of the rights of Jews and national minorities. Presenting these requests based on the need for international governance, Adolph Held made the struggle against anti-Semitism a precondition for the realization of an equitable future. The reconstruction of the cultural and economic life of the Jews could not take place without the guarantee of respect for fundamental freedoms. Accordingly the JLC demanded that incitement to racial hatred be considered a crime and that the rights of Jews in the countries where they resided be fully recognized; it demanded that refugees be repatriated or else welcomed in the country of their choice; and it demanded international aid for the reconstruction of Jewish life in countries where it had been destroyed, with the exclusive aim of integrating Jews into national economic life, establishing institutions for orphans, and furnishing aid to broken families. To this was added the request for the abrogation of the British *White Paper* that restricted emigration to Palestine.[107] These demands reflected the actions in which the JLC would be invested for years to come, including in the United States.

Immediately after the war, the reality of the Holocaust took a long time to penetrate minds and consciences. To make it concrete and save it from oblivion, ignorance, and indifference, the JLC organized an exhibition in New York, the first of its kind, that assembled statistics, facts, and images on the annihilation of the Jews of Poland. Titled "Martyrs and Heroes of the Ghetto" and inaugurated on April 19, 1945, the exhibition was opened on a date expressly chosen to commemorate the Warsaw Ghetto uprising. It was supported by a group of eminent personalities, including First Lady Eleanor Roosevelt, New York governor Thomas Dewey, New York City mayor Fiorello La Guardia, Herbert Lehman (now director of UNRRA), the presidents of the AFL and the CIO, and a number of anti-Nazi activists. Presenting some 2,500 photos, documents, and objects received from various private and government agencies, barely a few months after the first discovery of the camps, the exhibition illustrated the Nazi barbarity responsible for the extermination of five million Jews (the estimate at the time) and highlighted the resistance by the fighters in the Warsaw Ghetto. Ending on a note of hope for the reconstruction of Jewish life in Europe, it testified to the JLC's desire to struggle against any discrimination and any form of anti-Semitic exclusion, including in the United States itself. During the exhibition's inauguration Albert Einstein had stressed that the goal of the project was to furnish "enlightenment, education! We must be able to face the horrible reality in order to more effectively build a better future."[108]

Philo-fascist or clearly anti-Semitic sentiments had been expressed in the United States before the war, and it was far from certain that these prejudices had disappeared, despite the American democratic commitment, despite the full employment that the war industries had procured, and despite the revelations about the Final Solution since the end of 1942. Then came the discovery of the death camps by the U.S. Army when it reached Poland after the Russians. But could the European tragedy really have replicas in the United States? The JLC perceived anti-Semitism as a real threat there. It feared that, just as had happened after World War I, the war's end would be followed by a period of unemployment that would foster an explosion of racial hatred or overt anti-Semitism; many people thought that the war had been "a Jew war, fought for the Jews."[109] To better detect these prejudices, the JLC commissioned a sociological study that was carried out in the defense industries between July and December 1944. According to this study, nearly 50 percent of industrial workers were susceptible of being influenced by anti-Semitic propaganda, with some of them proffering statements very hostile to Jews.[110] The sociologists of the Institute of Social Research at Columbia University who had conducted the study were none other than the German scholars from the Frankfurt School directed by Max Horkheimer and Theodor Adorno. As Jews and Marxists, these scholars had emigrated to the United States in the 1930s. They noted that before Hitler took power, the German working class had been better equipped ideologically to struggle against anti-Semitic prejudices than had the American working class in 1944. And yet totalitarianism had demolished any resistance among German workers. "Will American workers, so much more easily swayed by racial prejudice, prove a stronger bulwark against totalitarianism?" they wondered.[111]

Accordingly, the JLC intensified its struggle against racial and ethnic prejudice and any form of discrimination. It remained vigilant by arranging conferences and joint sensitization training with AFL and CIO unions, publishing articles, and conducting radio programs and press interviews to educate the union base and reach a wavering public opinion.[112] According to Jacob Pat during the inauguration of the exhibition: "There were times when the world thought that anti-Semitism is the exclusive problem of the Jews. The years of blood and terror have finally brought home the lesson that anti-Semitism constitutes a deadly poison for nations, for peoples, and for the whole of humanity. Let the world learn now that the nests of anti-Semitism and racism must be eradicated forever throughout the universe."[113]

Reconstructing Jewish Life in Poland

American humanitarian aid was crucial for helping Jewish survivors after the war. "Without it the Jewish community in Poland could not be rebuilt. But relief is not sufficient," affirmed Jacob Pat when he went to Poland in the winter of 1946.[114] The JLC naturally targeted precise objectives. A Central Committee of the Jews of Poland had been founded in February 1945 in Warsaw and sent an appeal to the JLC. Directed by Dr. Emile Sommerstein, this committee represented some 80,000 Jewish survivors of various political orientations and spoke for the remaining Jewish community.[115] In response to their request, the JLC sent a first gift of $120,000 in August 1945 destined for the reconstruction of the Medem Sanatorium that had been destroyed by the Nazis, as well as for the relief of other labor and Jewish institutions, including libraries, for which $20,000 was earmarked. It also organized a collection of new clothing, shoes, food, books, and medicine with a total value of half a million dollars. This aid-in-kind, transported to Poland by UNRRA, was distributed to the Central Committee. The ILGWU, whose president, David Dubinsky, had been directly asked by Jan Stanczyk, minister of social welfare in the provisional Polish government, contributed $100,000 for this campaign.[116]

At the same time the JLC provided assistance to desperate survivors in Poland, it was also working on behalf of other Jewish communities in Europe. The JLC supported the rehabilitation of social work in France and Belgium, both socialist and Jewish. It also helped refugees in Sweden, Switzerland, Russia, Romania, Hungary, and Shanghai, as well as providing relief for Norwegian workers' institutions.[117] In the American zones of occupation in Germany and Austria, two JLC envoys (Paul Goldman and William Wolpert) had the task of investigating the situation of Jews in refugee camps and cooperating with UNRRA and American Jewish organizations to address the appalling lack of food, clothing, and lodging. They also asked for vocational training for the interned. Help in orienting these Displaced Persons (DPs) toward Palestine or the United States became one of the JLC's priorities in the postwar years.[118]

Visiting Poland during two months in the winter of 1946, Jacob Pat felt his "head and heart drift in an endless sea of desolation. All around me is the scene of the greatest Jewish disaster since Jewish history went into the making. I have seen Jews in thousands, and every one of them is a miracle of survival." An immense kaddish for a whole people, Pat's account also mentions his personal quest to find out the fate of his sisters and their children. From town to town, he heard the story of those who were last seen leaving for the death camps. He met the survivors of the ghettos and those who had lived in hiding, partisans and leaders of struggles with heroic and tragic memories, and those repatriated from the Soviet Union. He met with religious leaders, heads of associations, and statesmen, including Prime Minister Osubka Muravsky, political leaders, and diplomatic representatives of the United States, Great Britain, Sweden, and Norway. He was entrusted with hundreds of messages from persons who were trying to establish contact with relatives in America. He witnessed the arrival of help sent by the JLC and its distribution in towns where a Jewish community was starting to reappear.[119]

Everywhere he asked about what was needed to help resume economic, social, and cultural life. And he committed the JLC to financing projects: here the purchase of sewing machines, there a printing press, and there again the inauguration of a workers' cooperative. Everywhere, too, he heard stories of new anti-Semitic violence against children and adults, as well as murder, blackmail, looting, and threats of pogroms. And everywhere he heard about the desire to leave:

> What would 80,000 Jews do if they were presented with 80,000 certificates for Palestine? What would they do if they were given 80,000 visas for America? They would sail with the least possible delay. And yet . . . simultaneous with their frontier-sneaking towards German DP camps, towards Palestine, or the beckoning Eden of America, goes the upbuilding of producer-cooperatives, trade courses, schools, kindergartens, newspapers, magazines and theaters.[120]

Upon his return, Jacob Pat engaged the JLC in financing these sorts of projects. He "redeemed" a thousand children who had been hidden with Polish peasants by paying the families who had saved them. He proposed supporting the creation of workers' cooperatives. Among the survivors in Poland and the arrivals from Russia, 50 percent were skilled young men ready to work—if only they had the necessary tools and machines. They also needed to be housed in collective lodgings. The JLC assumed responsibility for one of these homes for 700 young people in Lodz equipped with a library and other services. On the matter of emigration, the JLC sponsored the departure of 75 persons for Sweden and promised to help those who had particular reasons (labor or political) to call upon the JLC. Jacob Pat wanted to revive cultural life: "It is our task to ensure the financial aid in this vital domain" by supporting artists and the theater, journalists and the publication of a new magazine (*Yiddische Schriften*), and contributing to the Jewish Historical Commission of Lodz, which was gathering testimonies on the Jewish martyrdom. Likewise, it offered aid to the search for (and preservation of) the Ringelblum archives hidden deep within the ruins of the Warsaw Ghetto.[121] For all these projects, Pat proposed a budget of $250,000 for Poland during 1946. More generally, the JLC started to collect a million dollars to finance all its humanitarian projects, reconstruction in Europe, and the struggle against anti-Semitism. In 1947, it further strengthened its activity in defense of the rights of Jews where this was necessary, promising a budget of $1.7 million.[122]

The year 1947 marked a high point in the work of the JLC, a caesura between two periods: that of the fight against Nazism, "twelve years of darkness (1933–1945)," and that of the defense of the Jewish people in the world to be reconstructed. The national convention of the JLC that took place in February 1947 in Atlantic City, the first since the war, was the conclusion of one era and the start of another. The JLC had assembled representatives of the various groups and political movements it had supported or with which it had collaborated throughout the hostilities. Accompanied by Fajwel Schrager, his Yiddish translator, who also represented Paris's Cercle Amical-Arbeter Ring, Daniel Mayer was there to express the gratitude of the Socialists of France. Haakon Lie thanked the JLC for its help during and after the war in the name of Norwegian, Danish, and Swedish labor parties.[123] Three Judeo-Polish delegates represented parties or groups from Poland: Ignacy Falk for the Bund, Szymon Rosenberg the Left Poale Zion, and Leon Finkelstein the union of Jewish writers. And three heroes from this country, among the very rare survivors of the ghettos' resistance, were there to testify to the JLC's help in their struggle: Bernard Goldstein, Vladka Meed, and Joseph Zygielbojm (son of Arthur). They expressed the desire for Socialist reconstruction, which had been bequeathed to them by their murdered comrades.[124]

Liebman Hersch had written from Geneva: he saw the American Jews as henceforth the guardians of the existence of Jewish people all over the world and asked them, despite their marginal geographical position, to be the new homeland from where Jewish culture would be reborn in the world. Among other foreign guests were Paul Olberg, JLC's correspondent in Sweden, Joseph Friedman, leader of the Left Poale Zion of France, and Marc Somerhausen for the Belgian Socialist Party. Alexander Kahn, director of the *Jewish Daily Forward*, brought messages from other Jewish American organizations recalling the JLC's specific action. Of course, he said, while the American Jewish Joint Distribution Committee had supplied most of the humanitarian aid for the Jews of Europe, the JLC played a unique role that only it could have assumed. He cited the saving of some 1,500 people of the European social-democratic world in 1940–1941, the parachuting of money for the ghettos' undergrounds in Poland, and the uninterrupted maintenance of contacts with resistants in Europe, signs of the political vision, the determination, and the political ties that the JLC had been able to maintain.[125]

THE JLC AND PALESTINE

In February 1947, in addition to its contribution to the renaissance of Jewish communities in Europe, the JLC now encouraged emigration to Palestine as one of the solutions for survival and renewal. It promised to set aside $250,000 (out of the $1.7 million it hoped to raise) for the settlement of 100,000 Jewish refugees in Palestine. In this sense, it was supporting a request made by the Anglo-American Commission and President Truman to the British Labour government and reiterating the necessity of abrogating the *White Paper* that limited entry to Palestine to 20,000 people per year.[126] Until then the JLC had not sought to finance emigration to Palestine. Was this a volte-face? Several reasons explain this change of heart. The pogrom perpetrated in Kielce, Poland, in July 1946 confirmed the already manifest sign of the return of anti-Semitism, which would destroy Jewish Polish life even more. After the Kielce pogrom, the JLC received 300 requests from

Bundists who were seeking to leave Poland.[127] Moreover, in the DP camps, where Zionists predominated among the Jewish refugees, Bundists were not being favored for Palestine. France, Belgium, Sweden, and Norway were welcoming refugees, as did Australia, where 42 former escapees from the Polish workers' movement stranded in Shanghai had been established. But in Germany and Austria the situation stagnated, with 250,000 refugees desperate to leave the camps. Among American Jews, including JLC members, majority opinion now favored the creation of a state in Palestine. The JLC, which had refrained from a decisive position on the subject in order to avoid conflict between pro- and anti-Zionists in its ranks, now took a new turn by establishing contact with the labor movement in Palestine (Histadrut) to help with settling refugees. "The Jewish Labor Committee acted on the premise that it had to support and sustain Jewish life everywhere, that every corner of the world and every country where Jewish life is sprouting, is hallowed ground." By this pragmatic and fervent position, it dissociated itself from the Bund Representation in New York, which remained ideologically opposed to the creation of a Jewish state and considered settling DPs in Palestine as implicit approval of the Zionist project.[128] Jacob Pat pointed out that it was important that 1.5 million Jews remain in Europe "if only because we do not wish to see the realization of Hitler's wish to rid this continent of its Jewish population! . . . It [would imply] that Jews cannot live among non-Jews under any circumstances; and the importation of the anti-Semitic poison into countries which today contain large Jewish settlements." Refuge in the Soviet Union, moreover, was impossible; it was not admitting anybody, and the 150,000 Jews who had been forced to live there under Soviet rule were now urgently trying to get out, even if this meant going back to Poland. By 1948, Jacob Pat had become convinced that "the state of Israel was necessary and positive."[129]

After the elections of January 1947, the Communist grip on Polish political life put an end to the Bund's independence as a party and to the possibility of intervention by foreign (especially American) organizations there. This ineluctable evolution explains the end of the JLC's aid to Poland and its support of reconstruction in France and in Belgium, which had become countries of European Jewish revival. The transatlantic link with Poland was broken for the duration of the Cold War. For Bundists in the United States, their original home had disappeared in the murderous Nazi terror and was now hopelessly closed for renewal because of Communist oppression. The Bundists' initial hostility to the two totalitarian ideologies was again justified.

Throughout the war and in its aftermath the JLC never abandoned Poland. Its aid was both humanitarian and political through its choice of means of action, its channels of transmission, and its beneficiaries. The possibility of official communication with the Soviets that began in the summer of 1941 permitted sending and distributing help in kind to Jews and Poles compelled to live under Soviet occupation. Providing relief to these populations brought the JLC closer to the Joint Distribution Committee, a humanitarian organization. More "political" in nature had been the rescue of Bundist leaders and militants who had taken refuge in Lithuania and help given to the combatants of the Warsaw Ghetto, even if in both cases survival was at stake. The nature of the ties binding the JLC to the Polish Bundists put it in a position to be able to intervene with American and Polish government institutions. And among the latter, the JLC was in contact with both the Polish resistance (officially represented by the government in exile in London) and the underground resistance inside Poland. Thanks to its original ties with members of the Bund in both instances, the JLC was the first American institution to be informed about the massacres of the Jewish population perpetrated in Poland. Unlike American government officials and public opinion it believed in the veracity of this information. As a consequence, it continued to act by sending money to the inhabitants of the ghetto for weapons for their defense and for the survival of those who managed to escape outside the ghetto walls. To accomplish this, the JLC adopted underground methods and helped finance the resistants' final struggles. Eventually, after 1944, with the creation of the War Refugee Board, the JLC's overall contribution to the survival of Jewish communities in Europe was officially recognized by the State Department.

AFTERWORD

Memory and Silence

The Jewish Labor Committee, which still exists in the United States, has never commemorated its rescue operations and other political activities on behalf of opponents of fascism and Nazism, nor its contributions to the reconstruction of Jewish life after the Holocaust.[1] To this day scholars have not traced the JLC's history in a substantial way. Of course, its most important actions took place under the seal of silence. The organization of rescue channels in 1940–1941 demanded absolute discretion. Its origin and mechanisms had to remain secret so that the operation would not collapse. The survivors themselves did not necessarily know to whom they owed their salvation. In Washington's administrative language, they were mentioned simply as persons on "the AFL list." Some of them did not even know of the existence of the Jewish Labor Committee. Similarly, the underground operations to assist resistance networks were by nature secret and never made publicly explicit. Consequently, the JLC's work during World War II is rarely, or only marginally, recorded in most institutions' archives, except its own. Yet on a historical level, one might have expected that the JLC could have legitimately laid claim to its meritorious actions or that historians attentive to resurrecting the political and social engagement of American labor and Jewish American activists might have celebrated what the JLC had done.

Apart from the linguistic reasons that make these archives difficult to read, and the late date at which they were deposited, historiographical questions have contributed to the fact that they have not been thoroughly examined. Intrinsically transnational, the history of the JLC exceeds the national framework of historical narrative and crosses over the thematic divisions that usually characterize it. Does it belong to Jewish history or to labor history? To American or European history? And as part of both the history of U.S. immigration and that of World War II, the JLC was involved in these mass movements of ideas and persons, in these momentous events that transformed the Western world. But the ways and means of international connections do not always follow obvious paths and may remain hidden for a long time. For instance, while there is a direct link between the emigration of early Bundist militants to the United States and the JLC's support of fighters in the Warsaw Ghetto, the aid it gave to the French Resistance was more circuitous.

Among the historiographic blind spots that have concealed the history of the JLC, a major one derives from the classic account of American labor unionism in the 1930s, which has long concentrated on the split between the AFL and the CIO, and on major domestic labor issues. Historians have scarcely addressed the subject of the two federations' positions concerning international relations during the 1930s and 1940s—apart from their support of the war effort. Therefore, the nominal but symbolic agreement extended by William Green for the rescue of European socialist and social-democratic leaders has remained unknown. The same is true of the AFL and CIO Joint Committee that was organized to support the underground labor movement in European countries during the war.[2] Since the 1960s, by contrast, political and historiographic debates on the AFL's (and then the AFL-CIO's) role in international relations during the Cold War have prevailed. This has certainly contributed to the neglect of the JLC in collective memory, and as a consequence the organization has suffered from the critical attention paid by many American and European historians to the AFL's postwar obsessive anti-communism, which weighed heavily on both national and international labor relations.[3] Some have speculated that the JLC's work during the 1930s and World War II might be seen as an introduction to the AFL's role in Cold War international relations.

PRELUDE TO THE AFL'S ROLE IN THE COLD WAR ?

According to historian Roy Godson, the AFL's interventionism in foreign policy partly originated with the JLC, notably because it brought together exiled European political leaders in New York. He adds that the Labor League for Human Rights, created under the aegis of AFL vice president Matthew Woll, was also an antecedent for international cooperation.[4] It does appear that the JLC brought knowledge of left-wing European politics to the attention of William Green and Matthew Woll, who had previously been quite ignorant of it. The chain of contacts created by the JLC reinforced the AFL's opposition to Nazism and led to its defense of socialist or social-democratic leaders, even though its distrust of any kind of left-wing ideology had kept it out of the international labor movement (IFTU and LSI). Thanks to the JLC's anti-Nazi and anti-fascist struggle, the AFL broke through this wall of voluntary isolation and insularity.

Yet it would be more correct to cite the Labor Desk of the OSS as the institutional initiator of relations between the U.S. intelligence services, the State Department, and the American labor movement. The JLC itself remained independent from these governmental institutions, even if the refugees it gathered in the Council for the Underground Labor Movement (CULM) widely contributed to the OSS with their knowledge of the political and social terrain in their home countries. Thus it was thanks to contact with political refugees close to the labor movement that the American intelligence services learned the value of union networks in the subversion of political regimes. During the Cold War, such contacts were sometimes cynically manipulated and turned against organized labor's normal social objectives. However, during World War II, establishing links with anti-Nazi resistance networks served democratic goals.[5]

The influence of some European exiles whom the JLC had exfiltrated on the AFL's postwar foreign policy was obvious and eventually vindicated. For example, the American Labor Conference on International Affairs, founded by ex-Menshevik Raphael Abramovitch, was one of its major sources of inspiration. Its founder would devote his life in America to fighting communism. In advance of the conference in London where the World

Federation of Trade Unions was created in 1945, and in which Soviet labor unions would take part, Abramovitch persuaded American labor leaders to distrust the "false prophets" and the "tricks of their language" when the Soviets spoke about unity. In reality, he claimed, "for the Communists, the number one enemies are not the capitalists or even the reactionaries, they are the Socialists and democratic organized labor."[6]

It also cannot be denied that some American trade unionists who had distinguished themselves with the JLC in the anti-fascist struggle would pursue their international activity with the AFL against communism. A case in point was David Dubinsky, who after the war became one of the leading figures of anti-communism.[7] In this domain, he acted principally in conjunction with Matthew Woll and George Meany, the AFL secretary-general. Inheriting the taste for secrecy that had been necessary during the war, these men prepared the reign of Jay Lovestone over undercover operations. This former secretary-general of the American Communist Party, who had been excluded from the Comintern in 1929 on Stalin's order, had changed sides and would for twenty-five years dominate operations in collaboration with the CIA to counter the spread of communism in the labor movements of Europe and Latin America. Practically in control of the AFL's international policy, these men thought that stability in Europe would only be guaranteed by the weakening of Communist influence over the working classes. Exceeding the limits of the unions' national orbit and their economic role, they were thus engaged in an eminently political international struggle. They precipitated the 1947 schism that took place within the CGT—the main federation of labor in France, with a strong Communist influence—which led to the creation of the more moderate Force Ouvrière (FO).[8] Similarly, in Italy they also paid substantial subsidies in order to break the Communist impact on the Italian Labor Confederation (CGIL), which had been founded in 1944.[9]

For the JLC leaders, anti-communism had not begun with the Cold War. Anchored in their history since the opposition between Bundists and Bolsheviks, it was accentuated by the Soviet grip over the countries of Central Europe, which put an end to any hope of political pluralism and the reconstruction of Jewish life in Poland, as well as in other satellite countries of the USSR. On this level, it can be said that in the McCarthy era, the JLC scarcely differed from the entire American labor movement, which was now uniformly anti-Communist.[10] Nor could it be distinguished from the major Jewish American organizations that were just as opposed to communism, to the point that none of them passed a resolution opposing the death sentence of the Rosenbergs. The JLC has even been described as "one of the most stridently anti-Communist American Jewish organizations."[11] In this context, the JLC's socialist specificity became less discernable, particularly since leftist or liberal political identities were being altered, or even erased, by pressure from the anti-Communist consensus in American political life. In sum, the left wing of the labor movement was silenced by the political repression exerted by McCarthyism and the Cold War.

Yet the methods and objectives of the JLC differed from the American imperialist ambitions to which the AFL subscribed. The help the JLC gave to socialist parties and movements in Europe as an extension of its prewar interventions was firmly independent of the State Department. In all its enterprises, the JLC continued to value the autonomy of direct relationships with labor, fraternal, and progressive groups across the ocean. The change of focus from anti-Nazism to anti-communism, substituting one totalitarian regime for another, did not modify this posture. In fact, the struggle against anti-Semitism was the keystone of this position, which was devoted to defending democracy. The JLC leaders were well-placed to condemn both the Nazi and the Soviet terrors that had jointly devastated their country of origin since 1939 and, when the war was over, had submitted it to Communist oppression.[12]

In the tense context of international relations that followed the Holocaust, the JLC acted for the defense and reconstruction of the Jewish world in a democratic environment. Accordingly, it was concerned with the fate of Displaced Persons and participated in their reintegration into their nations of origin or their emigration to the countries of their choice—Europe, Israel, or the Americas. It financed children's homes for orphans of the Holocaust and the reconstruction of secular Jewish life. And early in the 1950s, as a sign of its continuous civic and political commitment, it was one of the first organizations to draw international attention to the destruction of Jewish culture in the USSR. Forever convinced that all totalitarian regimes would destroy civil liberties, its leaders now associated the struggle against anti-Semitism with the condemnation of Communist tyranny, two keystones of the JLC's historic engagement.[13]

WITH VISION AND FORESIGHT

The complex nature of the JLC also may have inhibited the posterity of its message. In their own description, JLC leaders recognized their ambiguous position. "We are not a political party," they had asserted in a memo to the British Labour Party in 1941. "We do not conduct any independent political activity, but we are devoted to the principles of socialism."[14] And yet, in 1947, during the first JLC convention after the war, the Norwegian Labor Party leader, Haakon Lie, readily emphasized the political aspect of the JLC's involvement in international cooperation. He summarized the JLC's role by rendering it an eminently political homage. Recalling that it had been the first organization to support the Resistance in Norway, he stated: "The Jewish Labor Committee represents one of the strongest factors for international cooperation in the American labor movement." In other words, Haakon Lie regarded the JLC as belonging to the Labor and Socialist International community. He even went further, suggesting that "as long as America does not have a labor party, the Jewish Labor Committee has a pioneering task to fulfill and maintain relations between the American and European labor organizations."[15]

Was the JLC functioning as a quasi-socialist or labor party? Haakon Lie stressed that it was with the JLC that European labor movements and parties had found an interlocutor speaking the same language, with the same commitment to solidarity and to "international cooperation." Certainly JLC leaders had a different conception of social and international relations than most other segments of the U.S. labor movement. Indeed, a non–classically American consciousness was necessary to understand the relative positions of the various European socialist parties, whether majoritarian or dissident, which had been crushed by fascist repression. It also required experience with clandestine work (to which Vladeck, Dubinsky, Hillman, and several other JLC leaders had been exposed) to grasp the importance of networks and of how resistance movements came into existence. To give credence to information brought by such diverse people as Paul Hagen, the SPD dissident and member of Neu Beginnen, Paul Vignaux, a French Christian trade-unionist, and Ewa Lewinski-Pfister, internationalist activist from the ISK—who were young isolated bridgeheads of underground networks in Germany and in France—required an understanding of political efficiency, regardless of religious faith and traditional party politics. It also required the obstinacy of the Polish Bundists, Jacob Pat and Benjamin Tabachinsky, to be able to sustain the insurgents in the Warsaw Ghetto in their last stand, as well as their contacts outside the walls. The JLC exercised unlimited solidarity within socialist or social-democratic orbits ranging from Norway to Italy, from France to Poland. Their solidarity was circumscribed, of course, to that circle, excluding persons and movements of Communist affiliation, but here again this was the mark of a strong political identity.

Concerning the JLC's humanitarian gestures, Jacob Pat certified, in a 1943 letter to his counterpart at the Joint, that clearly the JLC was "not a relief organization": "It is neither our desire nor our practice to duplicate the work of the JDC. . . . The sphere of activity of the Jewish Labor Committee is very clearly defined. We are a civic-protective organization doing our best to combat anti-Semitism in the ranks of organized labor. Our overseas program is just as clearly defined."[16] And in enumerating the goals of this program Pat emphasized its political objectives while recognizing the humanitarian dimension it implied: "Support of the underground labor movement in all Nazi-occupied countries; Support to and maintenance of Jewish Labor institutions wherever they exist; Attempts to maintain a nucleus of a Jewish organized mass life in Hitler's Europe by rescuing labor leaders and liberal intellectuals, and by supplying them with the material means to carry on their work; and Aid to political refugees." From this perspective, when the JLC delivered humanitarian aid to populations in distress it was to serve vital political objectives concerning the survival of Jewish and democratic labor institutions.[17]

This duality—political *and* humanitarian work—was also replicated in the ambivalence of the very name "Jewish Labor Committee." Was the JLC primarily a Jewish organization acting against anti-Semitism or a labor organization acting in defense of labor? Originally, in the defense of the Jewish workers of Poland, the Bundist identity made these two objectives actually one. This dual mission still made sense among the Jewish proletariat as it existed in Poland and in the United States in the 1930s. And it was fundamental as an axis of struggle against Nazism, whose victims were primarily Jewish and political. But after the war, these two elements had less common resonance, with respect to the international labor movement and in the American national context. The JLC's two circles of belonging were now dissociated. After 1948 the Bund no longer existed in Polish political life. And after the incommensurable tragedy of the Holocaust, the goal of defending the Jewish world as a whole might have made the defense of labor institutions seem secondary. These differences in scale and ideological identity may have been part of the reason why contemporary and later commentators have paid so little attention to the JLC. JLC activists themselves were only too aware of the limits of what they had accomplished.

The scope of the tragedy humbled them. Were they taken over by this "strange silence," which several historians have claimed seized the Jewish and gentile world in America, but also in France and Europe for over twenty years after the Holocaust?[18] Yet, as Hasia Diner has documented, during those years Jewish Americans commemorated the tragedy. Whether they expressed themselves in English, Yiddish, or Hebrew, in print or oratory, they incorporated the catastrophe into the fabric of their public lives.[19] At the heart of the communities where the Workmen's Circle and the JLC were founded, as well as among other Jewish communities, the work of memory was vivid. Countless commemorations took place in the Bronx, in Manhattan and Brooklyn, especially as Displaced Persons were now reaching the United States.[20] The exhibition "Martyrs and Heroes of the Ghetto," which the JLC staged in April 1945, was an early expression of their will to memorialize. Yet it was not followed by other large public manifestations on the Holocaust aimed at informing and bringing together larger communities. More precisely, over the following decades, the JLC did not wish to commemorate its own action. Instead, it proceeded with reconstruction projects in Europe, as well as with programs of education against anti-Semitism and all forms of racial discrimination at home.[21]

For all the above-mentioned reasons the JLC was not celebrated in American political life after the war, nor does it belong to collective memory as Varian Fry does today in narratives of exile and exfiltration. Yet one voice did underline the JLC's discreet but efficient role, that of Attorney General Tom C. Clark, who early recognized its merits. Present at the occasion of the launching of the JLC's $1 million drive for rehabilitation abroad in 1946, he first transmitted a message from President Truman, who recognized the "silent services [the JLC had rendered] to the people, to democracy and to humanity." Clark then paid a vibrant homage to the JLC in his own words:

> Your instinct was truly democratic
>> You carried your work without clashing cymbals of self-righteousness
>> To you must be extended the accolade for vision and foresight
>> You heard the rising wind when many others were asleep
>> [The money you raised] came from the pockets of working men, whose
> anguished hearts responded to the summons for aid.[22]

This was the only official acknowledgment the JLC ever received for its wartime accomplishments.

Since the end of the 1970s, after decades of silence, the memory of the Holocaust in the United States has occupied an exceptional dimension in public space and has acquired a paradigmatic value for the expression of collective identities.[23] It has become a veritable civil religion, the standard that measures the degree of consciousness, of the universal justice of nations or groups who practice it in their museums, public memorials, and commemorations. Developed against the background of the struggle for civil rights for African Americans, this transformation has foregrounded ethnic and individual identities. Jews, blacks, and other minorities each demanded public recognition of the wrong done to them. At the same time, the impact of the labor movement in the United States, like everywhere in the Western world, has declined in both numbers and collective action, no longer serving as a strong symbolic, political, and social counterpower. Deindustrialization, economic liberalism, and the development of the middle class have together contributed to this decline. A general shift in identities has taken place, deeply transforming the sense of belonging by ethnicity and class—to the favor of the former and to the detriment of the latter.

In this context, the particular identity of the Jewish Labor Committee, both a Jewish and a workers' movement, can only be understood with reference to its historical origin and Bundist principles. But in the postwar decades, these particular sources of identity did not have the same value. The end of the Bund in Poland was the sign of its failure to defend the Jewish people and its culture. More generally, labor and socialist internationalism would have no place in the political culture of Cold War America—or even in the 1960s. Moreover, Jewishness in the diaspora was being transformed by the Americanization of the subsequent generations. The irremediable eradication of the original milieu, the *yiddishkeit* of Poland, abolished the transatlantic link between Central Europe and the United States. After 1948, the foundation of Israel gave rise to another source of identity for the American Jewish community but one whose existence the JLC leaders had not favored. In these conditions, memory of the JLC's work against Nazism remained dim and unexplored. The JLC's international achievements had been the acts of a generation of men experienced in political life on two continents. Looking to the future, their "vision and foresight" had been anchored in the memory of their own history.

APPENDIX I

The following pages reproduce an American Federation of Labor letter signed by William Green (AFL president), David Dubinsky (ILGWU president), Alexander Kahn (manager of the *Jewish Daily Forward*), and Isaiah Minkoff (JLC executive director), on July 2, 1940, to Secretary of State Cordell Hull, asking for temporary visas to the United States for persons in imminent danger of arrest and deportation by the Gestapo in Occupied France or by the Soviet NKVD in Lithuania. JLC R, Rescue Series, reproduced in Arieh Lebowitz and Gail Malmgreen, eds., *Robert F. Wagner Labor Archives, New York University, The Papers of the Jewish Labor Committee*, vol. 14 of *Archives of the Holocaust, An International Collection of Selected Documents*, edited by Henry Friedlander and Sybil Milton (New York: Garland, 1993), 99–100.

AMERICAN FEDERATION OF LABOR

Washington, D. C.
July 2, 1940.

Hon. Cordell Hull,
Secretary of State,
Washington, D. C.

Honorable Sir:

   In the name of the American Federation
of Labor, the Jewish Labor Committee, and representatives of organized labor in the United States, we wish
to appeal to you in a matter of great urgency.

   The Nazi occupation of France and the
Soviet seizure of Lithuania have placed in jeopardy the
lives of a great number of men and women prominent in
the democratic and labor movements in Europe.

   Permit us to impress upón you, Honorable
Sir, that unless these men and women find immediate
temporary haven in the United States, they are in danger
of being imprisoned, placed in concentration camps, or
shot, whether it be by the Gestapo or the GPU.

   The men and women in whose behalf we are
now appealing are world-famous writers, editors, labor
leaders, former government officials, and ministers.
Some of them are in intimate contact with the trade union
movement, and are well-known to organized labor in the
United States. Should they fall into the clutches of the
German Gestapo or the Soviet GPU, they will face certain
death, and their loss would be irreparable for the
civilized world.

   Because of their opposition to Fascism,
Naziism, and Communism, the majority of these men and
women were forced to flee their countries - Germany,
Austria, Czecho-Slovakia, Italy, Russia, Poland. Most of

them were until recently in Paris. Now they have found
a temporary refuge in Toulouse and other parts of France.
But, as you are undoubtedly aware, the present French
government, acceding to the demands of the government of
Germany, has agreed to hand over all these pro-democratic
refugees to the Gestapo.

This, Honorable Sir, will be the fate of
great and noble men and women, whose only crime is their
firm belief in Democracy, Freedom, and Tolerance, unless
they find an immediate place of refuge in the United States –
the traditional haven of all hunted and persecuted, and
the only remaining one in this sad and tragic world.

Similar will be the fate of those who are
stranded in Lithuania, which, for all practical purposes
is now a Soviet dependency. Those in Lithuania were
originally forced to flee Poland, because, as prominent
leaders of labor unions and anti-Nazi and anti-Communist
organizations, they were faced with the severest punishments
in the areas occupied both by Germany and Russia.

In view of the above, we earnestly appeal to
the State Department and sincerely urge you, Mr. Secretary,
to do all within your power, in line with American tradition,
to make it possible for these people to enter the United
States as visitors.

Enclosed kindly find a list of names, on
whose behalf we appeal:

Sincerely yours,

President,
American Federation of Labor.

President, International Ladies'
Garment Workers' Union.

General Manager,
Jewish Daily Forward.

Executive Secretary,
Jewish Labor Committee.

ME

APPENDIX 2

The following pages reproduce lists of labor and Socialist or Social Democratic Party leaders and activists to be rescued from France for whom the JLC required temporary visas. The JLC compiled these lists, organizing them by country and political origin. Submitted to the State Department in July and August 1940, the lists were modified several times before the end of August. JLC R, Rescue Series, reproduced in Arieh Lebowitz and Gail Malmgreen, eds., *Robert F. Wagner Labor Archives, New York University, The Papers of the Jewish Labor Committee*, vol. 14 of *Archives of the Holocaust, An International Collection of Selected Documents*, edited by Henry Friedlander and Sybil Milton (New York: Garland, 1993), 101–10.

1. Russian Refugees

List I

IN FRANCE

Rep. to Wash DAN, FEODOR, Age 68. Writer, leader of Russian Social-Democrats, member   *2*
    JD   of the Executive of the Labor and Socialist International, and
    his wife, LYDIA, Age 63.

Dept. to Wash ABRAMOWITSCH-REIN, RAFAEL, Age 60. Writer, leader of Russian Social-   *3 —*
    B JD   Democrats, member of the Executive of the Labor and Socialist
    International, his wife ROSA, daughter LEA, and sister SOFIA. *½ clear paid*
    Last known address: Hotel Regina, Toulouse, France.

JR AVKSENTIEV, NICOLAI, former minister of the Provisional Government in   *2 paid*
    Russia, and his wife.   *himself*

JR ZENZINOFF, VLADIMIR, Age 58, journalist. Editor Sovremennya Zapiski. *¼ in Finland*

Reported to SOLOVEITCHIK, S. Journalist-lawyer and his wife.   *3*   Doc. 72
Wash

JR VICHNIAC, MARK, Professor and political author, and his wife.   *2*

JR BERLIN, PETER, journalist and economist, editor Novaya Rossya   *2*   101

JR RUDNEV, V., Physician, former city mayor of Moscow after the Revolution, *may not*
    and his wife.   *go.*

Reported to ARONSON, GREJOR, journalist—poet, editor "Socialist Vestnik", his wife   *3½*
Wash. BJD   ANNA, and daughter MARIA.

JR VOLSKY, (YURJEWSKY), NICOLAI, statistician and economist, and wife.   *may not go*

JR STALINSKY, E., journalist, in French and Russian Press.   *may not go 2*

JR SLONIM, MARK, Journalist, and daughter.   *2*

JR SUCHOMLIN, BASIL. Journalist in French and Russian Press.   *1*

JD SCHWARTZ, SOLOMON, Age 57, economist and statistician, leader of Russian   *2*
    Trade Union Movement, and his wife VERA.   *will pay himself in am.*

JD JUGOV, AARON, Age 58, economist and statistician, and his wife JUGOV-DOMA-   *2*
    NEVSKAYA, OLGA.   *will pay part himself*

In France   - 2 -

GUREVITSCH, BORIS, journalist, his wife SOFIA, and son LEV.   *3 may go. will*
2 pay, if goes

JUDIN, NADEZHDA, and daughter.

DUBOIS, ANATOLE, Age 57, Sculptor. Former Commissioner of Russian XIIIth   *2*
    Army, during the World War, and DUBOIS-JACOBSON, FANNI.

PISTRAK, LAZAR, Volunteer in the French Army, his wife RAISA, and two   *3½*
    daughters ZINA and VERA.

Rjarle's BSD
Work
GINZBURG, DR. RAFAEL, Psychiatrist, Leader of Workmen's Circle Groups in   *2*
    Paris, and his wife FANNI.   *will pay he.*
himself

ESTRIN, LILLY, Age 41. Archivist Amsterdam Historical Institute in Paris.   *1*

HOICHGELERTER, Historian, and wife and son.   ————   *3 will pay*
½ to us

MENES, A., author and editor, his wife and two sons.   *3½*   *1 will pay*

KLATSCKO, CONSTANTIN.   ————

102   RUBINSTEIN, TATIANA, Age 60.   ————   *2 will pay he.*
Reforder it
Wark
TABACHNIK, MARK, 35, and wife NINA 33.   *works at   not at   1 will pay*

GARVY-BRONSTEIN, PETER, Age 60. Born in Odessa, Russia, political writer
    and journalist, Foreign Editor of "Zukunft" Monthly Publication   *3*
    in New York, his wife SOFIA, son GEORGE, 27.

GUREVITSCH, ALEXANDER, Chemist, Volunteer in French Army, and his wife,
    GUREVITSCH-GARVY, SILVA, Chemist, Age 26.   *2*

NICOLAYEWSKI, BORIS, Age 57, famous historian and author, Head of Amsterdam
    Historical Institute in Paris.   *will pay part*

TSERETELLI, IRACLI........,Age 59, Born in Caucasus, leader of Russian   *1*
    and Georgian labor movement, lawyer, former minister in the
    Russian Provisional Government.

WOLIN, (LEVIN), SIMON, economist, volunteer in the French Army.   *1*

In France   - 3 -

Rep to Wash ROSIN (BEN ADIR), ABRAHAM, Outstanding Jewish author, and his wife SARA. *murdered* 5

KIN, ABRAHAM, editor of Jewish Encyclopedia, and wife BRONISLAWA. *2 sisters will be here*

POTRESOVA, EKATERINA. Age 60, Widow of famous Russian Socialist Leader. *1 may not go*

PORTUGEIS (IVANOVITSCH), SIMON, journalist, and wife and son. Foreign *not on list*
    Editor of Jewish Daily Forward in New York.

MEKSIN, HIRSH, and WIFE BELLA. ————————————— 2

MERRING, BERTA, her husband, son JAKOB, and son's wife. ——— *not on list*

BERS, LIPA, Leader of Latvian Labor Movement, Educator, and wife. 2 *(mother here*

DALIN-LEVIN, DAVID, Age 57, economist and journalist, his wife EUGENIA, 2
    and son.

DKINIKE, GEORGE, Age 55, journalist. ————————————— 1

PESKIN, MATVEY, his wife SOFIA, and son. ——————————— 3

Rep to Wash KAMMERMACHER, MARK (KEFALI), Age 58, leader of trade-union movement in 2   103
    Russia, and his wife JULIA.

PESKIN, JAKOB, his wife and son. ———————————— *will not go / not on*

MENDELSON, MEYER. —————————————————— 1 *(may not go)*

EINHORN, DAVID, journalist and poet, Foreign Editor of Jewish Daily Forward
    in New York, his wife and son. 3

Rep to Wash EVENSKA, ESTERA, outstanding leader of Labor Movement in Poland. 1

Rep to Wash SIEGELBAUM, ARTUR, member of the Polish government abroad. 1

CHERNOV, W., Famous Political Author, former minister of Agriculture in 2
    Russian Provisional government, and his wife.

Rep to Wash SHIFRIN, ALEXANDER, Age 43, journalist, and his mother. ——————— 2

CHARNEY, DANIEL, journalist and poet, and his wife. *will not go*

In France   - 4 -

KURSKI, FRANZ, historian and archivist, Leader of Jewish Labor movement.   *1*

ETKIN, JAKOB, Age 27, his wife NATALIE, and ~~child~~.   *2*

CHERIKOVER, ILIA, historian, editor of the Jewish Encyclopedia, and his *2*
    wife.   *(James Bernstein)*

SARTISOVA, EUGENIE, and daughter TATIANA.   *2*

KROLL, M., Professor, and his wife.   *may not go*

FUNDAMINSKI, ILIA, journalist.   *+ may not go*

·LANDE, LEV, Age 39, Born in Warsaw, Poland, and his wife and two children. *4*
    Last address: Hilversum, Holland

SAPIR, BORIS, Age 37, Born Lodz, Poland. Archivist, Leader of Democratic *1*
    Youth Movement in Europe. Last address: Amsterdam, Holland.

BRAMSON, LEONTI, President of "ORT" Federation.   *not on list*

SINGALOFSKI, AARON, Vice-President of "ORT" Federation.   *not in list*

104   *Rep to Wash* LEBEDEFF, MARGARETTE, and daughter IRENE. Husband in New York.   *2*

Most of these people can be reached through
Rafael Abramowitsch-Rein

Hotel Regina
Toulouse, France

accepted July 4 1941

2. Germans and Austrians

List I

* VOGEL, HANS, age 60, Born in Bavaria, Chairman of the Executive of the German
  Social Democratic Party

* STAMPFER, FRIEDRICH, born September, 1874 in Brunn, Dzechoslovakia, former
  Chief Editor of "Vorwarts," member of the Executive of the German
  Social Democratic Party, his wife and daughter, MARIANNA.

Reported to West. * BREITSCHEID, DR. RUDOLF, born in Cologne, Germany, February, 1875, member of
  the Executive of the German Social Democratic Party, former member
  of Reichstag, his wife TONY, same age.

Reported to West * HILFERDING, DR. RUDOLF, born in Czechoslovakia, age 60, physician, famous
  economist, former Minister of Finances, member of the Executive of
  the German Social Democratic Party.

* GEYER, DR. KURT, member of the Executive of the German Social Democratic Party,
  economist, born in Leipzig, age 40-45, editor of "Neue Vorwarts" in   105
  Paris, wife ANNA,(has sister, Mrs. Peter Ehlen, in New York).

* RINNER, DR. ERICH, age 40, member of the Executive of the German Social Democratic Party, economist, editor of "Deutschland Berichte."

* HEINE, FRIEDRICH, member of the Executive of the German Social Democratic Party.

* OLLENHAUER, ERICH, age 35, member of the Executive of the German Social Democratic
  Party and Socialist Youth International, wife and at least one child.

- - - - -

* The last known address of the above was Agen, Lot et Garonne, Hotel Jasmin-
  Terminus.

- -

BRAUN, MAX, born in Magdeburg, Germany, and wife ANGELE, leader of German Democratic movement in the Saar, former Editor of Social-Democratic
  Volkstimme in Saarbrucken, both have Saar passports.

KIRSCHMANN, EMIL, former member of the Reichstag, born in Oberstein, Germany,
  age 50, active Social-Democrat in the Saar, last address Moulhouse,
  Haut-Rhin, France.

In France   - 2 -

HIRSCHFELD, HANS, born November 26, 1895 in Harburg, German Social Democrat,
since June 1939 "Prostataire" with a labor batallion of the French
Army near Tours, his wife BELLA and daughters DORLE and EVA, their
last address c/o Mlle. Pujos, 15, Rue du XIV Guillet, Lectaure, Gars,
have brother in United States, Dr. Kurt Hirschfeld, 1410 Grand Con-
course, Bronx, New York.

JUCHACZ, MARIE, former member of the Executive of the German Social Democratic
Party, and of the Reichstag.

HAMBURGER, DR. ERNST, age 43, born in Berlin, former member of the Prussian
Diet, editor of "Comier de Presse" in Paris, now in a French camp,
his wife, LOTTE, and daughter, EVA, in a French camp for women.

WEICHMANN, DR. HERBERG, age 40, born in Leipzig, former Prussian government official, worked for the "Europe Nouvelle," his wife ELSBERTH, born in
Brunn, Czechoslovakia.

JURKAT, DR., age 35, Social Democrat, until 1939 active in German Underground
movement, volunteered in the French Army Labor Batallion, his wife,
DORA, son and mother-in-law, age 65.

KAHN, MAX JOSEF, age 55-60, born in Nuremberg, wife, GERTIE, German, Social
Democrat.

BOCK, GEORG, German Social Democrat, lived in Paris.

SENDER, BENEDICT, dentist, evacuated from Belgium, now in camp in Garonne.

ADLER, FRIEDRICH, age 62, born in Vienna, Austria, secretary of the Labor and
Socialist International, and his wife, KADJA.

HOFFMAN, MAX, former Vice-President of the Reichbanner (German Republican Guard),
Social Democratic, active in the Saar.

Rep to Wash HEIDEN, KONRAD, author of history of National Socialism and other books about
Hitler, formerly of the "Frankfurter Zeitung."

STOLZ, JOSEPH, born in Czechoslovakia, secretary of the International Federation of Trade Unions.

106

In France — 3 —

HARTIG, VALTIN, secretary of the International Union of Office and Municipal
      Workers, German Social Democrat.

FERL, GUSTAV, Secretary of the German Social Democratic group in Belgium, former
      member of Reichstag, with him MARIE ARMING, also former member of
      Reichstag.

Rep to Wet SCHWARSCHULD, editor of the Neues Tagebuch.

BERNHARD, GEORG, former editor of the Vossische Zeitung, later of the Pariser
      Tageblatt.

MISCH, *Carl* GEORG, editor of the Pariser Tageblatt.

STEIN, ALEXANDER, age 65, born in Baltic Provinces, former Editor of the
      "Vorwarts," outstanding writer and leader of the German Labor Movement.

107

3. Italian Anti-fascists

Italian List I

NITTI, H.E. FRANCESCO, wife and one son. Formerly prime minister of Italy, delegate of Italy to the peace conference of 1919. Author of "Democracy".

SFORZA, H.E. Count CARLO, wife, son and daughter. Formerly Minister of Foreign Affairs, Italian Ambassador to France, well-known author and lecturer in American universities.

LUSSU, EMILIO, Age 50, and wife. Formerly member of Italian parliament. One of the leaders of the liberal group, Justice and Liberty. Author.

VENTURI, FRANCO, Age 26. Historian. Assistant Editor of Justice and Liberty. Father in United States, Professor at John Hopkins University.

CIANCA, ALBERTO, Age 55, wife and two sons. One of the foremost Italian journalists, of IL MONDO, Rome, and of Justice and Liberty, Paris.

TRENTIN, SILVIO, wife, two sons and daughter. Formerly Professor of Economics in Padua. Well-known author and scholar.

TARCHIANI, ALBERTO, wife and three daughters. Formerly editor of the largest Italian newspaper, "Corriere della Sera."

GAROSCI, ALDO, writer on the history of political theory. Assistant Editor of Justice and Liberty, Paris.

MODIGLIANI, GIUSEPPE EMANUELE, Age 67, and wife. Formerly member of Italian Parliament. Well-known author and lecturer. Just received address: Communicate through Paul Bertolussi, 27 Boulevard Riquet, Toulouse, France.

108

In France   - 2 -

PACCIARDI, RANDOLFO, Age 42-43. Lawyer. Head of the Italian Republican
     Party, Paris. Was a visitor in United States before.

LEVI, MARIO, Age 30. Professor and writer.

CAFFI, ANDREAS. Historian, writer. Born in Russia, lived in Italy, later
     in Paris.

CAMPOLONGHI, LUIGI, Age 70 and wife. Formerly editor of "Secolo," Milan,
     President of Italian League for Rights of Man.

ALBINI, MARIA. Well-known writer and novelist.

BOCCONI, Age 65. Formerly member of the Italian parliament.

FACCHINETTI, Age 50. Formerly member of the Italian parliament, one of
     the leaders of the Republican Party.

NENNI, PIETRO, Age 64. Formerly member of the Italian parliament. Leader
     of Italian Socialists.

TASCA (A. ROSSI), ANGELO, Age 50. Born in Italy, French citizen.

FARABOLI, GIOVANNI, Age 65. Head of the Italian Cooperative Movement in
     France. Head of the Relief Committee of the Italian Federation
     of Labor abroad. Now in Toulouse.

BUOZZI, BRUNO. Former President of the Italian Federation of Labor.

FANTOZZI, ENZO. Head of the Relief Committee for Refugees.

ZAVARONI, ENZO, Age 35. Administrative Secretary of the Italian Socialist
     Party abroad.

MARGARI, ODDINO, Age 76. Leader of Italian Socialist Party.

FARAVELLI, JOSEPH. Labor leader. Ardent anti-Fascist, in great danger.

FARAGAT, GIUSEPPE, Age 45. Journalist, member of Executive of Italian
     Socialist Party.

109

In France   - 3 -

AMEDEO, FILLIPO, Age 60. Lived in Marseilles, leader of Metal Workers
            Union. Former member of Italian Parliament.

TONELLO, ANGEIO, Age 72. Leader of Italian Teachers Union, former member
            of Parliament.

ROSENFELD. Editor of Populaire, <u>French citizen</u>,

SOUVAZINE, BORIS. Famous author and political leader, <u>French citizen</u>.

110

Most of these people can be reached through
Paul Bertolussi
27 Boulevard Riquet
Toulouse, France

APPENDIX 3

The following pages reproduce a report of the meeting between President Roosevelt and the leaders of four Jewish American organizations, December 8, 1942. The report was written by JLC president Adolph Held. JLC R, B1, F17, in Arieh Lebowitz and Gail Malmgreen, eds., *Robert F. Wagner Labor Archives, New York University, The Papers of the Jewish Labor Committee*, vol. 14 of *Archives of the Holocaust, An International Collection of Selected Documents*, edited by Henry Friedlander and Sybil Milton (New York: Garland, 1993), 224–26.

Slegation to the President

_— 3_

REPORT ON THE VISIT TO THE PRESIDENT

The Committee consisted of Rabbi Stephen S. Wise, of the Jewish Congress; Mr. Monsky, of Bnai Brith; Rabbi Rosenberg, of the Agudath, and Adolph Held, of the Jewish Labor Committee.

The meeting with the President was arranged for Tuesday, December 8, 1942, at 12 o'clock. We were originally notified that the President would give us 15 minutes, but the conference lasted 29 minutes. The purpose of the conference was to present a prepared memorandum on the German atrocities in Poland consisting of an appeal to the President for immediate action against the German extermination of Jews, and also a 12 page memorandum citing the facts that have been gathered on this subject.

We were taken into the President's office in the White House by General Watson, the President's personal military aide, exactly at 12 o'clock. The President was seated at his desk; in front of the desk were lined up five chairs for the delegation.

The President sat behind the desk smoking a cigaret in a long cigaret-holder. The desk was full of all sorts of trinkets — ash trays, brass and porcelain figures, etc. There was not an empty spot on his desk. The figures were of all shapes and sizes.

As we filed in, the President greeted Rabbi Wise: "How have you been, Stephen? You are looking well. Glad to see you looking well". Rabbi Wise then introduced each of us separately. The President shook hands with each of us, repeated the name, and then asked: "How do you do, Mr. Monsky?", etc, following which he asked us to sit down.

When we were seated, the President opened the conversation by saying: "I am a sadist, a man of extreme sadistic tendencies. When I appointed Governor Lehman as head of the new Office of Relief and Rehabilitation, I had some very sadistic thoughts in my head. I know that Governor Lehman is a great administrator, and I wanted a great administrator for this post. I had another thought in my mind, however. I had hopes that, when God spares my life and the war is over, to be able to go to Germany, stand behind a curtain and have the sadistic satisfaction of seeing some "Junkers" on their knees, asking Lehman for bread. And, by God, I'll urge him to give it to them".

Rabbi Wise then said: "Mr. President, we have an orthodox Rabbi in our midst. It is customary for an orthodox rabbi to deliver a benediction upon the head of his country, when he comes in his présence. Will you, therefore, permit rabbi Rosenberg to say the prayer of benediction?"

Doc. 148

224

−2− 4−

"Certainly" ± the President answered.

Rabbi Rosenberg rose and put on his scull-cap. We all rose. The President remained seated, and, as rabbi Rosenberg commenced to recite the prayer in Hebrew, the President bowed his head.

"O, God Lord of Kings, blessed be Thy name that Thou bestowest a share of Thy glory upon the son of men".

"Thank you very much" - the President said.

The President seemed to be moved, and so were we all.

Rabbi Wise then read the declaration by the committee.

Rabbi Wise did not read the details but simply said: "Mr. President, we also beg to submit details and proofs of the horrible facts. We appeal to you, as head of our government, to do all in your power to bring this to the attention of the world and to do all in your power to make an effort to stop it".

The President replied: "The government of the United States is very well acquainted with most of the facts you are now bringing to our attention. Unfortunately we have received confirmation from many sources. Representatives of the United States government in Switzerland and other neutral countries have given us proof that confirms the horrors discussed by you. We cannot treat these matters in normal ways. We are dealing with an insane man — Hitler, and the group that surrounds him represent an example of a national psychopatic case. We cannot act toward them by normal means. That is why the problem is very difficult. At the same time it is not in the best interests of the Allied cause to make it appear that the entire German people are murderers or are in agreement with what Hitler is doing. There must be in Germany elements, now thoroughly subdued, but who at the proper time will, I am sure, rise, and protest against the atrocities, against the whole Hitler system. It is too early to make pronouncements such as President Wilson made, may they even be very useful. As to your proposal, I shall certainly be glad to issue another statement, such as you request".

225

The President turned toward the delegation for suggestions. All, except rabbi Rosenberg, put in suggestions. Mine was about the possibility of getting some of the neutral representatives in Germany to intercede in behalf of the Jews. The President took notice of that but made no direct replies to the suggestions. The entire conversation on the part of the delegation lasted only a minute or two. As a matter of fact, of the 29 minutes spent with the President, he addressed the delegation for 23 minutes.

The President then plunged into a discussion of other matters. "We had a Jewish problem in North Africa"— he said. "As you know, we issued orders to free all the Jews from concentration camps, and we have also advised our representatives in North Africa to abolish all the special laws against the Jews and to restore the Jews to their rights. On this occasion I would like to mention that it has been called to our attention that prior to the war, Jews

-3- _ 5

and Frenchmen enjoyed greater rights than moslems in some of the
North African states. There are 17 million moslems in North
Africa, and there is no reason why anyone should enjoy greater
rights then they. It is not our purpose to fight for greater
rights for anyone at the expense of another group. We are for
freedom for all and equal rights for all. We consider the
attack on the Jews in Germany, in Poland, as an attack upon our
ideas of freedom and justice, and that is why we oppose it so
vehemently". -- "Now you are interested in the Darlan matter.
I can only illustrate this by a proverb, I recently heard from
a Yugoslav priest -- "When a river you reach and the devil you
meet, with the devil do not quarrel until the bridge you cross".

Apparently, at the end of this quotation the President must
have pushed some secret button, and his adjutant appeared in th e
room. His eyes and broad shoulders showed determination. We
rose from our seats, and, as we stood up, the President said:
"Gentlemen, you can prepare the statement. I am sure that you
will put the words into it that express my thoughts. I leave
it entirely to you. You may quote from my statement to the
Mass-Meeting in Madison Square Garden some months ago, but
please quote it exactly. We shall do all in our power to be of
service to your people in this tragic moment".

226

The President then shook hands with each of us, and we
filed out of the room.

APPENDIX 4

The following pages reproduce "Eye Witness Report from a Secret Courier Fresh from Poland." Jan Karski transmitted his report on the Warsaw Ghetto and on the Belzec death camp orally to the two Jewish representatives of the Polish government in exile in London, I. Schwartzbart and Szmul Zygielbojm, in December 1942. Zygielbojm then transmitted the report to the Bund Representation in New York and to the Jewish Labor Committee, which published it in the first issue of *Voice of the Unconquered*, March 1943, pp. 5, 8. Arieh Lebowitz and Gail Malmgreen, eds., *Robert F. Wagner Labor Archives, New York University, The Papers of the Jewish Labor Committee*, vol. 14 of *Archives of the Holocaust, An International Collection of Selected Documents*, edited by Henry Friedlander and Sybil Milton (New York: Garland, 1993), 240–41.

The Blackest Massacre of Jews in All Human History

Eye-Witness Report of a Secret Courier Fresh from Poland

At the end of October 1942 a secret courier of the United Polish Underground Organizations succeeded in getting out of Nazi-invaded Poland.

He reached London at the beginning of December, 1942.

FOR OVER A YEAR "THE COURIER" HAD BEEN A DISGUISED MEMBER OF THE POLICE FORCE OF POLAND THAT WAS ORGANIZED BY THE NAZI AUTHORITIES.

He brought with him the following documents: (1) A detailed report on the conditions in Poland to the Polish Government in London; (2) A message to the Jews from Agent "B" of the Underground General Jewish Workers Union of Poland; (3) A personal eye-witness account.

* * * * *

Immediately upon the arrival of "the Courier" in London, the Polish Government summoned the two Jewish members of the Polish National Council in London, Sh. Zygelbojm, representative of the General Jewish Workers Union, and Dr. J. Szwartzbart, Zionist representative, and turned over these documents to them. They were at once transmitted by the American Delegation of the General Jewish Workers Union of Poland to the JEWISH LABOR COMMITTEE which, ever since it was organized in 1933 to combat fascism, anti-Semitism and other forms of racial discrimination both in the United States and abroad has maintained intimate contact with the anti-Fascist and pro-Democratic underground forces of Europe. The eye-witness account follows:

Statement of the Secret Courier

I was in Poland from the month of October, 1941, until the end of October, 1942, on an official mission to the Polish Underground movement. Throughout this period I was in ~~ very midst of Polish underground activi—~ and I have been charged to transmit to ~u official information and also facts which I saw with my own eyes and which "B" of the Underground General Jewish Workers Union of Poland has requested me to tell you and to all Jews with whom I may come in contact when I get out of Poland.

What "B" Requested Me to Tell the Jews of the Free Countries

"B" requested me to inform you, Mr. Zygelbojm, and all other Jews the following: "Tell them 'there' (outside the Nazi-invaded countries) that there are moments when we hate them all; we hate them because they are safe 'there' and do not rescue us... Because they don't do enough. We are only too well aware that in the free and civilized world outside, it is not possible to believe *all* that is happening to us. Let the Jewish people, then, do *something* that will force the other world to believe us...

"We are all dying here. Let them not retreat until the civilized world will believe us—until it will undertake some action to rescue those of our people who will remain alive. Merely protests or threats are not sufficient."

Death in the Warsaw Ghetto

Long before the orgy of mass murder which commenced in the middle of July, 1942, conditions in the Warsaw Ghetto were desperate. The hunger was so great that the people became crazed. They refused to share their ~rumbs. Children would permit their old ~nts to starve to death. There was nothing to share.

The aged and children, by the hundreds, would drop dead in the streets and no one paid any attention to them. Dead corpses lying about in the streets no longer made an impression upon the inhabitants of the Ghetto. Every morning in front of practically every gate there would lie naked corpses. They were stripped of their clothes which were badly needed by the living and cast into the street to avoid funeral expenses. All of the dead gathered during the day would be buried in nameless common graves.

Hunting Jewish Children

There were thousands of children, whose parents were either murdered or dead of hunger, roaming the streets of the ghetto. The Germans organized actual hunting parties of these children and shot them in the thousands. In general the Germans demonstrate a particular brutality towards Jewish children. One can cite thousands of cases of people, who upon returning home from a day of forced labor, no longer found their children alive. Like beasts, the Germans comb the ghetto during the day, drag children out of their homes or off the streets and shoot them before the ghetto gates or outside of it. The Nazi authorities distributed arms to the Hitler Youth of 15 and 16, who go in hordes through the streets of the ghetto and kill all whom they meet in their path. They do not chose; children or grown ups. And when the streets are finally deserted they go into the yards, homes or shoot through the windows.

Numbering Corpses With Chalk

German soldiers and agents of the Gestapo are running the Hitler murder with a close second in this orgy of murder. They come to the ghetto in an interminable stream. For amusement they run competitions to determine who is the better shot. Some degenerates even mark their corpses with chalk, so as to be able to check the number they have killed. One Gestapo man by the name of Krause is known to enter a home, lock the door and murder an entire family. Then he marks in chalk on the door the number of persons he had shot that day. In the month of October alone, this Krause had marked in chalk on the door of a home the figure 1006—a thousand and six persons he had personally shot.

10,000 Jewish Children Murdered in One Day

It was since July 8, however, when the Germans first introduced special "Squads for the Destruction of Jews" (Juden Vernichtungs Kolonnen), which at once commenced the mass slaughter, that literally an atmosphere of hell began to permeate the ghetto. On that day, the Nazi authorities demanded of Dr. Czerniakow, head of the Jewish Ghetto Council, that he select 6000 Jews for "deportation". The following day they demanded 10,000 more and again 10,000 a day after and also 10,000 children. Czerniakow's wife was arrested and he was warned that she would be tortured and shot if he would not comply with the demand. When he inquired of the Germans what they intended to do with the Jews marked for "deportation" they laughed to his face and replied that they would do with them what one should do with Jews. On July 25, during one of these sessions with the Nazi authorities, Dr. Czerniakow excused himself, went into another room, and took poison.

The Polish policemen who usually guarded the gates of the Ghetto, both on the inside and the outside were removed a few days previously and substituted with German, Ukrainian, Latvian and Lithuanian guards.

After Czerniakow's death, all members of the Jewish Council were arrested and the aged engineer, Lichtenbaum, was appointed as the elder of the Ghetto. A hunt for Jews commenced. Whole streets were blockaded and all the inhabitants forcibly evacuated. In some cases, they even forced special Lithuanian, Polish and Jewish policemen to do the bloody work. These, on the one hand, were terrorized by the Nazi threat that if they would not round up daily a definite number of Jews in their district they themselves and their families would be executed—a threat which the Germans carried out in many districts—while,

(Continued on Page 8)

Eye-Witness Report of a Secret Courier Fresh from Poland

(Continued from Page 5)

on the other, they were promised to be spared if they would round up the required quota.

Anyone Who Looks Like a Jew Is Shot Outright

When the "Destruction Squads" begin their "liquidation" activities street after street, city after city is completely emptied of Jews. They simply disappear. No one can save them. Only a few outside the Ghetto escape with their lives. But even on the street outside the Ghetto, anyone who looks like a Jew is shot outright. There are many cases when the victims are Poles and even Germans who look like Jews.

Before I left, the Germans already began to settle Poles in the Warsaw Ghetto which was practically stripped of inhabitants by the "Destruction Squads." Our friends fear that when there will be no longer any Jews left in the Ghetto, the "Destruction Squads" will go after the Poles.

Scenes in the Valley of Death

Every day one can see thousands of Jews being led from the concentration points to the trains. On various pretexts dozens are shot during the march so as "to teach the Jews order before they die". Since July 8th the desperation of the ghetto has increased a hundred-fold. Total starvation is now reigning there. All smuggling of food stuffs which previously, too, was accompanied by great difficulties, has ceased completely. Before the mass slaughter commenced it was still possible for people outside the Ghetto to drop at specially designated places packages of food which were distributed to the Jews. Now it is no longer possible or safe to do this.

A particularly tragic problem are the children of the Ghetto. I have already related how thousands of children whose parents had died roamed the Ghetto streets, were hunted and killed out, like beasts. Thousands of them attempted to escape from the Ghetto but most were shot. It is known, however, that about 150 Jewish children are now roaming the streets outside the Ghetto begging in the houses of Poles. I saw some of these children on numerous occasions. I shall never forget them. They look less human than little monsters, dirty ragged with eyes that will haunt me forever—eyes of little beasts in the last anguish of death. They trust no one and expect only the worse from human beings. They slide along the walls of houses looking about them in mortal fear. No one knows where they sleep. From time to time they knock at the door of a Pole and beg for something to eat. Most of them follow a similar procedure: they knock at a door and run away to a distance ready to flee since no one can predict what kind of a creature would emerge from behind the locked door. If a human face appears they do not beg but without changing their pose they almost all repeat the same words in bad Polish: "Poles are kind people. Poles do not want to see human beings die of hunger. I am dying, *Paniusha*. Long live Poland."

Roads Paved With Dead

I want to return to the question of "deportations": I saw in Warsaw the first part of this act and later on the outskirts of Belzec the second and last part. From Warsaw the Jews are driven to the tracks on the outskirts of the city where a long train of cattle cars is already waiting for them. Before they reach the tracks, however, many are shot for one reason or another. Particularly those who lag behind. The whole route is literally strewn with corpses. When they finally reach their destination they are robbed of all their possessions (officially the deportees are urged to take along their most valuable possessions). Then they are loaded in cars, a hundred people in a car, and the first lap of the journey which lasts from two to eight days begins. Not once during the journey are the doors of the cars opened with the result that many die before they reach the "sorting point" (Obóz Rozdzielczy) which is located about fifty kilometers from the city of Belzec. Nevertheless the first stage of this journey is mild, almost human, in comparison with what awaits them at the second stage.

Belzec the Slaughter House

In the uniform of a Polish policeman I visited the sorting camp near Belzec. It is a huge barrack only about half of which is covered with a roof. When I was there about 5,000 men and women were in the camp. However, every few hours new transports of Jews, men and women, young and old, would arrive for the last journey towards death.

It is humanly impossible to convey the impression that these 5,000 people made upon me: they are no longer in the image of men. Skeletons with eyes dead with resignation. Naked, frightened, they are in constant motion with convulsive, nervous movements. A child is lying with its face towards the roof. It is in the last agony of death. But no one pays any attention to it. I spot amidst this indistinguishable mass an old man completely nude. He was probably stripped of his rags. No one looks at him. He makes no impression upon the people that surround him. The guards keep on shooting at the throng. Corpses are scattered everywhere. Men, in their convulsive moving about, step over them. They hardly notice the dead. Every few minutes the guards pick a number of men to clear the dead which are piled up alongside the fence. This, too, is done without any emotion, without a single expression in their faces as though they are completely oblivious of what they are doing. These are no longer normal beings but one large convulsive mass breathing its last.

The people are kept in this camp for several days. By the time they start on the last leg of their death-journey most of them have had nothing to eat for days since they are not given any food and have to subsist on whatever they manage to bring along with them.

The second and the most gruesome stage of their journey commences. Accompanied by the lashing of whips and the shooting of guns the "deportees" are suddenly, without any warning, beginning to be driven to the railroad tracks which are several dozen meters from the camp. A wild stampede of human beings begin. In the meantime, the Germans have made all the preparations to intensify their torture.

The route from the camp to the tracks is a specially constructed narrow passage lined by a weak fence of boards. On both sides of the fence are stationed armed guards. From behind the people are driven by guards who lash out mercilessly with their whips. Everything is designed to create a panic and a stampede. But at the same time "order" is demanded and no one dare touch the fence. Anyone who as much as touches the fence is shot at by the guards who are lined alongside of it. The shooting, the blood and the groans and shrieks of those who have been hit only increases the stampede and this gives the guards additional reason for shooting. In this manner, hundreds are killed on a stretch of several meters. But these are the lucky ones. An even more horrible death awaits the survivors.

The narrow passage leads to an open door of a cattle car. These are the famous cars designed for "40 people or 8 horses". We have measured these cars and found that if human beings were to be loaded there tightly pressed together and completely nude they could hold only 90. Yet 140 people are loaded in these cars. On both sides of the entrance are stationed special S.S. men with guns and whips. It is their job to force the people into the cars.

In Area of 50 Kilometers Corpses of Jews Are Being Burned Day and Night

In panic and fear the emaciated skeletons perform acrobatic feats. A moment comes when the last inch of a car is loaded to capacity. But human beings are still being driven into it: *einsteigen, einsteigen!* People begin to climb over the heads of their neighbors holding on by the hands, feet of hair of those who are already inside. Thus fifty more manage to get into the car which is then locked. Soon another takes its place . . .

A long train thus packed with several thousand men, women, and children is switched to a side line where it remains from two to eight days. The doors are never opened. Those inside suffer inhuman agony. They have to perform natural functions over the heads of the others. Many cars are painted with lime which begins to burn from the dampness of the urine and increases the tortures of the barefooted and nude.

Because there are not enough cars to kill the Jews in this relatively inexpensive manner many of them are taken to nearby Belzec where they are murdered by poison gases or by the application of electric currents. The corpses are burned near Belzec. Thus within an area of fifty kilometers huge stakes are burning Jewish corpses day and night.

The Cry of the Ghettos

Throughout my conversation with "B" he was composed and calm. Towards the end, however, he broke down. Banging his fist on the table he cried out: "I cannot, I cannot speak about these things. I am going mad. . . ." His last words were: "I am well aware that 'there', in the world of freedom civilized beings don't believe what they hear. Tell them that *we are all dying*. Let them rescue all those who will still be alive when the report reaches them. . . . We shall never forgive them for not having supplied us with arms so that we might have died like men, with guns in our hands."

NOTES

INTRODUCTION

1. American Federation of Labor, *Report of Proceedings of the 1934 Convention* (Washington, DC), 444.
2. The JLC's international focus was notable compared to the resolutely domestic emphasis of the AFL and even of the Congress of Industrial Organizations (CIO), the rival federation that from 1936 was engaged in formidable organizing struggles in the core sector of American industry. As we shall see, the JLC was connected to both federations by the two major garment workers' unions.
3. Enzo Traverso has argued that it was primarily exiled German Jews who reflected on Auschwitz: *La pensée dispersée: Figures de l'exil judéo-allemand* (Paris: Lignes/Éditions Léo Scheer, 2004), 11.
4. The rich bibliography on this subject is presented in chapter 1.
5. Varian Fry, *Surrender on Demand* (New York: Random House, 1945). Subsequent references to this book cite the edition jointly published with the United States Holocaust Memorial Museum, Varian Fry, *Surrender on Demand* (Boulder, CO: Johnson Books, 1997).
6. Fry, *Surrender on Demand*, 11.
7. Jean-Marie Guillon, editor of the conference held in Marseille, 1999, *Varian Fry du refuge à l'exil* (Arles: Actes Sud, 2000); Mona Bismarck Foundation, *Varian Fry à Marseille, 1940–1941: Les artistes et l'exil*, exhibition catalogue (Arles: Actes Sud, 2000); Andy Marino, *A Quiet American: The Secret War of Varian Fry* (New York: St. Martin's, 1999); Rosemary Sullivan, *Villa Air-Bel: World War II, Escape, and a House in Marseille* (New York: Harper, 2007).
8. Rudolf Hilferding, an Austrian-born economist who served as finance minister in the Weimar Republic, died in February 1941 in a Gestapo cell in Paris; Rudolf Breitscheid, a leading member of the German Social Democratic Party and legislator during the Weimar Republic, died at Buchenwald in August 1944.
9. David Wyman, the most widely known of a series of American historians who incriminated the Roosevelt administration for its slowness in accepting the reality of the destruction of the Jewish people, is the author of *Paper Walls: America and the Refugee*

Crisis, 1938–1941 (New York: Pantheon, 1968); and *The Abandonment of the Jews: America and the Holocaust, 1941–1945* (New York: New Press, 1998). See also Arthur Morse, *While Six Million Died: A Chronicle of American Apathy* (New York: Random House, 1968); Henry L. Feingold, *Politics of Rescue: The Roosevelt Administration and the Holocaust, 1938–1945* (New Brunswick, NJ: Rutgers University Press, 1970); Feingold, *Bearing Witness: How America and Its Jews Responded to the Holocaust* (Syracuse, NY: Syracuse University Press, 1995); Richard Breitman and Alan M. Kraut, *American Refugee Policy and European Jewry, 1933–1945* (Bloomington: Indiana University Press, 1987); Richard Breitman and Allan J. Lichtman, *FDR and the Jews* (Cambridge, MA: Harvard University Press, 2013).

10. Feingold, *Bearing Witness,* 239.

11. Isaac Deutscher, *The Non-Jewish Jew and Other Essays,* edited by Tamara Deutscher (London: Oxford University Press, 1968), 25–42.

12. For this statement, see Yuri Slezkine (*The Jewish Century* [Princeton: Princeton University Press, 2004], 85–86), citing in particular Istvan Deak, *Weimar Germany's Left Wing Intellectuals: A Political History of the Weltbühne and Its Circle* (Berkeley: University of California Press, 1968). See also Enzo Traverso, *Jews and Germany: From the "Judeo-German Symbiosis" to the Memory of Auschwitz,* translated by Daniel Weissbort (Lincoln: University of Nebraska Press, 1995).

13. Olivier Wieviorka has emphasized the multifaceted nature of the idea of resistance in *Histoire de la Résistance en France, 1940–1945* (Paris: Editions Perrin, 2013), 14–15.

14. François Bédarida, "Sur le concept de Résistance," in Jean-Marie Guillon and Pierre Laborie, eds., *Mémoire et Histoire: La Résistance* (Toulouse: Privat, 1995), 45–53; Frithjof Trapp argued that exile is in itself a form of resistance: "L'exil en tant que résistance, ébauche d'une typologie," in Gilbert Krebs and Gérard Schneilin, eds., *Exil et résistance au national-socialisme, 1933–1945* (Paris: Publications de l'Institut Allemand, Université Sorbonne Nouvelle, 1998), 15–59.

15. Eminent historian of the Holocaust Yehuda Bauer has underlined that the work of resistance included unarmed actions, such as providing food, medical care, and cultural support, to enable individual and group survival, as well as armed rebellion: "Resistance Myth and Reality," in *Rethinking the Holocaust* (New Haven: Yale University Press, 2001), 119–43. Concerning France, several historians have stressed the importance of Jewish resistance: Lucien Lazare, *Rescue as Resistance: How Jewish Organizations Fought the Holocaust in France,* translated by Jeffrey Green (New York: Columbia University Press, 1996); Asher Cohen, *Persécutions et sauvetages: Juifs et Français sous l'occupation et sous Vichy* (Paris: Editions du Cerf, 1993); Renée Poznanski, "Résistance juive, résistants juifs, retour à l'Histoire," in Guillon and Laborie, eds., *Mémoire et Histoire: La Résistance,* 227–45.

16. Poznanski, "Résistance juive."

17. Holocaust Era Records of the Jewish Labor Committee, Series I, 1934–1947, Robert F. Wagner Labor Archives, Tamiment Library, New York University (hereafter cited as JLC R, followed by Box [B] and Folder [F] number). The entire collection is available for consultation on 168 microfilm rolls.

18. Gail Malmgreen, "Labor and the Holocaust: The Jewish Labor Committee and the Anti-Nazi Struggle," *Labor's Heritage* 3, no. 4 (1991): 20–35; Malmgreen, "Comrades and Kinsmen: The Jewish Labor Committee and Anti-Nazi Activity," in Christine Collette and Stephen Bird, eds., *Jews, Labour and the Left, 1918–1948* (London: Ashgate, 2000), 4–20; Arieh Lebowitz and Gail Malmgreen, eds., *Robert F. Wagner Labor Archives, New York University, The Papers of the Jewish Labor Committee*, vol. 14 of *Archives of the Holocaust, An International Collection of Selected Documents*, edited by Henry Friedlander and Sybil Milton (New York: Garland, 1993) (hereafter cited as *Papers of the JLC*).

19. George L. Berlin, "The Jewish Labor Committee and American Immigration Policy in the 1930s," in *Studies in Jewish Bibliography, History and Literature in Honor of Edward Kiev*, edited by Charles Berlin (New York: Ktav, 1971), 45–73; David Kranzler, "The Role in Relief and Rescue during the Holocaust by the Jewish Labor Committee," in Seymour Finger, ed., *American Jewry during the Holocaust* (New York: Holmes and Meier, 1984), appendix 4-2, 1–29.

20. Jack Jacobs, "A Friend in Need: The Jewish Labor Committee and Refugees from the German-Speaking Lands, 1933–1945," *Yivo Annual* 23 (1996): 391–417.

21. Irving Howe, *World of Our Fathers: The Journey of the East European Jews to America and the Life They Found and Made* (New York: Simon and Schuster, 1976). The *Encyclopedia of the American Left*, edited by Mari Jo Buhle, Paul Buhle, and Dan Georgakas (New York: Oxford University Press, 1998), does not include an article on the JLC.

22. Moshe R. Gottlieb has studied the JLC's role in the boycott movement of German goods: *American Anti-Nazi Resistance, 1933–1941: An Historical Analysis* (New York: Ktav, 1982). Robert D. Parmet, David Dubinsky's biographer, has recorded his role with the JLC: *The Master of Seventh Avenue: David Dubinsky and the American Labor Movement* (New York: New York University Press, 2005), 193–94, 199–204, 241–42.

23. Wyman, *Paper Walls*, 55, 138; Wyman, *Abandonment of the Jews*, 161–62, 166, 170; Breitman and Kraut, *American Refugee Policy and European Jewry*, 95–96, 101, 104–5.

24. Yehuda Bauer, *My Brother's Keeper: A History of the American Jewish Joint Distribution Committee, 1929–1939* (Philadelphia: Jewish Publication Society, 1974); Bauer, *American Jewry and the Holocaust: The American Jewish Joint Distribution Committee, 1939–1945* (Detroit: Wayne State University Press, 1981); Sybil Milton and Fred Bogin, *American, Jewish Joint Distribution Committee*, vol. 10 of *Archives of the Holocaust*, edited by Henry Friedlander and Sybil Milton (New York: Garland, 1995); Laura Hobson Faure, *Un "plan Marshall juif": La présence juive américaine en France après la Shoah, 1944–1954* (Paris: Armand Colin, 2013).

25. Constance Pâris de Bollardière's Ph.D. dissertation focuses on the role of the JLC in France after the war: "'La pérennité de notre peuple': Une aide socialiste juive américaine dans la diaspora yiddish, le Jewish Labor Committee en France, 1944–1948" (Ph.D. diss., Ecole des Hautes Etudes en Sciences Sociales, 2017); Pâris de Bollardière, "Mutualité, fraternité et travail social chez les bundistes de France," *Archives juives, Revue d'histoire des Juifs de France*, 45, no. 1 (2012): 27–42.

26. For practical purposes, the names of persons of Jewish origin in Poland or elsewhere are spelled according to the English transliteration that has been used to establish the catalogue Holocaust Era Records of the Jewish Labor Committee.

CHAPTER 1: FOUNDATIONS

1. Saul Friedländer, *Nazi Germany and the Jews*, vol. 1, *1933–1939: The Years of Persecution* (New York: Harper Collins, 1997), 10, 17.
2. Despite differing interpretations of the specific characteristics and chronology of the Nazi movement, Holocaust historians concur that anti-Semitism was the central element of Nazi ideology. Arno Mayer has noted the specific link between anti-communism and anti-Semitism. In Hitler's discourse, which heavily influenced the thinking of Nazi-era military and civilian leaders, "the annihilation of Marxism from head to toe" was a precondition for the new order. Two unequal temporal and causal frameworks shaped this conjunction. See Arno Mayer, *Why Did the Heavens Not Darken?: The Final Solution in History* (New York: Pantheon, 1988) and Dan Michman, *Pour une historiographie de la Shoah: Conceptualisation, terminologie, définitions et problèmes fondamentaux* (Paris: In Press Editions, 2001), 48–51.
3. Deborah E. Lipstadt, *Beyond Belief: The American Press and the Coming of the Holocaust, 1933–1945* (New York: Free Press, 1986).
4. Moshe R. Gottlieb, *American Anti-Nazi Resistance, 1933–41: An Historical Analysis* (New York: Ktav, 1982), 28–34.
5. *New York Times*, August 22, 1933, cited in Daniel J. Tichenor, *Dividing Lines: The Politics of Immigration Control in America* (Princeton: Princeton University Press, 2002), 156. In *Nazi Germany and the Jews*, vol. 1, Saul Friedländer estimates that 525,000 Jews were living in Germany in 1933.
6. *New York Times*, May 3, 1933, 1, and May 5, 1933, 9.
7. Paul Pasteur, *Pratiques politiques et militantes de la social-démocratie autrichienne: 1888–1934* (Paris: Belin, 2003).
8. See, for example, *New York Times*, February 13, 1934, 2–3; February 15, 1934, 2; February 16, 1934, 1; February 17, 1934, 1–3; February 18, 1934, 1, section 8, xx; February 19, 1934, 14. Unlike their response to similar events in Germany in May 1933, the *New York Times* published articles accompanied by photographs showing the cruel fate of the Austrian labor movement.
9. Julius Braunthal reported that the Soviet newspaper *Pravda* asserted that "the Austrian social democrats, like their German comrades, had prepared the way for the triumph of fascism." *History of the International*, vol. 2, *1914–43* (London: Nelson, 1967), 403–14.
10. *Justice*, March 1934, 2–3; *New York Times*, February 18, 1934, 32.
11. Vladeck had initially reserved a hall at the New Yorker Hotel, but an employee strike at the hotel prompted him to cancel, informing the hotel management that it was unthinkable for a labor union meeting to cross a picket line. JLC R, B2, F1.
12. JLC R, B1, F1.

13. "Affiliated organizations may not at the same time be members of other Jewish inter-organizational central bodies who are engaged in activities similar to those which are engaged in by the Jewish Labor Committee." JLC R, B1, F1.

14. *New York Times*, April 5, 1934, 10.

15. AFL, *Proceedings of the 1934 Convention*, 443.

16. AFL, *Proceedings of the 1934 Convention*, 443–45.

17. The National Industrial Recovery Act (NIRA) (1933) was the first federal law to regulate labor relations. It encouraged competing businesses to work with worker representatives to draft codes of fair competition (such as banning child labor and regulating the length of the workday). Section 7(a) guaranteed workers the right to unionize and engage in collective bargaining. The NIRA was replaced by the Wagner Act, which reinforced labor rights, in 1935.

18. Melech Epstein, *Jewish Labor in U.S.A.: An Industrial, Political and Cultural History of the Jewish Labor Movement, 1914–1952* (New York: Trade Union Sponsoring Committee, 1953), 192–203; Robert D. Parmet, *The Master of Seventh Avenue: David Dubinsky and the American Labor Movement* (New York: New York University Press, 2005), 81–93; Irving Bernstein, *Turbulent Years: A History of the American Worker, 1933–1941* (Boston: Houghton Mifflin, 1970), 84–89.

19. Epstein, *Jewish Labor*, 203–11; Bernstein, *Turbulent Years*, 66–77; Steven Fraser, *Labor Will Rule: Sidney Hillman and the Rise of American Labor* (New York: Free Press, 1991), 284–93.

20. Epstein, *Jewish Labor*, 261–82; Joseph Brandes, "From Sweatshop to Stability: Jewish Labor between Two World Wars," *Yivo Annual of Jewish Social Science* 16 (1976): 1–150; Isaiah Trunk, "The Cultural Dimension of the American Jewish Labor Movement," *Yivo Annual of Jewish Social Science* 16 (1976): 342–93; Daniel Katz, *All Together Different: Yiddish Socialists, Garment Workers, and the Labor Roots of Multiculturalism* (New York: New York University Press, 2011), 123–64.

21. Brandes, "From Sweatshop to Stability," 105; Katz, *All Together Different*, 98–123.

22. Tony Michels, *A Fire in Their Hearts: Yiddish Socialists in New York* (Cambridge, MA: Harvard University Press, 2005), 179–216; Daniel Soyer, *Jewish Immigrant Associations and American Identity in New York, 1880–1939* (Cambridge, MA: Harvard University Press, 1997), 129–37.

23. The Poale Zion movement was divided into two factions: a rightist group with social-democratic tendencies that underestimated conflict in the Palestinian settlements and a smaller leftist branch inspired by Ber Borochov that was close to Communist parties. The left-leaning group had sided with the Bolsheviks during the Russian revolution but, like the Bund, strongly supported Yiddish culture.

24. ILGWU, *Proceedings of the 1934 Convention*, 250.

25. Jonathan Frankel, *Prophecy and Politics: Socialism, Nationalism and the Russian Jews, 1862–1917* (New York: Cambridge University Press, 1981), 185–257; Henri Minczeles, *Histoire générale du Bund: Un mouvement révolutionnaire juif* (Paris: Denoël, 1999); Enzo Traverso, *Les marxistes et la question juive: Histoire d'un débat (1843–1943)* (1990;

Paris: Éditions Kimé, 1997), 114–31; Jack Jacobs, ed., *Jewish Politics in Eastern Europe: The Bund at 100* (New York: New York University Press, 2001).

26. According to one argument offered during the Bund's Fourth Congress in 1901, "National does not signify nationalism, but merely the desire to belong to a determined nation, whereas nationalism signifies, in the short or long term, the domination of one nation by another." Cited in Minczeles, *Histoire générale du Bund*, 74.

27. Minczeles, *Histoire générale du Bund*, 124; Jack Jacobs, *On Socialists and "the Jewish Question" after Marx* (New York: New York University Press, 1992), 118–42.

28. Frankel, *Prophecy and Politics*, 141–47.

29. Vladimir Medem, *Fun mayn Lebn* (New York, 1923); Henry Tobias, *The Jewish Bund in Russia from Its Origins to 1905* (Stanford: Stanford University Press, 1972), 326–43.

30. Traverso, *Les marxistes et la question juive*, 120–31; Frankel, *Prophecy and Politics*, 183–85.

31. Minczeles, *Histoire générale du Bund*, 260–70; Emanuel Nowogrodzki, *The Jewish Labor Bund in Poland, 1915–1939: From Its Emergence as an Independent Political Party until the Beginning of World War II* (Rockville, MD: Shengold, 2001), 33–35.

32. Antony Polonsky, "The Bund in Polish Political Life, 1935–1939," in Ezra Mendelsohn, ed., *Essential Papers on Jews and the Left* (New York: New York University Press, 1997), 166–98. After initially being tempted to join the Third International (communist), the Polish Bund ultimately joined the LSI after years of fruitless discussions with the Comintern and the Polish Communist Party. Nowogrodzki, *The Jewish Labor Bund*, 28–74; Abraham Brumberg, "The Bund: History of a Schism," in Jacobs, ed., *Jewish Politics*, 81–90; Mario Kessler, "The Bund and the Labour and Socialist International," in Jacobs, ed., *Jewish Politics*, 183–94.

33. Claudie Weill, "Russian Bundists Abroad in Exile, 1898–1925," in Jacobs, ed., *Jewish Politics*, 46–55.

34. Samuel A. Portnoy, introduction to the English translation of Medem, *Fun mayn Lebn*: Vladimir Medem, *The Life and Soul of a Legendary Socialist* (New York: Ktav, 1979).

35. On Anton Litvak, see Epstein, *Jewish Labor*, 388–90; on Raphael Abramovitch, see André Liebich, *From the Other Shore: Russian Social Democracy after 1921* (Cambridge, MA: Harvard University Press, 1997), 100.

36. "Baruch Charney Vladeck," in Melech Epstein, *Profiles of Eleven* (Detroit: Wayne State University Press, 1965), 323–57; Epstein, *Jewish Labor*, 384–88. The most complete portrait of Vladeck was written by John Herling, "Vladeck," *Survey Graphic* 18, no. 11 (November 1939): 663–701, and 19, no. 1 (January 1940): 29–47.

37. The People's Relief Committee, the immediate ancestor of the JLC, had been formed by a garment trade union, the Workmen's Circle, the Association of the *Forward*, and leftist Zionist groups. Brandes, "From Sweatshop to Stability," 100–150.

38. Herling, "Vladeck," *Survey Graphic*, vol. 19; *Justice*, November 15, 1938, 1; Vladeck Memorial Meeting, December 11, 1938, JLC R, B13, F12.

39. Two biographies of these leaders are Robert D. Parmet, *The Master of Seventh Avenue: David Dubinsky and the American Labor Movement* (New York: New York University Press, 2005); Steve Fraser, *Labor Will Rule: Sidney Hillman and the Rise of American Labor* (New York: Free Press, 1991). See also the special issue of the journal *Labor*

History devoted to Dubinsky in the spring of 1968; and David Dubinsky and A. H. Rankin, *Dubinsky: A Life with Labor* (New York: Simon and Schuster, 1977), and "Sidney Hillman," in Epstein, *Profiles of Eleven*, 269–95.

40. During the New Economic Policy in Russia (1922–1924), Hillman had organized an industrial collaboration (the Russian American Industrial Corporation) with the USSR, sending machines and workers to develop textile and garment factories there. Fraser, *Labor Will Rule*, 185–88.

41. Fraser, *Labor Will Rule*, 441–539.

42. In a letter to Vladeck on August 27, 1937, Schlossberg claimed that the Palestinian Question was the only issue on which he disagreed with the Bund. Joseph Schlossberg Correspondence, ACWA Records Kheel Center for Labor-Management Documentation and Archives, Catherwood Library, Cornell University, Ithaca, New York (hereafter Schlossberg Correspondence), B140, F4.

43. For biographical information about these two leaders, see *Papers of the JLC*, xxvii, xxix, xix, xx.

44. Cited in Polonsky, "The Bund in Polish Political Life," 166–97.

45. Epstein, *Jewish Labor*, 124–56; Fraser, *Labor Will Rule*, 178–97; Parmet, *Master of Seventh Avenue*, 3.

46. Fraser, *Labor Will Rule*, 198–205.

47. There were only 9,300 members in 1929, far fewer than earlier in the decade. As many as 80 percent of its members were of working-class origin and many were employed in the garment industry. The replacement of the head of the American Communist Party, Jay Lovestone, with William Foster—who was imposed by Stalin—was a clear indication of Comintern authority. Harvey Klehr, *The Heyday of American Communism: The Depression Decade* (New York: Basic Books, 1984), 5–10.

48. Allan Wald, *The New York Intellectuals: The Rise and Decline of the Anti-Stalinist Left from the 1930s to the 1980s* (Chapel Hill: University of North Carolina Press, 1987), 46–50.

49. Nathan Chanin to Moses Schenkman, president of the Menorah Society, February 23, 1934, JLC R, B2, F1.

50. *New York Times*, April 5, 1934, 10.

51. Georges Haupt, Michael Lowy, and Claudie Weill, *Les marxistes et la question nationale, 1848–1914* (Paris: Maspéro, 1974); Jacobs, *On Socialists*; Traverso, *Les marxistes et la question juive*; Henry Tobias, "The Reassessment of the National Question," in Ezra Mendelsohn, ed., *Essential Papers*, 101–21; Nowogrodzki, *The Jewish Labor Bund*, 174–216.

52. Karl Kautski, "Der Kampf der Nationalitäten und das Staatsrecht in Oestereich," *Die Neue Zeit* 16 (1897–1898): 557–64; Otto Bauer, *Die Nationalitätenfrage und die Sozialdemokratie* (Vienna: Ignaz Brand, 1907) (which includes a chapter about Jewish nationality); works cited in Jacobs, *On Socialists*.

53. Haupt, Lowy, and Weill, *Les marxistes et la question nationale*; Jacob S. Hertz, "The Bund's Nationality Program and Its Critics in the Russian, Polish and Austrian Socialist Movements," *Yivo Annual of Jewish Social Science* 14 (1969): 53–67; Norbert Leser,

"Austro-Marxism: A Reappraisal," in Walter Laqueur and George L. Mosse, eds., *The Left Wing Intellectuals between the Wars, 1919–1939* (New York: Harper Torchbooks, 1966), 117–35.

54. Friedrich Adler to Henryk Erlich, October 15, 1929, cited in Kessler, "The Bund and the Labour and Socialist International," 183–94.

55. Jack Jacobs, "Austrian Social Democracy and the Jewish Question in the First Republic," in Anson Rabinbach, ed., *The Austrian Socialist Experiment: Social Democracy and Austro-Marxism, 1918–1934* (Boulder, CO: Westview Press, 1985), 157–68.

56. Louisa and Karl Kautski to Vladeck, June 1, 1938, JLC R, B6, F26. Vladeck left no records concerning his trips to Palestine or the USSR during the summer.

57. AFL, *Proceedings of the 1933 Convention*, 466–71.

58. AFL, *Proceedings of the 1933 Convention*, 466–71.

59. CIO, *Proceedings of the 1938 Convention*, 9–12; Leroy J. Lenburg, "The CIO and American Foreign Policy, 1935–1955" (Ph.D. diss., Pennsylvania State University, 1973); Robert H. Zieger, *John L. Lewis: Labor Leader* (Boston: Twayne, 1988). Lewis's strident isolationism led him to abandon President Roosevelt during the 1940 campaign and in turn to be replaced by Philip Murray as CIO president.

60. AFL, *Proceedings of the 1934 Convention*, 434–41.

61. The AFL was only affiliated with the IFTU between 1913 and 1919. The connection was not renewed after the war because the AFL feared being marginalized by socialist, labor, and social-democratic majorities.

62. See, for example, Alexander Saxton, *The Indispensable Enemy: Labor and the Anti-Chinese Movement in California* (Berkeley: University of California Press, 1971); Gwendolyn Mink, *Old Labor and New Immigrants in American Political Development: Union, Party and State, 1875–1920* (Ithaca: Cornell University Press, 1986); Catherine Collomp, *Entre classe et nation: Mouvement ouvrier et immigration aux Etats-Unis, 1880–1920* (Paris: Belin, 1998).

63. One indication of the Jewish presence in local higher education is that 93 percent of the student body at the Washington Square campus of New York University was Jewish at the time, with 80–90 percent Jewish at City College and Hunter College in 1920, and 40 percent at Columbia University. Henry L. Feingold, *A Time for Searching: Entering the Mainstream, 1920–45* (Baltimore: Johns Hopkins University Press, 1992), 15; Jeffrey S. Gurock, ed., *American Jewish History*, vol. 6, *Anti-Semitism in America* (New York: Routledge, 1998).

64. One ILGWU member in St. Louis alerted David Dubinsky of the likeliness that anti-Semitism would arise from Coughlinites among Italian members of the union. David Dubinsky Correspondence, ILGWU Records, 5780/002, Kheel Center for Labor-Management Documentation and Archives, Catherwood Library, Cornell University, Ithaca, New York (hereafter DDC), 5780/002, B6, F6c.

65. Ronald Bayor, "Klans, Coughlinites and Aryan Nations: Patterns of American Anti-Semitism in the 20th Century," in Gurock, ed., *American Jewish History*, 6:579–94; Sander A. Diamond, *The Nazi Movement in the United States, 1924–1941* (Ithaca: Cornell University Press, 1974).

66. Arthur D. Morse, *While Six Million Died: A Chronicle of American Apathy* (New York: Random House, 1968); David Wyman, *Paper Walls: America and the Refugee Crisis, 1938–1941* (New York: Pantheon, 1968); Henry L. Feingold, *The Politics of Rescue: The Roosevelt Administration and the Holocaust, 1938–1945* (New Brunswick, NJ: Rutgers University Press, 1970); Saul Friedman, *No Haven for the Oppressed: United States Policy toward Jewish Refugees, 1938–1945* (Detroit: Wayne State University Press, 1973); David Wyman, *The Abandonment of the Jews: America and the Holocaust, 1941–1945* (New York: New Press, 1998). Richard Breitman and Allan Lichtman have nuanced these judgments emphasizing Roosevelt's positive gestures toward refugees: *FDR and the Jews* (Cambridge, MA: Harvard University Press, 2013). Rebecca Erbelding, by focusing on the creation of the War Refugee Board, has also produced a more positive vision of the Roosevelt administration's reactions to the knowledge of the extermination of the Jews: *Rescue Board: The Untold Story of America's Efforts to Save the Jews of Europe* (New York: Anchor, 2019).

67. *Historical Statistics of the United States* (Washington, DC: U.S. Department of Commerce/Bureau of the Census, 1970), 105.

68. Maurice Davie, *Refugees in America: Report of the Committee for the Study of Recent Immigration from Europe* (New York: Harper and Brothers, 1947), 28.

69. Maurice Davie contends that nearly all immigrants from countries under Nazi and fascist domination were actually refugees, with a significant proportion of them Jewish, depending on the country (*Refugees in America*, 33–35). Henry Feingold provides a lower estimate of 157,000 refugees, including 110,000 Jews, for the years 1933–1944 (*The Jewish People in America*, 234).

70. As I was writing these lines, a similar situation was occurring in Europe. Faced with the uninterrupted flow of Syrians desperately fleeing the civil war in their country, European nations have been divided as to welcoming refugees. A combination of economic and cultural arguments were used by countries that only reluctantly admitted small numbers of refugees, while others have been more generous. Stringent admission regulations for asylum seekers and reinforced border controls have not reduced the flow of migrants but left many of them in desperate situations. As soon as nation-states establish quotas, ceilings, or other regulations to control the migratory flow to their countries, they face dilemmas when refugee crises occur that necessitate adapting or loosening quotas.

71. Laura Fermi (Enrico Fermi's wife) was among the first to attract attention to this particular source of immigration: *Illustrious Immigrants: The Intellectual Migration from Europe, 1930–1941* (Chicago: University of Chicago Press, 1968); Donald Fleming and Bernard Bailyn, *The Intellectual Migration: Europe and America, 1930–1960* (Cambridge, MA: Harvard University Press, 1969); Stuart H. Hughes, *The Sea Change: The Migration of Social Thought, 1930–1965* (New York: Harper and Row, 1975); Anthony Heilbut, *Exiled in Paradise: German Refugee Artists and Intellectuals in America from the 1930s to the Present* (New York: Viking, 1983); Martin Jay, *Permanent Exiles: Essays on the Intellectual Migration from Germany to America* (New York: Columbia University Press, 1985); Jean-Michel Palmier, *Weimar in Exile: The Antifascist Emigration in Europe and*

America, translated by David Fernbach (London: Verso, 2017); Claus-Dieter Krohn, *Intellectuals in Exile: Refugee Scholars and the New School for Social Research* (Amherst: University of Massachusetts Press, 1993); Stephanie Barron, ed., *Exiles + Emigrés: The Flight of European Artists from Hitler* (Los Angeles: Los Angeles County Museum of Art, Harry Abrams, 1997); Laurent Jeanpierre, "Des hommes entre plusieurs mondes: Étude sur une situation d'exil, Intellectuels français réfugiés aux États-Unis pendant la Deuxième Guerre mondiale" (Ph.D. diss., Ecole des Hautes Etudes en Sciences Sociales, 2004); Emmanuelle Loyer, *Paris à New York: Intellectuels et artistes français en exil, 1940–1947* (Paris: Grasset, 2005).

72. Laurent Jeanpierre, "Système de l'exil: L'exemple des Français réfugiés aux États-Unis pendant la Seconde Guerre Mondiale, 1940–1942," in Catherine Collomp and Mario Menéndez, eds., *Exilés et réfugiés politiques aux Etats-Unis, 1789–2000* (Paris: CNRS Editions, 2003), 113–35.

73. Aristide Zolberg, *A Nation by Design* (New York: Russell Sage Foundation, 2006), 275. See also Richard Breitman and Alan M. Kraut, *American Refugee Policy and European Jewry, 1933–1945* (Bloomington: Indiana University Press, 1987), 34–38; Tichenor, *Dividing Lines*, 156–59.

74. According to Henry Feingold, Breckinridge Long "viewed his fight against the refugees as primarily a battle against Jewish Communist agitators who were trying to ruin his political career": *Bearing Witness: How America and Its Jews Responded to the Holocaust* (Syracuse, NY: Syracuse University Press, 1995), 81.

75. The story of the *Saint Louis* created a scandal. Of the 933 passengers onboard a ship that sailed from Hamburg, 743 were German Jews with pending applications for American immigration visas. They had filed the required affidavits for their visas to be processed and hoped to wait in Cuba to fall inside the quotas. The Department of State, however, refused to approve this approach, arguing that pre-admitting Jewish visa applicants would pre-assign places in the German quota, to the detriment of already registered applicants. The ship eventually sailed back to Europe after its passengers were refused permission to disembark while the ship was anchored in the port of Havana.

76. Feingold, *A Time for Searching*, 229.

77. Feingold, *Bearing Witness*, 10.

78. According to Breitman and Lichtman, "Oddly enough FDR did more for the Jews than any other world figure, even if his efforts seemed inefficient in retrospect" (*FDR and the Jews*, 2).

79. ACWA, *Proceedings of the 1934 Convention*, 400; *Proceedings of the 1936 Convention*, 189; ILGWU, *Proceedings of the 1934 Convention*, 414; *Proceedings of the 1937 Convention*, 329; *Proceedings of the 1940 Convention*, 685.

80. AFL, *Proceedings of the 1935 Convention*, 603; George L. Berlin, "The Jewish Labor Committee and American Immigration Policy in the 1930s," in Charles Berlin, ed., *Studies in Jewish Bibliography, History and Literature in Honor of Edward Kiev* (New York: Ktav, 1971), 45–71.

81. In 1936, the JLC Executive Office reported that it was "physically impossible under present circumstances to transport the 450,000 remaining Jews in Germany to other countries." JLC R, B1, F2.

CHAPTER 2: CONSTRUCTING INTERNATIONAL LINKS, 1933–1937

1. Victor Silverman, *Imagining Internationalism in American and British Labor, 1939–1949* (Urbana: University of Illinois Press, 2000), 17–20. Jean Yves Saunier has underlined the heuristic importance of circulations, personal contacts, voyages, and material exchanges on the impact of cultural, political, and scientific transfers: "Circulations, connexions et espaces transnationaux," *Genèses* 57 (December 2004): 110–26.

2. On the weakness of the LSI, see Bruno Groppo, "L'Internationale ouvrière social-iste en 1933," in Serge Wolikow and Michel Cordillot, eds., *Prolétaires de tous les pays unissez-vous? Les difficiles chemins de l'internationalisme (1848–1956)* (Dijon: Centre de documentation sur les internationales ouvrières, 1993), 153–67; Michel Dreyfus, "Les sept causes de la crise de l'IOS en 1939," in Wolikow and Cordillot, eds., *Prolétaires de tous les pays unissez-vous*, 177–83; Julius Braunthal, *History of the International*, vol. 2, *1914–43* (London: Nelson, 1967), 399–402, 469–92. On the IFTU, see Geert van Goethem, "Conflicting Interests: The International Federation of Trade Unions, 1919–1945," in Anthony Carew, Michel Dreyfus, et al., eds., *The International Confederation of Free Trade Unions* (Berne: Peter Lang, 2000), 123–47.

3. Such as the members of the Socialist Labor Party in the 1890s or of Eugene Debs's Socialist Party of America in the 1900s.

4. Lewis L. Lorwin, *The International Labor Movement, History, Policies, Outlook* (New York: Harper and Brothers, 1953), 127; Lewis Lorwin, *FSI: L'œuvre de la Fédération syndicale Internationale dans les années 1927–1930* (Amsterdam, 1931), 240–41.

5. On the fruitless postponement of an anti-fascist agreement between the LSI and the Comintern, see Gerd-Rainer Horn, *European Socialists Respond to Fascism: Ideology, Activism and Contingency in the 1930s* (New York: Oxford University Press, 1996), 37–50.

6. Walter Schevenels, *Forty-Five Years: The International Federation of Trade Unions, 1901–1945* (Brussels: International Federation of Trade Unions, 1956), 204–5; Braunthal, *History of the International*, 402–14; AFL, *Proceedings of the 1933 Convention*, 470.

7. Selig Perlman, himself an immigrant of Russian origin, had noted the pragmatism of the American worker, more "job conscious" than "class conscious," caring little about intellectual and political matters: *A Theory of the Labor Movement* (New York: Macmillan, 1928).

8. See the diary that Abraham Plotkin wrote during his stay in Berlin: *An American in Hitler's Berlin: Abraham Plotkin's Diary, 1932–1933*, edited by Catherine Collomp and Bruno Groppo (Urbana: University of Illinois Press, 2009).

9. Abraham Plotkin Collection, Kheel Center for Labor-Management Documentation and Archives, Catherwood Library, Cornell University, Ithaca, NY (hereafter Plotkin Collection), B2, F9.

10. Abraham Plotkin, "The Destruction of the Labor Movement in Germany," *American Federationist* (August 1933): 811–26, article reproduced in *An American in Hitler's Berlin*, 175–95. In his correspondence, Plotkin noted that the article was also published in Yiddish during the month of July in the *Jewish Daily Forward*. Plotkin to Stolz, July 1, 1933, Plotkin Collection, B2, F15.

11. Plotkin, *An American in Hitler's Berlin*, 185.

12. *New York Times*, May 5, 1933, 5: "Mr. Green announced that the American Federation of Labor had received information from a confidential source of the ruthless suppression of the German trade unions, whose offices were raided without warning, their property confiscated, the elected officers arrested and representatives of the Hitler Government placed in full control."

13. Plotkin to Stolz, November 14, 1933, Plotkin Collection, B2, F15.

14. Lefkowitz to Plotkin, May 23, 1933, Plotkin Collection, B1, F14.

15. Plotkin to Plettl, July 14, 1933, October 31, 1933, November 1, 1933, all in Plotkin Collection B2, F9. See also the *New York Times*, October 31, 1933, 10.

16. Schevenels to Plotkin, June 3, 1933, Plotkin Collection, B2, F15.

17. Dubinsky, November 9, 1933, circular to the sections in Cleveland, Chicago, Baltimore, Philadelphia, Boston, Newark, DDC, 5780/002, B134, F4B); *Justice*, November 1933, 21, December 1933, 27, March 1934, 17; *New York Times*, February 16, 1934, 5.

18. German text of Plettl's speech to the ILGWU Convention, DDC, B8, F2B; ILGWU, *Proceedings of the 1934 Convention*, 166; ACWA, *Proceedings of the 1934 Convention*, 189–93.

19. Plettl to Vladeck, July 8, 1934, DDC, B39, F3B.

20. Plettl to Dubinsky, August 10, 1935, February 1, 1936, DDC, B134, F4B; Albrecht Ragg, "The German Socialist Emigration in the United States, 1933–1945" (Ph.D. diss., Loyola University-Chicago, 1977), 101–6.

21. Plettl to Vladeck, July 8, 1934, and Vladeck to Dubinsky, July 19, 1934, DDC, B39, F3B; AFL, *Proceedings of the 1934 Convention*, 434–45.

22. AFL, *Proceedings of the 1934 Convention*, 434–45.

23. Walter Citrine, *Men and Work: The Autobiography of Walter Citrine* (London: Hutchinson, 1964), 346–47. See also "Journey to America," 1934, Walter Citrine Papers, London School of Economics.

24. Labor Chest for the Liberation of Workers of Europe, JLC R, B16, F14; DDC, B134, F4B.

25. By comparison with Citrine's tour that had brought in $2,063, and that of Julius Deutsch ($1,102), Seger's furnished only $228 to the Labor Chest. See 2nd Convention of the JLC, October 1935, JLC R, microfilm roll 160.

26. Seger to Minkoff, June 27, 1938, JLC R, B3, F4.

27. Ragg, "The German Socialist Emigration," 109–20.

28. ILGWU, *Proceedings of the 1934 Convention*, 162–66, 330–31.

29. On Giuseppe Modigliani, see A. Thomas Lane, ed., *Biographical Dictionary of European Labor Leaders* (Westport, CT: Greenwood Press, 1995), 2:65; *Enciclopedia dell' Antifascismo e della Resistenza* (Milano: La Pietra, 1968), 491. Giuseppe was the older brother of the painter Amedeo Modigliani.

30. On Antonini and the Italian dressmaking locals in New York, see Charles Anthony Zappia, "Unionism and the Italian American Worker: A History of the New York City 'Italian Locals' in the ILGWU" (Ph.D. diss., University of California–Berkeley, 1994); Philip V. Cannistraro, "Luigi Antonini and the Italian Anti-fascist Movement in the United States, 1940–1943," *Journal of American Ethnic History* (Fall 1985): 21–40. On Local 89, see *La Strenna commemorativa del XV anniversario della fondazione della Italian Dressmakers Union, Locale 89, ILGWU,* compiled by the Italian Labor Education Bureau (New York, 1934). On fascist-leaning sympathies in the United States, see John Patrick Diggins, *Mussolini and Fascism: The View from America* (Princeton: Princeton University Press, 1972); Stefano Luconi, *La "Diplomazia Parallela": Il regime fascista e la mobilitazione politica degli italo-americani* (Milano: Franco Angeli, 2000). On radio WEVD: Nathan Godfried, "Struggling over Politics and Culture: Organized Labor and Radio Station WEVD during the 1930s," *Labor History* 42, no. 4 (2001): 347–69.

31. On Modigliani's tour, see Luigi Antonini Correspondence, ILGWU Records, Kheel Center for Labor-Management Documentation and Archives, Catherwood Library, Cornell University, Ithaca, New York (hereafter AC), 5780/023, Romualdi to Antonini, B118, F1; Antonini to Pietro Nenni, B35, F1; B36, F4; Modigliani-Antonini Correspondence, June 8, 1935, B35, F1; June 26, 1935, B35, F2; Augusto Bellanca Papers, ACWA Records, 5619, B146; *Justice*, December 1934, 16, January 1, 1935, 4, January 15, 1935, 5, February 15, 1935, 3. The list of cities where Modigliani made speeches is impressive: Buffalo, Rochester, Syracuse, Utica, Toronto, Cleveland, Cincinnati, Detroit, Chicago, Milwaukee, San Francisco, Los Angeles, Seattle, Portland, Scranton, Philadelphia, Pittsburgh, Baltimore, New York, Brooklyn, Boston, and Providence.

32. Dubinsky to Modigliani, March 22, 1935; Adler to Modigliani, April 2, 1935, DDC, B8 F2B; Antonini to Dubinsky, memorandum on Labor Chest contributions to Italian anti-fascists, June 1936, DDC, B8, F1C; excerpts from letters of Modigliani to Antonini, June 26, 1936, DDC, B8, F1 C.

33. Antonini's speech on radio station WEVD after his return from Belgium and France, November 12, 1935, AC, B46, F4.

34. *Justice*, October 1, 1935, 7; October 15, 1935, 6; November 1, 1935, 3; November 15, 1935, 6.

35. ILGWU, *Proceedings of the 1937 Convention,* 187; *Justice*, August 15, 1936, 7; DDC, B34, F1.

36. Schevenels, *Forty-Five Years,* 248–49; Dubinsky, "To all local unions and joint boards of the ILGWU," August 17, 1936, DDC, B164, F3D; Dubinsky's speech on WEVD addressed to ILGWU members, August 14, 1936, DDC, B39, F6.

37. New York State District of Communist Party, August 18, 1936, "All funds will be turned over, upon receipt, to David Dubinsky, President of the ILGWU, who heads the Trade Union Committee which has set itself the goal of raising $100,000 for the support of the cause of the Spanish workers"; Dubinsky to Israel Amter, organizer of

the Communist Party for New York state, August 19, October 29, 1936; Dubinsky to
the *Daily Mirror*, September 26, 1936, DDC, B164, F3D; Harvey Klehr, *The Heyday of
American Communism: The Depression Decade* (New York: Basic Books, 1984), 219.

38. Dubinsky to Citrine, telegram of September 9, 1936, informing him of the campaign
led by the Catholic Church against the Spanish Republicans, DDC, B47, F1B; B164,
F3D; *Justice*, October 1, 1936, 3 and 16; "You rotten dog of a Jew, here is your warning"
was a typical insult, this one signed "A Christian"; Dubinsky responded to Reverend
Francis J. Healy, editor of the *Brooklyn Tablet* (a leading Catholic weekly): "Permit me
to say that the ILGWU, the third largest trade union in the United-States is not composed of any single ethnical group or religious following. We have in our membership
as many of the Catholic faith as of the Jewish, and a substantial number of Protes-
tants." DDC, B164, F3D; Robert D. Parmet, *The Master of Seventh Avenue: David
Dubinsky and the American Labor Movement* (New York: New York University Press,
2005), 137–39.

39. Walter Schevenels noted that Citrine's trip to the United States had the goal of
correcting the image of the loyal Spanish Republicans in American public opinion
(*Forty-Five Years*, 25).

40. Citrine to Dubinsky, September 1, 1936, DDC, B47, F1B.

41. "Report of Committee on International Labor Relations," AFL, *Proceedings of the 1937
Convention*, 628–30.

42. AFL, *Proceedings of the 1937 Convention*, 628–30; William Green, *American Federationist*, December 1937, 1293–94; *Justice*, August 1, 1937, 16. Correspondence from Matthew
Woll to Dubinsky indicates that he had reason to complain about a certain contempt
for him shown by some European delegates during the meeting in Warsaw, notably
on the part of Adolf Staal, representing the textile unions at the International Labor
Organization; Woll to Dubinsky, August 13, 1937, DDC, B47, F4.

43. Schevenels to Lipschitz, coordinator of Trade Union Relief for Spain, August 2, 1938,
announcing his decision not to go to Mexico; Jouhaux to Dubinsky, August 4, 1938,
DDC, B166, F3A–3B; Stolz to Dubinsky, August 16, 1938, DDC, B166, F3A–3B; Vla-
deck, "Remarks at luncheon to Pena, Jouhaux, Fimmen," August 24, 1938, DDC, B166,
F2B and F3B. This trip was the occasion for Léon Jouhaux to meet William Green
in Washington, and also to obtain an interview with President Roosevelt. Georges
Bernard and Denise Tintant, *Léon Jouhaux dans le mouvement syndical français* (Paris:
Presses Universitaires de France, 1979), 415.

44. "American Fund for Political Prisoners and Refugees," New York, August 10, 1938,
appeal signed by figures from the American progressive, socialist, or anarchist world,
including: Baruch Charney Vladeck, John Dos Passos, Max Eastman, Benjamin Stol-
berg, Suzanne La Follette, John Dewey, Sidney Hook, Dwight McDonald, Norman
Thomas, Carlo Tresca, Sidney Hillman, Charles Zimmerman, Joseph Schlossberg,
David Dubinsky; Julian Gorkin, political secretary of the POUM, to Dubinsky, Paris,
May 5, 1939, thanking him for his "active solidarity," DDC, B166, F2A, F3B.

45. Calls for solidarity with the Spanish Republic had also multiplied in England in the
form of a popular front that apparently diminished the initial role of the unions: Tom

Buchanan, *The Spanish Civil War and the British Labour Movement* (Cambridge: Cambridge University Press, 1991), 140.

46. "Trade Union Relief for Spain," DDC, B166, F2A; Lipschitz to Zimmerman, July 5, 1938, B166, F3B; Dubinsky to Schevenels, August 6, 1937, DDC, B47, F2B; Charles Zimmerman Papers, ILGWU Records, Kheel Center for Labor-Management Documentation and Archives, Catherwood Library, Cornell University, Ithaca, New York, 5780/014, B12, F9; *Justice*, June 15, 1937, 3; *New York Times*, April 27, 1939. The Friends of the Abraham Lincoln Brigade assembled sympathizers with the Republican cause—workers, the unemployed, and intellectuals—on a much wider scale than what could be achieved by the American Communist Party acting alone. Peter N. Carroll, *The Odyssey of the Abraham Lincoln Brigade: Americans in the Spanish Civil War* (Stanford: Stanford University Press, 1994).

47. Trade Union Relief for Spain, meeting, September 21, 1938, DDC, B166, F2B; Edo Fimmen, August 24, 1938, DDC, B166, F3B; Dieter Nelles, "ITF Resistance against Nazism and Fascism in Germany and Spain," in Bob Reinalda, ed., *The International Transportworkers Federation, 1914–1945: The Edo Fimmen Era* (Amsterdam: Stichting beheer IISG, 1997), 174–98.

48. Since 1936, the ILGWU had supported the Italian combatants of the Garibaldi Brigade in Spain: Pietro Nenni to Antonini, March 9, 1937, thanking him for the $2,000 received, DDC, B8, F1C; Dubinsky to Schevenels, September 2, 1937, sending $2,500 intended for them, DDC, B8, F1C. In 1939, Friends of the Garibaldi Brigade requested aid for the sixteen Italian refugees in France of which the Friends were aware; DDC, B166, F2A.

CHAPTER 3: POLITICS OF ANTI-NAZISM, 1935–1939

1. Jacques Droz, *Histoire de l'antifascisme en Europe* (Paris: La Découverte, 1985).

2. The massive demonstration at Madison Square Garden in New York on March 27, 1933, had gathered many prominent personalities (Jewish and non-Jewish) from the city, and their speeches were broadcast on the radio throughout the United States and in Europe. Simultaneously assemblies were taking place in all the major American cities. The blackmail practices by the Nazi authorities are described by Saul Friedländer, *Nazi Germany and the Jews*, vol. 1, *1933–1939: The Years of Persecution* (1997; New York: Harper Collins, 2009), 19–23.

3. The American Jewish Committee and the B'nai B'rith were opposed to the boycott because they thought this form of action, like mass demonstrations, could only inflame the situation in Germany and be used against Jewish residents. The Jewish War Veterans in the United States were among the first to mobilize in favor of a boycott. On this subject, see Moshe R. Gottlieb, *American Anti-Nazi Resistance, 1933–1941: An Historical Analysis* (New York: Ktav, 1982); William Orbach, "Shattering the Shackles of Powerlessness: The Debate Surrounding the Anti-Nazi Boycott of 1933–41," *Modern Judaism* 2, no. 2 (1982): 149–69; Henry L. Feingold, *A Time for Searching: Entering the Mainstream, 1920–1945* (Baltimore: Johns Hopkins University Press, 1992), 234–39.

4. In December 1934, Vladeck had rejected the AJC's proposal to affiliate: Gottlieb, *American Anti-Nazi Resistance*, 181–85. After corrections, the November 27 agreement was ratified by both parties on February 3, 1936, JLC R, B9, F39.

5. Gottlieb, *American Anti-Nazi Resistance*, 185–90; Cordell Hull, *The Memoirs of Cordell Hull* (New York: Macmillan, 1948), 1:236–42.

6. "Agreement between the American Jewish Congress and the Jewish Labor Committee, entered upon February 3, 1936," JLC R, B9, F39. The document established a list of businesses and unions to which it was sent.

7. Dr. Joseph Tenenbaum, "Three Years of the Anti-Nazi Boycott," 1936 brochure, JLC R, B9, F40.

8. Robert Dallek, *Franklin D. Roosevelt and American Foreign Policy, 1932–1945* (Oxford: Oxford University Press, 1979), 124–25; William R. Allen, "The International Trade Philosophy of Cordell Hull, 1907–1933," *American Economic Review* 43, no. 1 (1953): 101–16.

9. Dallek, *Franklin D. Roosevelt and American Foreign Policy*, 92–93, 124–25. Cordell Hull clearly explained that these German export subsidies came from the money the Third Reich was recuperating by refusing to pay the whole interest sum on the war reparations debt (for which it had borrowed from American banks and which was paid over to German exporters). *The Memoirs of Cordell Hull*, 1:239–40.

10. "Boycott Nazi Goods and Services," bulletin of the Joint Boycott Council, January 1938; "Report of Activities of the Joint Boycott Council, January–June 1938," JLC R, B9, F41.

11. Joseph Tenenbaum, "Boycott can defeat Hitlerism," in *Six Years of Anti-Nazi Boycott*, May 7, 1939, JLC R, B9, F42; Tenenbaum, "The boycott in the light of war experiences," September 1939, JLC R, B9, F42.

12. Moshe Gottlieb, "In the Shadow of War: The American Anti-Nazi Boycott Movement in 1939–41," *American Jewish History* 62, no. 2 (1972): 146–61.

13. Allen Guttmann, *The Olympics: A History of the Modern Games* (Urbana: University of Illinois Press, 1994), 53–71; Deborah E. Lipstadt, *Beyond Belief: The American Press and the Coming of the Holocaust, 1933–1945* (New York: Free Press, 1986), 63–85.

14. Brundage was firmly won over to the holding of the Games in Berlin even before going there for his inspection, "believing what they wanted him to believe." Guttmann, *The Olympics*, 56–62.

15. Lipstadt, *Beyond Belief*, 74–78; Edward Shapiro, "The World Labor Athletic Carnival of 1936: An American Anti-Nazi Protest," *American Jewish History* 59 (March 1985): 255–73.

16. Founded in 1888, the AAU established sporting norms and the rules of competition, and thus represented the athletes during national and international meetings, notably during the Olympic Games.

17. World Labor Athletic Carnival, JLC R, B13, F6; Isaiah Minkoff to Meyer Weinrib, JLC representative in Chicago, July 8, 1936, affirming that the event should also be a success on the sporting level, *Papers of the JLC*, 17.

18. We might add that the vogue for sport in the education offered in youth movements had also developed in Poland under the aegis of the Bund in the 1930s: Jack Jacobs, *Bundist Counterculture in Interwar Poland* (Syracuse, NY: Syracuse University Press, 2009), 48–49.

19. New York City newspaper clippings in JLC R, microfilm roll 49, B20; JLC R, B13, F6; daily *New York Times* entries for World Labor Athletic Carnival in sports sections; see, for instance, June 3–July 31, August 1–29.

20. In the United States it was noticed that Hitler had not saluted the African American hero, but the silence of the press in the southern states prevented national pride from being displayed. Deborah Lipstadt stresses that the critical opinion of the American newspapers, including the *New York Times*, was overshadowed by enthusiastic coverage of the grandeur of the Games, even though Germany had begun to rearm in 1935 and had occupied the Rhineland in March 1936, i.e., between the Winter and Summer Games (*Beyond Belief*, 63–85).

21. "Baruch Charney Vladeck," in Melech Epstein, *Profiles of Eleven* (Detroit: Wayne State University Press, 1965), 323–57; Epstein, *Jewish Labor in U.S.A.: An Industrial, Political and Cultural History of the Jewish Labor Movement, 1914–1952* (New York: Trade Union Sponsoring Committee, 1953), 240–52; John Herling, "Vladeck," *Survey Graphic* 19, no. 1 (January 1940): 29–47.

22. On the American Labor Party, of which Hillman was also one of the initiators, see Steven Fraser, *Labor Will Rule: Sidney Hillman and the Rise of American Labor* (New York: Free Press, 1991), 363–65; Kenneth Waltzer, "The American Labor Party: Third Party Politics in New Deal–Cold War New York" (Ph.D. diss., Harvard University, 1977).

23. Vladeck Houses, an ensemble of twenty buildings of six stories containing 1,523 apartments, began construction in 1939.

24. The 1936 elections have been characterized as "a referendum on the New Deal." V. O. Key, *Politics, Parties and Pressure Groups* (New York: Th. Crowell, 1958), 207–9; Feingold, *A Time for Searching*, 189–224. The SPA lost over half of its members in this election.

25. "Memorandum submitted to the British Labour Party and British Labour Congress (TUC) by the National Executive of the Jewish Labor Committee," New York, July 1941, DDC, B50, F3C.

26. Claus-Dieter Krohn, "L'exil politique allemand aux Etats-Unis après 1933," *Matériaux pour l'histoire de notre temps*, no. 60 (October–December 2000): 9–15. According to Albrecht Ragg, a number of Germans exiled in Europe or in the United States recognized Vladeck's central role in the success of their emigration: "The German Socialist Emigration, 1933–1945" (Ph.D. diss., Loyola University-Chicago, 1977), 43–44, 96, 129.

27. Miles (the pseudonym of Walter Löwenheim), *Neu Beginnen! Faschismus oder Sozialismus: Diskussionsgrundlage zu den Streitfragen des Sozialismus in unsere Epoche* (Prague: Graphia, 1933); two editions of the English version appeared, one in England (the National Council of Labour Colleges, London, 1934), and the other in the United States, published by the League for Industrial Democracy (New York, 1934).

28. Paul Hagen dedicated his book, *Will Germany Crack?* (New York: Harper and Brothers, 1942), "to the memory of B. Charney Vladeck, courageous and perspicacious friend of the clandestine movement"; Krohn, "L'exil politique allemand," 9–16; Ragg, "The German Socialist Emigration," 114–44; Droz, *Histoire de l'Antifascisme en Europe,* 83–84.

29. Paul Hagen to Vladeck, October 3, 1937, Baruch Charney Vladeck Papers, Robert F. Wagner Labor Archives, Tamiment Library, New York University (hereafter Vladeck Papers), R. 1859. Support from abroad was the only option for Neu Beginnen, whose domestic strength had already been annihilated by the Gestapo; see Gilbert Badia, "Panorama des Résistances allemandes, 1933–1945," in Françoise Knopper and Alain Ruiz, eds., *Les résistants au Troisième Reich en Allemagne et dans l'exil* (Toulouse: Presses Universitaires du Mirail, 1997), 17–37; Barbara Koehn, *La résistance allemande contre Hitler, 1933–1945* (Paris: Presses Universitaires de France, 2003), 49; Hans Mommsen, "German Society and the Resistance against Hitler," in Christian Leitz, ed., *The Third Reich: The Essential Readings* (Oxford: Blackwell, 1999), 255–75.

30. Neu Beginnen received the support of the Norwegian Labor Party and of the Socialist League of Sir Stafford Cripps in Great Britain; in France, Léon Blum and part of the CGT procured 40,000 francs for it. See "Autobiographical Data," Karl Frank Papers, Hoover Institution, Stanford University (hereafter Frank Papers), B6, F4. I thank Bruno Groppo for sharing these documents with me.

31. Ragg, "The German Socialist Emigration," 15; Françoise Knopper, "Paramètres de la résistance de la SOPADE," in Knopper and Ruiz, eds., *Les résistants au Troisième Reich,* 189–201.

32. "Autobiographical Data"; Richard Wightman Fox, *Reinhold Niebuhr, A Biography* (New York: Pantheon Books, 1985), 201.

33. "Report on Conditions of Illegal Socialist Activity in Germany, Report for the Friends of German Freedom, submitted by the Foreign Bureau of Neu Beginnen," sent by Vladeck to David Dubinsky, DDC, B7, F1A.

34. Hagen to Vladeck, Prague, October 3, 1937, Vladeck Papers, R. 1859. While seeking information about his son, Abramovitch had written to Vladeck several times. Hagen's trip to Barcelona was in response to these requests. Abramovitch also asked Leon Blum to intervene. Raphael Abramovitch Papers, Hoover Institution, Stanford University (hereafter Abramovitch Papers), 589–3; André Liebich, *From the Other Shore: Russian Social Democracy after 1921* (Cambridge, MA: Harvard University Press, 1997), 261–63.

35. On these inglorious confrontations, see Ragg, "The German Socialist Emigration," 89–144; "Autobiographical Data."

36. JLC, minutes of the meeting of the Executive Committee, March 7, 1940, JLC R, B1, F3.

37. Cahan at the JLC National Executive Committee's meeting, March 7, 1940, JLC R, B1, F3. Schlossberg of the JLC Executive Committee mentioned in his diary (dated March 7, 1940) that Cahan had been abusive, whereas Paul Hagen, Neu Beginnen's representative, wished to collaborate with SOPADE, which the latter obstinately

refused; Schlossberg Diary, Microfilm EMKA, Jerusalem, microfilm roll 2, Schlossberg Correspondence.

38. Minutes of the meetings of the Office Committee, April 19, May 11, and July 21, 1939, February 1 and March 23, 1940, JLC R, B1, F6; minutes of the meeting of the National Executive Committee, February 15 and March 7, 1940, JLC R, B1, F3; Ragg, "The German Socialist Emigration," 114–44; Frank Papers, B6, 7.

39. *Justice* (ILGWU), May 1, 1935, 10; August 15, 1936, 6; June 1, 1937, 9; *Advance* (ACWA), May 1937; Dubinsky to Schlossberg, June 10, 1935, requesting his agreement to provide $3,000 to help the Polish unions, Schlossberg Correspondence, 5619, B140.

40. "Campaign against Pogroms," JLC R, B17, F5; Antony Polonsky, "The Bund in Polish Political Life, 1935–1939," in Ezra Mendelsohn, ed., *Essential Papers on Jews and the Left* (New York: New York University Press, 1997), 166–98; Jacobs, *Bundist Counterculture in Interwar Poland*, 5–6; Pawel Korzec, *Juifs en Pologne: La question juive pendant l'entre-deux guerres* (Paris: Presses de la Fondation Nationale des Sciences Politiques, 1980), 239–75.

41. JLC 1938 Convention, "Auditor's Report of Special Drive Fund," February 1937–April 1938, JLC R, microfilm roll 160.

42. Memorandum sent for agreement to Schlossberg; Schlossberg Correspondence, 5619, B140, F4. See also JLC R, B1, F2. The meeting with Cordell Hull did indeed take place in April 1936 and not in 1937, contrary to what Charles Berlin notes in "The Jewish Labor Committee and American Immigration Policy in the 1930s," in *Studies in Jewish Bibliography, History and Literature in Honor of Edward Kiev*, edited by Charles Berlin (New York: Ktav, 1971), who is followed by Richard Breitman and Alan M. Kraut, *American Refugee Policy and European Jewry, 1933–1945* (Bloomington: Indiana University Press, 1987), 101.

43. After the Peel Commission on the British mandate that recommended the partition of Palestine into a Hebrew state and an Arab state, the British White Paper of 1939 limited the number of immigrants to Palestine to some 12,000 per year.

44. Vladeck to Dubinsky, July 2, 1937, "What American Jews should do to Help the Jews in Poland," DDC, B51, F1A; Korzec, *Juifs en Pologne*, 253.

45. David Wyman, *Paper Walls: America and the Refugee Crisis, 1938–1941* (New York: Pantheon, 1968).

46. Minutes of the meeting of the Executive Committee, September 7, 1939, JLC R, B1, F3.

47. Among some 16,000 Jewish refugees from Poland in Lithuania, about 400 were members of the Bund. Daniel Blatman, *For Our Freedom and Yours: The Jewish Labour Bund in Poland, 1939–1949* (London: Vallentine Mitchell, 2003) (Paris: 19–22).

48. Minutes of the meeting of the Office Committee, December 6, 1939 (wrongly dated 1940 in the original), JLC R, B1, F6; Executive Committee meeting, November 8, 1939, JLC R, B1, F3.

49. Minutes of the meeting of the Executive Committee, December 28, 1939, JLC R, B1, F3; Blatman, *For Our Freedom and Yours*, 20–21.

50. Minutes of the meeting of the Executive Committee, December 28, 1939, JLC R, B1, F3.

CHAPTER 4: TRAJECTORIES OF EXILE, RESCUE OPERATIONS

1. Varian Fry, *Surrender on Demand* (New York: Random House, 1945). References in this book are to the 1997 edition (Boulder CO: Johnson Books; reprinted Plunkett Lake Press, 2017). Fry's story has inspired many writers. However, stressing the rescue of artists and writers, none of the works published about Varian Fry cites or explores the relation between Fry's agency, the Emergency Rescue Committee, and the JLC: Andy Marino, *A Quiet American: The Secret War of Varian Fry* (New York: St. Martin's Press, 1999; Jean-Marie Guillon, editor of the conference held in Marseille, 1999, *Varian Fry du refuge à l'exil* (Arles: Actes Sud, 2000); Mona Bismarck Foundation, *Varian Fry à Marseille, 1940–1941: Les artistes et l'exil* (Arles: Actes Sud, 2000); Jean-Marie Guillon, "La Provence refuge et piège: Autour de Varian Fry et de la filière américaine," in Max Lagarrigue, ed., *1940, La France du repli, l'Europe de la défaite* (Toulouse: Privat, 2001), 269–88; Sheila Isenberg, *A Hero of Our Own: The Story of Varian Fry* (New York: Random House, 2001); Rosemary Sullivan, *Villa Air-Bel: World War II, Escape and a House in Marseille* (New York: Harper, 2007).

2. Approximately 20,000 people were interned, according to Denis Peschanski, *La France des camps: L'internement, 1938–1946* (Paris: Gallimard, 2002), 76–80; Anne Grynberg, *Les camps de la honte, les internés juifs des camps français* (Paris: La Découverte, 1999); Vicky Caron, *Uneasy Asylum: France and the Jewish Refugee Crisis, 1933–1942* (Stanford: Stanford University Press, 1999), 244–62. On the conditions of internment, see the gripping stories of writers Lion Feuchtwanger interned in Les Milles, *Devil in France: My Encounter with Him in the Summer of 1940* (New York: Viking, 1941), and Arthur Koestler at Le Vernet, *Scum of the Earth* (1941; New York: Macmillan, 1968).

3. Jean-Louis Panicacci, *L'occupation italienne: Sud-Est de la France, juin 1940–septembre 1943* (Rennes: Presses Universitaires de Rennes, 2010).

4. Minkoff to Dubinsky, JLC R, B12, F2, reprinted in *Papers of the JLC*, 96–97.

5. *Papers of the JLC*, 99–100. This letter is reproduced in its entirety in Appendix 1.

6. Breckinridge Long to William Green, AFL, July 3, 1940, JLC R, B39, F1.

7. To this list should be added a large number of associations that provided rescue or material aid, such as the American Jewish Joint Distribution Committee, the American Friends Service Committee (Quakers), the Unitarian Service Committee, and the Hebrew Immigration Aid Society (HIAS).

8. The PACPR had been appointed with a view to preparing the Evian Conference in 1938 and was especially interested in collective solutions for accepting Jewish refugees, notably one proposed by the government of the Dominican Republic.

9. Starting in June 1940, the Immigration and Naturalization Service, previously under the authority of the Labor Department, which was considered too lax, came under the joint authority of the State Department and the Department of Justice. The rationale for this change was the search for Communist or Nazi infiltrators. David Wyman, *Paper Walls: America and the Refugee Crisis, 1938–1941* (New York: Pantheon, 1968), 137–45.

10. The recent reaffiliation of the ILGWU to the AFL (in 1940) bolstered the federation's support for this operation, thus lending greater weight to the JLC's request to the State Department.

11. *The War Diary of Breckinridge Long: Selections from the Years 1939–1944*, edited by Fred L. Israel (Lincoln: University of Nebraska Press, 1987), 131.

12. Previously (June 24, 1940), Thomas Mann had compiled a hundred names of German exiles, JLC R, B38, F19; Thomas Mann to Dubinsky, July 16, 1940; Stefan Zweig to Adolph Held, July 9, 1940, JLC R, B39, F1.

13. Lionello Venturi, memo to Isaiah Minkoff, July 28, 1940, JLC R, B39, F1.

14. Seals had been put on the door of Raphael Abramovitch's apartment in Paris by the German police during the first days of the Occupation. Biographical data, Abramovitch Papers, 588–1.

15. André Liebich, *From the Other Shore: Russian Social Democracy after 1921* (Cambridge, MA: Harvard University Press, 1997), 10–26.

16. In the United States since 1939, ex-Menshevik Samuel Estrin had left the USSR in 1923, had gone to Latvia, and then to Berlin and to France in 1933, where he was active in helping anti-Nazi refugees.

17. See Appendix 2. Claudie Weill, "Mencheviks et Socialistes-révolutionnaires en exil," in *Mélanges pour Mark Ferro, de Russie et d'ailleurs* (Paris: Institut d'Etudes Slaves, 1995), 417–26.

18. R. Rein (Abramovitch) in Marseille to Chanin in New York, July 19, 1940, Minkoff to Abramovitch-Rein, Marseille, August 5, 1940, both in JLC R, B39, F1.

19. Abramovitch was accompanied by his wife, Rosa, his daughter Lia, and his sister Sofia. JLC R, B39, F2. Telegram from J. Pat to N. Chanin: List of arrivals on September 12, JLC R, B39, F3.

20. In the end the JLC furnished a list of 77 "Russian, Jewish, Polish" names to Washington for whom it was requesting visas. Telegram, Minkoff to Nicolaevski at the Lux-hotel, Marseille, August 24, 1940, JLC R, B39, F2.

21. Abramovitch to G. L. Warren, December 24, 1940, *Papers of the JLC*, 142.

22. "All persons included in list submitted by American Federation of Labor are covered by assurances of support and assurances regarding arrangements to proceed to foreign destination." Adolph Berle (A. B.), telegram to the Consul of Marseille, July 26 and August 1, 1940, National Archives and Records Administration (hereafter NARA), RG 59, 811/111.

23. See Appendix 2.

24. Modigliani, telegram to Romualdi, July 31, 1940; Modigliani to the American Consul in Marseille, July 31, 1940, both in JLC R, B39, F1.

25. Gaetano Salvemini, founder of the Mazzini Society, an anti-fascist organization in the United States in which Max Ascoli and Lionello Venturi, among others, participated. Romualdi to Modigliani in Marseille, August 1, 1940, and Romualdi to Minkoff in New York, August 16, 1940, both in JLC R, B39, F2.

26. Quoted in Carlo Vallauri, "Le retentissement en Italie de l'action de Silvio Trentin en exil," in Nicoletta Pannocchia, ed., *Silvio Trentin e la Francia: Saggi e testimonianze* (Venice: Marsilio Editori, 1991), 79–96.

27. Excerpts of a letter from G. E. Modigliani, Marseille, August 5, 1940, DDC, B8, F1C; Vera Funaro to David Dubinsky, December 27, 1940, JLC R, B39, F2. Joyce Lussu (Emilio's wife) helped Modigliani escape to Switzerland.

28. See Appendix 2. On the making of the German/Austrian list and the political battles in New York among the several factions of socialist exiles, see Jack Jacobs, "A Friend in Need: The Jewish Labor Committee and Refugees from German-Speaking Lands, 1933–1945," *Yivo Annual* 23 (1996): 391–417.

29. Rudolf Katz to Minkoff, June 24, July 11, 13, and 14, 1940, JLC R, B39, F1; Katz to Minkoff, August 1, 13, and 16, 1940, JLC R, B39, F2.

30. G. Stolz asked that his visa be transferred to London where he was located and to have his wife evacuated from France; the JLC obtained a U.S. visa for her.

31. The JLC sent Heine and Fry $1,000 per month to help refugees who were waiting for visas. Office Committee, December 7, 1940, JLC R, B1, F6.

32. Modigliani did not want to part with the fur coat he had been given during his visit to New York in 1935 by the ILGWU. Fry, *Surrender on Demand*, 51.

33. Rudolf Katz Diary, July 10–16, 1940, Rudolf Katz collection, microfilm roll 115, Leo Baeck Institute, German Jewish History, New York; State Department, telegram to American consul in Marseille, July 22 and 23, 1940, NARA, RG 59, 811/111.

34. The JLC requested visas and paid the transatlantic passage for Franz Boegler, Gerhard Danies, Heinrich Ehrmann, Erna Franke, Sigmund Jeremias, Erik Schmidt, Thomas Schocken, and Elsa Gronenberg, members of Neu Beginnen; they were added to the "third AFL list." July 24, 1940, JLC R, B38, F23. Albrecht Ragg, "The German Socialist Emigration in the United States, 1933–1945" (Ph.D. diss., Loyola University-Chicago, 1977), 157–60; Carlo Tresca to Romualdi, letter forwarded to Minkoff, New York, [October] 1940, JLC R, B39, F5.

35. Anna Stein, New York, August 29, 1940, thanking Minkoff for the help given to save Ewa Lewinski, JLC R, B39, F2.

36. Hagen to Minkoff, August 8 and 19, 1940, JLC R, B39, F2; Hagen to Minkoff, October 2, 1940, JLC R, B39, F5; List, JLC R, B38, F19; Hagen to David Dubinsky, July 30, 1941, DDC, B6, F6B.

37. Fry, *Surrender on Demand*, 11.

38. Telegrams, State Department to the American consul in Marseille, July 23, 1940; State Department to the American Consul in Lisbon, August 2, 1940, both in NARA, RG 59, 811/111. During the war in Spain, Frank Bohn had been in charge of a committee to welcome 500 children from Bilbao. May 1937, DDC, B164, F2A; *New York Times*, June 7, 1937.

39. Frank Bohn, telegrams sent from Vichy to the Secretary of State, August 6, 1940, NARA, RG 59, 811/111, France 13.

40. Telegram to the JLC, September 3, 1940, JLC R, B39, F3.

41. Frank Bohn, cable to William Green, September 13, 1940, via the American embassy in Vichy, NARA, RG 59, 811/111/267.

42. On these episodes, see Fry, *Surrender on Demand*, 79–93.

43. Fry, *Surrender on Demand*, 163–78.
44. State Department to U.S. Embassy, Vichy, France, September 16, 1940, NARA, RG 59, 811/111/267; quoted also in Fry, *Surrender on Demand*, 81.
45. Bohn to Rudolf Katz, September 6, 1940, and Katz to Minkoff, September 28, 1940, Isaiah M. Minkoff Papers, Robert F. Wagner Labor Archives, Tamiment Library, New York University (hereafter Minkoff Papers), B6, F10.
46. Bohn to William Green, September 12, 1940, JLC R, B39, F3. According to the August 23, 1940, agreement with the Vichy government, President Lazaro Cardenas had offered to welcome to Mexico all the Spanish refugees in France who asked to be evacuated. The German occupation forces, however, prevented this Spanish emigration form taking place.
47. Excerpt from airmail from Marseille, Frank Bohn, September 3, 1940, JLC R, B39, F3; Frank Bohn to William Green, September 12, 1940, JLC R, B39, F3.
48. Wyman, *Paper Walls*, 143–47; Long, *War Diary*, October 3, 1940, 128, 134.
49. Fry, *Surrender on Demand*, xiii.
50. The dedication also mentions "For Frank Kingdon who lent it support; For Ingrid Warburg and Harold Oram who made it possible; and for all those who in Switzerland, France, Spain, Portugal, and Africa, who, forgetful of self and sometimes at risk of their lives, carried it out."
51. On the political nature of Fry's mission, see Laurent Jeanpierre, "Varian Fry et le sauvetage des réfugiés aux États-Unis," in Jean-Marie Guillon, ed., *Varian Fry du refuge à l'exil* (Arles: Actes Sud, 2000), 2:58–73; Anne Klein, "Droit d'asile ou sauvetage: L'activité du Centre américain de secours et la politique internationale des réfugiés," in Guillon, ed., *Varian Fry du refuge à l'exil*, 2:74–87.
52. "Among the refugees who were caught in France were many writers and artists whose work I had enjoyed. . . . Now that they were in danger, I felt obliged to help them, if I could, just as they, without knowing it, had often in the past helped me." Fry, *Surrender on Demand*, xii–xiii, 257.
53. Victor Serge, a libertarian socialist, had joined the Russian Revolution; as a long-time Trotskyist, he denounced Stalinism, was deported to Siberia, and was liberated by a campaign of French and Belgian intellectuals. *Memoirs of a Revolutionary 1905–1941*, translated by Peter Sedgwick (New York: NYRB Classics, 2012), 426.
54. Albert Hirschman, *Crossing Boundaries: Selected Writings* (New York: Zone Books, 1998). See also the story Hirschman tells of his meeting with Fry: "Albert O. Hirschman, Albert Herman, Beamish," in Guillon, ed., *Varian Fry du refuge à l'exil*, 12–16, and the biography of him by Jeremy Adelman, *Worldly Philosopher: The Odyssey of Albert O. Hirschman* (Princeton: Princeton University Press, 2013).
55. Lisa Fittko, *Escape through the Pyrenees*, translated by David Koblick (Evanston, IL: Northwestern University Press, 1991); Fittko, *Solidarity and Treason, Resistance and Exile, 1933–1940* (Evanston, IL: Northwestern University Press, 1993).
56. Daniel Bénédite, *La Filière marseillaise* (1984), and "L'aventure du Pélenq: On fait feu de tout bois," reproduced in J. M. Guillon and J. M. Guiraud, eds., *Un chemin vers la liberté*

sous l'occupation (Paris: Le Félin, 2017); Daniel Bénédite, "Administrative Report," in Karen Greenberg, ed., Columbia University Library, Varian Fry Papers, vol. 5: *Archives of the Holocaust: An International Collection of Selected Documents*, edited by Henry Friedlander and Sybil Milton (New York: Garland, 1990), 4–15. The Centre Américain de Secours is generally abbreviated as CAS in many studies on Varian Fry. We choose, however, to mention it as CAmS in order to avoid confusion with another institution, the Comité d'Action Socialiste (chapter 5), abbreviated as CAS.

57. The writer Alfred Döblin figured among the nine Germans on this list. JLC R, B39, F5; "Persons Rescued by the Jewish Labor Committee," Minkoff Papers, B6, F10.

58. Ragg, "The German Socialist Emigration," 174–77.

59. Ragg, "The German Socialist Emigration," chap. 5, especially 145, 181, 185–89, 478. "The attitude of the GLD towards the ERC and NB confirmed the opinion of the JLC that the GLD lacked interest in the task of rescue" (189). Heine had been in contact with some 240 members of German parties and unions waiting in the southern zone at the end of 1940 (174). Jack Jacobs also underlines that the SOPADE would be reorganized in England rather than in the United States ("A Friend in Need," 403); Françoise Knopper, "Paramètres de la résistance de la SOPADE," in Françoise Knopper and Alain Ruiz, eds., *Les résistants au Troisième Reich en Allemagne et dans l'exil* (Toulouse: Presses Universitaires du Mirail, 1997), 189–201.

60. Hagen to Minkoff, October 2, 1940; ERC to Minkoff, October 8, 1940, both in JLC R, B39, F5.

61. Adolph Held to Friedrich Adler, 336 Central Park West, October 26, 1940, JLC R, B39, F6.

62. Julius Deutsch to Adolph Held, Havana, October 12, 1940, JLC R, B39, F3; A. S. Lipsett to Dubinsky, September 17, 1940, JLC R, B39, F4; "Persons Rescued by the Jewish Labor Committee," Minkoff Papers, B6, F10.

63. Emilio Lussu, *Diplomazia Clandestina* (Florence: La Nuova Italia, 1956).

64. Lussu, *Diplomazia Clandestina*, 13–21; "Persons Rescued by the Jewish Labor Committee," Minkoff Papers, B6, F10, B9, F38; Lussu to Dubinsky, Lisbon, June 21, 1941, eight-page letter explaining the achievements and failures of the Italian evacuation and asking Dubinsky to help finance the transatlantic crossing of the refugees waiting in Casablanca, DDC, B151, F3B; Antonini to Vera Modigliani, announcing the arrival of Cianca, Natoli, Chiaromonte, and the Pianas, AP, 57080/023, B35, F4. Leo Valiani, an ex-Communist, received a visa for Mexico; Varian Fry also describes parts of this episode in *Surrender on Demand*, 189–91, 233–34.

65. Daniel Blatman, *For Our Freedom and Yours: The Jewish Labour Bund in Poland, 1939–1949* (London: Vallentine Mitchell, 2003), 16–18.

66. According to Daniel Blatman, there were 94 names (*For Our Freedom and Yours*, 27); later, he mentions 200 party militants (125). The archives of the Bund Representation in New York show a series of lists revised or completed during the summer of 1940: Bund Archives, Papers of the Representation of the Bund, RG 1404, F37A, F41. In fact, the sources do not correspond with each other, including those of the JLC, where

the figures sometimes refer to visas requested for a family or for *"people"* whose numbers largely exceed those of the visas and changed from day to day. See, for example, "Office Committee," March 22, 1941, JLC R, B1, F6; "Executive Committee," March 6 and April 16, 1941, JLC R, B1, F3.

67. JLC R, B38, F19. On the evacuation of Polish and Lithuanian Jews via the Far East, see David Kranzler, *Japanese, Nazis and Jews* (New York: Yeshiva University, 1976), 309–46; Yehuda Bauer, *American Jewry and the Holocaust: The American Jewish Joint Distribution Committee, 1939–1945* (Detroit: Wayne State University Press, 1981), 119–28.

68. The American Jewish Congress had obtained visas for this "list of rabbis" via the PACPR.

69. Bauer, *American Jewry and the Holocaust*, 119–20; Kranzler, *Japanese, Nazis and Jews*, 309–46. A few other diplomats also used their authority as consuls to provide visas in order to save hundreds or thousands of refugees, including Aristide Sousa Mendes, the Portuguese consul in Bordeaux, and Raoul Wallenberg at the Swedish embassy in Budapest.

70. Wyman, *Paper Walls*, 146.

71. According to Jacob Pat, the situation became all the more urgent because on January 30, 1941, the refugees in Lithuania would be forced to accept Soviet citizenship, which would have prevented them from departing. Office Committee, January 9, 1941, JLC R, B1, F6.

72. In January 1941, the JLC was seeking $14,000 on behalf of sixty-two persons in transit to Japan ($200 per person according to Pat's estimate; JLC R B1, F6). The cost of transporting and caring for the JLC protégés was ultimately split with the Joint. In June 1941 the latter asked the JLC for its share of $39,000: Harrietta Buchman (JDC) to Jacob Pat, June 13, 1941, JLC R, B7, F25; I. Minkoff to Moses Leavitt, Joint Distribution Committee, September 9, 1940, JLC R, B7, F25.

73. Wyman, *Paper Walls*, 146–47; Bauer, *American Jewry and the Holocaust*, 121–24; JLC R, B33, F29. Actually, the Jewish Polish refugees in Japan were collectively deported to Shanghai starting in September 1941. In the end, the JLC had approximately sixty protégés in Shanghai that it tried to get out of this ghetto after the war; see, for example, the Goldsztejn case, JLC R, B48, F6. The JLC paid sums through the International Red Cross to support many other Jewish Polish refugees in Shanghai. David Kranzler, "The Role in Relief and Rescue during the Holocaust by the Jewish Labor Committee," in Seymour Finger, ed., *American Jewry during the Holocaust* (New York: Holmes and Meier, 1984).

74. "Persons Rescued by the Jewish Labor Committee," Minkoff Papers, B6, F10.

75. Minkoff to "Dear friend" in Seattle, November 1, 1940, JLC R, B5, F18.

76. Minkoff Papers, B6, F10; I. F. Wixon, Department of Justice, Memorandum to Mr. Pritchard, November 9, 1940, NARA, RG 85, ACC 58A734, B1936, F56054/954: "Mr. Minkoff has requested that we advise our Pacific Coast districts, Seattle, San Francisco, Los Angeles, to admit without regard to the public charge features or otherwise,

aliens sponsored by the American Federation of Labor to whom visas have been issued at the instance of the State Department. . . . Mr Minkoff has since arranged with the State Department to furnish a list of all of the aliens coming in the conditions mentioned."

77. "Persons Rescued by the Jewish Labor Committee," Minkoff Papers, B6, F10. Among these 86, however, a dozen had not yet arrived in July 1941; perhaps they arrived in the United States before the attack on Pearl Harbor, but if not their chances of survival were low. Executive Committee, March 6, 1941, JLC R, B1, F3. In April 1941 Minkoff had announced higher figures than those in July: 123 persons who had come from Japan and "about" 400 from France. JLC Executive Committee, April 16, 1941, JLC R, B1, F3.

78. Jacob Pat, Office Committee, March 22, 1941, JLC R, B1, F6.

79. Isaiah Minkoff to Joseph Tuvim, November 13, 1940; Adoph Held and Isaiah Minkoff, circular announcing the conference and presence of "eminent" European labor leaders, December 13, 1940, both in JLC R, B2, F5.

80. The White House, Franklin D. Roosevelt, telegram to Adolph Held, January 16–17, 1941, JLC R, B2, F5.

81. Address to the JLC by Friedrich Adler, JLC R, B2, F6.

82. David Dubinsky's address, JLC R, B2, F6.

83. Adolph Held, memorandum to William Green, JLC R, B2, F5.

84. Knopper, "Paramètres de la résistance de la SOPADE," 189–201.

85. Hagen to Minkoff, January 7, 1941, JLC R, B2, F5.

86. Stéphane Dufoix, Politiques d'exil: Hongrois, Polonais et Tchécoslovaques en France après 1945 (Paris: Presses Universitaires de France, 2002), 30–41.

87. "We Refugees" (1943); "The Jew as Pariah: A Hidden Tradition" (1944), in Hannah Arendt, Jewish Writings, edited by Jerome Kohn and Ron H. Feldman (New York: Schocken, 2009). Hannah Arendt was one of the persons saved by the Emergency Rescue Committee.

88. It was not until the spring of 1942 that the U.S. Office of Strategic Services (OSS) collaborated with associations of political refugees whose knowledge of the terrain was fruitful. This subject is developed in the following chapter.

89. For example, the institution created by Raphael Abramovitch in 1943, the American Labor Conference on International Affairs, whose goal was anticipating the postwar period, warned the American labor movement against any international alliance that would include the Soviet Union, thus foreshadowing Cold War labor politics. Varian Fry, who had by then returned to the United States, found in this organization (of which he briefly became the secretary) the place where he could use his knowledge of the émigré milieux and the European context. On this subject, see Abramovitch's correspondence with David Dubinsky, DDC, B173.

90. Caron, Uneasy Asylum, 331–38; Michael Marrus and Robert Paxton, Vichy France and the Jews (New York: Basic Books 1981), 70; Peschanksi, La France des camps, 219–21.

91. Wyman, Paper Walls, 148–51.

92. Caron, Uneasy Asylum, 332.

93. "Persons Rescued by the Jewish Labor Committee" is an undated document, but the information it contains situates the writing between the end of June and the start of August 1941. Minkoff Papers, B6, F10; JLC R, B1, F3.

94. "Individuals on AFL List whose families have not yet arrived in the United States," July 8, 1941, Minkoff Papers, B6, F10.

95. "Individuals on AFL List not yet arrived in America," June 30, 1941, Minkoff Papers, B6, F10.

96. In 1942, the JLC and other rescue organizations affirmed that the Vichy government had refused exit visas to some 800 persons who had received an American visa. JLC R, B32, F11.

97. The Italian refugees were supported by the ILGWU, which along with the JLC had sent them $4,750 during 1941. Jacob Pat to Dubinsky, April 24, 1942, DDC, B51, F2B.

98. The JLC and the ILGWU had appealed to the State Department and to President Roosevelt demanding that the American embassy in Vichy intervene with Marshal Pétain to obtain the liberation of Breitscheid and Hilferding, and then of Buozzi. Their request, which was unsuccessful, also concerned other arrested figures: Guido Miglioli, Catholic representative of the Italian Chamber of Deputies; Signora Bernerini, widow of Professor Bernerini who had been assassinated in Barcelona during the Civil War; and Largo Caballero, former Spanish prime minister and leader of the Spanish Labor Confederation arrested in France. DDC, B151, F3A, March, April 1941.

99. Memorandum submitted to the British Labour Party and to the Trades Union Congress by the executive of the Jewish Labor Committee, New York, July 1941, DDC, B50, F3C.

100. "The Jewish Labor Committee in 1941," DDC, B50, F3C.

101. "Visas cabled from Mexico to France, but not issued in Marseilles"; "List submitted by the Jewish Labor Committee"; "List of Austrian Trade Unionists submitted by the Jewish Labor Committee"; these three lists are dated August 13, 1942, Minkoff Papers, B6, F10, F1; "The Jewish Labor Committee in 1942," JLC R, B44, F8. In addition, on November 16, 1942, Jacob Pat affirmed to Jacob Potofsky, vice president of the ACWA, that it had obtained, with the help of a Mexican committee, 173 visas for this country and had requested that these visas be sent to Portugal, hoping that the refugees in France corresponding to these names could reach that country (JLC R, B11, F34). In 1945 the JLC asserted that it had saved 1,500 labor and political leaders, intellectuals, and other opponents of fascism and Nazism. The total cost of the operation rose to $355,568. A. Held, J. Pat, B. Tabachinsky, Memorandum, January 18, 1945, JLC R, B1, F19.

102. Fry was not only recalled by the State Department and the ERC but expelled by Vichy's Ministry of the Interior.

103. Bénédite, Filière marseillaise, 251; Fry proposes the number of 300 persons saved between his departure in September 1941 and the month of June 1942 when the offices of the Centre Américain de Secours were raided by the police (Surrender on Demand, 236).

104. Elisabeth Kessin Berman, afterword to Fry, *Surrender on Demand*, 256. Daniel Bénédite affirms there were "about 1,200 persons" who thus escaped Nazi pursuit; he counts separately the 300 British officers and soldiers that the ERC helped to evacuate (*Filière marseillaise*, 246). In 1943 Frank Kingdon, president of the ERC, affirmed that this organization had saved some 2,000 persons. "The Work of Refugee Relief Trustees," JLC R, B44, F8.

105. "Summary statement of receipts and disbursements for year ending 1940," December 31, 1940, *Papers of the JLC*, 144; "The Jewish Labor Committee in 1941," JLC R, B9, F17; "The Jewish Labor Committee in 1942," JLC R, B9, F17; mail between the International Rescue and Relief Committee and the JLC on the financing of expenses incurred on one side or the other, JLC R, B49, F3.

106. Minutes of the meeting of the Executive Committee, April 16, 1941, JLC R, B1, F3; Minutes of the meeting of Office Committee, June 3, 1941, JLC R, B1, F6.

107. Harold Oram, the ERC's public relations officer, January 22, 1941, quoted in Jean-Marie Guillon, "La Provence refuge et piège: Autour de Varian Fry et de la filière américaine," in Max Lagarrigue, ed., *1940, La France du repli, l'Europe de la défaite* (Toulouse: Privat, 2001), 269–88.

108. Minutes of the meeting of the Executive Committee, April 16, 1941, JLC R, B1, F3. "The people come to us for aid. . . . To us requests are coming the whole time about questions and cases of political emigration, about people who are just as important as those who were on our lists."

109. "The general humanitarian relief work of the other organizations does not include the political rescue activities which only we conduct." Memorandum of the Executive Committee, "Our Rescue project and the new immigration regulations," DDC, B50, F3C.

110. Although specific exceptions were issued from 1950 to 1980 to accept refugees from Hungary, Cuba, Vietnam, Cambodia, and the Soviet Union, it was only in 1980 that the United States fully recognized the international definition of political refugees adopted by the Geneva Convention of 1951: "persons who could not without danger of persecution return to their country of origin due to their race, their religion, or their political opinions."

111. Jacob Pat to Dubinsky, November 25, 1941, DDC, B50, F3B; Dubinsky to President Roosevelt, March 17, 1941, asking for the government's intervention in favor of Caballero and Bruno Buozzi, DDC, B151, F3A.

112. Anne Grynberg suggests that 40,000 Jews were interned in February 1941 (*Les camps de la honte*, 95). Vicky Caron suggests 33,910 were interned in January 1941 (*Uneasy Asylum*, 342).

CHAPTER 5: WITH THE FRENCH RESISTANCE

1. Daniel Mayer, former secretary-general of the Socialist Party, retrospectively used the expression "privileged ties" to explain the influence of Bundist militants on the French Socialists in learning about underground activism: Georges Wellers, André Kaspi,

and Serge Klarsfeld, eds., *La France et la question juive, 1940–1944* (Paris: Editions Messinger, 1981), 379–80. The fact is also mentioned in Martine Pradoux, *Daniel Mayer: Un socialiste dans la Résistance* (Paris: Editions de l'Atelier-Editions Ouvrières, 2002), 91.

2. Section Française de l'Internationale Ouvrière (SFIO), the official name of the party.

3. Decrees of August 16 and November 9, 1940.

4. Few militants and even fewer French labor leaders were included on the JLC lists in 1940. Among those who were: Boris Souvarine (1895–1984, ex-Bolshevik, French citizen, excluded from the Communist Party in 1926 as the author of a very critical biography of Stalin) and William Rosenfeld, editor of the *Populaire* (organ of the Socialist Party), whose two names were added to the Italian list. The names of Odette Bigard and Juliette Blanc (SFIO), too, appeared in the correspondence between Modigliani and the JLC. Later on, the JLC submitted the names of many Jewish Bundists residing in France although the likelihood of obtaining a visa for them was even less at the time: "List submitted by the Jewish Labor Committee," August 13, 1942, Minkoff Papers, B6, F10.

5. Jean-Louis Crémieux-Brilhac was the former head of the Free France broadcasting service in London; he also wrote *La France Libre* (Paris: Gallimard, 2001), 1:350. On the political divisions among French emigrants during the war, see Laurent Jeanpierre, "Des hommes entre plusieurs mondes: Étude sur une situation d'exil, Intellectuels français réfugiés aux Etats-Unis pendant la deuxième guerre mondiale" (Ph.D diss., Ecole des Hautes Etudes en Sciences Sociales, 2004), 184–241; Emmanuelle Loyer, *Paris à New York: Intellectuels et artistes français en exil, 1940–1947* (Paris: Grasset, 2005), 167–202.

6. Laurent Jeanpierre, "Paul Vignaux inspirateur de la deuxième gauche: Récits d'un exil français aux États-Unis pendant la Seconde Guerre Mondiale," *Matériaux pour l'histoire de notre temps* 60 (October–December 2000): 48–56; Jean Lecuir, "Paul Vignaux à Toulouse: Résistance spirituelle et politique en zone non-occupée (juin 1940–juin 1941)," in O. Boulnois, ed., *Paul Vignaux, citoyen et philosophe* (Turnhout: Brepols, 2013), 51–121.

7. In September 1939 the CGT began excluding from its ranks the Communist sections supporting the German-Soviet Pact; it remained a reformist labor federation, with half a million members in June 1940 before it was dissolved by Vichy authority. Léon Jouhaux had been part of the moderate minority.

8. Frank Georgi, "Les relations entre Léon Jouhaux et le syndicalisme chrétien, 1940–1954," in Mairie d'Aubervilliers, *Léon Jouhaux: D'Aubervilliers au Prix Nobel* (Paris: Documentation Française, 2010), 131–43; Georges Bernard and Denise Tintant, *Léon Jouhaux et le mouvement syndical français* (Paris: Presses Universitaires de France, 1979), "Discours de Saint Nazaire," 416–23; Olivier Wieviorka, *Histoire de la Résistance en France, 1940–1945* (Paris: Editions Perrin, 2013), 61–64.

9. Paul Vignaux, "Testimonianza," in N. Pannochia, ed., *Silvio Trentin e la Francia: Saggi e testimonianze* (Venice: Marsilio Editori, 1991), 197–200.

10. Vignaux, "Testimonianza," 197–200.

11. Lecuir, "Paul Vignaux à Toulouse," 107.

12. Vignaux, "Testimonianza," 200; Léon Jouhaux had met William Green when he came to New York in 1938. The CGT has no records for the war period, but a copy of Léon Jouhaux's letter to William Green, dated June 19, 1941, is contained in Archives de la CFDT, 3H1/10; JLC invitation to hear the report, "Professor Vignaux on the Situation in France," August 19, 1941, Archives de la CFDT, 3H1/10.

13. Joseph Botton, secretary of the Metal Workers' Federation in France, had been an early activist of the CFTC network of resistance in the Lyon area before joining Vignaux in the United States.

14. Jouhaux gave the gathering of non-Communist labor unionists who had chosen to resist the name Mouvement Ouvrier Francais (French Labor Movement). The move-ment was recognized by France Libre as a force independent from the organized Resis-tance movements and political parties. Colonel Passy (André Dewavrin), *Mémoires du chef des services secrets de la France Libre* (Paris: Odile Jacob, 2000), 487–88.

15. "French Labor Movement Committee, Statement of Policies," *France Speaks*, Septem-ber 1941, JLC R, B40, F35.

16. In January 1943, Vignaux, recognizing that "it is in large part thanks to your help that we have been able to pursue our work," asked the JLC to raise the amount of its sub-sidy to *France Speaks*. JLC R, B32, F12.

17. This was the execution of 48 interned Resistants, including 27 from Chateaubriant, among whom were Guy Môquet and Jean Pierre Timbaud, and 50 hostages from Souge near Bordeaux as a reprisal for attacks on the German officers Karl Hotz and Hans Reimers. *France Speaks*, November 1941.

18. "French Workmen against the Corporate State," "The Manifesto of Twelve," *France Speaks*, September–December 1941, JLC R, B40, F35.

19. *France Speaks*, September 26, 1941.

20. *France Speaks*, February 9, March 2, 1942, JLC R, B41, F8; June 5, 1943, JLC R, B41, F21.

21. Hauck had been named by Jouhaux as labor attaché at the French embassy in London in May 1940. After the armistice he rallied to De Gaulle, who appointed him Labor delegate for France Libre in September 1941. In his speech to the ILO, Hauck under-scored the unity established between the CGT and the CFTC. *France Speaks* 1, no. 11 (November 8, 1941).

22. Henry Hauck to Adolph Held, November 29, 1941, JLC R, B32, F9, letter reproduced in *Papers of the JLC*, 184–85. Officially valued at 50 francs during the war, the dollar was traded at up to 150 francs on the black market.

23. Lawyer and journalist Robert Jean Longuet was the son of Jean Longuet (in other words he was Karl Marx's grandson), an anticolonialist militant, and engaged in the defense of victims of fascism. He had come to the United States on the eve of the war.

24. Henry Hauck to Adolph Held, November 29, 1941, JLC R, B32, F9. On the question of financing the Resistance, see Passy, *Mémoires*, 480–90, 749–51; Daniel Cordier, *Jean Moulin: La République des Catacombes* (Paris: Gallimard, 1999), 632–33, 641; Jean-Luc Binot and Bernard Boyer, *L'argent de la Résistance* (Paris: Larousse, 2010).

25. Charles de Gaulle, *The Complete War Memoirs of Charles de Gaulle*, translated by Richard Howard (New York: Simon and Schuster, 1967), 405; Daniel Mayer, *Les Socialistes dans la Résistance* (Paris: Presses Universitaires de France, 1968); Marc Sadoun, *Les Socialistes sous l'occupation: Résistance et collaboration* (Paris: Presses de la Fondation Nationale des Sciences Politiques, 1982), 115–18; Robert Verdier, *La vie clandestine du parti socialiste* (Paris: Editions de la Liberté, 1944); Wieviorka, *Histoire de la Résistance*, 56–61. On Daniel Mayer, see also the issue devoted to him by *Matériaux pour l'histoire de notre temps*, "Daniel Mayer, l'idéal et le réel en politique," no. 51–52, July–December 1998. Mayer liked to define himself as "primarily a socialist, then a Frenchman, and finally a Jew." Anne Grynberg, ed., *Les Juifs dans la Résistance et la Libération: Histoire, témoignages, débats* (Paris: Editions du Scribe, 1985), 53–77.

26. Léon Blum presided over the Popular Front governments (1936 and 1938) based on a coalition of socialist and communist representatives, a position that in addition to his Jewish identity attracted full-blown antagonism and anti-Semitism from right-wing opponents.

27. Pradoux, *Daniel Mayer*, 84–89; Serge Bernstein, *Léon Blum* (Paris: Fayard, 2006), 673–87; Sadoun, *Les Socialistes sous l'occupation*, 133–45. Blum's speeches had an impact even in the United States.

28. A former militant in the German Union of Employees, Ewa Lewinski-Pfister had emigrated to France in 1933 where she participated in the ISK information network on labor resistance in Germany. In the United States (which she reached in October 1940 thanks to the JLC), she was close to Paul Hagen and Neu Beginnen; as a result of this contact, in 1942 she became secretary of the International Rescue and Relief Committee, which succeeded the Emergency Rescue Committee.

29. "Léon Blum Answers His Accusers," *France Speaks*, February 20, 1942, JLC R, B40, F35.

30. Ewa Lewinski-Pfister to Jacob Pat, July 16 and December 11, 1942, JLC R, B32, F11. Along with Blum, Edouard Daladier and other prominent statesmen of the Third Republic governments were indicted by Pétain at the Riom trial. Daladier, like Blum, had been Président du Conseil (a function equivalent to prime minister) from 1938 to 1940. They were able to reverse the charges incriminating them against their accusers, thus preventing the prosecution from continuing.

31. A group of Léon Blum's friends in the United States, including former U.S. ambassador to France William C. Bullitt, quickly published a book that reproduced articles by the Socialist leader and some passages of his defense: Léon Blum, *L'Histoire jugera* (Montréal: Editions de l'Arbre, 1943). Suzanne Blum, not related to Léon Blum but sister of André Blumel, his former cabinet secretary, a lawyer in exile in New York, was the force behind this publication: Suzanne Blum, *Vivre sans la patrie, 1940–1945* (Paris: Plon, 1975), 116–17.

32. Ewa Lewinski to Jacob Pat, September 1, 1942, and Jacob Pat to Ewa Lewinski, September 2, 1942, JLC R, B5, F28. *Le Populaire* came out on May 15, 1942, in mimeographed version, with the mention, "First issue since the last known on 18 June 1940." After July 15 it was printed. The help of the JLC was only partial, but it preceded what Jean Moulin obtained from France Libre. Cordier, *Jean Moulin*, 632.

33. Ewa Lewinski to Jacob Pat, September 16, 1942, JLC R, B32, F11.
34. Ewa Lewinski to Jacob Pat, October 29 and November 9, 1942, JLC R, B32, F11.
35. Ewa Lewinski and Paul Vignaux to the JLC, October 3, 1942, JLC R, B32 F11; Executive Committee meeting, JLC R, B1, F7: "R" is René Bertholet, a socialist comrade in Zurich who transmitted funds for the evacuation of refugees or aid to resistants. "Ryba Nathan" refers in fact to two Jewish resistants, Rafael Ryba and Nathan Frenkel, bridgeheads of a network of Jewish refugees in the southern zone. This subject is developed later in this chapter.
36. E. Lewinski, March 1943, JLC R, B32, F12. Arrested on December 26, 1942, Jouhaux was delivered to the Germans in May 1943. On the date this news arrived, "conscripted labor" refers to the Service du Travail Obligatoire (STO) instituted in February 1943 or the *Relève* program that preceded it. *France Speaks* rebelled against the STO: "Mass Deportation of French Workers," March 1943, 8. The term "deportation" used in France about workers sent to Germany is confusing, since it also refers to the roundups and deportations of Jews in convoys to Poland.
37. Following Léon Blum's advice, in order not to divide the Resistance, Daniel Mayer promised not to create an autonomous socialist resistance movement. The CAS "poured" its militants into existing organizations, especially Libération Sud. The Communist Party, on the other hand, created its own organizations (Mayer, *Les Socialistes dans la Résistance*, 62–73).
38. Sadoun, *Les Socialistes sous l'occupation*, 173, 184–85; Crémieux-Brilhac, *La France Libre*, 1:499; see also Léon Blum's letter to Général de Gaulle, March 15, 1943, in Mayer, *Les Socialistes dans la Résistance*, 211; Henri Michel, *Les courants de pensée dans la Résistance* (Paris: Presses Universitaires de France, 1962), 431.
39. Crémieux-Brilhac, *La France Libre*, 1:503–4. Carlton Gardens was the seat of the Free French government in London.
40. *France Speaks*, no. 41, August 19, 1942, no. 48, April 7, 1943, no. 51, June 5, 1943.
41. Robert Jean Longuet, June 23, 1943, to *New Leader* and copied to the JLC (JLC R, B32, F13): "Albert Grand, Rollin and Vignaux transformed *France Speaks* into a publication which seems to criticize systematically the Gaullist movement. However almost the whole French Labor Movement is now behind de Gaulle.... They manifest quite an obvious sympathy for General Giraud who represents the old reactionary forms which we have always opposed." Laurent Jeanpierre has stressed, on the other hand, that Vignaux was equally opposed to General Giraud and hoped that the principle of unity of the French Labor Movement represented "a chance for workers to organize an independent force": "Paul Vignaux inspirateur de la 'Deuxième Gauche,'" *Matériaux pour l'Histoire de notre temps* 60 (October–December 2000): 48–56.
42. Giraud's trip to the United States in June 1943 while De Gaulle was governing in Algiers, giving the latter more leeway to establish his power, marked the start of this switch. Crémieux-Brilhac, *La France Libre*, 2:857–77.
43. *Voice of the Unconquered*, no. 1 (March 1943): 1. The microfilmed collection of the monthly is recorded in JLC R, microfilm roll 159.
44. *Voice of the Unconquered*, Correspondence, JLC R, B20, F3.

45. In this action, the JLC was allied with the group of French émigrés to the United States known as France Forever: Paul Weill to Samuel Estrin, October 25, 1943; Adolph Held to Honorable Henri Hoppenot, minister plenipotentiary, Comité Francais de Libération Nationale, Washington, October 28, 1943, JLC R, B32, F13; *Voice of the Unconquered*, November 1943, 1, 3. The Crémieux Decree of 1870, granting French citizenship to the Jews of Algeria, had been abrogated by Vichy on October 7, 1940. On March 18, 1943, General Giraud invalidated the status of Jews decreed by Vichy but abolished the Crémieux Decree on the pretext that it established a racial distinction for Jews without taking the Arabs into account. Only the restoration of the Crémieux Decree completely reestablished civil equality for the Jews of Algeria.

46. *Voice of the Unconquered*, April 1943, 1, 8; May 1943 1, 4; the July–August 1943 issue (p. 8) reproduced a full page of *Le Populaire* from March 1943.

47. Léon Blum was handed over to the Nazis and transferred to Buchenwald in March 1943. In trying to liberate him, the JLC, in collaboration with France Forever, asked the president of the Czech government in exile in London, Edouard Benes, to intervene with President Roosevelt and Winston Churchill so they would influence Hitler on Blum's fate. But Benes affirmed, ironically, that he did not have the means to do so. Adolph Held, Paul Weill, and Ladislas Fenyes to Dr. Edouard Benes, July 6, 1943; and Edouard Benes's reply, August 12, 1943, both in JLC R, B32, F13.

48. Telegram written in French, May 8, 1945, JLC R, B32, F16. On the occasion of the announcement of Blum's liberation, the JLC also affirmed that in 1941 it had tried to extricate him from his place of detention and exfiltrate him from France, but given Blum's refusal to leave France, the plan was abandoned. Yet no trace of this effort remains in the JLC records. *Voice of the Unconquered*, April–May 1945, 2.

49. Léon Blum and Daniel Mayer, Radiogram in French, JLC R, B32, F16. This notion of "United Socialist States of the world" was not a figure of speech but reflected the widespread idea that the defeat of Nazism would enable the advent of socialism in Western democracies.

50. "Special Conference of the Socialist Parties of Europe," Bund Archives, New York, RG 1404, F98–103.

51. Note the use of the singular to refer to the resistance movements in occupied countries as if they were unified! The struggle against the Nazi occupation was their only common denominator.

52. Jacob Walcher to the Jewish Labor Committee, April 4, 1943, JLC R, B8, F12.

53. CULM, Minkoff speech, June 11, 1943, JLC R, B8, F12; List of members, JLC R, B8, F12.

54. The initiative for this fundraising came from Matthew Woll of the AFL, who suggested to Sidney Hillman that the equivalent of the AFL's Labor War Chest be created by the CIO and that the two organizations pool what they raised into a "Greater War Chest for New York" with a humanitarian objective for war victims, including Americans: Matthew Woll to Sidney Hillman, November 25, 1942, Sidney Hillman Papers, ACWA Records, Kheel Center for Labor-Management Documentation and Archives, Catherwood Library, Cornell University, Ithaca, New York (hereafter Hillman Papers),

5619 B210 F1. Most of the research concerning this fund has been based on the papers of Sidney Hillman, who was essentially its architect.

55. "IFTU quite willing [to] collaborate in aiding anti-Nazi movement in occupied Europe. Have cabled Month ago to Matthew Woll our readiness to participate with Labor War Chest for this purpose." IFTU telegram to JLC and to David Dubinsky, April 10, 1943, JLC R, 17, B8, F12; CULM Meeting, May 12, 1943, JLC R, B8, F12.

56. CULM Meeting, May 12, 1943, JLC R, B8, F12.

57. Abraham Bluestein, representative of the AFL, was secretary of the Labor League for Human Rights, Freedom and Democracy, which had been founded by Matthew Woll in 1938. He was convinced by the CIO's arguments about the matter of the transfer of this money and of its humanitarian nature, CULM Meeting, October 18, 1943, JLC R, B8, F13.

58. CULM Meeting, October 18, 1943, JLC R, B8, F13.

59. CULM Meetings, September 27, 1943, October 18, 1943.

60. A CULM meeting of July 6, 1944, demonstrated the dysfunction of the Council on this matter, in *Papers of the JLC*, 291; see also minutes of September 27, 1943, A. Bluestein to the CULM Secretariat, JLC R, B8, F13. A CIO report itemizes these administrative constraints: CIO, *Proceedings of the 1943 Convention*, 97–98. See especially the correspondence received by Sidney Hillman on the subject: "1943–1944: Agreements between the National CIO War Relief Committee and the National War Fund, American Red Cross," ACWA, Hillman Correspondence, B210, F2.

61. On these conditions, see Nelson Lichtenstein, *Labor's War at Home: The CIO in World War II* (New York: Cambridge University Press, 1982); Philip Taft, *The A.F.L. from the Death of Gompers to the Merger* (New York: Harper, 1959), 219–32.

62. A. Bluestein also announced that $20 million would be collected by the Labor War Chest, of which one million would be targeted to the Council. These sums would only arrive in January 1944, he added. The CIO representative took the same position. CULM meetings, September 27 and October 18, 1943, JLC R, B8, F13.

63. "AFL Opens Drive to Aid Foreign Labor," *Voice of the Unconquered*, November 1944, 2.

64. Hillman Papers, B210, F1–3.

65. "Financial statement," 1942, 1943, 1944, JLC R, B1, F16, F17, F18; Memorandum, "Activities of the JLC in the United States and Abroad," January 18, 1945, JLC R, B1, F19.

66. Adolph Held, "Report for 1943," JLC R, B1, F17; JLC, "Report for 1944," JLC R, B1, F18.

67. Félix Gouin, former Socialist deputy from Aix en Provence, had participated with Daniel Mayer in the formation of the CAS. He arrived in London in September 1942.

68. "French labor movement," CULM, April 1943, JLC R, B8, F12; Paul Vignaux and Ewa Lewinski Pfister to the JLC, April 29, 1943, JLC R, B32, F12. They based their rate of exchange on 100 to 120 francs to the dollar.

69. Georges Buisson, confederal secretary of the CGT, active with his wife, Suzanne Buisson, in the formation of the CAS in the southern zone, had reached London in the spring 1943. Albert Guigui-Théral, called "Guigui," originally a mechanic and active in the Metal Workers' Federation, accepted a job from the executive body of the underground CGT "in order to go to London to confirm to De Gaulle the workers' support

of the Free French." Marcel Poimboeuf, one of the founders of the CFTC in 1919, had become a member of confederal office. At the end of 1943 he would sit on the Consultative Assembly in Algiers. Biographies of these leaders can be found in Jean Maitron and Claude Pennetier, eds., *Dictionnaire Biographique du Mouvement ouvrier français, 1914–39* (Paris: Editions de l'Atelier, 1999), http://maitron-en-ligne.univ-paris1.fr. General de Gaulle recognized their "active representation" in the fight for Free France in London (*The Complete War Memoirs of Charles de Gaulle*, 404).

70. Albert Guigui and Georges Buisson to Sidney Hillman, April 22, 1943, and Hillman's complementary note, both in Hillman Papers, B73, F38.

71. Albert Guigui to Samuel Estrin, May 27, [1943], JLC R, B32, F12.

72. Albert Guigui, CGT, Transport House, London SW1, June 25, 1943, to Paul Vignaux (in French), Fonds Paul Vignaux, 14, P2, Archives de la CFDT, Paris. In other passages of this letter Guigui tries to convince Vignaux to join the Gaullist movement. The Robert mentioned in this letter was no doubt the famous "R," "Robert," or René Bertholet, Agent 328, of which we speak below.

73. Vignaux to Albert Guigui, CGT Delegation, Transport House, undated letter (in French), but responding point by point to the preceding one from Guigui, Fonds Paul Vignaux, Archives de la CFDT, Paris. This exchange of letters was sent through the Office of Strategic Services, which had established a branch in London. The Paul Vignaux family archives also contain a document in Vignaux's hand that confirms a division of the remittances arriving between August 1942 and August 1943 by the JLC, the ACWA, and the New York War Labor Chest (AFL-CIO) monies destined for the CGT ($11,900), the CFTC ($10,200), and the Socialist Party ($10,100). I thank Jean Lecuir for sharing this document with me.

74. CULM meeting, December 10, 1943, "Report of G. Stolz," JLC R, B8, F13; Albert Guigui to Adolph Held, September 12, 1944, JLC R, B32, F14. Guigui had gone in April/May 1944 to the ILO congress in Philadelphia. Georges Buisson and Lucien Midol (who had come from Algiers) were part of this delegation. Paul Vignaux and Ewa Lewinski-Pfister to the JLC, July 24, 1943, Minkoff Papers, B1, F3; Daniel Mayer thanked the Jewish Labor Committee (*Voice of the Unconquered*, December 1944, 6); JLC National Convention, 1947, JLC R, B2, F13.

75. Georges Buisson and Albert Guigui for the CGT, message for Sidney Hillman and Matthew Woll, AFL-CIO Joint Relief Committee. This message apparently translated from French recorded a request for $15,000 per month. Hillman Papers, undated, B73, F38.

76. The OSS succeeded the Office of Coordinator of Information that was already operational in July 1941. On the OSS, see, for example, Bradley F. Smith, *The Shadow Warriors: OSS and the Origins of the CIA* (New York: Basic Books, 1983); Barry M. Katz, *Foreign Intelligence: Research and Analysis in the Office of Strategic Services, 1942–1945* (Cambridge, MA: Harvard University Press, 1989); Fabrizio Calvi and Olivier Schmidt, *OSS, La guerre secrète en France, 1942–1945: Les services spéciaux américains, la Résistance et la Gestapo* (Paris: Hachette, 1990); Gildas Le Voguer, *Le Renseignement américain entre secret et transparence, 1947–2013* (Rennes: Presses de l'Université de Rennes, 2014).

77. Geert Van Goethem has described the foundation of the Labor Desk, its branch in London, and its first contacts with the European labor movements: "Conflicting Interests: The International Federation of Trade Unions, 1919–1945," in Anthony Carew, Michel Dreyfus, et al., *The International Confederation of Free Trade Unions* (Berne: Peter Lang, 2000), 73–163, in particular 151–53.

78. NARA, Records of the Foreign Nationalities Branch, RG 226.17.1; Records of the New York Office; Records of the Special Operation Branch, RG 226, Entry 106; Jeanpierre, "Des hommes entre plusieurs mondes," 270–84; Loyer, *Paris à New York*, 319–25.

79. "The Italian Underground movements"; "Information about Germany and German émigrés written by Paul Hagen"; "Records relating to Omer Bécu manager of ITF"; "Labor situation in Norway": all in NARA, RG 226, Entry 210, B70; OSS, Special Intelligence Operations, NARA, RG 226, Entry 106, B67. These reports are not always signed.

80. NARA, OSS, Special Intelligence Operations, RG 226, Entry 106, B67, F352.

81. NARA, RG 226, Entry 100, INT French 12FR 1 to 12FR 1080: see, for example, INT-12FR-92; INT-12FR-225; 231; 284; 294; 314; 409, 417; etc. Adolph Held, president of the JLC, communicated to the OSS some documents coming from the Resistance in Europe (France, Poland, Germany, Austria): "List of Documents given by Mr. Held to the Donovan Committee," JLC R, B4, F45.

82. Passy, *Mémoires*, 289–92.

83. Cable from Omer Bécu and John Marchbank to Jacobus Oldenbroek, March 5, 1943, copies to IFTU, CIO, AFL, and ITF. On May 25, Bécu informed Oldenbroek that the money had indeed been received: "International Transportworkers' Federation," NARA, OSS, RG 226, Entry 106, B67, F345.

84. Van Goethem, "Conflicting Interests," 152; George Pratt to Albert Guigui, May 11, 1943, NARA, RG 226, Entry 211, B16; "International Transportworkers' Federation," NARA, OSS, RG 226, Entry 106, B67, F345.

85. Arthur Goldberg to Gerry Van Arkel, July 1, 1943, NARA, OSS, RG 226, Entry 210, B81, document WN 3669/018.

86. Arthur Goldberg to George Pratt, June 24, 1943, OSS, RG 226, Entry 210, B81, document WN 4009.

87. A former high-ranking civil servant dismissed by the Vichy government, Jean Moulin served the Resistance as the intermediary between General de Gaulle in London and the internal movements in southern France (Combat, Libération Sud, Franc Tireurs). In May 1943 he was able to rally them to De Gaulle's authority and to coordinate their action by forming the Conseil National de la Résistance (CNR). In June he was arrested and tortured by the Gestapo in Lyon and died shortly thereafter in July 1943.

88. Michel Dreyfus indicates that the CGT "received financial aid from the French Committee for National Liberation and from American unions": *Histoire de la CGT: Cent ans de syndicalisme en France* (Brussels: Editions Complexe, 1995), 210. Albert Guigui, who supplied elements of his own biography to Jean Maitron, noted: "In the days following his arrival in London, Guigui, accompanied by André Philip, was received by Général de Gaulle who congratulated him on the support that the clandestine CGT

was bringing to fighting France. As for Guigui, he tried to solve the urgent problem of bringing material aid to the unions in occupied France: an agreement was reached for the creation of a Fund of tripartite support (French, British and American) under the aegis of a representative of the Comité national de la France combattante. Thus from March 1, 1943, to July 1, 1944, the BCRA transmitted 'at each moon' a Franco-Anglo-American envelope to a representative designated by the underground CGT to enable it to pursue its various activities." Jean Maitron and Claude Pennetier, eds., *Dictionnaire biographique du Mouvement ouvrier francais, 1997*, http://maitron-en-ligne.univ-paris1. fr/spip.php?article155669.

89. Neal H. Petersen has studied the career of Dulles in Berne and reproduced a number of his messages: *From Hitler's Doorstep: The Wartime Intelligence Reports of Allen Dulles, 1942–1945* (University Park: Pennsylvania State University Press, 1996), 1–7.

90. The subject remains controversial: Wieviorka, *Histoire de la Résistance*, 304–7; Robert Belot and Gilbert Karpman, *L'Affaire suisse: La Résistance a-t-elle trahi de Gaulle?* (Paris: Armand Colin, 2009); Cordier, *Jean Moulin*, 350–61; Crémieux-Brilhac, *La France Libre*, 1:688–92; Henri Frenay, *La nuit finira: Mémoires de résistance, 1940–1945* (1973; Paris: Michalon, 2006), 465–80.

91. Crémieux-Brilhac, *La France Libre*, 1:692.

92. "We have not broken things off, but we are all bruised and outraged." Frenay, *La nuit finira*, 482. Out of the 37 million francs that Dulles was said to have promised Frenay, the latter had already received 8 million. Passy, *Mémoires*, 382, 616, 622; Cordier, *Jean Moulin*, 361.

93. Petersen, *From Hitler's Doorstep*, 7, 544; Philippe Adant, *René Bertholet, 1907–1969: Parcours d'un Genevois peu ordinaire* (Lausanne/Paris: Fondation pour le Progrès de l'Homme, 1995), 76–78. Bertholet is also mentioned by Daniel Bénédite, who, after Varian Fry's departure, tried to exfiltrate refugees from France via Switzerland. *La filière marseillaise: Un chemin vers la liberté sous l'occupation*, edited by J. M. Guillon and J. M. Guiraud (Paris: Le Félin, 2017), 297. He is cited as the most important activist in the network established by the International Transportworkers' Federation. Dieter Nelles, "ITF Resistance against Nazism and Fascism in Germany and Spain," in Bob Reinalda, *The International Transportworkers Federation, 1914–1945: The Edo Fimmen Era* (Amsterdam: Stichting beheer IISG, 1997), 175–99. Michael Richard D. Foot, *SOE in France: An Account of the Work of the British Special Operations Executive in France, 1940–1944* (London: HMSO, 1966), 156–57, 218–19.

94. Petersen, *From Hitler's Doorstep*, 23.

95. Allen Dulles, telegram 6-10, November 24, 1942 (NARA, RG 226, B171), document 1-3 in Petersen, *From Hitler's Doorstep*, 23.

96. Allen Dulles, telegram 610-12, Agent 328 to Eva, August 16, 1943 (NARA, RG 226, B273), document 1-115 in Petersen, *From Hitler's Doorstep*, 102. This telegram of thanks was responding to the dispatch by "Dominique" [Paul Vignaux] on August 10, 1943 (NARA, RG 226, B341). The JLC had furnished in this sum the share that was to be paid to the Socialist Party ($3,000), whereas the shares destined for the CGT ($6,500) and the CFTC ($3,000) came from "New York labor."

97. "The following persons are been deported: Brechenmacher, Eugen Epstein and his wife, Riess and Walter Bregner. Relatively sheltered are Seehof, Orozlan, Zienau, Hardekopf, Kloth, Cohenreuss, Hirschberg and Schwalbach." Telegram 621-22, from "328" to Eva, August 19, 1943 (NARA, RG 226, B273), document 1-119 in Petersen, *From Hitler's Doorstep*, 104–5.

98. Dulles, telegram 1085-87, November 17, 1943, "message concerning the financing of the European labor movement by OSS, at Berne" (NARA, RG 226, B341), document 2-65 in Petersen, *From Hitler's Doorstep*, 160; telegram 2541-43, March 22, 1944 (NARA, RG 226, B191), document 3-61, Petersen, *From Hitler's Doorstep*, 248, 602. About these difficulties, "Dominique [Paul Vignaux]" and Eva had indicated that American labor was about to send significant sums of money designed to help French labor. They suggested these sums be transferred by an individual who was not an OSS member in order not to overburden the OSS account for "328." One of Dulles's superiors told him Washington agreed that he could remunerate "328" in proportion to the value of intelligence provided. Dieter Nelles confirms that Bertholet refused to be paid for services rendered to the underground movements ("ITF Resistance against Nazism and Fascism").

99. Dulles, telegram 2054-56, February 15, 1944 (NARA, RG 226, B170), document 3-13 in Petersen, *From Hitler's Doorstep*, 218; "328 to Eva," telegram 3750-51, June 7, 1944 (NARA RG 226, B192), document 3-144 in Petersen, *From Hitler's Doorstep*, 303, 610.

100. Jewish Labor Committee, "Report for 1944," 4, JLC R, B1, F18. In 1945, Adolph Held summarized the total financial aid for the year 1944 to underground movements in France, Italy, Belgium Norway, and Poland that had been raised by the JLC to the amount of $321,260. Adolph Held, Jacob Pat, B. Tabachinsky, Memorandum, January 18, 1945, JLC R, B1, F19.

101. "List submitted by the Jewish Labor Committee," August 13, 1942. This list contained the names of 83 people, the majority of whom were Jews born in Poland who had managed to flee to the southern zone, since the address given for many of them was that of the Centre Américain de Secours in Marseille, at the time managed by Daniel Bénédite. Mentioned on this list are persons linked to the Cercle Amical-Arbeter Ring. The Yiddish writer Wulf Wieviorka, his two sons, and his daughter are mentioned on this list. Arrested in 1943, Wieviorka would die in Auschwitz in January 1945. Several other persons on this list died in concentration camps. Minkoff Papers, B6, F10. A list of the same names can be found in the Papers of the American Representation of the Bund, Bund Archives, New York, RG 1404, F37A–41.

102. The Bund in Paris at the end of the 1930s included about a thousand members, of whom 500–600 belonged to the Arbeter Ring, plus a section of about a hundred young people. Henri Minczeles, "La résistance du Bund en France pendant l'occupation," *Revue d'histoire de la Shoah* 54 (May–August 1995): 138–53. I retain here the name Arbeter Ring, the Yiddish form of Workmen's Circle, rather than the French version, Cercle Amical.

103. On July 16 and 17, 1942, the roundup at the Vélodrome d'Hiv (the winter cycling arena) was the most massive ever held in Paris or in France during the Occupation.

Arrested by French police and gendarmes, 13,152 Jewish persons of foreign origin, including 4,115 children of all ages, were held up in the Vélodrome d'Hiver for a few days in horrendous conditions before being deported to detention camps near Paris and finally to Auschwitz. Less than 100 persons, and no children, survived the deportation.

104. On the Amelot Committee, see Jules Jacoubovitch, *Rue Amelot, Aide et Résistance* (1948; Paris: Editions du Centre Medem, 2006); Lucien Lazare, *La Résistance juive en France* (Paris: Stock, 1987), 30–31; Asher Cohen, *Persécutions et sauvetages: Juifs et Français sous l'occupation et sous Vichy* (Paris: Editions du Cerf, 1993), 83–85, 366–72; Grynberg, *Les Juifs dans la Résistance et la Libération*, 115–21. On the Union Générale des Israëlites de France (UGIF) created at the request of the Germans by the intermediary of Vichy, see especially Michel Laffitte, *Un engrenage fatal: L'UGIF face aux réalités de la Shoah, 1941–1944* (Paris: L. Lévi, 2003).

105. Fajwel Schrager, *Un militant juif*, translated from Yiddish by H. Bulawko (Paris: Editions Polyglottes, 1979).

106. Constance Pâris de Bollardière, "Fajwel Schrager (né Ostrynski), bundiste, directeur de l'ORT-France et du bureau parisien de l'Union mondiale-ORT," *Archives juives, Revue d'histoire des Juifs de France* 48, no. 1 (2015): 136–39.

107. Schrager went to Marseille in April 1942 to take advantage of this visa, which had been requested at the end of 1941 under his official name, Fajwel Ostrynski, but according to the consul the visa had expired (*Un militant juif*, 103). "List submitted by the Jewish Labor Committee," Minkoff Papers, B6, F10; JLC R, B48, F12, 13, 14. Apart from Fajwel Ostrynski, we find on this list the names of several contributors to the Bundist organ *Unzer Stimme*: Rafal Ryba and his wife, Dyna, Natan Frenkel, his wife and son, Jacques and Berthe Mering, and Shulim Honikman.

108. Schrager thus miraculously escaped the roundup of the Rue Sainte Catherine in February 1943 when several militants were arrested, as he would escape a *rafle* in the suburbs of Lyon in August 1944 (*Un militant juif*, 111–13, 126).

109. Schrager, *Un militant juif*, chaps. 11 and 12; Lazare, *La Résistance juive en France*, 208.

110. Telegrams from Adolph Held and Jacob Pat to Boris Tschlenoff, February 26, 1943, International Red Cross, Geneva, and memo 66, JLC R, B38, F7. The spelling of the names cited is no doubt corrupted by their telegraphic transmission ($10,000 = 30,000 Swiss francs, according to a message from Boris Tschlenoff).

111. The families of Aronovitch, Roth, Cieshinsky [Cisinky], Rafal [Ryba], Nathan [Frenkel], Cuba, Goldberg, Cahan (Brussels) Yelin, Hayblum, Peskin Anna, Chornobroda [Czarnobroda], Stark, "memo 65": September 1943; "memo 68," JLC R, B38, F7.

112. Copy of a telegram received from Emanuel Scherer in London, January 27, 1944, JLC R, B38, F7; telegram from Jacob Pat to Leo Puder, May 2, 1944, "Professor Hersch received the money directly from the JLC for your needs, see Bertholet for arrangements," JLC R, B38, F7.

113. Throughout the war the Swiss government is said to have admitted some 51,100 refugees, of whom 19,495 were Jews, the majority arriving in 1943 and 1944. Commission

indépendante d'experts, *La Suisse et les réfugiés à l'époque du national-socialisme* (Paris: Fayard, 2000), 31.

114. Schrager, *Un militant juif*, 119; Rachel Minc, *L'enfer des innocents: Les enfants juifs dans la tourmente nazie* (Paris: Le Centurion, 1966), 89; Yehuda Bauer, *American Jewry and the Holocaust: The American Jewish Joint Distribution Committee, 1939–1945* (Detroit: Wayne State University Press, 1981), 230; Liebman Hersch to Jacob Pat, April 7 and 12, 1944, June 21, 1945, JLC R, B38, F9. The exact list of Bundist refugees from France aided by Liebman Hersch has been established by Daniel Bitter, "Liebmann Hersch: Un bundiste genevois face aux épreuves de la Seconde Guerre Mondiale" (Master's thesis, INALCO, 2017), 366–72.

115. Laura Hobson Faure, *Un "plan Marshall juif": La présence juive américaine en France après la Shoah, 1944–1954* (Paris: Armand Colin, 2013), 55; according to Yehuda Bauer, the Joint spent $1,748,500 and $1,657,223 in 1943 and 1944, respectively, on France (*American Jewry and the Holocaust*, 217–34, 242–44).

116. Schrager, *Un militant juif*, 119.

117. George Weill, "Un pionnier russe de la médecine sociale, le docteur Boris Tschlenoff, président de l'Union-OSE," in Laura Hobson Faure et al., eds., *L'oeuvre de secours aux enfants et les populations juives au XXᵉ siècle: Prévenir et guérir dans un siècle de violence* (Paris: A. Colin, 2014), 127–47; Boris Tschlenoff's correspondence, JLC R, B38, F7.

118. Liebman Hersch's thesis has been translated into Yiddish and his articles appeared in English, German, French, Polish, and Yiddish. After the war, Hersch would maintain that it was the Diaspora that saved the Jews from total extinction. "We have no guarantee that we will not be the prey to some other catastrophe [if we are assembled] in one country or another," he noted when Israel was created, while recognizing the lift that the Jewish colonists were giving the region. Gur Alroey, "Demographers in the Service of the Nation: Liebman Hersch, Jacob Lestchinsky and the Early Study of Jewish Migration," *Jewish History* 4 (2006): 265–82.

119. "Report from Geneva representative," JLC R, B1, F18.

120. Bitter, "Liebmann Hersch"; *Voice of the Unconquered*, January–February 1946, 4; Adolph Held and Benjamin Tabatchinsky to Professor Hersch, March 7, 1946, JLC R, B38, F9.

121. Schrager, *Un militant juif*, 127.

122. *Voice of the Unconquered*, November 1944, 1 and December 1944, 6. Esther Rivka Richter (Ika) had run the canteen in the Rue Vieille du Temple until her arrest in March 1941. She died in prison in Fort de Romainville in 1942. From the beginning of the occupation the JLC had supported several canteens in Paris, for example, sending $500 for this purpose in June 1941: minutes of the meeting of the Office Committee, June 20, 1941, JLC R, B1, F6. On the Arbeter Ring at the end of the war, see Constance Pâris de Bollardière, "Mutualité, fraternité et travail social chez les bundistes de France," *Archives Juives, Revue d'histoire des Juifs de France* 45, no. 1 (2012): 27–43.

123. "Relief, France," JLC R, B45, F6.

124. *Voice of the Unconquered*, December 1944, 1, 6 and October–November 1945, 8; the appeal of 1945 was renewed in 1946. *Voice of the Unconquered*, May–June 1946, 1.

125. Serge Klarsfeld has established that whatever the exact number of deported Jews, which he situates at 75,721, the total number could not be lower than 75,500 or higher than 76,000. The total number of survivors is tiny: 2,569. *Vichy-Auschwitz: Le rôle de Vichy dans la solution finale de la question juive en France, La Shoah en France* (Paris: Fayard, 2001), 359. Jacques Sémelin has focused on how 75 percent of the Jews in France survived: *The Survival of the Jews of France*, translated by Cynthia Schoch and Natasha Lehrer (New York: Oxford University Press, 2018).

126. On this subject, see Hobson Faure, *Un "plan Marshall juif,"* and Katy Hazan, *Les orphelins de la Shoah: Les maisons de l'espoir, 1944–1960* (Paris: Les Belles Lettres, 2000).

127. Nathan Chanin's correspondence, JLC R, B4, F24.

128. Office Committee, JLC R, B1, F9; B32, F18, F21; *Voice of the Unconquered*, September–October 1945, 3.

129. *Voice of the Unconquered*, November 1944, 1, February 1945, 7; Katy Hazan suggests that eight to ten thousand Jewish children found themselves abandoned after the war (*Les orphelins de la Shoah*, 71).

130. Katy Hazan counts about eighty children's homes, set up by various religious or political groups of the French Jewish world (*Les orphelins de la Shoah*, 397–402).

131. The names given to these homes celebrated the memory of important figures in the labor and Polish Bundist movements and in the Diaspora: Morris Sigman, David Dubinsky's predecessor as president of the ILGWU; Shlomo Mendelsohn, Bundist director of Yiddish schools in Poland and survivor of the Lithuania-Siberia-Japan-USA itinerary, who died in Los Angeles in 1948; Emanuel Ringelblum (Poale Zion), historian and martyr of the Warsaw Ghetto. Constance Pâris de Bollardière has studied the JLC's role in the creation of these homes: "'La pérennité de notre peuple': Une aide socialiste juive américaine dans la diaspora yiddish, le Jewish Labor Committee en France, 1944–1948" (Ph.D. diss., Ecole des Hautes Etudes en Sciences Sociales, 2017); Pâris de Bollardière, "The Jewish Labor Committee's Bundist Relief Network in France, 1945–1948," *Jewish History Quarterly* 246, no. 2 (2013): 293–301; "Nathan Chanin's Visit to Les Buissons," *Voice of the Unconquered*, October–November 1945, 3.

132. Ernst Papanek and Edward Linn, *Out of the Fire: How an Eminent Educator Saved Children from the Hitler Onslaught* (New York: William Morrow, 1975); Jean Christophe Coffin, "Ernst Papanek (1900–1973): Une pédagogie à l'épreuve de la violence," in Hobson Faure et al., *L'oeuvre de secours aux enfants*, 148–65; Pâris de Bollardière, "'La pérennité de notre people,'" 181–96.

133. *Voice of the Unconquered*, January–February 1949, 5.

134. Pâris de Bollardière, "'La pérennité de notre people,'" 193–96.

135. Fajwel Schrager, "The Jewish Labor Committee Rehabilitation Work in France," *Voice of the Unconquered*, October–November 1946, 9; "Our Institutions in France," *Voice of the Unconquered*, March 1948, 6; Schrager, *Un militant juif*, 7–10, 158, 213–24.

136. By this agreement, Blum obtained a reduction of four-fifths on the French debt, a loan of $550 million from the Import/Export Bank for the purchase of equipment

and raw materials. These agreements also opened French cinema halls to American movies.

137. "Here I Feel at Home," speech at the Waldorf Astoria, April 13, 1946, JLC R, B62, F32.

138. Schrager, *Un militant juif*, 213–24.

139. Maison de la Culture Yiddish, Paris, Schrager Archives, eight manuscript and typed articles by Léon Blum for the *Forward*, quotation from first article (December 1, 1949) (French version).

CHAPTER 6: FIRE AND ASHES IN POLAND

1. Jacob Pat, *Ashes and Fire*, translated from Yiddish by Leo Steinberg (New York: International Universities Press, 1947), 7, 16.

2. "Jacob Pat" (1890–1966), in *Papers of the JLC*, xvii–xviii; Constance Pâris de Bollardière, "Ecritures de la destruction et reconstruction: Yankev Pat auteur et acteur du monde yiddish," in Judith Lindenberg, *Premiers savoirs de la Shoah* (Paris: CNRS Editions, 2017), 275–93.

3. "Tabachinsky," *Papers of the JLC*, xxix, 404–5.

4. Stalin-Hitler Pact, JLC statement, September 1939, JLC R, B19, F27, translated from Yiddish by Erez Lévy.

5. According to the Molotov-Ribbentrop Pact, Poland was divided into three main parts: the western provinces were directly incorporated into the Reich, the eastern ones, including Byelorussia and Ukraine, were integrated into the USSR, while the central region extending between Warsaw, Lublin, and Krakow to the south formed the General Government under German rule.

6. The food rations in 1941 were calculated by the Nazi Occupiers to guarantee the extinction of the Jews by famine: 2,613 calories for Germans, 699 for Poles, 184 for the Jews: see Samuel D. Kassow, *Who Will Write Our History?: Rediscovering a Hidden Archive from the Warsaw Ghetto* (Bloomington: Indiana University Press, 2007), 108.

7. Pawel Korzec, *Juifs en Pologne: La question juive pendant l'entre-deux-guerres* (Paris: Presse de la Fondation Nationale des Sciences Politiques, 1980); David Engel, *In the Shadow of Auschwitz: The Polish Government in Exile and the Jews, 1939–1942* (Chapel Hill: University of North Carolina Press, 1987); see also Dariusz Libionka, "L'Etat polonais clandestin et la 'question juive,' 1942–1944," in Jean Charles Szurek and Annette Wieviorka, *Juifs et Polonais, 1939–2008* (Paris: Albin Michel, 2009), 61–79.

8. Emanuel Ringelblum of the Left Poale Zion and his collaborators met in the manner of a secret society called Oyneg Shabes to collect and preserve methodically and almost religiously the underground press and testimonies on life in the Warsaw Ghetto before disappearing themselves. Samuel Kassow's *Who Will Write Our History* is an analysis of these archives rediscovered after the war. Daniel Blatman has presented a thematic selection of extracts of the news clippings thus assembled: *En direct du ghetto: La presse clandestine juive dans le ghetto de Varsovie, 1940–1943* (Paris: Editions du Cerf, 2005), translated from Hebrew.

9. Yehuda Bauer, *American Jewry and the Holocaust: The American Jewish Joint Distribution Committee, 1939–1945* (Detroit: Wayne State University Press, 1981), 67–106. Bauer notes that in the spring of 1941 half of the 1.8 million Jews of Poland under Nazi domination were in need of help and that at most 300,000 received it (Kassow, *Who Will Write Our History?* 107, 112–19).

10. Originally a glovemaker, Zygielbojm had joined the Bund after World War I. In Warsaw he was secretary of the Trade Union Federation, then, transferring to Lodz, he was elected to this city's council while keeping his seat as a member of the Bund's Central Committee. Fleeing Warsaw in December 1939, he reached Brussels just in time for the meeting of the Executive Bureau of the LSI, which he informed about the situation in Poland. Bernard Goldstein, *The Stars Bear Witness*, translated from Yiddish by Leonard Shatzkin (New York: Viking Press, 1949), 33, 38; Daniel Blatman, *For Our Freedom and Yours: The Jewish Labour Bund in Poland, 1939–1949* (London: Vallentine Mitchell, 2003), 7–11.

11. Goldstein, *The Stars Bear Witness*, 71–72, 86–88.

12. Essentially this meant aid to the Jewish workers' movement of Poland. But as we will see, the JLC helped the Bund and the Polish Socialist Party underground. Blatman, *For Our Freedom and Yours*, 123–25; JLC, minutes of the meeting of the Executive Committee, September 7 and November 8, 1939, JLC R, B1, F3.

13. Minutes of the meeting of the Office Committee, December 26, 1939, JLC R, B1, F6.

14. Jacob Pat to David Dubinsky, February 9, 1940, July 3, 1941, thanking him for contributing $10,000 for the operation of the Medem Sanatorium. JLC R, B12, F2.

15. Szygielbojm in the United States, JLC R, B19, F29.

16. The hesitancy to nominate Zygielbojm came from both the Bund Representation, which did not trust him, and the government in exile, which took a long time to accept a Bundist representation and had agreed to appoint Henryk Erlich before hearing of his tragic fate (discussed below). Blatman, *For Our Freedom and Yours*, 129–39; Engel, *In the Shadow of Auschwitz*, 115–56.

17. Minutes of the meeting of the Office Committee, July 28, 1941, JLC R, B1, F6.

18. Jacob Pat to H. Buchman (representing the Joint), December 29, 1941, JLC R, B17, F25: "I am herewith sending you a translation of a telegram sent by the Polish ambassador in Kuybishev to the Polish ambassador in Washington."

19. Adolph Held, Jacob Pat to His Excellency Constantin Oumansky, USSR Ambassador, Washington, DC, August 28, 1941, September 12, 1941; Benjamin Tabachinsky to the Chargé d'Affaires of the Soviet Embassy, September 17, 1941, all in JLC R, B19, F4; Jacob Pat to the General Consul of Poland, September 5, October 2, and November 12, 1941, JLC R, B17, F7.

20. "Budget for year ending December 1942," JLC R, B44, F7; "The Jewish Labor Committee in 1942," JLC R, B44, F8; Stanislaw Kot to JLC, undated, JLC R, B17, F6.

21. JLC R, B6, F13, 14; Jacob Pat to David Dubinsky, October 3 and 9, 1942, JLC R, B12, F2.

22. Jacob Pat to UNRRA, September 6, 1944, JLC R, B44, F12; A. Held, J. Pat, and B. Tabachinsky, "Memorandum," 1945, JLC R, B1, F19. In 1943 and 1944, the JLC

furnished, respectively, $45,113 and $21,346 for aid to Russia (*Papers of the JLC*, 311). Jacob Pat to the Consul-General of Poland, lists of names of Polish refugees in Russia to whom packages must be sent, letters of September 3, 8, 16, and 30, 1941, October 7 and 22, 1941, JLC R, B17, F7.

23. Polish Embassy, Memorandum, September 18, 1942, on the citizenship of refugees in the USSR and the distribution of aid, JLC R, B17, F8; Memo from the Jewish Labor Committee (September?) 1942, JLC R, B17, F6; Jacob Pat to Ambassador S. Kot, in Kuybishev, June 22, 1942, JLC R, B17, F8. Regarding the ambivalence of the Polish government, it should be recalled that the number of Jews was very limited in the Polish Army led by General Anders in Russia and that the Jewish soldiers suffered from severe discrimination in the Polish Army stationed in Great Britain, to the point of causing their desertion. Engel, *In the Shadow of Auschwitz*, 129–31; David Engel, *Facing a Holocaust: The Polish Government in Exile and the Jews* (Chapel Hill: University of North Carolina Press, 1993), 129–37.

24. Blatman, *For Our Freedom and Yours*, 69–89; Engel, *Facing a Holocaust*, 55–62.

25. Among them, Philip Murray, secretary-general of the CIO, Wendell Willkie, Republican opponent of Roosevelt in the 1940 election and Roosevelt's envoy to Moscow, Albert Einstein, Frank Kindgdon of the International Rescue and Relief Association, theologian Reinhold Niebuhr, Paul Kellogg of *Survey Graphic*, Alvin Johnson, director of the New School for Social Research, and Abraham Cahan of the *Jewish Daily Forward*. Brochure published after the commemoration, March 30, 1943, DDC, B36, F4A and F4C.

26. Blatman, *For Our Freedom and Yours*, 81–89.

27. Jacob Pat to Dubinsky, February 25, 1943, JLC R, B12, F3.

28. "Declaration adopted by standing vote by 3,500 unionists at Erlich-Alter Protest meeting," Mecca Temple, March 30, 1943, JLC R, B13, F32, reproduced in *Papers of the JLC*, 251.

29. Engel, *Facing a Holocaust*, 70–72.

30. Walter Laqueur, *The Terrible Secret: An Investigation into the Suppression of Information about Hitler's "Final Solution"* (London: Weidenfeld and Nicolson, 1980); Walter Laqueur and Richard Breitman, *Breaking the Silence* (New York: Simon and Schuster, 1986); David Wyman, *The Abandonment of the Jews: America and the Holocaust, 1941–1945* (New York: New Press, 1998); Richard Breitman and Alan M. Kraut, *American Refugee Policy and European Jewry, 1933–1945* (Bloomington: Indiana University Press, 1987), 146–66; Richard Breitman, *Official Secrets: What the Nazis Planned, What the British and Americans Knew* (New York: Hill and Wang, 1998).

31. According to Wyman, among other revelations, it was the report from the Bund that became the decisive factor in the first breakthrough of extermination news (*Abandonment of the Jews*, 21, 40, 53).

32. The text of this message does not figure in the JLC records; its contents appear in Blatman, *For Our Freedom and Yours*, 138. Leon Feiner is described in Goldstein, *The Stars Bear Witness*, 100–101; Jan Karski also paints a striking portrait of Feiner, an elegant

lawyer and businessman on the Aryan side and a harassed Jew in the ghetto: *Story of a Secret State: My Report to the World* (1944; London: Penguin, 2012), 347–48.

33. Blatman, *For Our Freedom and Yours*, 95–96 2.

34. Engel, *In the Shadow of Auschwitz*, 179–85.

35. Laurel Leff, *Buried by the Times: The Holocaust and America's Most Important Newspaper* (New York: Cambridge University Press, 2005), 139–41; David Wyman notes that the *Boston Globe* was the first to speak of this report, on June 26 (*Abandonment of the Jews*, 22).

36. Heydrich was the coordinator of the deportation of Jews to the death camps.

37. Minutes of the meeting of the Office Committee, June 17, 1942, JLC R, B1, F7 (translated from Yiddish by Erez Lévy).

38. "Directly contrary to international law and [in violation] of every tenet of humanity and morality, has been the deliberate massacre of some one million European Jews by the Nazi government. These million dead cannot be brought to life. But further insensate and brutal bloodshed can yet be stopped; and we ask you Mr. President, to issue a declaration, concurred in by the various leaders of civilized humanity to demand a reckoning of the leaders and people of Germany for any further excesses committed against the Jewish civilized population of Europe. We respectfully request you, Mr. President, to again raise the voice of America and its allies in the defense of the most defenseless people in Europe." "Petition to President Roosevelt," JLC R, B17, F1.

39. Wyman, *Abandonment of the Jews*, 24; President Roosevelt to Stephen Wise, July 17, 1942, JLC R, B17, F1.

40. The Bund Representation even refused to let Zygielbojm write a major article for the *Jewish Daily Forward* (Blatman, *For Our Freedom and Yours*, 140–41).

41. Minutes of the Executive Committee, August 26, 1942, JLC R, B1, F3. The minutes of the Executive Committee from 1942 to 1945 are in Yiddish and have been translated for me by Erez Lévy. Blatman, *For Our Freedom and Yours*, 141–42, also mentions that Leon Feiner managed to send a second report to the West at the end of August 1942, while noting that Zygielbojm had official knowledge of it only at the end of November 1942; see notes 53, 54.

42. Gerhart M. Riegner, "Témoignage de mes activités en Suisse pendant la Seconde Guerre Mondiale," *Revue d'histoire de la Shoah* 163 (May–August 1998): 91–100; Wyman, *Abandonment of the Jews*, 42–45; Laqueur, *Breaking the Silence*, 119–41.

43. Goldstein, *The Stars Bear Witness*, 113–59; Bauer, *American Jewry and the Holocaust*, 325–27; Saul Friedländer, *Nazi Germany and the Jews*, vol. 2, *1939–1945: The Years of Extermination* (New York: Harper Perennial, 2007), 426–33.

44. Minutes of the Executive Committee, August 26, 1942, JLC R, B1, F3. See also "Memorial meeting for Czerniakow," August 26, 1942, JLC R, B13, F29 (translated from Yiddish by Erez Lévy).

45. Minutes of the Executive Committee, September 24, 1942, JLC R, B1, F3.

46. Minutes of the Executive Committee, September 24, 1942, JLC R, B1, F3.

47. Adolph Held read the same report to the JLC Convention on December 18, 1942, JLC R, B2, F7.

48. American Federation of Labor, *Proceedings of the 1942 Convention*, October 5–14, Washington, DC, 1942, 637–43. David Wyman, in his detailed reconstitution of the stages of the dissemination of information in the United States, does not mention this report.

49. AFL unions had local branches in Canada, hence the holding of this convention in Toronto.

50. Karski, *Story of a Secret State*, 337. Karski's testimony to the government in exile in London is reproduced in Laqueur, *Terrible Secret*, 232–38. It was also recorded in 1978 by Claude Lanzmann for his film *Shoah* (1985).

51. Karski, *Story of a Secret State*, 351, 355–56.

52. Karski, *Story of a Secret State*, 356.

53. Minutes of the Executive Committee, December 2, 1942, JLC R, B1, F7.

54. "Memorandum from the Underground Labor Groups in Poland," JLC R, B35, F1. Simultaneously Zygielbojm had sent a telegram to the JLC in which he announced the massacre of 250 children from the Medem Sanatorium as well as the staff looking after the children. Telegram from Jacob Pat echoing the news to Tabachinsky, December 3, 1942, JLC R, B6, F18.

55. Wyman, *Abandonment of the Jews*, 42–53, figures cited in the *New York Herald Tribune* and *New York Times*, November 25, 1942; Breitman and Kraut, *American Refugee Policy*, 157.

56. Minutes of the Executive Committee, December 2, 1942, JLC R, B1, F7.

57. Stephen Wise (American Jewish Congress), Henry Monsky (B'nai B'rith), Israel Rosenberg (Union of Orthodox Rabbis), and Maurice Wertheim (American Jewish Committee).

58. Adolph Held, "Report on the Visit to the President," JLC R, B1, F17. The report by Adolph Held in the JLC records is the only one known about this meeting.

59. Resolution of the Jewish Labor Committee on the Declaration of the Eleven United Nations, December 18, 1942, JLC R, B2, F7. In its resolution the JLC added the demand that "practical measures be taken at once to save the Jews of Europe." On the signatories of this declaration (the governments of Belgium, Czechoslovakia, Greece, Luxembourg, the Netherlands, Norway, Poland, the Soviet Union, Great Britain, the United States, Yugoslavia, and the National Committee of the Fighting French), see Laqueur, *Terrible Secret*, 224–28.

60. Shlomo Mendelsohn in JLC Executive Committee, August 26, 1942, JLC R, B1, F3.

61. The Jewish combat unit Zhydowska Organizatzia Boyova (ZOB) had been founded by members of the Hashomer Hatzaïr, Poale Tzion, and Dror HeHaluts. The Bund participated but remained outside the Jewish National Committee that was trying to coordinate various groups politically on the pretext that this association would alter its representation to the government in exile and its relations with the PPS. On these oscillations, see Blatman, *For Our Freedom and Yours*, 102–5.

62. Blatman, *For Our Freedom and Yours*, 115–17.

63. Goldstein, *The Stars Bear Witness*, 186.

64. Nevertheless, the Nazis killed several thousand people during this interrupted roundup, when many Bundist comrades died, like Isaac Guiterman, director of the Joint in Warsaw; see Goldstein, *The Stars Bear Witness*, 177, 186.

65. Shmuel Krakowski, *The War of the Doomed: Jewish Armed Resistance in Poland, 1942–1944* (London: Holmes and Meier, 1984), 176; Vladka Meed (Feigele Miedzyrzecki), *On Both Sides of the Wall: Memoirs from the Warsaw Ghetto* (1993; Washington, DC: U.S. Holocaust Memorial Museum, 1999), 123.

66. Meed, *On Both Sides of the Wall*, 94, 133; Daniel Blatman, "A Hesitant Partnership: The Bund and Polish Socialists during the Holocaust," in David Bankier and Israel Gutman, eds., *Nazi Europe and the Final Solution* (Jerusalem: Yad Vashem, 2003), 199–214.

67. The telegram destined for Zygielbojm was transmitted to the JLC (JLC R, B11, F24). According to Daniel Blatman, the second signatory of the telegram was Bund leader Maurycy Orzech. The foreign minister of the Polish government, Raczinski, transmitted this appeal to Pius XII (*For Our Freedom and Yours*, 147).

68. *Voice of the Unconquered*, June 1943, 1, 8.

69. JLC Report for 1943, p. 14, JLC R, B1, F17.

70. Bauer, *American Jewry and the Holocaust*, 329–34.

71. JLC R40, B17, F6. An article in *Voice of the Unconquered*, June 1944, p. 6, gives figures that partly corroborate the preceding ones: the underground Jewish labor movement of Warsaw acknowledged having received from the JLC $43,000 between October 1942 and June 1943, and $38,000 from July to November 1943.

72. Blatman, *For Our Freedom and Yours*, 155–56; Jacob Pat's letter to JDC vice president, Joseph Hyman, on the transmission of funds, March 8, 1943, JLC R, B47, F12.

73. Marek Edelman, *The Ghetto Fights: Warsaw, 1943–1945* (London: Bookmarks, 2014). In an article from 1947, Jacob Pat mentions the parachuting of money from flights from England: "The Jewish Labor Committee and the International Anti-Nazi Resistance Movement," *Labor and Nation* (January–February 1947).

74. Meed, *On Both Sides of the Wall*, 181. About thirty thousand Jewish survivors were living in hiding in Warsaw and the region.

75. Meed, *On Both Sides of the Wall*, 182. Meed's story on Jews on the Aryan side matches the chapter Jacob Pat devoted to the young Bundist militant, "Underground Marisha," in *Ashes and Fire*, 162–79. Jacob Pat to Joseph Hyman, November 18, 1943, informing him of the sums spent to support Jews escaped to the Aryan side and the partisans who protected them, JLC R, B47, F12.

76. "Address by Vladke, Feige Mendzczecki [sic] to the National Convention of the JLC," 1947, JLC R, B2, F14.

77. Bauer, *American Jewry and the Holocaust*, 332. Kenneth Waltzer also indicated that the Joint and the JLC were the only American organizations to support the Jews of Poland: "American Jewish Labor and Aid to Polish Jews during the Holocaust" (paper presented at the United States Holocaust Memorial Council, Washington, DC, March 1987).

78. See chapter 5.

79. American Representation of the General Jewish Workers' Union of Poland, to the Council for the Underground Labor Movement (CULM), April 9, 1943, JLC R, B8, F12.

80. American Delegation Left Poale Zion, to Council, June 5, 1943, JLC R, B8, F12.

81. "Financial Assistance Sent to Poland," JLC R, B1, F17, reproduced in *Papers of the Jewish Labor Committee*, 310.

82. Polish Labor Group to Council for the Underground Labor Movement, April 15, 1943, JLC R, B8, F12.

83. Jacob Pat to W. Malinowski, New York, June 23, 1943, JLC R, B17, F6.

84. Wladyslaw Malinowski to Jacob Pat, May 17 and June 26, 1942; Arthur Salman to Jacob Pat, August 26, 1942, all in JLC R, B17, F8.

85. Malinowski to Jacob Pat, August 5, 1943; Jacob Pat to "Dear friend," August 6, 1943, both in JLC R, B17, F6. Jacob Pat was invited to "hear a representative of the Polish Underground, who recently got through to this country, [whose] report is of the utmost importance, so much so, as to merit his giving it over to the highest authorities in Washington." Jan Karski, in his memoirs, reports elements of his conversation with President Roosevelt on July 28, 1943 (*Story of a Secret State*, 418–19).

86. Malinowski to Jacob Pat, August 23, 1943, December 13, 1943, February 9, 1944, JLC R, B17, F6.

87. A. Held and J. Pat to Jan Kwapinski, vice prime minister of the government in London, September 28, 1943, JLC R, B17, F6; J. Pat to Jan Cziechanowski, Polish Ambassador, August 10, 1944, JLC R, B17, F10.

88. Jacob Pat to Malinowski, August 10, 1944, JLC R, B17, F6.

89. JLC Report 1942–43, "We stood before a wall," JLC R, B1, F17.

90. Deborah Lipstadt asserts that in 1943 and in the early months of 1944 the main American daily papers "ignored" or only marginally covered reports on the Final Solution (*Beyond Belief*, 218–40).

91. Leon Dennen to the editor of the *New York Times*, February 18, 1943, JLC R, B4, F26; *Voice of the Unconquered*, March 1943, 5, 8.

92. *Voice of the Unconquered*, March 1943, 5; April, May, June 1943, 1; July 1943, 1, 7; November 1943, 1; February 1944, 1; June 1944, 7; August and September 1944, 1; October 1944, 1, 7. Orzech and Ringelblum were both murdered in the Paviak Prison, the former in August 1943, the latter in March 1944.

93. *Voice of the Unconquered*, November 1943, 1. To support and honor this gesture, the JLC made a gift of $10,000 to the Swedish labor movement, which had taken on the task of feeding and protecting these refugees.

94. "American Labor's Memorandum to State Department on Aid to Jews in Nazidom," *Voice of the Unconquered*, November 1943, 6; Adolph Held, "Report for Year Ending 1943," JLC R, B1, F17. On the failure of the Bermuda Conference, see, for example, Wyman, *Abandonment of the Jews*, 104–23.

95. Stephen Wise, *Challenging Years* (London: East and West Library, 1951), 190–94.

96. Wyman, *Abandonment of the Jews*, 209–15; Breitman and Kraut, *American Refugee Policy*, 182–91; Wise, *Challenging Years*, 190–94; Bauer, *American Jewry and the Holocaust*, 401; Rebecca Erbelding, *Rescue Board: The Untold Story of America's Efforts to Save the Jews of Europe* (New York: Anchor, 2019).

97. Memorandum, January 1, 1945, JLC R, B1, F19: in this note Held, Pat, and Tabachinsky recalled that they had sent $400,000 to resistance movements in Poland, and $150,000 more recently.

98. *Voice of the Unconquered*, February 1944, 1, 3, 5. Breckinridge Long estimated that 580,000 "refugees" had entered the United States since the start of Hitler's regime (1933–1943). According to the Bureau of Labor, cited by Held, this figure was actually the total number of visas granted by the immigration services, including to immigrants coming from non-European countries and not occupied by the enemy. Subtracting these cases, 296,632 Europeans had entered the United States, some of whom were on temporary visas. Of this figure it was estimated that 163,756 were Jews.

99. Wyman, *Abandonment of the Jews*, 267; *Voice of the Unconquered*, July 1944, September 1944, 5, 6.

100. Wyman, *Abandonment of the Jews*, 285; Bauer, *American Jewry and the Holocaust*, 400–407. Erbelding, *Rescue Board*, 276.

101. "Just informed 400 thousand Hungarian Jews deported Poland. Annihilation 350 Thousand facing liquidation next days Stop." Emanuel Scherer, member of the Polish National Council, *Papers of the JLC*, 293. *Voice of the Unconquered*, August 1944, 1.

102. "Agreement between JLC and IRRC," February 2, 1944, *Papers of the JLC*, 278.

103. *Voice of the Unconquered*, September 1944, October 1, 1944, 4; "Message received from Leon Denenberg," August 1, 1944; Denenberg to Sheba [Strunksy, IRRC], July 11, 1944; "Report Regarding Mr. Denenberg's activities in Turkey," October 19, 1944, JLC R, B4, F26.

104. JLC drive to raise $1 million, December 1944, JLC R, B1, F20.

105. "JLC Plenary Session's Resolutions," *Voice of the Unconquered*, December 1944, 6.

106. *Voice of the Unconquered*, January 1944, 1; February 1944, 6.

107. *Voice of the Unconquered*, April–May 1945.

108. "Outline of JLC Sponsored Exhibit," JLC R, B14, F14; Message from Albert Einstein to the JLC, *Papers of the JLC*, 320, 32; *Voice of Unconquered*, March 1945, 5; April–May 1945, 5–11.

109. Expression often heard among American workers, reported in the study cited in the following note.

110. "Anti-Semitism among American Labor," Report on a Research Project Conducted by the Institute of Social Research of Columbia University, 4 vols., mimeographed, in JLC R, microfilm roll 161–64. According to this study 30.7 percent held violent, even virulent, views against Jews, and 19.1 percent of them expressed a marked anti-Jewish hostility without mentioning what the Nazis had done. Inversely, 50.2 percent of the others expressed a degree of tolerance, even more or less friendship, for Jews. On

this study, see Catherine Collomp, "Anti-Semitism among American Labor: A Study by the Refugee Scholars of the Frankfurt School of Sociology at the End of World War II," *Labor History* 52, no. 4 (2011): 417–39.

111. In Collomp, "Anti-Semitism among American Labor"; JLC R, microfilm roll 161, vol. 1, 13.

112. During the war it had spent $321,851 for this purpose. "Report of the Department of American Activities of the JLC," March 8, 1945, JLC R, B1, F9; *Voice of the Unconquered*, June 1943, 3; December 1944, 4; January 1945, 4, 6; March 1945, 3; April–May 1945, 4, 9.

113. *Voice of the Unconquered*, April–May 1945, 9.

114. Pat, *Ashes and Fire*, 31.

115. To the approximate figure of 80,000 survivors should be added some 150,000 repatriated from the Soviet Union.

116. *Voice of the Unconquered*, August–September 1945, 1; October–November 1945, 1.

117. Rescue work, 1946, National Convention, 1947, JLC R, B2, F12.

118. *Voice of the Unconquered*, October–November 1945, 5, January–February 1946, 6; May–June 1946, 4. Charles Zimmerman of the ILGWU fulfilled another reconnaissance mission on the human and political needs of the liberated countries. After going to the Scandinavian countries and France and having visited the DP camps in Germany, he saw Poland, its ruins, and the devastated cities and ghettos. He reported what he had seen to the JLC in January 1946, JLC R, B1, F20.

119. Pat, *Ashes and Fire*, 7–16; *Voice of the Unconquered*, January–February 1946, 3.

120. Pat, *Ashes and Fire*, 38, 112, 118, 249.

121. Samuel Kassow notes that it was effectively with the money sent by the Jewish Labor Committee that the excavations really began to unearth the Ringelblum archives during the summer of 1946; see Kassow, *Who Will Write Our History?* 206; Pat, *Ashes and Fire*, 65.

122. *Voice of Unconquered*, May–June 1946, 1, 5; March–April 1947, 1.

123. The Norwegian, Danish, and Swedish governments had invited an American labor delegation in 1945 to thank the JLC for its support during the war. This delegation included Charles Zimmerman from the ILGWU and Irving Brown from the AFL.

124. A hundred survivors of the labor movement of Poland who had been in DP camps in Germany were admitted to the United States in 1946 with the help of the JLC. Vladka Meed and Bernard Goldstein were among them: "Rescue of Democratic and Labor Leaders from Nazi Occupation Forces," *Labor and Nation*, January–February 1947.

125. 1947 National Convention, JLC R, B2, F14.

126. 1947 National Convention, JLC R, B2, F14.

127. Blatman, *For Our Freedom and Yours*, 182. According to Jean-Charles Szurek, 60,000 Jews suddenly left Poland after Kielce: "Les Juifs en Europe de l'Est depuis 1945," in Antoine Germa, Benjamin Lellouch, and Evelyne Patlagean, *Les Juifs dans l'histoire* (Seyssel: Champ Vallon, 2011), 767–84; Jan T. Gross, *Fear: Anti-Semitism in Poland after Auschwitz* (New York: Random House, 2006).

128. "Highlights of the report of executive secretary Jacob Pat," 1947 Convention, JLC R, B2, F13; Blatman, *For Our Freedom and Yours*, 262–63.
129. Jacob Pat's nuanced position is explained in "Problems of Jewish Rehabilitation," in "International Postwar Problems" (1945), 353–60, publication of the American Labor Conference on International Affairs, JLC R, B5, F31. On Jacob Pat and the Zionist question, see David Slucki, *The International Jewish Labor Bund after 1945: Toward a Global History* (New Brunswick, NJ: Rutgers University Press, 2012), 23–25, 184–85.

AFTERWORD

1. Two brief exceptions to this statement appeared in organs of the labor movement. One article, "Rescue of Democratic and Labor Leaders from Nazi Occupation Forces," was partly written by Jacob Pat; it summarized the JLC's important achievements: saving 1,500 anti-fascists and support for the resistance in Europe, *Labor and Nation*, January–February 1947 (courtesy of the Inter-Union Institute, 4 unpaginated pages). The second is a much later and brief article in the AFL-CIO organ written by Thomas R. Brooks, "The Jewish Labor Committee, Fighters for Freedom," *AFL-CIO American Federationist* 71, no. 7 (1963): 18–21. Writing in the context of the civil rights movement, the author stressed the JLC's activities on this subject while recalling its actions since 1934.

   In December 1984, on the occasion of the visit to Germany by AFL-CIO president Lane Kirkland, the German union confederation DGB published a brochure mentioning that some German anti-Nazi leaders had been rescued by the AFL. This forty-five-page brochure was also published in English in 1985 under the title "German-American Trade Union Solidarity in the Struggle against Fascism, 1933–1945: How the American Trade Unions Helped Their Persecuted German Colleagues, A Report." The JLC is mentioned in this brochure on pages 18 and 27. George Meany Memorial Archives, RG 34–002, AFL-CIO Publications, Box 26.
2. The William Green Papers do not mention the JLC, and they include no mention of the rescue episodes, despite their being designated by the State Department as the "AFL list." Nor do they make any reference to the AFL and CIO Joint Committee for financing European labor movements under Nazi occupation (*American Federation of Labor Records, Part II, President's Office Files, Series A: William Green Papers 1934–1952*, published from the holdings of the State Historical Society of Wisconsin, general editor, Melvyn Dubofsky, project editor, Randolph Boehm, Guide compiled by Martin Schipper, Microfilm project, University Publications of America). Similarly, records of the CIO secretary-general, Philip Murray, contain no reference to the AFL and CIO Joint Committee: Philip Murray Papers 1936–1952, Records of the Congress of Industrial Organizations (CIO), 1943–1944, American Catholic History Research Center and University Archives, Catholic University, Washington, DC.
3. Ronald Radosh, *American Labor and United States Foreign Policy* (New York: Random House, 1969); Roy Godson, *American Labor and European Politics: The AFL as a Transnational Force* (New York: Crane, Russak, 1976); Ronald Filippelli, *American*

Labor and Postwar Italy, 1943–1953 (Stanford: Stanford University Press, 1989); Federico Romero, *The United States and the European Trade Union Movement, 1944–1951* (Chapel Hill: University of North Carolina Press, 1992); Peter Weiler, "The United States, International Labor and the Cold War: The Break-up of the World Federation of Trade Unions," *Diplomatic History* 5, no. 1 (1981): 1–22; Gary Bush, *Political Currents in the International Trade Union Movement* (London: Economist Publications, 1980); Leroy J. Lenburg, "The CIO and American Foreign Policy, 1935–1955" (Ph.D. diss., Pennsylvania State University, 1973); Anthony Carew, "The American Labor Movement in Fizzland: The Free Trade Union Committee and the CIA," *Labor History* 39, no. 1 (1998): 25–42; Robert Anthony Waters and Geert Van Goethem, *American Labor's Global Ambassadors: The International History of the AFL-CIO during the Cold War* (New York: Palgrave Macmillan, 2013).

4. Godson, *American Labor and European Politics*, 35–36.

5. Geert Van Goethem, "Conflicting Interests: The International Federation of Trade Unions, 1919–1945," in Anthony Carew, Michel Dreyfus, et al., *The International Confederation of Free Trade Unions* (Berne: Peter Lang, 2000), 152–53.

6. Abramovitch to Dubinsky, November 22, 1944, DDC, B173, F4B; Abramovitch to Dubinsky, June 9, 1946, DDC, B173, F3A. The memorandum he sent in 1946 to Matthew Woll and to Dubinsky advocated the essential methods by which the AFL functioned and intended to oppose the World Federation.

7. Robert D. Parmet, *The Master of Seventh Avenue: David Dubinsky and the American Labor Movement* (New York: New York University Press, 2005), 224–42.

8. Interpretations differ as to the impact of American pressure on the creation of FO. Radosh, *American Labor and United States Foreign Policy*, 304–48, and Annie Lacroix-Riz attribute a lot of influence to Irving Brown (agent of the AFL) in this schism, "Autour d'Irving Brown: L'AFL, le Free Trade Union Committee, le département d'Etat et la scission syndicale française," *Le Mouvement Social* 151 (April–June 1990): 79–118. Others analyze the importance of local factors, and international ones like the Marshall Plan, which led in parallel to the division within the World Federation of Trade Unions: Jean Marie Pernot, "Les relations internationales et les débuts de la CGT-FO," in Michel Dreyfus, Gérard Gautron, and Jean Louis Robert, *La naissance de Force Ouvrière* (Paris: Presses Universitaires de Rennes, 2003), 199–213; Denis MacShane, *International Labour and the Origins of the Cold War* (Oxford: Clarendon Press, 1992), 79–96; Jack Kantrowicz, "L'influence américaine sur Force Ouvrière: Mythe ou réalité?" *Revue française de science politique* 28, no. 4 (1978): 717–39.

9. Romero, *The United States and the European Trade Union Movement*, 31–81; Filippelli, *American Labor and Postwar Italy*, 33–50.

10. The Taft-Hartley Act of 1947 imposed on all American labor organizations the obligation to swear an oath of non-affiliation with any Communist organization, thus muzzling any political opposition to economic liberalism, capitalism, and the Marshall Plan.

11. The Jewish American organizations kept a low profile during the McCarthy era so as not to feed the common public opinion that associated communism with left-wing

Jewish unions or intellectual circles. Several organizations, including the JLC, distrusted the Rosenbergs' defense team and considered it merely a Communist facade. Edward Shapiro, *A Time for Healing: American Jewry since World War II* (Baltimore: Johns Hopkins University Press, 1992), 36–38; JLC R, II, B66, F25; Hasia R. Diner, *We Remember with Reverence and Love: American Jews and the Myth of Silence after the Holocaust* (New York: New York University Press, 2009), 279.

12. The JLC's interpretation of totalitarianism was confirmed by that given by Hannah Arendt in 1951. For the German Jewish philosopher who had been a refugee in the United States since 1941, the totalitarian regimes in Germany and the Soviet Union relied on the arbitrariness of anti-Semitism, the weapon by which modern dictatorships imposed their terror. "Terror as we know it today strikes without any preliminary provocations, its victims are innocent even from the point of view of the persecutor. This was the case in Nazi Germany, where full terror was directed against Jews.... In Soviet Russia, the situation is more confused, but the facts, unfortunately, are all too obvious." *The Origins of Totalitarianism* (New York: Harcourt Brace Jovanovich, 1975), 6. The Slansky trial in Prague (1952), like the "doctors' plot" in the Soviet Union (1953), would soon unmask the use of state anti-Semitism in Stalin's regime.

13. In a petition addressed to the United Nations in 1951, the JLC called on the "conscience of mankind," but this would not bear fruit until the 1970s and 1980s: "An Appeal to the Conscience of Mankind," JLC R, B66, F39; Pauline Peretz, *Let My People Go: The Transnational Politics of Soviet Jewish Emigration during the Cold War* (New Brunswick, NJ: Transaction, 2015).

14. "Memorandum submitted to the British Labour Party and British Labour Congress (TUC) by the National Executive of the Jewish Labor Committee," July 1941, DDC, B50, F3C.

15. Speech by Haakon Lie to the JLC Congress, February 1947, JLC R, B2, F14, reproduced in *Voice of the Unconquered*, March–April 1947, 7. Charles Zimmerman of the ILGWU, who went to Norway in 1945, also testifies to the fact that the JLC was the first organization to help the clandestine struggle in that country. "Zimmerman's Report," January 1946, JLC R, B1, F20. See also Parmet, *Master of Seventh Avenue*, 204.

16. Jacob Pat to Joseph Hyman (JDC), November 18, 1943, JLC R, B47, F12.

17. Laura Hobson Faure has noted that if the Joint theoretically did not mingle in political activity, "the boundary between caring action and résistance was blurry." *Un "plan Marshall juif": La présence juive américaine en France après la Shoah, 1944–1954* (Paris: Armand Colin, 2013), 56–57, 70. Lucien Lazare estimates that the Joint had financed 60 percent of the Jewish resistance in France: *La Résistance juive en France* (Paris: Stock, 1987), 282.

18. Peter Novick, *The Holocaust in American Life* (New York: Houghton Mifflin, 1999). See also Gerald Sorin, *Tradition Transformed: The Jewish Experience in America* (Baltimore: Johns Hopkins University Press, 1997), 217. Renée Poznanski has analyzed this "strange silence" in postwar France: *Propagande et persécutions* (Paris: Fayard, 2008), 552–95. Tony Judt has described this silence in European countries: *Postwar: A History of Europe since 1945* (London: Heineman, 2005), 803–31.

19. Diner, *We Remember with Reverence and Love.*

20. David Slucki, *The International Jewish Labor Bund after 1945: Toward a Global History* (New Brunswick, NJ: Rutgers University Press, 2012), 123–24.

21. Among other causes, the JLC was active in the 1960s civil rights movement.

22. "Attorney General Clark Commends JLC Accomplishments," *Voice of the Unconquered,* May–June 1946, 1.

23. Novick, *The Holocaust in American Life.*

BIBLIOGRAPHY

ARCHIVES

Robert F. Wagner Labor Archives, Tamiment Library, New York University
    Holocaust Era Records of the Jewish Labor Committee, Series I, 1934–1947
    Isaiah M. Minkoff Papers, 1930–1984
    Jacob Pat Papers, 1935–1978
    Baruch Charney Vladeck Papers, 1907–1938

YIVO Institute for Jewish Research, New York
    Bund Archives: Jewish Labor Committee, Jewish Labor Movement and Jewish Socialists in North America, RG 117
    Papers of the American Representation of the Jewish Labor Bund in Poland, RG 1404

Leo Baeck Institute, German Jewish History, New York
    Rudolf Katz Collection

Kheel Center for Labor-Management Documentation and Archives, Catherwood Library, Cornell University, Ithaca, New York
    Amalgamated Clothing Workers of America Records, 1914–1980
        Sidney Hillman Papers, 1930–1946
        Joseph Schlossberg Correspondence, 1930–1940
    International Ladies' Garment Workers' Union Records, 1884–2006
        Luigi Antonini Correspondence, 1919–1968
        David Dubinsky Correspondence, 1932–1966
        Charles Zimmerman Papers, 1919–1958
    Abraham Plotkin Collection

Butler Library Rare Book and Manuscript Library, Columbia University, New York
    Varian Fry Papers, 1940–1967, correspondence and subject files

Hoover Institution, Stanford University, California
    Karl Frank Papers, 1937–1961

National Archives of the United States, College Park, Maryland
    Department of Justice, Immigration and Naturalization Service, RG 85, 2.5, 56054/525; 56.054/954
    Department of State Records, RG 59, 811/111, Refugees, France

Office of Strategic Services
    Records of the Foreign Nationalities Branch RG 226, Entry 106, E.210
    OSS Bern, Special Funds Reports, RG 226, Entry 210, B159, 160; RG 226, Entry
        216, Bern, Switzerland Office
    President's Advisory Committee on Political Refugees, RG 85, 56.054/954

London School of Economics
    Walter Citrine Papers

Centre Medem-Arbeter Ring, Paris
    Archives du Bund, dossier F. Schrager
    Collection Photographique

Maison de la Culture Yiddish, Paris
    Archives F. Schrager

Archives de la CFDT, Paris
    Archives Confédérales
    Fonds Paul Vignaux

Fondation Nationale des Sciences Politiques, Paris, Centre d'histoire: Archives d'Histoire
        Contemporaine
    Archives Cletta et Daniel Mayer
    Fonds Léon Blum

PRINTED DOCUMENTS
Organized Labor Conventions

Amalgamated Clothing Workers of America, *Proceedings of the Biennial Conventions*,
    1934–1944.
American Federation of Labor, *Reports of Proceedings of Conventions*, 1933–1945.
Congress of Industrial Organizations, *Proceedings of Conventions*, 1938–1944.
International Ladies' Garment Workers' Union, *Reports and Proceedings of Conventions*,
    1934–1944.

Anthology of Jewish Labor Committee Documents

Arieh Lebowitz and Gail Malmgreen, eds. *Robert F. Wagner Labor Archives, New York
    University, The Papers of the Jewish Labor Committee*, vol. 14 of *Archives of the Holocaust,
    An International Collection of Selected Documents*, edited by Henry Friedlander and
    Sybil Milton. New York: Garland, 1993.

BOOKS AND ARTICLES

Adant, Philippe. *René Bertholet, 1907–1969: Parcours d'un Genevois peu ordinaire*. Lau-
    sanne/Paris: Fondation pour le Progrès de l'Homme, 1995.

Adelman, Jeremy. *Worldly Philosopher: The Odyssey of Albert O. Hirschman*. Princeton: Princeton University Press, 2013.

Affoumado, Diane. *L'exil impossible: L'errance des Juifs du Paquebot Saint Louis*. Paris: L'Harmattan, 2005.

Arendt, Hannah. *The Origins of Totalitarianism*. 1951. New York: Harcourt Brace Jovanovitch, 1975.

———. *Jewish Writings*. Edited by Jerome Kohn and Ron H. Feldman. New York: Schocken, 2007.

Bankier, David, and Israel Gutman, eds. *Nazi Europe and the Final Solution*. Jerusalem: Yad Vashem, 2003.

Bankier, David, and Dan Michman, eds. *Holocaust Historiography in Context: Emergence, Challenges, Polemics and Achievements*. New York: Berghahn, 2009.

Barron, Stephanie, ed. *Exiles + Emigrés: The Flight of European Artists from Hitler*. Los Angeles: Los Angeles County Museum of Art, Harry Abrams, 1997.

Bauer, Yehuda. *My Brother's Keeper: A History of the American Jewish Joint Distribution Committee, 1929–1939*. Philadelphia: Jewish Publication Society, 1974.

———. *American Jewry and the Holocaust: The American Jewish Joint Distribution Committee, 1939–1945*. Detroit: Wayne State University Press, 1981.

———. *Rethinking the Holocaust*. New Haven: Yale University Press, 2001.

Belot, Robert, and Gilbert Karpman. *L'Affaire suisse: La Résistance a-t-elle trahi de Gaulle?* Paris: Armand Colin, 2009.

Bénédite, Daniel. *La filière marseillaise*. 1984. In J. M. Guillon and J. M. Guiraud, eds., *Un chemin vers la liberté sous l'occupation*. Paris: Le Félin, 2017.

Berlin, George. "The Jewish Labor Committee and American Immigration Policy in the 1930s." In *Studies in Jewish Bibliography, History and Literature in Honor of Edward Kiev*, edited by Charles Berlin, 45–73. New York: Ktav, 1971.

Bernard, Georges, and Denise Tintant. *Léon Jouhaux dans le mouvement syndical français*. Paris: Presses Universitaires de France, 1979.

Bernstein, Irving. *Turbulent Years: A History of the American Worker, 1933–1941*. Boston: Houghton Mifflin, 1970.

Bernstein, Serge. *Léon Blum*. Paris: Fayard, 2006.

Binot, Jean-Luc, and Bernard Boyer. *L'argent de la Résistance*. Paris: Larousse, 2010.

Bitter, Daniel. "Liebman Hersch: Un bundiste genevois face aux épreuves de la Seconde Guerre Mondiale." Master's thesis, INALCO, 2017.

Blatman, Daniel. "On a Mission against All Odds: Samuel Zygielbojm in London, April 1942–May 1943." *Yad Vashem Studies* 20 (1990): 237–71.

———. *For Our Freedom and Yours: The Jewish Labour Bund in Poland, 1939–1949*. London: Vallentine Mitchell, 2003.

———. *En direct du ghetto: La presse clandestine juive dans le ghetto de Varsovie, 1940–1943*. Paris: Editions du Cerf, 2005.

Blum, Léon. *L'Histoire jugera*. Montréal: Editions de l'Arbre, 1943.

———. *L'œuvre, Mémoires, La prison, et le procès, A l'Echelle Humaine, 1940–1945*. Paris:

Editions Albin Michel, 1955. Vol. 7, translated by W. Pickles as *For All Mankind*. Gloucester, MA: P. Smith, 1969.

Blum, Suzanne. *Vivre sans la patrie, 1940–1945*. Paris: Plon, 1975.

Brandes, Joseph. "From Sweatshop to Stability: Jewish Labor between Two World Wars." *Yivo Annual of Jewish Social Science* 16 (1976): 1–150.

Braunthal, Julius. *History of the International*. Vol. 2, *1914–43*. London: Nelson, 1967.

Breitman, Richard, and Alan M. Kraut. *American Refugee Policy and European Jewry, 1933–1945*. Bloomington: Indiana University Press, 1987.

Breitman, Richard. *Official Secrets: What the Nazis Planned, What the British and Americans Knew*. New York: Hill and Wang, 1998.

Breitman, Richard, and Allan J. Lichtman. *FDR and the Jews*. Cambridge, MA: Harvard University Press, 2013.

Broszat, Martin. *L'Etat hitlérien*. Paris: Editions Pluriel, 2012.

Calvi, Fabrizio, and Olivier Schmidt. *OSS, La guerre secrète en France, 1942–1945: Les services spéciaux américains, la Résistance et la Gestapo*. Paris: Hachette, 1990.

Cannistraro, Philip V. "Luigi Antonini and the Italian Anti-fascist Movement in the United States, 1940–1943." *Journal of American Ethnic History* 5 (Fall 1985): 21–40.

Carew, Anthony. "The American Labor Movement in Fizzland: The Free Trade Union Committee and the CIA." *Labor History* 39, no. 1 (1998): 25–42.

Carew, Anthony, Michel Dreyfus, et al. *The International Confederation of Free Trade Unions*. Berne: Peter Lang, 2000.

Caron, Vicky. *Uneasy Asylum: France and the Jewish Refugee Crisis, 1933–1942*. Stanford: Stanford University Press, 1999.

Citrine, Walter. *My American Diary*. London: Routledge, 1941.

———. *Men and Work: The Autobiography of Walter Citrine*. London: Hutchinson, 1964.

Cohen, Asher. *Persécutions et sauvetages: Juifs et Français sous l'occupation et sous Vichy*. Paris: Editions du Cerf, 1993.

Collomp, Catherine. *Entre classe et nation: Mouvement ouvrier et immigration aux Etats-Unis, 1880–1920*. Paris: Belin, 1998.

———. "I nostri compagni d'America: The Jewish Labor Committee and the Rescue of Italian Antifascists, 1934–1941." *Altreitalie* 28 (January–June 2004): 66–83.

———. "The Jewish Labor Committee, American Labor and European Socialists, 1934–1941." *International Labor and Working Class History* 68 (Fall 2005): 112–34.

———. "Anti-Semitism among American Labor: A Study by the Refugee Scholars of the Frankfurt School of Sociology at the End of World War II." *Labor History* 52, no. 4 (2011): 417–39.

Collomp, Catherine, and Bruno Groppo, eds. *An American in Hitler's Berlin, Abraham Plotkin's Diary, 1932–1933*. Urbana: University of Illinois Press, 2009.

Collomp, Catherine, and Mario Menéndez, eds. *Exilés et réfugiés politiques aux Etats-Unis, 1789–2000*. Paris: CNRS Editions, 2003.

Cordier, Daniel. *Jean Moulin: La République des Catacombes*. Paris: Gallimard, 1999.

Crémieux-Brilhac, Jean-Louis. *La France Libre*. 2 vols. Paris: Gallimard, 2001.

Czerniakow, Adam. *The Warsaw Diary of Adam Czerniakow: Prelude to Doom*. Edited by Raul Hilberg, translated by Stanislas Staron. New York: Stein and Day, 1979.

Davie, Maurice. *Refugees in America: Report of the Committee for the Study of Recent Immigration from Europe*. New York: Harper and Brothers, 1947.

Dawidowicz, Lucy. *The War against the Jews, 1933–1945*. London: Weifenfeld and Nicolson, 1975.

Deutscher, Isaac. *The Non-Jewish Jew and Other Essays*. Edited by Tamara Deutscher. London: Oxford University Press, 1968.

Diamant, David. *La résistance juive: Entre gloire et tragédie*. Paris: L'Harmattan, 1993.

Diggins, John Patrick. *Mussolini and Fascism: The View from America*. Princeton: Princeton University Press, 1972.

Diner, Hasia. *We Remember with Reverence and Love: American Jews and the Myth of Silence after the Holocaust, 1945–1962*. New York: New York University Press, 2009.

Dreyfus, Michel. "Les sept causes de la crise de l'IOS en 1939." In *Prolétaires de tous les pays unissez vous: Les difficiles chemins de l'internationalisme*, edited by Serge Wolikow and Michel Cordillot, 177–83. Dijon: Centre de documentation sur les internationales ouvrières, 1993.

———. *Histoire de la CGT: Cent ans de syndicalisme en France*. Brussels: Editions Complexe, 1995.

Droz, Jacques. *Histoire de l'antifascisme en Europe*. Paris: La Découverte, 1985.

Dufoix, Stéphane. *Politiques d'exil: Hongrois, Polonais et Tchécoslovaques en France après 1945*. Paris: Presses Universitaires de France, 2002.

Edelman, Marek. *Mémoires du Ghetto de Varsovie: Un dirigeant de l'insurrection raconte*. Translated from Polish by Pierre Li and Maryna Ochab. Paris: Liana Levi, 1993.

———. *The Ghetto Fights: Warsaw, 1943–1945*. London: Bookmarks, 2014.

Engel, David. *In the Shadow of Auschwitz: The Polish Government in Exile and the Jews, 1939–1942*. Chapel Hill: University of North Carolina Press, 1987.

———. *Facing a Holocaust: The Polish Government in Exile and the Jews*. Chapel Hill: University of North Carolina Press, 1993.

Epstein, Melech. *Jewish Labor in U.S.A.: An Industrial, Political and Cultural History of the Jewish Labor Movement, 1914–1952*. New York: Trade Union Sponsoring Committee, 1953.

———. *Profiles of Eleven*. Detroit: Wayne State University Press, 1965.

Erbelding, Rebecca. *Rescue Board: The Untold Story of America's Efforts to Save the Jews of Europe*. New York: Anchor, 2019.

Feingold, Henry L. *Politics of Rescue: The Roosevelt Administration and the Holocaust, 1938–1945*. New Brunswick, NJ: Rutgers University Press, 1970.

———. *A Time for Searching: Entering the Mainstream, 1920–45*. Baltimore: Johns Hopkins University Press, 1992.

———. *Bearing Witness: How America and Its Jews Responded to the Holocaust*. Syracuse, NY: Syracuse University Press, 1995.

Fermi, Laura. *Illustrious Immigrants: The Intellectual Migration from Europe, 1930–1941*. Chicago: University of Chicago Press, 1968.

Feuchtwanger, Lion. *Devil in France: My Encounter with Him in the Summer of 1940.* New York: Viking, 1941.

Filippelli, Ronald. *American Labor and Postwar Italy, 1943–1953.* Stanford: Stanford University Press, 1989.

Fittko, Lisa. *Escape through the Pyrenees.* Translated by David Koblick. Evanston, IL: Northwestern University Press, 1991.

———. *Solidarity and Treason, Resistance and Exile, 1933–1940.* Evanston, IL: Northwestern University Press, 1993.

Fleming, Donald, and Bernard Bailyn. *The Intellectual Migration: Europe and America, 1930–1960.* Cambridge, MA: Harvard University Press, 1969.

Foot, Michael Richard D. *SOE in France: An Account of the Work of the British Special Operations Executive in France, 1940–1944.* London: HMSO, 1966.

Frankel, Jonathan. *Prophecy and Politics: Socialism, Nationalism and the Russian Jews, 1862–1917.* New York: Cambridge University Press, 1981.

Fraser, Steven. *Labor Will Rule: Sidney Hillman and the Rise of American Labor.* New York: Free Press, 1991.

Frenay, Henri. *La nuit finira: Mémoires de résistance, 1940–1945.* 1973. Paris: Michalon, 2006.

Friedländer, Saul. *Nazi Germany and the Jews.* Vol. 1, *1933–1939: The Years of Persecution.* New York: Harper Collins, 1997. Vol. 2, *1939–1945: The Years of Extermination.* New York: Harper Perennial, 2007.

Friedman, Saul. *No Haven for the Oppressed: United States Policy toward Jewish Refugees, 1938–1945.* Detroit: Wayne State University Press, 1973.

Fry, Varian. *Surrender on Demand.* New York: Random House, 1945. Reprint, Boulder, CO: Johnson Books, 1997.

Gaulle, Charles de. *The Complete War Memoirs of Charles de Gaulle.* Translated by Richard Howard. New York: Simon and Schuster, 1967.

Georgi, Frank. "Les relations entre Léon Jouhaux et le syndicalisme chrétien, 1940–1954." In Mairie d'Aubervilliers, *Léon Jouhaux: D'Aubervilliers au Prix Nobel,* 131–43. Paris: Documentation Française, 2010.

Giniewski, Paul. *Une résistance juive: Grenoble, 1943–1945.* Brest: Editions du Cheminement, 2009.

Godson, Roy. *American Labor and European Politics: The AFL as a Transnational Force.* New York: Crane, Russak, 1976.

Goldstein, Bernard. *The Stars Bear Witness.* Translated from Yiddish by Leonard Shatzkin. New York: Viking, 1949.

Gottlieb, Moshe R. *American Anti-Nazi Resistance, 1933–41: An Historical Analysis.* New York: Ktav, 1982.

Greenberg, Karen, ed. *Columbia University Library, Varian Fry Papers.* Vol. 5, *Archives of the Holocaust: An International Collection of Selected Documents,* edited by Henry Friedlander and Sybil Milton. New York: Garland, 1990.

Groppo, Bruno. "L'Internationale ouvrière socialiste en 1933." In Serge Wolikow and Michel Cordillot, eds., *Prolétaires de tous les pays unissez vous? Les difficiles chemins de l'internationalisme (1848–1956)*, 153–67. Dijon: Centre de documentation sur les internationales ouvrières, 1993.

———. "De Karl Frank à Paul Hagen: Itinéraire d'un exilé atypique." *Matériaux pour l'histoire de notre temps* 60 (October–December 2000): 31–33.

Gross, Jan T. *Fear: Anti-Semitism in Poland after Auschwitz.* New York: Random House, 2006.

Grynberg, Anne. *Les Juifs dans la Résistance et la Libération: Histoire, témoignages, débats.* Paris: Editions du Scribe, 1985.

———. *Les camps de la honte, les internés juifs des camps français.* Paris: La Découverte, 1999.

Guillon, Jean-Marie, editor of the conference held in Marseille in 1999. *Varian Fry du refuge à l'exil.* 2 vols. Arles: Actes Sud, 2000.

———. "La Provence refuge et piège: Autour de Varian Fry et de la filière américaine." In *1940, La France du repli, l'Europe de la défaite*, edited by Max Lagarrigue, 269–88. Toulouse: Privat, 2001.

Guillon, Jean-Marie, and Pierre Laborie. *Mémoire et Histoire: La Résistance.* Toulouse: Privat, 1995.

Gurock, Jeffrey S., ed. *American Jewish History.* Vol. 6, *Anti-Semitism in America.* New York: Routledge, 1998.

Gutman, Israël. *Resistance: The Warsaw Ghetto Uprising.* New York: Houghton Mifflin, 1994.

Guttmann, Allen. *The Olympics: A History of the Modern Games.* Urbana: University of Illinois Press, 1994.

Hagen, Paul. *Will Germany Crack?* New York: Harper and Brothers, 1942.

———. *Germany after Hitler.* New York: Farrar & Rinehart, 1944.

Haupt, Georges, Michael Lowy, and Claudie Weill. *Les marxistes et la question nationale, 1848–1914.* Paris: Maspéro, 1974.

Hazan, Katy. *Les orphelins de la Shoah, Les maisons de l'espoir, 1944–1960.* Paris: Les Belles Lettres, 2000.

Heilbut, Anthony. *Exiled in Paradise: German Refugee Artists and Intellectuals in America from the 1930s to the Present.* New York: Viking, 1983.

Herling, John. "Vladeck." *Survey Graphic* 18, no. 11 (November 1939): 663–701, and 19, no. 1 (January 1940): 29–47.

Hertz, Jacob S. "The Bund's Nationality Program and Its Critics in the Russian, Polish and Austrian Socialist Movements." *Yivo Annual of Jewish Social Science* 14 (1969): 53–67.

Hilberg, Raul. *The Destruction of the European Jews.* New Haven, CT: Holmes and Meier, 1985.

Hirschman Albert. *Crossing Boundaries: Selected Writings.* New York: Zone Books, 1998.

———. "Albert O. Hirschman, Albert Herman, Beamish." In *Varian Fry du refuge à l'exil*, edited by J. M. Guillon, 1:12–16. Arles: Actes Sud, 2000.

Hirschmann, Ursula. *Noi senza patria.* Bologna: Il Mulino, 1993.

Hobson Faure, Laura. Un "plan Marshall juif": La présence juive américaine en France après la Shoah, 1944–1954. Paris: Armand Colin, 2013. Translated as A Jewish Marshall Plan: The American Jewish Presence in Post-Holocaust France, 1944–1954. Bloomington: University of Indiana Press, forthcoming.

Hobson Faure, Laura, Mathias Gardet, Katy Hazan, and Catherine Nicault. L'oeuvre de secours aux enfants et les populations juives au XXᵉ siècle, prévenir et guérir dans un siècle de violence. Paris: Armand Colin, 2014.

Horn, Gerd-Rainer. European Socialists Respond to Fascism: Ideology, Activism and Contingency in the 1930s. New York: Oxford University Press, 1996.

Howe, Irving. World of Our Fathers: The Journey of the East European Jews to America and the Life They Found and Made. New York: Simon and Schuster, 1976.

Hughes, Stuart H. The Sea Change: The Migration of Social Thought, 1930–1965. New York: Harper and Row, 1975.

Hull, Cordell. The Memoirs of Cordell Hull. 2 vols. New York: Macmillan, 1948.

Isenberg, Sheila. A Hero of Our Own: The Story of Varian Fry. New York: Random House, 2001.

Jacobs, Jack. On Socialists and "the Jewish Question" after Marx. New York: New York University Press, 1992.

———. "A Friend in Need: The Jewish Labor Committee and Refugees from the German-Speaking Lands, 1933–1945." Yivo Annual 23 (1996): 391–417.

———, ed. Jewish Politics in Eastern Europe: The Bund at 100. New York: New York University Press, 2001.

———. Bundist Counterculture in Interwar Poland. Syracuse, NY: Syracuse University Press, 2009.

Jacoubovitch, Jules. Rue Amelot, Aide et Résistance. 1948. Paris: Editions du Centre Medem, 2006.

Jay, Martin. Permanent Exiles: Essays on Intellectual Migration from Germany to America. New York: Columbia University Press, 1985.

Jeanpierre, Laurent. "Paul Vignaux inspirateur de la deuxième gauche: Récits d'un exil français aux États-Unis pendant la Seconde Guerre Mondiale." Matériaux pour l'histoire de notre temps 60 (October–December 2000): 48–56.

———. "Varian Fry et le sauvetage des réfugiés aux Etats-Unis." In Varian Fry du refuge à l'exil, edited by J. M. Guillon, 2:58–73. Arles: Actes Sud, 2000.

———. "Des hommes entre plusieurs mondes: Etude sur une situation d'exil, Intellectuels français réfugiés aux Etats-Unis pendant la deuxième guerre mondiale." Ph.D. diss., Ecole des Hautes Etudes en Sciences Sociales, Paris, 2004.

Judt, Tony. Postwar: A History of Europe since 1945. London: Heineman, 2005.

Kantrowicz, Jack. "L'influence américaine sur Force Ouvrière: Mythe ou réalité?" Revue française de science politique 28, no. 4 (1978): 717–39.

Karski, Jan. Story of a Secret State: My Report to the World. 1944. London: Penguin, 2012.

Kassow, Samuel D. Who Will Write Our History: Rediscovering a Hidden Archive from the Warsaw Ghetto. Bloomington: Indiana University Press, 2007.

Katz, Barry. *Foreign Intelligence: Research and Analysis in the Office of Strategic Services, 1942–1945.* Cambridge, MA: Harvard University Press, 1989.

Katz, Daniel. *All Together Different: Yiddish Socialists, Garment Workers, and the Labor Roots of Multiculturalism.* New York: New York University Press, 2013.

Klarsfeld, Serge. *Vichy-Auschwitz: Le rôle de Vichy dans la solution finale de la question juive en France, La Shoah en France.* Paris: Fayard, 2001.

Klehr, Harvey. *The Heyday of American Communism: The Depression Decade.* New York: Basic Books, 1984.

Klein, Anne. "Droit d'asile ou sauvetage: L'activité du Centre américain de secours et la politique internationale des réfugiés." In *Varian Fry du refuge à l'exil*, edited by J. M. Guillon, 2:74–87. Arles: Actes Sud, 2000.

Knopper, Françoise, and Alain Ruiz, eds. *Les résistants au Troisième Reich en Allemagne et dans l'exil.* Toulouse: Presses Universitaires du Mirail, 1997.

Koehn, Barbara. *La résistance allemande contre Hitler, 1933–1945.* Paris: Presses Universitaires de France, 2003.

Koestler, Arthur. *Scum of the Earth.* 1941. New York: Macmillan, 1968.

Korzec, Pawel. *Juifs en Pologne: La question juive pendant l'entre-deux-guerres.* Paris: Presse de la Fondation Nationale des Sciences Politiques, 1980.

Krakowski, Shmuel. *The War of the Doomed: Jewish Armed Resistance in Poland, 1942–1944.* London: Holmes and Meier, 1984.

Kranzler, David. *Japanese, Nazis and Jews.* New York: Yeshiva University, 1976.

———. "The Role in Relief and Rescue during the Holocaust by the Jewish Labor Committee." In *American Jewry during the Holocaust*, edited by Seymour Finger, appendix 4-2, pp. 1–29. New York: Holmes and Meier, 1984.

Krebs, Gilbert, and Gérard Schneilin, eds. *Exil et résistance au national-socialisme, 1933–1945.* Paris: Publications de l'Institut Allemand, Université Sorbonne Nouvelle, 1998.

Krohn, Claus-Dieter. *Intellectuals in Exile: Refugee Scholars and the New School for Social Research.* Amherst: University of Massachusetts Press, 1993.

———. "L'exil politique allemand aux Etats-Unis après 1933." *Matériaux pour l'histoire de notre temps* 60 (October–December 2000): 9–15.

Laffitte, Michel. *Un engrenage fatal: L'UGIF face aux réalités de la Shoah, 1941–1944.* Paris: L. Lévi, 2003.

Lagarrigue, Max, ed. *1940, La France du repli: L'Europe de la défaite.* Toulouse: Privat, 2001.

Lane, A. Thomas, ed. *Biographical Dictionary of European Labor Leaders.* 2 vols. Westport, CT: Greenwood Press, 1995.

Laqueur, Walter. *The Terrible Secret: An Investigation into the Suppression of Information about Hitler's "Final Solution."* London: Weidenfeld and Nicolson, 1980.

Laqueur, Walter, and Richard Breitman. *Breaking the Silence.* New York: Simon and Schuster, 1986.

Laqueur, Walter, and George L. Mosse, eds. *The Left Wing Intellectuals between the Wars, 1919–1939.* New York: Harper Torchbooks, 1966.

Lazare, Lucien. *La Résistance juive en France.* Paris: Stock, 1987.

———. *Rescue as Resistance: How Jewish Organizations Fought the Holocaust in France.* Translated by Jeffrey Green. New York: Columbia University Press, 1996.

Lecuir, Jean. "Paul Vignaux à Toulouse: Résistance spirituelle et politique en zone non occupée (juin 1940–juin 1941)." In O. Boulnois, ed., *Paul Vignaux, citoyen et philosophe,* 51–121. Turnhout: Brepols, 2013.

Leff, Laurel. *Buried by the Times: The Holocaust and America's Most Important Newspaper.* New York: Cambridge University Press, 2005.

Lenburg, Leroy J. "The CIO and American Foreign Policy, 1935–1955." Ph.D. diss., Pennsylvania State University, 1973.

Libionka, Dariusz. "L'Etat polonais clandestin et la 'question juive,' 1942–1944." In *Juifs et Polonais, 1939–2008,* edited by Jean Charles Szurek et Annette Wieviorka, 61–79. Paris: Albin Michel, 2009.

Lichtenstein, Nelson. *Labor's War at Home: The CIO in World War II.* New York: Cambridge University Press, 1982.

Liebich, André. *From the Other Shore: Russian Social Democracy after 1921.* Cambridge, MA: Harvard University Press, 1997.

Lindenberg, Judith. *Premiers savoirs de la Shoah.* Paris: CNRS Editions, 2017.

Lipstadt, Deborah E. *Beyond Belief: The American Press and the Coming of the Holocaust, 1933–1945.* New York: Free Press, 1986.

Long, Breckinridge. *The War Diary of Breckinridge Long: Selections from the Years 1939– 1944.* Edited by Fred L. Israel. Lincoln: University of Nebraska Press, 1987.

Lorwin, Lewis L. *The International Labor Movement, History, Policies, Outlook.* New York: Harper and Brothers, 1953.

Loyer, Emmanuelle. *Paris à New York: Intellectuels et artistes français en exil, 1940–1947.* Paris: Grasset, 2005.

Luconi, Stefano. *La "Diplomazia Parallela": Il regime fascista e la mobilitazione politica degli italo-americani.* Milan: Franco Angeli, 2000.

Lussu, Emilio. *Diplomazia Clandestina.* Florence: La Nuova Italia, 1956.

Lussu, Joyce. *Fronti e frontiere.* Bari: Laterza, 1967.

MacShane, Denis. *International Labour and the Origins of the Cold War.* Oxford: Clarendon Press, 1992.

Maitron, Jean, and Claude Pennetier, eds. *Dictionnaire Biographique du Mouvement ouvrier français, 1914–39.* Paris: Editions de l'Atelier, 1999. http://maitron-en-ligne.univ-paris1.fr.

Malmgreen, Gail. "Labor and the Holocaust: The Jewish Labor Committee and the Anti-Nazi Struggle." *Labor's Heritage* 3, no. 4 (1991): 20–35.

———. "Comrades and Kinsmen: The Jewish Labor Committee and Anti-Nazi Activity." In *Jews, Labour and the Left, 1918–1948,* edited by Christine Collette and Stephen Bird, 4–20. London: Ashgate, 2000.

Marino, Andy. *A Quiet American: The Secret War of Varian Fry.* New York: St. Martin's, 1999.

Marrus, Michael, and Robert Paxton. *Vichy France and the Jews.* New York: Basic Books, 1981.

Mayer, Arno. *Why Did the Heavens Not Darken? The Final Solution in History.* New York: Pantheon, 1988.

Mayer, Daniel. *Les Socialistes dans la Résistance.* Paris: Presses Universitaires de France, 1968.

Medem, Vladimir. *Fun mayn Lebn.* New York, 1923. Translated by Samuel A. Portnoy. *The Life and Soul of a Legendary Socialist.* New York: Ktav, 1979.

Meed, Vladka (Feigele Miedzyrzecki). *On Both Sides of the Wall: Memoirs from the Warsaw Ghetto.* 1993. Washington, DC: U.S. Holocaust Memorial Museum, 1999.

Michel, Henri. *Les courants de pensée dans la Résistance.* Paris: Presses Universitaires de France, 1962.

Michels, Tony. *A Fire in Their Hearts: Yiddish Socialists in New York.* Cambridge, MA: Harvard University Press, 2005.

Miles (alias Walter Löwenheim). *Neu Beginnen! Faschismus oder Sozialismus: Diskussionsgrundlage zu den Streitfragen des Sozialismus in unsere Epoche.* Prague: Graphia, 1933. *Socialism's New Beginning: A Manifesto from Underground Germany.* New York: League for Industrial Democracy, 1934.

Milton, Sybil, and Fred Bogin. *American, Jewish Joint Distribution Committee.* Vol. 10 of *Archives of the Holocaust,* edited by Henry Friedlander and Sybil Milton. New York: Garland, 1995.

Minc, Rachel. *L'enfer des innocents: Les enfants juifs dans la tourmente nazie.* Paris: Le Centurion, 1966.

Minczeles, Henri. "La résistance du Bund en France pendant l'occupation." *Le Monde juif, Revue d'histoire de la Shoah,* no. 154 (May–August 1995): 138–53.

———. *Histoire générale du Bund: Un mouvement révolutionnaire juif.* Paris: Denoël, 1999.

Mommsen, Hans. "German Society and the Resistance against Hitler." In *The Third Reich: The Essential Readings,* edited by Christian Leitz, 255–75. Oxford: Blackwell, 1999.

Mona Bismarck Foundation. *Varian Fry à Marseille, 1940–1941: Les artistes et l'exil.* Arles: Actes Sud, 2000.

Morse, Arthur. *While Six Million Died: A Chronicle of American Apathy.* New York: Random House, 1968.

Mosse, George L. *Germans and Jews: The Right and the Left and the Search for a Third Force in Pre-Nazi Germany.* London: Orbach and Chambers, 1971.

Novick, Peter. *The Holocaust in American Life.* New York: Houghton Mifflin, 1999.

Nowogrodzki, Emanuel. *The Jewish Labor Bund in Poland, 1915–1939: From Its Emergence as an Independent Political Party until the Beginning of World War II.* Rockville, MD: Shengold, 2001.

Ottanelli, Fraser M. *The Communist Party of the United States: From Depression to World War II.* New Brunswick, NJ: Rutgers University Press, 1991.

Palmier, Jean-Michel. *Weimar in Exile: The Antifascist Emigration in Europe and America.* Translated by David Fernbach. London: Verso, 2017.

Panicacci, Jean-Louis. *L'occupation italienne: Sud-Est de la France, juin 1940–septembre 1943.* Rennes: Presses Universitaires de Rennes, 2010.

Pannocchia, Nicoletta, ed. *Silvio Trentin e la Francia: Saggi e testimonianze*. Venice: Marsilio Editori, 1991.

Papanek, Ernst, and Edward Linn. *Out of the Fire: How an Eminent Educator Saved Children from the Hitler Onslaught*. New York: William Morrow, 1975.

Pâris de Bollardière, Constance. "Mutualité, fraternité et travail social chez les bundistes de France." *Archives juives, Revue d'histoire des Juifs de France* 45, no. 1 (2012): 27–43.

———. "The Jewish Labor Committee's Bundist Relief Network in France, 1945–1948." *Jewish History Quarterly* 246, no. 2 (2013): 293–301.

———. "Fajwel Schrager (né Ostrynski), bundiste, directeur de l'ORT-France et du bureau parisien de l'Union mondiale-ORT." *Archives juives, Revue d'histoire des Juifs de France* 48, no. 1 (2015): 136–39.

———. "Ecritures de la destruction et reconstruction: Yankew Pat, auteur et acteur du monde yiddish: Le cas de Paris, 1946–1948." In Judith Lindenberg, *Premiers savoirs de la Shoah*, 275–93. Paris: CNRS Editions, 2017.

———. "'La pérennité de notre peuple': Une aide socialiste juive américaine dans la diaspora yiddish, le Jewish Labor Committee en France, 1944–1948." Ph.D. diss., Ecole des Hautes Etudes en Sciences Sociales, 2017.

Parmet, Robert D. *The Master of Seventh Avenue: David Dubinsky and the American Labor Movement*. New York: New York University Press, 2005.

Passy, Colonel (André Dewavrin). *Mémoires du chef des services secrets de la France Libre*. Paris: Odile Jacob, 2000.

Pasteur, Paul. *Pratiques politiques et militantes de la social-démocratie autrichienne, 1888–1934*. Paris: Belin, 2003.

Pat, Jacob. *Ashes and Fire*. Translated from Yiddish by Leo Steinberg. New York: International Universities Press, 1947.

Paxton, Robert O. *Vichy France: Old Guard and New Order*. New York: Knopf, 1972.

Peretz, Pauline. *Let My People Go: The Transnational Politics of Soviet Jewish Emigration during the Cold War*. New Brunswick, NJ: Transaction, 2015.

Peschanski, Denis. *La France des camps: L'internement, 1938–1946*. Paris: Gallimard, 2002.

Petersen, Neal H., ed. *From Hitler's Doorstep: The Wartime Intelligence Reports of Allen Dulles, 1942–1945*. University Park: Pennsylvania State University Press, 1996.

Phelan, Craig. *William Green: Biography of a Labor Leader*. Albany: State University of New York Press, 1989.

Plotkin, Abraham. *An American in Hitler's Berlin: Abraham Plotkin's Diary, 1932–1933*. Edited by Catherine Collomp and Bruno Groppo. Urbana: University of Illinois Press, 2009.

Polonsky, Antony. "The Bund in Polish Political Life, 1935–1939." In *Essential Papers on Jews and the Left*, edited by Ezra Mendelsohn, 166–98. New York: New York University Press, 1997.

Poznanski, Renée. "Résistance juive, résistants juifs, retour à l'Histoire." In *Mémoire et Histoire: La Résistance*, edited by Jean-Marie Guillon and Pierre Laborie, 227–45. Toulouse: Editions Privat, 1995.

———. *Jews in France during World War II*. Translated by Nathan Bracher. Waltham, MA: Brandeis University Press, 2001.

———. *Propagande et persecutions*. Paris: Fayard, 2008.

Pradoux, Martine. *Daniel Mayer: Un socialiste dans la résistance*. Paris: Editions de l'Atelier-Editions Ouvrières, 2002.

Pradoux, Martine, and Emmanuel Naquet. "Entretien avec Robert Verdier: Daniel Mayer secrétaire du Parti socialiste clandestin, à travers le regard d'un autre resistant." *Matériaux pour l'histoire de notre temps* 51 (July–December 1998): 9–17.

Rabinbach, Anson, ed. *The Austrian Socialist Experiment: Social Democracy and Austro-Marxism, 1918–1934*. Boulder, CO: Westview Press, 1985.

Radosh, Ronald. *American Labor and United States Foreign Policy*. New York: Random House, 1969.

Ragg, Albrecht. "The German Socialist Emigration in the United States, 1933–1945." Ph.D. diss., Loyola University-Chicago, 1977.

Reinalda, Bob. *The International Transportworkers Federation, 1914–1945: The Edo Fimmen Era*. Amsterdam: Stichting beheer IISG, 1997.

Riegner, Gerhart M. "Témoignage de mes activités en Suisse pendant la Seconde Guerre Mondiale." *Revue d'histoire de la Shoah* 163 (May–August 1998): 91–100.

Romero, Federico. *The United States and the European Trade Union Movement, 1944–1951*. Chapel Hill: University of North Carolina Press, 1992.

Sadoun, Marc. *Les Socialistes sous l'occupation: Résistance et collaboration*. Paris: Presses de la Fondation Nationale des Sciences Politiques, 1982.

Saunier, Jean Yves. "Circulations, connexions et espaces transnationaux." *Genèses* 57 (December 2004): 110–26.

Schevenels, Walter. *Forty-Five Years: The International Federation of Trade Unions, 1901–1945*. Brussels: International Federation of Trade Unions, 1956.

Schrager, Fajwel. *Un militant juif*. Translated from Yiddish by H. Bulawko. Paris: Editions Polyglottes, 1979.

Sémelin, Jacques. *The Survival of the Jews of France*. Translated by Cynthia Schoch and Natasha Lehrer. New York: Oxford University Press, 2018.

Serge, Victor. *Memoirs of a Revolutionary, 1905–1941*. Translated by Peter Sedgwick. New York: NYRB Classics, 2012.

Shapiro, Edward. "The World Labor Athletic Carnival of 1936: An American Anti-Nazi Protest." *American Jewish History* 59 (March 1985): 255–73.

———. *A Time for Healing: American Jewry since World War II*. Baltimore: Johns Hopkins University Press, 1992.

Silverman, Victor. *Imagining Internationalism in American and British Labor, 1939–1949*. Urbana: University of Illinois Press, 2000.

Slezkine, Yuri. *The Jewish Century*. Princeton: Princeton University Press, 2004.

Slucki, David. *The International Jewish Labor Bund after 1945: Toward a Global History*. New Brunswick, NJ: Rutgers University Press, 2012.

Smith, Bradley F. *The Shadow Warriors: OSS and the Origins of the CIA*. New York: Basic Books, 1983.

Snyder, Timothy. *Bloodlands: Europe between Hitler and Stalin*. New York: Basic Books, 2010.

Sorin, Gerald. *Tradition Transformed: The Jewish Experience in America*. Baltimore: Johns Hopkins University Press, 1997.

Soyer, Daniel. *Jewish Immigrant Associations and American Identity in New York, 1880–1939*. Cambridge, MA: Harvard University Press, 1997.

Sullivan, Rosemary. *Villa Air-Bel: World War II, Escape and a House in Marseille*. New York: Harper, 2007.

Szurek, Jean Charles, and Annette Wieviorka. *Juifs et Polonais, 1939–2008*. Paris: Albin Michel, 2009.

Taft, Philip. *The A.F.L. from the Death of Gompers to the Merger*. New York: Harper, 1959.

Tichenor, Daniel J. *Dividing Lines: The Politics of Immigration Control in America*. Princeton: Princeton University Press, 2002.

Tobias, Henry. *The Jewish Bund in Russia from Its Origins to 1905*. Stanford: Stanford University Press, 1972.

Traverso, Enzo. *Jews and Germany: From the "Judeo-German Symbiosis" to the Memory of Auschwitz*. Translated by Daniel Weissbort. Lincoln: University of Nebraska Press, 1995.

———. *Les marxistes et la question juive: Histoire d'un débat (1843–1943)*. 1990. Paris: Editions Kimé, 1997.

———. *La pensée dispersée: Figures de l'exil judéo-allemand*. Paris: Lignes, Editions Leo Scheer, 2004.

Trunk, Isaiah. "The Cultural Dimension of the American Jewish Labor Movement." *Yivo Annual of Jewish Social Science* 16 (1976): 342–93.

Van Goethem, Geert. "Conflicting Interests: The International Federation of Trade Unions, 1919–1945." In Anthony Carew, Michel Dreyfus, et al., *The International Confederation of Free Trade Unions*, 73–163. Berne: Peter Lang, 2000.

———. *The Amsterdam International: The World of the International Federation of Trade Unions (IFTU)*. Ashgate: Aldershot, 2006.

Verdier, Robert. *La vie clandestine du parti socialiste*. Paris: Editions de la Liberté, 1944.

Vignaux, Paul. "Testimonianza." In *Silvio Trentin e La Francia: Saggi e Testimonianze*, edited by N. Pannocchia, 197–200. Venice: Marsilio Editori, 1991.

Waltzer, Kenneth. "American Labor and Aid to Polish Jews during the Holocaust." Paper presented at the United States Holocaust Memorial Council, Washington, DC, March 1987.

Weill, Claudie. "Mencheviks et Socialistes-révolutionnaires en exil." In *Mélanges pour Mark Ferro, de Russie et d'ailleurs*. Paris: Institut d'Etudes Slaves, 1995.

Wellers, Georges, André Kaspi, and Serge Klarsfeld, eds. *La France et la question juive, 1940–1944*. Paris: Editions Messinger, 1981.

Wieviorka, Olivier. *Histoire de la Résistance en France, 1940–1945*. Paris: Editions Perrin, 2013.

Windmuller, John. *The International Trade Union Movement*. Boston: Deventer, 1980.

Wise, Stephen. *Challenging Years*. London: East and West Library, 1951.

Wyman, David. *Paper Walls: America and the Refugee Crisis, 1938–1941*. New York: Pantheon, 1968.

———. *The Abandonment of the Jews: America and the Holocaust, 1941–1945*. New York: New Press, 1998.

Zappia, Charles Anthony. "Unionism and the Italian American Worker: A History of the New York City 'Italian Locals' in the ILGWU." Ph.D. diss., University of California–Berkeley, 1994.

Zieger, Robert. *The CIO, 1935–1955*. Chapel Hill: University of North Carolina Press, 1995.

Zolberg, Aristide. *A Nation by Design*. New York: Russell Sage Foundation, 2006.

INDEX

CPSIA information can be obtained
at www.ICGtesting.com
Printed in the USA
LVHW111730130521
687356LV00006B/645